Bion

This is a book of 365 quotes from the work of the psychoanalyst Wilfred Bion. Something of an enigma, Bion often doesn't write in the way one would expect of a psychoanalyst, but is being read ever-increasingly around the world, in and outside the psychoanalytic community. Certain of his comments are often quoted, whilst swathes of his work lie almost untouched. How to make some of the detail of this work available? What he writes is often dense in the way the structure of a poem can be, and the book has the format of a "poem a day" collection – providing a way into his complete work one quote at a time. Alongside commentaries by Abel-Hirsch are thoughts on Bion's work drawn from papers by other analysts from the UK, the Americas, and Europe. The book is structured in a way that will inform and interest the general reader as well as giving something new to psychoanalysts and others who already know his work well.

Nicola Abel-Hirsch is a training and supervising analyst of the British Psychoanalytical Society and works in private practice in London. She has given clinical and theoretical papers and seminars on Bion in the UK; Taiwan (annually 2005–2012); the USA; and Europe. From 2013–2015 she was the Visiting Professor at the Centre for Psychoanalytic Studies, University of Essex. Her publications include *Eros* (2001); "The Life Instinct", in *The International Journal of Psychoanalysis* (2010); "A Note and a Short Story", in *The Bion Tradition* (2015); and "The Devil is in the Detail", in *The Melanie Klein Tradition* (2017). She is the editor of Hanna Segal's last book, *Yesterday, Today and Tomorrow* (2007).

Bion

365 Quotes

Nicola Abel-Hirsch

Routledge
Taylor & Francis Group

LONDON AND NEW YORK

First published 2019
by Routledge
2 Park Square, Milton Park, Abingdon, Oxon OX14 4RN

and by Routledge
52 Vanderbilt Avenue, New York, NY 10017

Routledge is an imprint of the Taylor & Francis Group, an informa business

© 2019 Nicola Abel-Hirsch

The right of Nicola Abel-Hirsch to be identified as author of this
work has been asserted by her in accordance with sections 77 and 78
of the Copyright, Designs and Patents Act 1988.

British Library Cataloguing-in-Publication Data
A catalogue record for this book is available from the British Library

Library of Congress Cataloging-in-Publication Data
A catalog record for this book has been requested

ISBN: 9781782205869 (pbk)
ISBN: 9780429400803 (ebk)

Typeset in Times New Roman
by Apex CoVantage, LLC
Printed and bound by CPI Group (UK) Ltd, Croydon, CR0 4YY

For Dennis
and my daughters Hannah and Naomi

Contents

Acknowledgements

My thanks to Dennis Duncan for his steady and insightful belief.

And to my daughters Hannah and Naomi, for more than I can say.

Susan Lawrence read the whole book, and with her I was able to discuss any detail of the quotes. She has an inestimable capacity to think deeply and clearly – in a relaxed way. My thanks also to the erudite and subtly amusing Annie Pesskin who wrote most of the glossary notes.

It was as a young philosophy/religious studies student that I first came across Bion's work, and a light was switched on! I embarked on analysis. It goes without saying that this book could not have come into being without the patient work over the years of my own analysts, Murray Jackson, Elizabeth Bott-Spillius and Caroline Polmear.

I want to thank my patients, who have been very present in my mind as I have done the book. The book contains clinical vignettes from our work.

I never met Bion myself, but I know a man who did! I am very fortunate to have been trained by people who were close colleagues of Bion, in particular Hanna Segal and Betty Joseph; and those who speak and write about Bion's work so clearly and whose support I greatly value, including: Ignês Sodré, David Bell, Ronald Britton, Michael Parsons, Priscilla Roth and Catalina Bronstein. The book includes excerpts from papers written by these analysts, and others in the United Kingdom, the Americas and Europe. I am warmly grateful for their agreement to be included.

Chris Mawson (Editor: *The Complete Works of Bion*) has throughout been very generous in his responses to my enquiries and his support of this endeavour – beyond the call of duty.

From 2005 to 2012 I spent a week each year in Taiwan, giving lectures and seminars on Bion, in hospital and university settings and to the general public. There, under the auspices of the newly developing Taiwan Centre for the Development of Psychoanalysis – now Taiwan Psychoanalytic Association (Study Group and Allied Centre) – I met people fully engaged in the development of psychoanalysis, with whom I spent a formative time exploring Bion's work. I would like to thank in particular: Jung-Yu Tsai (蔡榮裕), Chia-Chang Liu (劉佳昌), Nancy Pei-Ling Yu (游佩琳), Chun-Tse Chen (陳俊澤), Yi-Ching Lin (林怡青), Hsin-Wei Hsu (許欣偉), Hsien-Chih Chiou (邱顯智), Jen-Yu Chou (周仁宇), and Ming-Min Yang (楊明敏).

From 2013 to 2015 I was able to continue the work on Bion as Visiting Professor at The Centre for Psychoanalytic Studies Essex University. I would particularly like to thank Bob Hinshelwood, Chris Mawson, and Denis Flynn for our joint enquiries into "Bion on Observation". My thanks also to Sira Dermen and Jan Abrams for our debates on the links and differences between Bion and Winnicott. I have also been fortunate to be in contact with psychoanalysts from other countries with a shared interest in Bion's work, particularly Monica Horovitz and the other members of the Bion in Marrakech Seminar; Joseph Aguayo and the Regional Bion Symposium (Los Angeles); Howard Levine, and Rudy Vermote.

> I never realized before I tried that you don't just write a book – you have to *make* it as well.
>
> (*CWB II*, p. 197)

The making of the book began with Oliver Rathbone and the initial work done by the Karnac team; latterly it has been completed by the team at Routledge. My particular thanks to Adam Guppy, Senior Production Editor at Taylor & Francis, and Meridith Murray, who took on the index at short notice and has been good humored and thorough in relation to the complexities of the book.

Central to the making of the book has been copyeditor Klara King. It is with her that I have traversed the groundswell of details that underpin the book. She, with Eric King, is responsible for the visible structure of the book and the accuracy of its grammar and referencing. The depth of her commitment can be glimpsed in an early comment she made to me: "It always strikes me that there seems to be a strange parallel between psychoanalysis and editing: in editing, you also have to suspend memory, otherwise you will read what you know should be there rather than what is actually there..." (Klara King personal communication).

Copyright acknowledgements

From *The International Journal of Psychoanalysis*, published by Wiley, Copyright Institute of Psychoanalysis. All rights reserved. No part of these publications may be reproduced, stored, transmitted, or diseminated, in any form, or by any means, without prior permission from Taylor & Francis Group, to whom all requests to reproduce copyright material should be directed, in writing: D. Birksted-Breen, "Time and the après-coup"; R. Britton, "Publication Anxiety: Conflict Between Communication and Affiliation" and *"Taming Wild Thoughts*. By W. R. Bion"; L. D. Brown, "Bion's Discovery of Alpha Function: Thinking under Fire on the Battlefield and in the Consulting Room"; E. T. De Bianchedi, "Whose Bion? Who is Bion?"; D. Duncan, "A Thought on the Nature of Psychoanalytic Theory"; M. Eigen, "The Area of Faith in Winnicott, Lacan and Bion"; A. Green, "Cogitations: By Wilfred R. Bion", "On Negative Capability—A Critical Review of W. R. Bion's *Attention and Interpretation*" and "The Primordial Mind and the Work of the Negative"; H. Guntrip, "The Concept of Psychodynamic Science"; B. Joseph, "An Aspect of the Repetition Compulsion"; M. Klein, "Notes on Some Schizoid Mechanisms"; O. Lyth, "Wilfred Ruprecht Bion (1897–1979)"; E. O'Shaughnessy, "Whose Bion?" and "Relating to the Superego"; T. H. Ogden, "On Not Being Able to dream" and "Elements of Analytic Style: Bion's *Clinical Seminars*"; P. C. Sandler, "The Origins of Bion's Work"; H. Segal, "Symposium on Fantasy—Fantasy and Other Mental Processes"; E. B. Spillius, "Some Developments from the Work of Melanie Klein"; N. Symington, "The Possibility of Human Freedom and its Transmission (With Particular Reference to the Thought of Bion)"; D. Taylor, "Commentary on Vermote's 'on the Value of "Late Bion" to Analytic Theory and Practice'"; M. Teising, "Permeability and Demarcation in the Psychoanalytic Process: Functions of the Contact-barrier"; N. Tracey, "Thinking about and Working with Depressed Mothers in the Early Months of Their Infant's Life".

From *The Journal of Analytic Psychology,* published by Wiley: J. Culbert-Koehn, "An Analysis with Bion: An Interview with James Gooch".

From *The Psychoanalytic Quarterly,* published by Wiley: L. J. Brown, "The Cognitive Effects of Trauma: Reversal of Alpha Function and the Formation of a Beta Screen".

From the *Journal of the American Psychoanalytical Association* published by Sage Publications Inc.: R. Britton, "Common and Uncommon Ground: Panellist's Response"; H. B. Levine, "Truth, Growth, and Deception: The Late Seminars of Wilfred Bion: *The Italian Seminars*. By Wilfred R. Bion"; J. Steiner, "A Mind of One's Own: A Kleinian View of Self and Object".

From Journals published by Taylor and Francis: *Journal of Infant, Child, and Adolescent Psychotherapy:* Ron Britton, Judy Chused, Steve Ellman, et al., 'Panel II: The Oedipus Complex, the Primal Scene, and the Superego'. *Journal of Child Psychotherapy*: Edna O'Shaughnessy, "A Commemorative Essay on W.R. Bion's Theory of Thinking"; Hanna Segal, "The Importance of Symbol-Formation in the Development of the Ego' – in context"; Frances Tustin, "A Modern Pilgrim's Progress: Reminiscences of Personal Analysis with Dr. Bion". *International*

Forum of Psychoanalysis: Marco Conci "Bion and His First Analyst, John Rickman (1891–1951): A Revisitation of Their Relationship in the Light of Rickman's Personality and Scientific Production and Of Bion's Letters To Him (1939–1951)".
Psychoanalytic Inquiry: Michael Feldman, "Aspects of Reality, and the Focus of Interpretation"; Ignês Sodré, "Obsessional Certainty Versus Obsessional Doubt: From Two to Three'.

Reprinted with permission of Guilford Press from *The Psychoanalytic Review*: R. Britton, "Roundtable Discussion, 2, March 31, 2007" Publication year 2010.

The quotes from Karnac publications are with the permission of Karnac Books. An extract from *The Spontaneous Gesture: Selected Letters of D.W.Winnicott* (1987, Routledge) by permission of The Marsh Agency on behalf of The Winnicott Trust.

An extract from *The Dove that Returns, The Dove that Vanishes* (Parsons 2000) is reproduced with the kind permission of Michael Parsons.

Preface

This is a book of 365 quotes from the work of the psychoanalyst W.R. Bion. Something of an enigma, Bion often doesn't write in the way one would expect of a psychoanalyst, but he is being read ever increasingly around the world, within and outside the psychoanalytic community. Certain of his comments are often quoted, while swathes of his work lie almost untouched. How to make some of the detail of this work available? What he writes is often dense in the way a poem can be, and the book has the format of a "poem a day" collection – providing a way into his complete work a quote at a time.

Beginning with Bion's autobiography, *The Long Weekend: 1897–1919 (Part of a Life),* the book includes quotes from the best-known seminal papers of the 1950s; the increasingly unexpected content of the four books that followed; the International Seminars, and his novel, *A Memoir of the Future* (in which we see him relating to the turbulence his work has stirred in earlier years and talking "at the end of the day" still with a genius for observing human beings and how they can change – or not). Bion's more relaxed writings (personal notes, letters and the novel) throw light on the more condensed comments in his books, and where possible the two have been put together. On some pages there is more than one quote on the same subject – I have counted these as one. With the quotes are my commentaries and relevant excerpts from papers by analysts from the United Kingdom, the Americas and Europe. The book has more repetition of introductory material than is usual. This is in order to have it easily at hand when dipping into the book or reading a quote a day, as well as when reading it straight through.

It is hoped that the book will be accessible to those new to Bion's work, yet sufficiently detailed to offer something substantial to those who already know his work well. Bion was unusually interested in the understanding of human beings held by disciplines other than psychoanalysis, and it is hoped that the book will also be accessible to those outside the psychoanalytic professions.

Most of the Bion quotes are referenced to *The Complete Works of W.R. Bion,* Vols. I to XVI (edited by Chris Mawson; consultant editor, Francesca Bion; London, Karnac, 2014) and are abbreviated throughout as *CWB*. The remainder are from *Wilfred Bion: Los Angeles Seminars and Supervision* (edited by Joseph Aguayo & Barnet D. Marin; London, Karnac, 2013, and published after *CWB*), abbreviated throughout as *LASS*.

Introduction

"Why write then?" you may ask.
To prevent someone who KNOWS from filling the empty space.

(*CWB XIV*, p. 138)

The pleasure of doing this book is that the quotes give direct access to Bion's writings. The following notes are intended to provide a helpful "map".

The quote above is from the last lines of Bion's novel, *A Memoir of the Future,* written in his seventies. Also in his seventies, he wrote two volumes of autobiography, completed shortly before he died in 1979. His autobiography is perhaps the most accessible of all his writings and is so immediate and fresh, it is difficult to believe it was written long after the events it describes. I have put the autobiographical quotes at the beginning, as they recount his childhood, war experiences and some years after. Suffice it to say here that Bion was born in India and, from the age of 8, sent to Bishops Stortford boarding school in England. He left school in 1915 aged 17 and joined the Royal Tank Regiment as an officer – tanks being a new weapon. Bion was decorated with the DSO (Distinguished Service Order) and the French Legion of Honour. His first daughter, Parthenope (herself going on to become a psychoanalyst) made the following comment:

> It would, of course, be an excessive simplification to say that Bion became an analyst "because of" his war experiences – in fact, it might be equally true to say that he became one in spite of them; notwithstanding his exposure to mindless stupidity and the brutality of war, he still felt that there was enough goodness in mankind (and that it was thought-provoking enough) for it to be worth dedicating his life to the study of people.
>
> (Bion Talamo, "Aftermath", *CWB III*, p. 309)

After demobilisation in 1918, Bion studied history at Queen's College Oxford. He then went on to train as a doctor and psychiatrist at University College London. Bion had some psychotherapy in the years between the wars and worked as a psychotherapist himself (one patient being Samuel Beckett), but it was meeting the psychoanalyst John Rickman that made a real difference. He went into analysis with Rickman (I give more detail about Rickman in the book) and began the psychoanalytic training. Both analysis and training were interrupted by the advent of the Second World War in 1939. Bion joined the armed forces psychiatric services and with other psychiatrists, including Rickman, propounded a number of innovative schemes. Two were undertaken for the War Office Selection Board: devising new ways of selecting non-commissioned officers, and the Northfield Experiment (working with troops who had been invalided out of the war). The Northfield experiment was stopped by the military establishment after only six weeks, but it has had a considerable influence. Bion is said to have had little time for the military establishment, and himself comments that he was the only person he knew who was not promoted at all during the war years. The reader will find quotes on his work at Northfield hospital and the group work he went on to do at the Tavistock Clinic after the war.

When compiling the quotes from the First World War and then Northfield, I was struck by a pattern. Bion stood up to people and at the same time rallied them, together with him, against a common enemy. At the end of the First World War, the newly arrived guards (Welsh miners) were refusing to come out of their huts on parade. Bion has the guns turned on them, but made sure the guns were on their huts "with the hill behind". When they appeared – bristling with hostility and humiliation – he rallied them together against the "Boche" who could appear over the hill. In the Second World War, when he arrived at the Northfield hospital, he was dismayed by the state of things, and we find him using the same model of standing up to the men and uniting them against a common enemy: in this instance the enemy is identified as "neurosis". I think, too, that when he was so abrasive with the psychoanalytic community in the 1960s, he thought something was going wrong in psychoanalysis and was intent on uniting psychoanalysts against a common enemy: this time, "memory and desire".

Bion returned to his psychoanalytic training after the war and now to a training analysis with Melanie Klein that was to continue for eight years, until 1953. For some time between the completion of his analysis and her death in 1960, Bion was a member of a small group who met regularly with her – a remarkable group of people, which included Hanna Segal and Betty Joseph. When editing Hanna Segal's last book, I realised that during these years she and Bion were independently coming to some of the same key ideas at around the same time. An example is Segal's "repression barrier" and Bion's "contact barrier". When I pointed this out to Segal, she chuckled and said that Bion was always better at coming up with catchy names. Bion makes reference to very few psychoanalysts in his writing, but he does thank the people in this group.

Themes from the 1940s

In 1939 Freud arrived in London. To my knowledge, Bion did not meet him. However, Bion was always in an internal dialogue with Freud, and in Bion's 1940s papers on groups we find his most extended debate with Freud's views.

Freud thought of groups in terms of family dynamics. Bion extended this and argued that groups and societies operate at root to contain psychotic anxieties. In his group work Bion did not analyse the individual in the group; in fact, he says that "the individual must be allowed to get hanged". His analysis is of the functioning of the group. In the course of doing this, he was to identify what he calls the basic assumptions: forces that operate below the level of the group's reality-based work task.

Basic assumptions

One metaphor for the basic assumptions, although not a wholly satisfactory one, is that of the currents that run beneath the surface of the sea. Any particular area of sea is affected by different currents at different times. Sitting with the groups, Bion sensed underlying patterns operating in the themes that were presented on the surface. He came to the view that there were three identifiable patterns, and he called them basic assumption Dependency (*baD*), basic assumption Pairing (*baP*) and basic assumption Fight/Flight (*baF*). At any particular time, one assumption holds court, before being replaced by another. The change from one assumption to another is, at least in part, because none of the assumptions is satisfactory, and when in the ascendency, its defects also start to press on the group. There is more to be understood about why the basic assumptions are there, but Bion repeatedly comments that they are the repository of our wish to be able to develop and change without work or pain.

The enigmatic, brooding and questioning Sphinx

The description of the Sphinx as enigmatic, brooding and questioning is taken from a 1940s quote in which Bion describes the group's primitive anxiety about studying itself. I include it here to mark how, early in his thought, Bion was engrossed in the Oedipus myth. When Freud formulated the Oedipus complex in 1897 (the year following his father's death), his focus was on the passionate love and jealous hate felt towards one's parents in childhood. Bion altered the focus on the same myth and through it explored curiosity, knowing, thinking – a model for the way the mind itself works – and the hatred of all of these. The reader will find quotes on the Oedipus myth throughout the book.

By the end of the 1940s, Bion was in training as a psychoanalyst, and although he continued to think about groups (particularly in his 1970 book, *Attention and Interpretation*), he would not be working with groups again. Giving attention to the factors that promote or attack development and change would now be explored with his psychoanalytic patients.

Themes from the 1950s

I have begun the chapter on the 1950s with some of Bion's rather wry comments on his analysis with Klein. For example, on one occasion he wasn't sure of an interpretation given to him by Klein, and so he tried it out on one of his own patients!

Psychotic mechanisms

In the 1950s Bion and Segal and Herbert Rosenfeld embarked on working with psychotic patients in psychoanalysis. Segal had been in analysis with Klein during the years of Klein's formulation of the paranoid–schizoid position. Klein's ground-breaking paper "Notes on Some Schizoid Mechanisms" was published in 1946, and Segal said of this paper that it was "a bombshell and yet familiar". This may well have been true for Bion too, who was also in analysis with Klein at around this time. These analysts could draw on Klein's theory and clinical supervision and would also have been able to draw on her analysis of their own psychotic functioning.

Through the 1950s, Bion wrote a series of papers on psychotic illness and specific psychotic mechanisms, such as hallucination and attacks on linking. He explored in great depth the interplay between psychotic and non-psychotic functioning and what happens when there is a change in the balance of these. Quotes have been included from the majority of the papers, including a quote detailing the difference between Bion's analysis of a psychotic patient and Winnicott's own view of Bion's clinical material.

(Some ten years later Bion gave a number of seminars in Los Angeles in which he focused again on work with psychotic patients. Quotes from this time include excerpts from his somewhat heated debates with the Californian analyst Ralph Greenson.)

What brings about change?

In his first paper as a psychoanalyst, "The Imaginary Twin", we hear that Bion has been duly interpreting the Oedipal content, to little effect. He then describes his observation of the interaction happening between the patient and himself. This is an early example of what was to go on to become a substantial shift in psychoanalytic technique, from paying attention to content to paying more attention to the "actions" (enactments) that occur between patient and analyst.

On a later occasion, with a different patient, Bion takes seriously the patient's complaint that Bion is obstructing him. This leads to the realisation that projective identification is not only a way of getting rid of what is unwanted, but a mode of communication. Bion makes what is a mutative shift in perspective, from focusing solely on the level of disturbance in the patient to focusing on the analyst's capacity to take in the patient's projections. His recognition that allowing the patient's projection to "sojourn in my psyche" could result in some modification of the patient's bad feelings anticipated his soon-to-arrive thoughts about the container, the contained, and the relation between the two.

The evolution of a theory of thinking

Through his work with psychotic patients, Bion studied in detail the way people's thinking can fail. This can be either – or both – because of a failure in infancy in their having a more mature person to "contain" and process their raw experience, or an excess of intolerance of frustration and attacks on their own rudimentary thought. This work led Bion to propose the theory of thinking that is one of his key contributions to our understanding of human functioning.

Themes from the 1960s

During these years Bion held various positions: as Director of the London Clinic of Psychoanalysis (1956–62), as President of the British Psychoanalytical Society (1962–1965), and others. In 1960, on the death of Klein, he took over from her as Chairman of the Melanie Klein Trust. Oliver Lyth commented: "It was noticeable during this period that the conflicts between the different groups in the society diminished, not because of abandonment of honestly held opinions, but because the common elements of our work as psychoanalysts became more obvious" (Lyth 1980, p. 271).

In the early 1960s we see a change. He no longer wrote papers to be published in the *International Journal of Psychoanalysis,* but short books in which he seems freer to think in his own way. A part of this is the development of a new psychoanalytic language. It is not just that the terms are new, but Bion wanted it to function in a different way. He wanted the possibility of marking a phenomenon without saying conclusively what it is, so that it can then go on to be explored "for the rest of your life, if you so wish".

Alpha-function, alpha-elements, beta-elements

From the late 1950s, Bion had looked more closely at dreaming. We see his gradual departure from Freud's theory of dreaming (dreams as the protector of sleep, wish-fulfilment) to ideas about the function of dreams in the "digestion" and "suffering" (making personal) of emotional experiences. In early 1960 he drew a distinction between Freud's dream-work and what he called dream-work-α: the capacity to dream rests on the ability of dream-work-α to transform into α-elements that may be linked in a dream narrative. This was then replaced by simply "alpha-function" – although he also tended also to use alpha-function and "dreaming" somewhat interchangeably. In the 1960s, Bion was himself becoming able to think about the traumatic experiences he had suffered in the First World War, and this may have deeply informed the development of his work on alpha-function.

Beta-elements are the stuff before thought or the result of attacked thought, raw experience yet to be processed, or highly sophisticated manipulations produced by a mind that has become expert at "regulating" itself by evacuation. Beta-elements are transformed into alpha-elements by alpha-function – the name given to the absolutely key process in human functioning of the way something moves from not being thought at all (for example a psychosomatic symptom, an enactment,) to becoming thought.

Thinking and dreaming

Still in the early 1960s Bion was also coming to the view that we "dream" when awake as well as when asleep – even that night dreams may be the result of what we did not manage to "dream" during the day. In some psychoanalytic traditions we hear now of analysts speaking in terms of their work as "dreaming" with the patient.

Container–contained

Container–contained ($♀♂$) the concept that was to become so well known, is an aspect of alpha-function and is explored in the penultimate chapter of the first book of the 1960s, *Learning from Experience*. Freud had been well aware that without the care of the mother, self regulation through the pleasure principle could not operate; this, however, is different from Bion's model, in which the environment not only provides the conditions for an individual's self-regulation, but the regulation of the self is provided by the object. The relationship between container and contained is not always benign, and Bion goes into the detail of this particularly in the last book of the 1960s, *Attention and Interpretation*.

The Grid

Another major concern of the 1960s is Bion's attention to the science of psychoanalysis. He does not try to push psychoanalysis into the shape of other sciences – in fact, he is of the belief it has something to offer them – but he does want it to be as rigorous as possible. As part of his development of tools to this end, he produced the Grid. It has a vertical and a horizontal axis, and one can plot the level of development and use to which any material in a session is being put (both the patient and the analyst's material). This allows scrutiny and reflection – between sessions – on whether, for example, analyst and patient are stuck in a repeating pattern.

My own impression is that Bion may well have been "gridifying" what went on in his mind in any case. In reading his work, one can see that he has an unusual capacity to plot the "dance" between analyst and patient (perhaps with echoes of his group-work) and the palimpsest of different levels of functioning.

At the time of writing, use of the Grid hasn't really taken off – yet, anyway – when I was teaching a recent course on Bion, the people in the group who were working in IT were very interested in it.

Transformations and invariants

Transformations: Change from Learning to Growth, published in 1965, is held by many people to be Bion's most difficult book. Is it difficult because it is incomprehensible, or because it is disturbing? Bion talks about his psychotic patients with increasing depth, and this can be disturbing to read.

At the same time as drawing attention to the specific experience of the patient (i.e. it is not enough just to call something an hallucination), Bion is also concerned to identify underlying configurations that are mistakenly seen as different by the surfeit of theories in psychoanalysis. He does not want this book to add to psychoanalytic theory, but to aid observation. One of the most compelling clinical examples is of his identification of "invariants" through the breakdown of a psychotic patient in analysis. "Things" that appeared as psychosomatic symptoms suddenly become externalised. Having an understanding of the invariant elements supports the analyst's maintenance of the analytic setting.

Bion differentiates between different modes of transformation – in particular between "transference" and "transformations in hallucinosis". In transference we "transfer" as a current experience what is repressed, but in a way that allows some "intercourse" with the actual reality. As I write this, emails are arriving in my inbox between neighbours in my block about a cat who is pooing everywhere! The owners of the cat are sending friendly cute replies, but not dealing with the problem. I am imagining them as children, perhaps being rather spoilt and now expecting the world to behave as their parents did. I hope they are in for a shock, but they seem remarkably immune to anything that doesn't fit their expectation. Although the cat's owners seem immune, we do have the potential to "learn from experience" through our transferences as we register differences between our phantasies about the world and its reality. By contrast, "transformation in hallucinosis" is evacuative rather than explorative, and "in competition with", rather than in "intercourse" with the world.

Disturbing, too, is Bion's exploration of his own way of looking at things. He wants to broaden his observations beyond the model provided by the senses or deeply embedded in the culture (i.e. the model of cause and effect). He draws on the experience of the mystics in his analysis of the prevalence of pleasure principle functioning in what we assume to be our scientific thinking, and in the increasing attention he pays to "being" rather than "knowing". As psychoanalytic discourse, his religious language can be quite shocking. In this book, he does not civilise either psychosis or religion.

Some part company with Bion's work at *Transformations*. My own view is that he is thinking in a different way (not "deteriorating"). In the following book, *Attention and Interpretation: A Scientific Approach to Insight in Psycho-Analysis and Groups,* we see, for example, his most detailed thinking about his best-known earlier concept of container–contained, alongside his emerging most controversial work. Although there tends to be a split in how people see Bion's later work, I don't think this split was in him.

In 1968 Bion and his second wife, Francesca, moved to Los Angeles. One reason for the invitation was his expertise in working with psychotic patients. One reason he went was the pursuit of a greater freedom. It is extraordinary how much work/writing he did in his seventies.

Themes from the 1960s/1970s

Eschewing memory and desire

Bion most frequently presents eschewing "memory and desire" as the following of a rule. In his response to the discussants of his paper in Los Angeles, however, we see a different picture. He suggests that we take "memory" and "desire", see what *we* understand by them, and embark on a process of discovery. This is much more in the vein of the way he wants to use the term "alpha-function", to mark a process that can then be explored. So why did he say it so abrasively, and why did it have the effect it did? I suggested earlier that he may have been attempting to unite the psychoanalytic group against a common enemy. Not everyone was convinced that there was an enemy. Bion was convinced: he thought that we (as psychoanalysts) underestimate the subtle attacks on our own contact with psychic reality and the extent of our own defensiveness. I find myself reminded of his arrival at Northfield Hospital (back in the 1940s) to find his desk covered with request slips to either get away or stay away from the hospital. He was struck then by there being a lack of discipline. Did Bion think there was a lack of discipline in the psycho-analysis of the 1960s? A prevalent view in England is that from the mid 1960s on Bion is becoming increasingly less disciplined himself. Bion's view is, I think, the opposite.

On the nature of change and growth: "being" and "O"

Bion came to a question in later life that Freud also came to in his later life: why is change so difficult to achieve? In 1920 Freud's response was to consider the existence of an inherent destructiveness in human beings (the death instinct). His conclusions were part of Bion's psychoanalytic inheritance. Fifty years later, Bion's response went in a different direction: to the difference between "K" (knowing) and "O" (being). The use of the letters "K" and "O" again allows us to mark a subject that can then be enquired into.

   Up to this point Bion's work had been very much to do with thinking. His theory of thinking is a major contribution to psychoanalysis. Now "thinking" – understood as a profoundly "digestive" process – was construed as limited and contrasted with "being". In the 1950s Bion wrote particularly about his psychotic patients and their difficulties with thinking. In his 1970s book, *Attention and Interpretation,* he makes reference to a new group of patients: those who have difficulty "being" (suffering their experiences as part of being themselves). It is not only the patient's difficulty with "being" that concerns Bion, but also the analyst's "being" properly in the session with the patient. At its core, I think, he is indicating a way of being with the patient – that is, being *in* what is essential. It is worth mentioning – and the reader will see this in the quotes from his patients – Bion remained strict throughout about the analytic setting.

"F" (Faith)

In the late 1960s/1970s Bion began to use the term "F" (Faith) to describe the psychoanalyst's relation to the non-sensible world of psychic reality. How can a man so concerned with being in touch with reality take on the idea of faith as a key concept? From the point of view of science, even common sense, isn't faith delusional belief? I must confess a liking for conundrums and have grappled with this one for quite some time. Take, for example, "The Red Wheelbarrow", by American modernist poet William Carlos Williams (1883–1963). The poem describes the scene of a red wheelbarrow and white chickens after the rain. The scene painted for us is one that would be "seen" by the senses of sight, and perhaps smell. Yet we are also able to *sense* the weight of meaning held by the scene. In his use of the term F (Faith), I think Bion is talking about a faculty rather than a belief. It is not necessarily a precise faculty, there are different interpretations of the poem, but it is nonetheless a faculty.

The "Messianic idea" and the "Establishment"

In *Attention and Interpretation* Bion refers to the relationship between what he calls "the messianic idea" and the "establishment". Growth occurs if a new idea is allowed to be strong, while being rightly assessed and checked by the establishment to ascertain real worth, not just superficial daring. In order to do this, the establishment is required to allow its established ideas and practices to be put into question. Growth does not occur if the challenging idea is suppressed by the establishment through ridicule or avoidance, or if the establishment is dismissed as irrelevant or "blown up" by the idea.

It does seem that Bion had grown frustrated with the external establishment (or had always been frustrated with the external establishment?). The key question is whether he maintained a healthy robust internal establishment through which to scrutinise his emerging ideas. Here is a quote from Claudio Neri, who attended Bion's *Italian Seminars*:

> I realized that my own and my colleagues' idea of a "Bion of the generation of '68", an anarchic Bion, needed to be reconciled with the reality we had experienced of a "Colonel Bion", a "soldier Bion", and a "Bion who demands discipline". Bion's roots lay in Imperial Britain and India. He had a powerful sense of the establishment and of belonging. However, this also enabled him to be very original.
>
> (Neri 2015, pp. 26–27)

Themes from the 1970s

We move now into the 1970s. Bion was writing a novel and two volumes of his autobiography, and he was presenting lectures and seminars in the Americas and Europe. There are a large number of entries in the book from the 1970s, the format of his presentations in lectures and seminars being particularly suitable to be quoted. Bion addresses many subjects in this period, and the seminars and supervisions give us very good access to his clinical wisdom. Taking a step back, I realised that a central theme in his later work/writings was war.

War

In his seventies Bion wrote more about his experiences in the First World War than at any time, except for the *War Memoirs*, written immediately after the war. He was also keenly aware of the current dangers of war. What is it about human beings that contributes to their being creatures who go to war? It is of note that Parthenope Bion Talamo commented that Bion talked surprisingly little about man's aggression.

In his novel *A Memoir of the Future*, Bion makes the following statement:

> If the Oedipus story is the weapon that reveals homo, it is also the story
> that conceals, but does not reveal, that by which it will destroy itself.
>
> (*CWB XII*, p. 62)

What defensive armour does Oedipus have? Isn't Oedipus bravely pursuing the truth? Bion has held him up as a symbol of inquiry: he does, however, also refer to the arrogance of Oedipus.

From here, my own thoughts took the following path:

Oedipus, of course, doesn't just want to kill his father and marry his mother – he actually (if unknowingly) does it, and in so doing he breaches the generational divide between parents and children. Does Oedipus also go where he ought not to in his relation to knowledge? On the surface, he seems very justified in his pursuit of answers: he is trying to save Thebes from a plague, after all. His relation to knowledge, however, results in gaining information while lacking the wisdom – the developmental achievement of wisdom – to bear what he discovers. On realising his patricide and incest, he takes out his own eyes, and we see the deterioration of his character in the following book. This fits with what Bion says about humankind being "clever monkeys". At the time of his writing in the 1970s, he had particularly in mind the construction of nuclear weapons: the accumulation of knowledge without the wisdom to use it safely. The last line of his novel is: "Wishing you all a Happy Lunacy and a Relativistic Fission. . . ."

Beginnings and "wild thoughts"

Bion did not see himself as a messiah, but he was on a mission. The warfare he was engaged in was what he calls "the war of the mind". It could equally be called "the war for the mind". His "call to arms" is for people to allow themselves to have the thoughts that are actually there, both sophisticated and primitive, and to help their patients do this. He speaks of there being a spectrum in what we are open to. In his later work one hears him listening for what is most primitive, even embryonic, in adult patients, myths and human behaviour. On one occasion he paints a rather amusing picture of thoughts flying around and needing catching. At the same time, he conveys the weighty difficulty of living *in* the life that is one's own.

Religion and mysticism

There is much discussion of religion (God and the Devil) in Bion's novel, *A Memoir of the Future*, as well as poignant references to the lack of an "answering god" in his parents' and his own religious experience when growing up. Bion himself came from a Protestant missionary family, Swiss Calvinist of Huguenot origin on his father's side, and Anglo-Indian on his mother's (Bion Talamo 2005, p. 183). In both the novel and his seminars he elaborates on his view that human beings are, by nature, religious. On the question of whether there is a god: he does not put everything down to constructions made by the human mind.

Saying goodbye

In a number of his statements in these final years, one can hear him saying goodbye.

The Bions returned to England in 1979, and moved into a house in Oxford at the beginning of October. Bion became ill with myeloid leukaemia in the third week of October; he died on 8 November.

The book ends with six "Last Quotes". I end this Introduction from the last one of them:

> It is easy in this age of the plague – not of poverty and hunger, but of plenty, surfeit and gluttony – to lose our capacity for awe. It is as well to be reminded by the poet Herman Melville that there are many ways of reading books, but very few of reading them properly – that is, with awe. How much the more is it true of reading people.
>
> (From Bion's Introduction to his unfinished
> anthology of poems, *CWB II*, p. 263)

A list of the 365 quotes

I   *The Long Weekend: 1897–1919 (Part of a Life)*

(Written in Bion's seventies in the 1970s and first published in 1982, *The Long Weekend* is Bion's autobiography of the first 22 years of his life, including his childhood in India and the First World War.)

1   Ayah, and Mother's lap
2   Arf Arfer
3   Tiger
4   India
5   Arrival at boarding school
6   Wiggling
7   Holidays: the Hamiltons
8   Holidays: the Archers
9   Munden
10   Sublimation

2   Bion's war

(Quotes from *The Long Weekend, War Memoirs 1917–1919* (written immediately after the war) and other writings.)

11   War and parents
12   Weekend pass: Bion and his Mother
13   Tanks
14   Dante's Inferno
15   The Battle of Cambrai
16   Receiving the Distinguished Service Order (DSO)
17   The full force of passivity
18   In the dream I must have wished it was only a war
19   Like a small child
20   Sweeting

3   *All My Sins Remembered: Another Part of a Life*

(Written in the 1970s and published in 1985, *All My Sins Remembered* is Bion's autobiography from age 22 to 50.)

4   The 1930s and 1940s

(Including his group work papers published together in 1961 in *Experiences in Groups*.)

5 The Other Side of Genius

(Letters to his wife Francesca, and his children Parthenope, Julian and Nicola; written 1951–1979 and published in 1985.)

About Francesca Bion

(A number of quotes from *The Other Side of Genius* that refer to specific writings/ occasions have been included later in the book.)

6 Papers of the 1950s

(The papers of the 1950s and quotes from letters written during those years.)

7   *Cogitations*

(Notes written from February 1958 to April 1979; published in 1992.)

8   A theory of thinking

(Paper published 1962 and then again in *Second Thoughts* in 1967.)

9   Learning from Experience

(Published in 1962.)

10   The Grid

(Includes quotes from the whole of Bion's work.)

The Rows:

The Columns:

11 *Elements of Psycho-Analysis*

(Published in 1963.)

12 *Transformations: Change from Learning to Growth*

(Published in 1965.)

13   *"Memory and Desire" (1965)*

(Published in 1965.)

14   *Attention and Interpretation: A Scientific Approach to Insight in Psycho-Analysis and Groups*

(Published in 1970.)

15 Visiting Los Angeles: seminars and supervision

Letters

Further Cogitations, 1976–1968:

16   Brazilian Lectures, 1973–74

17   Clinical Seminars and Four Papers: "Brasilia 1975"

18   Bion in New York and São Paulo "New York, 1977"

23   "A Paris Seminar"

24   A Memoir of the Future: Book I – The Dream

25   A Memoir of the Future: Book 2 – The Past Presented

26   A Memoir of the Future: Book 3 – The Dawn of Oblivion

27   Last quotes

From Francesca Bion's "Envoi"
Francesca Bion after Bion's death

Part I

Autobiography

Chapter 1

The Long Weekend: 1897–1919 (Part of a Life)

Introduction

The Long Weekend and Bion's second volume of his autobiography, *All My Sins Remembered: Another Part of a Life*, were written when he was in his seventies, but as the record of Bion's first 50 years, the quotes have been put at the beginning of the book.

The Long Weekend begins with his childhood in Muttra in the United Provinces of Northwest India, where Bion's father was an irrigation engineer. The first four quotes are about India. In the fifth quote he has arrived in a boarding school in England, where he was sent at the age of 8, never to return to India.

From the age of 8, Bion grew up in groups. After being sent to boarding school, it was more than three years before he saw his mother again "and then, momentarily, did not recognise her" (Francesca Bion, 1994, pp. 91–92).

Bion left school in 1915, just before his eighteenth birthday, and joined the Royal Tank Regiment. *The Long Weekend* quotes about these years have been put together with his other writings on the war in Chapter 2: "Bion's War".

Quotes

1 Ayah, and Mother's lap
2 Arf Arfer
3 Tiger
4 India
5 Arrival at boarding school
6 Wiggling
7 Holidays: the Hamiltons
8 Holidays: the Archers
9 Munden
10 Sublimation

[1]   Ayah and Mother's lap

Our ayah was a wizened little woman who, in so far as I connected age with her at all, was assumed by my sister and me to be very old, much older than our father and mother. We were very fond of her, perhaps more fond than of our parents. On second thoughts, perhaps not. My mother was a little frightening. For one thing she might die because *she* was so old. She was not so old as our ayah; my sister and I agreed that she was not less than, say, two or maybe three hundred years old, and though this was a ripe age she did not seem likely to die. Our mother, on the other hand, was peculiar; it felt queer if she picked me up and put me on her lap, warm and safe and comfortable. Then suddenly cold and frightening, as it was many years later at the end of school service when the doors were opened and a cold draught of night air seemed to sigh gently through the sermonically heated chapel. Sermons, the Headmaster, God, The Father Almighty, Arf Arfer Oo Arf in Mphm, please make me a good boy. I would slip off her lap quickly and hunt for my sister.

(*CWB I*, p. 13)

Many years later Bion commented about a woman who had "married a man who had risen from the ranks. She had therefore lost caste and had become, like my dear ayah, an untouchable" (*CWB II*, p. 50).

Parthenope Bion Talamo

"Bion certainly absorbed a very great amount of Indian culture, much more than most of the, shall we say, colonialist children of the time did, precisely because of the work that his father did—he was a civil engineer who built some of the first railways in India and very long irrigation canals (1,600–1,700 kilometres) whose plotted course, like the railways, often passed through uninhabited areas (including the jungle).

So the family followed the construction site and moved month by month, as the construction site moved; practically a small European nucleus and a very large number of Indians so my father, when he was little, certainly for example spoke Hindustani fluently, something that he later forgot completely. A colleague from Bombay told me he heard Bion speaking in the last year of his life, giving a lecture in which he spoke about the *Bhagavad Gita*: speaking about sacred texts he had a very strong English accent, but when he quoted even a phrase of Hindustani he had no accent; so there was certainly a level, a stratification that had become entirely unconscious, of an Indo-European language that had been completely forgotten."

(1996 [2011] pp. 429–430)

[2]   Arf Arfer

In a sunny room I showed my father a vase of some yellow flowers for him to admire the skill with which I had arranged them.

"Yes", he said, "very good."

"But do look Daddy."

"I am; it's lovely."

Still I was not satisfied. "It's very pretty, isn't it?"

"Yes," he said, "it is."

"I'm not lying Daddy. I did it all myself."

That stopped him in his tracks. He was upset.

"Why did you say that?"

"What Daddy?"

"I never expected you to be lying."

"Well I wasn't", I replied becoming afraid that Arf Arfer would appear.

Arf Arfer was very frightening. Sometimes when I heard grown-ups talking they would indulge in bursts of meaningless laughter, "Arf! Arf! Arf!" they would go. This would happen especially when my sister or I spoke. We would watch them seriously, wide-eyed. Then we would go into another room and practice. Arf, arf, arf. . . .

(*CWB I*, pp. 16–17)

[3] Tiger

That night Arf Arfer came in terror "like the King of Kings". The hunt had killed a tiger and the body had been brought to our camp. His mate came to claim him and for the next two nights the camp was circled by fires and torches burning bright to keep her out. With her great head and mouth directed to the ground so as to disguise her whereabouts she roared her requiem. Even my fear was swallowed up in awe as almost from inside our tent there seemed to come a great cough and then the full-throated roar of the tigress's mourning. All that night and the next it continued while even our brave dogs shivered and snarled and cowered. No sooner had the sun set to release the orchestra of the tropical night than we were aware of the added diapason.

"She won't eat us Daddy? You are sure she won't?"

We slept safe in their tents for those nights. On the third night her vigil was short. She went away before midnight and came no more.

(CWB I, pp. 22–23)

[4]   India

None the less I loved India. The blazing, intolerable sun – how wonderful it was! The mid-day silence, the great trees with leaves hanging motionless in the breathless air, the brain-fever bird with its rising reiterated call, "Brain-fever, brain-fever, brain-fever ...", then silence again.

I discovered it was a marvellous place to play trains. The intense heat conspired to produce masses of fine white dust. Nonchalantly I kicked it up and was rewarded by a great cloud that rose into the air. I did it again. Before I had time to think I was racing around, kicking up huge clouds of ... steam ... in front of me like a huge "Ee Ay Ah" locomotive. The Devil entered into me: The Devil, unlike Arf Arfer, was a great friend of mine. "Go on! Do it again", he said. "Lead us not into temptation", I learned to pray, but only rather half-heartedly. Temptation, unlike heaven, was such fun. The immense speed at which I was travelling, the intoxicating sulphurous fumes of smoke which belched out from the pistons in front of me – glorious! And much superior to electric city with its old slug of buttered locomotive.

"What *have* you been doing?" my mother asked. "Just look at you! White ... from top to toe!"

I couldn't "look at me" but I saw what she meant. I was a bit dusty. She, poor woman, thought I had come in for a drink, but in fact it was the great E.I.R. express locomotive come to have its tank filled in its record-making run across India and there was not a moment to lose. I tried to make her understand that I had to go at once. It took her some time to make *me* understand – even now I can hardly believe it – that I was never to do it again. Never!....

Later, when the monsoon came, I found she was curiously blind about *that*.

"What rain?" I asked, not hopefully, as I stood before her "soaked to the skin" as she called it. It made it worse that I felt she was laughing – inside.

"You're laughing", I said. "No", she said looking very stern. So she wasn't sad; and she wasn't laughing either.

(CWB I, pp. 36–37)

[5] Arrival at boarding school

The train worked steadily, sometimes painfully over the stiffer gradients of the Western Ghats till it drew in to the terminus at Bombay. The railway station, like other architectural monuments of the British Raj, was a mixture of tawdry provincialism and Imperial domesticity which even in retrospect can evoke in me nostalgic feelings of great poignancy. I came in time to believe that these feelings were the substitute for what others called "homesickness". But I had no home for which I could feel sick – only people and things. Thus, when I found myself alone in the playground of the Preparatory School in England where I kissed my mother a dry-eyed goodbye, I could see, above the hedge which separated me from her and the road which was the boundary of the wide world itself, her hat go bobbing up and down like some curiously wrought millinery cake carried on the wave of green hedge. And then it was gone.

Numbed, stupefied, I found myself staring into a bright, alert face. "Which are you – A or B?" it said. Other faces had gathered.

"A", I said hurriedly in response to the urgency I felt in their curiosity.

"You're *not*! You jolly well say "B". You know nothing about it!" This was only too true.

"B", I said obediently.

"You dirty little liar!" said the first one. Appealing passionately to the rest, "He just said he was A. Didn't he?" That I had to admit.

"You can't go back on that", said the advocate of B. "You must stay B or you'll be a beastly little turn-coat!" he cried heatedly.

"All right. I'll stay B."

A fight developed. I heard the first one shouting, "He is a beastly turn-coat; and a liar anyway. We don't want him. Do we chaps?" The crowd had grown to formidable proportions, say, six or seven. "No", they shouted.

"Don't mind them", said the second boy. "You stick to B." And I did – for the rest of my life – though it took a long time before I discovered, and even then did not understand, that the main school was divided into Houses. School House, being bigger than all others, was divided into School House A and School House B-rivals. That was the immediate issue which had been solved by my becoming for ever B.

The storm subsided as if it had never been of the slightest interest to anyone. B, *not* A; not A – B; *that* was what I had to remember.

At last the ghastly day ended and I was able to get under the bedclothes and sob.

(CWB I, pp. 43–44)

[6] Wiggling

England. . . .

The day Thou gavest Lord is ended. Bed at – nearly – last. But first we had to say our prayers. Each knelt in prayer at the end of his bed. . . . Shod with the gospel of peace, which the moth could not corrupt nor gravel wear out, I was going to sleep. I would leap in to bed and there, if the bed did not creak too much, I could start wiggling. This was so delightful that a new danger crept in – I might laugh. The danger was real because no one had ever known me to laugh.

One day in class the master noticed that I was wiggling; it seems hard to believe now that I could ever have supposed he didn't, for my wiggling could hardly have been more anonymous than the Indian bear's progress through the forest. He was very gentle. "Don't do that Wilfred", he said, "or you will have to be sent away." I could hardly believe my ears. The other boys, witnesses of my rebuke, stared at me in stony innocence like the gods in the caves at Elephantine. . . .

(CWB I, pp. 49–50)

One night when I was lying on my bed with pyjamas on waiting for Dudley to get into his bed, he suddenly discarded the towel he had round his waist and jumped astride me as if challenging me to wrestle. "Now how do you feel?" he said. I felt nothing physically; mentally a sense of boredom and anti-climax, which soon communicated itself to Dudley who, after a few futile attempts to provoke a struggle, got off. I was bitterly disappointed. I had no idea what I wanted, but I did know – and the realization grew with time – that I wanted it badly. I wished I had encouraged Dudley to go on and then I would have found out what he was going to do. But now I think Dudley did not know any more than I did.

When I expressed this to my psychoanalyst years later he was convinced I knew. This seems to me now to be a failure to understand the horrible and painful nature of frustration, its powerful contribution, with fear and guilt, to an absolute hatred and loathing of sexuality in any shape or form. Furtive-ness, guilt, frustration, in alternation or all together – such was my experi-ence for many years, the most impressionable years of my life, the matrix from which passionate love supposedly will spring.

(CWB I, p. 87)

[7]   Holidays: the Hamiltons

Rhodes's and Hamilton's "people" used to ask me to their houses for occasional – I now think most generously frequent – holidays. . . .

Mrs Hamilton and Mrs Rhodes, both in their different ways, helped to make my last year at the prep school one in which I began to break through what I see in retrospect to have been an intolerable exoskeleton of misery. . . .

Mr Hamilton was a good business man and a good employer, judging by the respect in which he was held by his employees. His shrewdness frightened me though I admired his keen, alert manner. . . .

I remember his once describing at table that someone had gone over Niagara Falls in a barrel on some kind of money-making wager. "And if he had got through that, then the next fool would have had to go over in a paper-bag." This so tickled me that although as a small boy, and a guest at that, I should have been seen and not heard, I laughed so undisguisedly that Mr Hamilton, Mrs Hamilton and several adult friends could not help catching the infection. "Paper bag!" I repeated, and would start off again, the others being swept in by my amusement.

That holiday was a revelation. I could not have believed I could ever be so happy. I was not pleased when the time came for me to go to Archer Hall where the Rhodes's lived. I was taken in the car – not that it was called a car. It was referred to, that glorious creamcoloured, brassembellished confection distilled out of Heaven itself, as The Leon Bollet – the one and only in our world, a world made radiant by its presence in our midst.

(*CWB I*, pp. 65–66)

Léon Bollée Automobiles: French company founded by Léon Bollée in Le Mans. It built automobiles between 1895 and 1931, and around the time that Bion was at the Hamiltons, it built about 600 cars a year.

[8]   Holidays: the Archers

Archer Hall was at the top of a hill and was approached by a long drive which led from a lane to the valley of the river Rib, then climbed to the farmhouse....

Mrs Rhodes would express a shrill, explosive, but immediately muted laugh; this she did as she gave me a welcoming kiss. She asked after my parents whom I had forgotten; thinking of them was inseparable from home-sickness. To all such inquiries I used to reply that they were "very well thank you"; no more "summer suns are glowing" for me. In fact they were in India, my mother having returned with my sister at the beginning of the year; they were a nuisance – the cause of having to write a letter once a week.

Life at Archer Hall was austere in a way that was new to me. I always picture the Hamiltons in summer time with the lawns brooded over by their magnificent cedar....

When I see Archer Hall it is as a great farmhouse lying amidst fields, deserted, sleeping its winter sleep. Mr Rhodes, weathered, striding from field to field, stopping now and then to talk to a farm-hand, seemed to typify the ruthless and austere character of farm life in prosperous England. It *was* prosperous, but the prosperity did not conceal the relentless struggles with an impenetrable cloak of comfort – as did the wealth of the Hamiltons.

(*CWB I*, pp. 67–69)

[9]   Munden

"You two boys haven't anything to do", said Mr Rhodes briskly one fine morning, not so much formulating and reporting an observed fact as premising a definitory hypothesis. "Just drive Curly [the cow]. over to Mundens for me...."

(*CWB I*, p. 70)

Cousin Bob met us at Munden. He would not allow us in the pigeon-cote because "the mess had not been cleared up".

"What mess?"

"Oh, it was a bad business! One of my foremen went up there last night with a gun and blew his head off. It was a terrible mess."

This time neither Heaton nor I wanted to see.

The sun shone brightly through the soft golden haze, the doves strutted and cooed, Bob spoke quietly to Heaton and me, but "up there" was a "mess".

(*CWB I*, pp. 72–73)

This incident may provide the setting of a key scene in Bion's novel *A Memoir of the Future*. In the novel there is a man hiding from an invading force in a pigeon cote. He is then joined by a friend. When one of the invaders enters, the friend kills the invader by smashing in his skull.

[10]   Sublimation

"Sublimation", not yet a Freudian term, was used by some for what in fact was a substitution. Games were substituted for sex; even religion was thought of by the more advanced as if it were some harmless substitute. No one thought that sublimation could mean the reaching for, yearning for games which were sublime, a religion that was sublime and not a stopper that could dam back the noxious matter till it stank, or bury the growth of personality till it turned cancerous.

(*CWB I*, p. 108)

Chapter 2

Bion's war

Introduction

Bion wrote about the First World War at a number of different times in his life.

To the quotes from *The Long Weekend*, I have added quotes from his *War Memoirs*: "Diary", "Commentary", and "Amiens".

War Memoirs 1917–1919

Bion's first writings on the war are his *War Memoirs*. Bion had kept a diary during the war, but this had been lost. The *War Memoirs* were written soon after the end of the war, when he went up to Queen's College, Oxford. Hand-written and contained in three hardbound notebooks, it was offered to his parents as compensation, as he had found it impossible to write letters to them during the war. To my knowledge there is no record of their response. The *Memoirs* are a factual record of Bion's war service in France in the Royal Tank Regiment between June 1917 and January 1919.

On the opening page is a hand-written note to his parents: "In place of letters I should have written! – from Wilfred".

Diary of Amiens

Nearly 40 years later, in August 1958, Bion (now in his early sixties) and Francesca, his second wife, visited France and the battlefields of the First World War. Bion wrote a narrative in the third person of his experience as a young man (he attributes some of his own actions to others and imagines the experiences that others may have had). The account ends in mid-sentence. Francesca Bion suggests that this was because "other more pressing commitments intervened" (he was working on *Learning from Experience* at the time), but mid-sentence seems more abrupt than this might account for. Here are the last sentences:

"I think his nerve must have gone", said de Freine.

"It's very likely, sir. He had had continuous action since the time the battalion came out here."

"Well, for that matter, so have you, but you don't show any signs of crack-
ing up, I'm glad to say."

Bion did not believe him. He felt that people who cracked up were merely
those who did not allow the rest of the world to....

[*Ends here – no more written.*]

(*CWB III*, p. 305)

The "Commentary"

Some 10 or so years later, now in California, Francesca Bion made a typescript
of the original *War Memoir* diaries, and Bion read it for the first time in 50 years.
He wrote a "Commentary" in the form he was to use in his novel, *A Memoir of the
Future*: the conversation is between "Bion", the inexperienced young man of 21,
and "Myself", the wise old man of 75.

The Long Weekend and A Memoir of the Future

The Long Weekend (from which the quotes of his childhood have been taken) was
written in Bion's seventies. It includes a long section on the war. The war is also
very present in his novel, *A Memoir of the Future,* also written in his seventies.
The text written immediately after the war contains more factual details, diagrams
and maps. Those written in his seventies give voice to his having taken on the
experience of war, within himself, over the intervening years of his adult life.

Quotes

11   War and parents
12   Weekend pass: Bion and his Mother
13   Tanks
14   Dante's Inferno
15   The Battle of Cambrai
16   Receiving the Distinguished Service Order (DSO)
17   The full force of passivity
18   In the dream I must have wished it was only a war
19   Like a small child
20   Sweeting
21   "To die for a squabble"
22   Writing to Sweeting's Mother
23   Asser
24   Get out
25   Leave
26   Refusal to parade
27   Bion, Myself and Asser
28   Who had gone mad?

[11]   War and parents

From *The Long Weekend*

As the train drew into Liverpool Street station I knew I would shortly meet my father and mother. Thank God, thank God! And then I thought, for what?....

(CWB I, p. 118)

War

...I got there. In my parent's bedroom the electric light cast its livid warmth; they were glad to see me – that I knew. But I could feel that her boy's precocious departure for the war left my mother kissing a chitinous semblance of a boy from whom a person had escaped. But I was imprisoned, unable to break out of the shell which adhered to me. "Couvre-toi de gloire!", but how loudly my unjesting soul said, "Couvre-toi de flannelle", despite the prickliness of those hated Indian stockings. The roar of traffic in the streets below "bore all its sons away". Although fanned by its waves yet I remained tenuously held by a thread, my father praying that I would join the Church's communion; my mother praying, as I knew she must be, that I would not be swept away and lost. Often I have wondered whether it had not been better if those invisible bands had not been so steely strong, or whether, had they been any weaker, I should have lost my hold on sanity.

(CWB I, pp. 121–122)

Bion's parents came to London at the time of his enlisting. Initially turned down, Bion obtained a commission through a contact of his fathers.

[12]   Weekend pass: Bion and his Mother

From *The Long Weekend*

My first and only week-end pass from that camp was a horror which plucked harshly and cruelly at chords which I had forgotten – my week-end of respite from the daily misery of the prep school. I loathed it; I hated every moment of it. I have no recollection of how I spent the day; I must have been conscious – my psychoanalytical bible tells me so. What it was like for my mother I do not know and cannot remember caring. I was cut off from my base. And the enemy was in full occupation of my mother.

(*CWB I*, p. 131)

[13]   Tanks

From *The Long Weekend*

Haig and his Staff have been blamed for thinking that such terrain was suitable for tanks, for not reconnoitring the ground personally, for not understanding the capacities and limitations of tanks. Well, we three *did* know the tanks and we were reconnoitring the ground on the spot. But I do not remember that any of us for a moment thought that a fortyton tank could float; the mud must have seeped into the place where our minds were supposed to be....

(CWB I, p. 143)

With the engine's roar silenced we could appreciate the racket outside, like an inferno of slamming doors. And now I was aware of a novel sensation; the tank with which I was familiar as a solid mass of steel was shaking continuously like a wobbling jelly. No protection more solid than a figment of the imagination.

I was not aware of being afraid, which, from the point of view of comfort, is as good as not being afraid. The tank continued to wobble and the doors to slam; sometimes the slam and the wobble were instantaneous. When I realized that both violent slam and wobble occurred at intervals which were rhythmically connected, I knew we were very near the bursting point of a heavy shell. I felt we should move; there was nowhere to go.

Since it was dark the enemy were firing blind on their established barrage lines and, so far, we had not been hit. Could a shell fall short or over? It could – so I gave up thinking about it, thus taking shelter instinctively in mindlessness.

(CWB I, p. 147)

After some months of what he describes as a good training in the United Kingdom, Bion sees his first action at the third battle of Ypres, the Battle of Passchendaele July/August 1917. It was known as the "Battle of Mud". Constant shelling had churned the clay soil and smashed the drainage systems. Within a few days, the heaviest rain for 30 years had turned the soil into a quagmire. It became so deep that men and horses drowned in it. The tanks could not function in the mud; Bion's own tank ends up sinking into it.

[14]   Dante's *Inferno*

From *The Long Weekend*

Sometimes it stopped for a minute or so and then the chorus broke out again, not raucous or crude – gentle. Dante's Inferno – but how much better we do these things now.

"Do you mean no stretcher bearer gets them?"

"No stretcher bearer would be such a fool. Your unit might save you. . . ."

"Shut up! Shut up! you noisy sods, you bleeding pieces of Earth."

But they didn't; and they don't. And still the warning voices sound in answer to the sufferers of bereavement, depression, anxiety. "Don't go off the beaten track. Don't do as the psychoanalysts do. Haven't you heard? Pay Stills Your Conscience Here. Don't go off the beaten Church. Remember Simon Magnus. Leave your mind alone. Don't go down the Unconscious Daddy: Let the Gold Mine come up to you." How wise! How very wise!

(CWB I, p. 170)

Bion was later instructed to go back and see whether the sunken tank was salvageable. He describes great difficulty finding his way back to it, and coming across exhausted soldiers collapsed, asleep on the duck boards. He had been warned not to stray off the duck boards and realised that the sounds he could hear were men drowning in the mud.

Simon Magus: Early convert to Christianity in the first century AD, Simon Magus is the man posterity has used to coin the sin of simony, which involves the paying of monies for influence or positions within the church hierarchy.

Dante's Inferno: Dante Alighieri was a fourteenth-century Florentine poet and the author of Italy's most famous work of literature: *The Divine Comedy*, written between 1308 and 1320. Composed of three *cantiche* or parts, *L'Inferno, Purgatorio* and *Paradiso*, this long poem is an allegory of the journey of the human soul towards God. In the first canto, *Inferno*, Dante loses his way in a dark wood, meets the Roman poet Virgil, and embarks with him on a journey through the nine concentric circles of suffering composing Hell. Each circle of Hell contains a different category of sinner whose eternal torment most befits their crime – for example, soothsayers must walk with their heads on backwards, destined never to see where they are going.

[15] The Battle of Cambrai

From *War Memoirs*

But just at this time the enemy seemed to be opening fire on us again from all sides, and we didn't quite know where they were. I was very excited at this time. I had sent back Colombe and Allen with Pell to get him out of the way.

I decided the chief fire was coming from the wood in front from behind the wall. So I took my Lewis gun with two drums of ammunition (we only had four left) and got on top of the tank behind the facine. . . . I fired into the wood over the facine and saw the enemy begin to run about and clear out. They all cleared out or stopped firing pretty quickly, and then my gun jammed and became too hot to hold.

At this moment the enemy led a counter-attack through the gap between the lodge and the wood. I only saw an officer run out in front waving a small stick and pointing at me. I decided it was time to leave, and I came off that tank in record time. . . .

I met Edwards there, and he said everything was going splendidly. A moment later a sniper got him through the head, and he died a bit later. I thereupon took over the company. . . . Their ammunition had practically run out, so that we were still in a rotten position. I got hold of an enemy machine-gun, which we had taken previously, and as there was a lot of ammunition, we opened fire. The enemy had stopped . . . and we kept their heads down with this fire. I subsequently took the lock out of this gun and that I also sent back to you.

(*CWB III*, pp. 57–58)

At Passchendaele, after his tank had sunk, Bion and his crew had set up their guns on the ground, but they were ordered to retreat. Bion decided afterwards that he was not going to retreat again. Some months later (Nov/Dec 1917), at the Battle of Cambrai described above, Bion again had to abandon his tank; but he did not retreat, he embarked on action for which he was nominated for the Victoria Cross and earned both the Distinguished Service Order and the French Légion d'Honneur.

"Amiens", the battle that is to haunt him for the rest of his life, was yet to come.

[16]   Receiving the Distinguished Service Order

From *The Long Weekend*

I was by far the youngest officer to be up for the DSO so a large, fierce and extremely important colonel addressed me personally. . . .

(CWB I, p. 218)

After the ceremony, Bion and his mother hear news of a German attack. Bion knows that the British defensives being lauded do not in fact exist. Although he attempts to reassure his mother he knows her to be "no fool", and both are "stiff upper lipped" about the danger he is to return to the following day.

By eight that evening I felt neither of us could stand any more. Pleading the excuse of an early morning and a long day I suggested we should go to bed. She agreed – like an automaton.

As I entered my bedroom and closed the door I felt I had entered Hell. I have entered it since, not often, but too often. To others who have to do the same I can say: it's not so bad if you stick it out. After the first three or four times it's not so bad, but don't do it till after twenty-one – nineteen is too early.

The next morning when I saw my mother's white powdered face I recognized misery. We did not talk; we had withdrawn. We said good-bye in the hotel and a taxi took me to Waterloo.

"Everybody suddenly burst out singing" – I did not; not even after the war. Never, never again. I was not unhappy – indeed I often felt I was much happier than most. But no more singing; never.

(CWB I, p. 220)

"Everybody suddenly burst out singing": the line comes from a poem written by Siegfried Sassoon just after the Armistice was signed.

Siegfried Sassoon

Everyone Sang

Everyone suddenly burst out singing;
And I was filled with such delight
As prisoned birds must find in freedom,
Winging wildly across the white
Orchards and dark-green fields; on – on – and out of sight.
Everyone's voice was suddenly lifted;

And beauty came like the setting sun:
My heart was shaken with tears; and horror
Drifted away. . . . O, but Everyone
Was a bird; and the song was wordless; the singing will never be done.

(Sassoon, 1948)

Siegfried Sassoon (1886–1967): Soldier, poet and writer, was one of the few poets who described the First World War and survived it. He was highly critical of the generals who sent so many men to slaughter, and he became a trenchant voice of dissent, publishing his protest against the war in an anti-war letter, entitled "Soldier's Declaration", in 1917. This led to him being sent to Craiglockhart Hospital under the care of W. H. R. Rivers, where he met the great poet Wilfred Owen. Their time there was fictionalized in Pat Barker's 1991 novel, *Regeneration*.

[17]   The full force of passivity

From *War Memoirs*

The days were fairly awful. There was a blazing sun most of the time, and this used to beat down on the piece of elephant iron that made my H.Q. and make the inside intolerably stuffy and hot. Here I used to lie, tired out after the night [supervising his men who were positioned in a number of farms near the front line], in a kind of stupor, which served instead of sleep. It was a weird business – the heat, and the nightmares out of which one started up suddenly in a kind of horror to find the sweat pouring down one's face. It was almost impossible to distinguish dream from reality. The tat–tat–tat of the German machine-guns would chime in with your dream with uncanny effect, so that when you awoke you wondered whether you were dreaming. The machine-gun made you think everything was genuine, and only by degrees you recovered yourself to fall into uneasy sleep again.

It did not take long for interest in life to die out. Soon I found myself almost hopeless. I used to lie on my back and stare at the low roof. Sometimes I stared for hours at a small piece of mud that hung from the roof by a grass and quivered to the explosion of the shells. Then suddenly one day I heard that the South Africans on our left were playing the fool. They used to crawl out onto the road on their left at night and try to get hit by the German machine-gun that fired down the road. This news had a curiously bracing effect. I don't know now whether the tale was true – certainly it had been common enough in the earlier part of the war – but I felt things now could get no worse and that actually a gleam of hope had appeared – it was always possible to get badly wounded or perhaps even killed.

This may seem hardly possible to you. But the fact remains that life had now reached such a pitch that horrible mutilations or death could not conceivably be worse. I found myself looking forward to getting killed, as then, at least, one would be rid of this intolerable misery. These thoughts were uppermost with me then and excluded all others – and I think many were in the same state. After all, if you get a man and hunt him like an animal, in time he will become one. I am at a loss now to tell you of our life. Such worlds separate the ordinary human's point of view from mine at that time, that anything I can write will either be incomprehensible or will give a quite wrong impression. Briefly, I felt like this: I didn't care tuppence whether we held the "line" or not. Germany's victory or defeat was nothing. Nevertheless, I would do my job by my men as well as I could, as there was nothing else to do. I wasn't interested in religion or world politics or any rot like that. I was merely an insignificant scrap of humanity that was being intolerably persecuted by unknown powers, and I was going to score off those powers by dying. After all, a mouse must feel that it is one up on the playful cat when it dies without making any sport for its captor. With this new idea before me, I felt better. I didn't feel afraid any more, and I walked about doing my job feeling as if I had scored off Providence.

(CWB III, pp. 98–101)

In late Spring 2018, with six guns under his command, Bion was to cover a section of the line on ground that had been torn up by the shell-fire of the old battles of Messines. His nights were spent moving – under fire – between the three derelict farms his men were stationed in. During the day, he was alone.

[18] In the dream I must have wished it was only a war

From *The Long Weekend*

I went off to lie on the ground and get some sleep. The ground was hard, but I was tired. So I slept and I had a terrible dream. I awoke just as I was about to go into battle; it was unnerving to find that I was.

The dream was grey, shapeless; horror and dread gripped me. I could not cry out, just as now, many years later, I can find no words. Then I had no words to find; I was awake to the relatively benign terrors of real war. Yet for a moment I wished it was only a dream. In the dream I must have wished it was only a war.

(*CWB I*, p. 269)

[19]   Like a small child

From *War Memoirs*

We walked slowly in front of the tanks and waited for shells. The strain had a very curious effect; I felt that all anxiety had become too much; I felt just like a small child that has had rather a tearful day and wants to be put to bed by its mother; I felt curiously eased by lying down on the bank by the side of the road, just as if I was lying peacefully in someone's arms.

I went to the back of the column and talked to Asser. As we went past French H.Q., I went in and collected a couple of extremely tired looking pigeons with which to send back information to the French. Whether they ever took a message back or not I don't know. When I *did* release them, they looked more like making a separate peace with the enemy than anything else.

(CWB *III*, pp. 127–128)

[20]   Sweeting

From *The Long Weekend*

"Mother ... Mother ... Mother. ..." Then he saw me looking. "Why can't I cough sir?"

I could not stand it. Those tanks – perhaps they were enfilading the Canadian Corps? – the French First Army without support looking for that joke Englishman who understood French? I began to whimper.

"Sweeting, *please* Sweeting ... please, please *shut up*." He shut up. I knew he would start again. I caught a glimpse of the poplars, waving. There must be a strong wind. Why did it not blow the fog away?

"Why can't I cough sir?"

Why can't you cough it away? Why can't ... I began to vomit but I had nothing to vomit.

"Mother ... Mother ... Mother", he was muttering. How then could I hear him? I looked up. The shelling had stopped. The sun was shining. The fog, the night, had gone.

The Amiens–Roye road had resumed its proper place on our left. We were in a shell hole at the edge of a cart track and the track was edged on the other side by tall grasses, not the poplars of the Amiens–Roye road.

I was not relieved. "God damn it God! That was not funny." Utterly exhausted, I said "Sweeting, I'm very sorry. There will be some bearers shortly. They will take you to the casualty clearing station. You've got a Blighty."

He was too far gone to call me a liar. His eyes were glazed over. Enough life flickered into them at my words for him to say, "You will write to my mother? You *will* write sir, won't you?" He was alive now and urgent. "Sir! You will write to my mother? Won't you?"

"Yes, of course."

"Her address is ..."

"Don't. I have it. We have it in the office."

And then I think he died. Or perhaps it was only me.

(*CWB I*, pp. 280–281)

It is to the Battle of Amiens – on 8 August 1918 and ensuing days – that Bion most refers throughout his life. In the novel of his seventies he says that he "died" on the Amiens–Roye road: "For though the Soul should die, the Body lives for ever" (*CWB XIII*, p. 38). In military history, Amiens was a successful battle, and it is cited as a turning point in the war. So what happened on the Amiens–Roye Road? Bion was now a captain and on foot between his tanks, rather than in charge of one tank. He had just been inside one of the tanks talking to its commander when the German battery started up. The tank he had been in moments earlier was blown up; Bion grabbed Sweeting's belt (his runner), and they threw themselves into a shell hole. Barely able to function in the bombardment, Bion looked out of the shell hole and became extremely anxious that the Amiens–Roye Road was not where he had thought it was, and that had he had sent the tanks in the wrong direction – towards their own lines, rather than the enemy's. He made Sweeting look, to check. Bion did not see it happen, but he realised that Sweeting was horribly wounded in the chest.

[21] "To die for a squabble"

From *War Memoirs*

The bombardment was now dying down, so I sent the other runner to take him to the dressing station. He actually walked there with their support and reached the dressing station before dying. This incident upset Hauser and me very badly, and we were very sick. I mention it in such detail, horrible as it is, because it had a great effect on me. The look in his eyes was the same as that in the eyes of a bird that has been shot – mingled fear and surprise. I didn't see then, and I don't see now, why that fellow and many like him should have been taken from their English homes (and their German homes) to die for a squabble they didn't understand and couldn't realize. It was simply the distrust, so frivolously sown by grown-up children who wanted to satisfy their childish ambitions, that led to Hell for us and misery for so many homes. The sooner people realize the criminal folly of their leaders the better.

(*CWB III*, pp. 131–133)

[22] Writing to Sweeting's Mother

From *The Long Weekend*

"Finished?" It was Cook again. "Good God, what have you been up to?" I told him I wouldn't be long and scribbled furiously.

"Hero and strumpet voluntary – One of the best" (Mother, Mother, Mother) "Always could be relied upon" (Mother, Mother, Mother) "We shall miss him". Chorus: (all letters) "Luckily he died instantly and could not have experienced pain." ...

"Dear Madam, I am sorry I have not been able to write to you before about the death of your son. He was a good lad and you must have been a very good mother to him. I was with him at the end when he knew he was dying. You were the person who was in his mind in those last hours and it was your name that was on his lips. I hope you will feel proud that he loved you so much. I am, dear Madam, his officer that day. ..."

(*CWB I*, p. 288)

[23] Asser

From *The Long Weekend*

I was met by Asser, a spectacled, cheerful lad who had joined us a week earlier. I suppose he reminded me of what I and my friends had been like in England. He was about a year younger than I. I had told him to act as second in command to me and to take over if I was killed. . . . If it had not been out of date by that time to be aware of patriotism one would have said it burned in him with a pure flame. A brother, whom he adored, and a father who was an even greater though more romantically shadowy figure, had both been killed in action, his father in late 1914.

(*CWB I*, pp. 266–267)

From *All My Sins Remembered*

I had never forgotten that Asser did not surrender and was shot through the heart. We, who are left, grow old – Asser did not.

(*CWB II*, p. 63)

In the hours and days that followed Sweeting's death, Bion repeatedly asked about a second man, whose death – along with that of Sweeting – was never to leave him. The man's name was Asser – a youthful, hopeful, and capable newish arrival. Bion was somewhat anxious about whether Asser would be all right in his new position.

Asser died at Amiens. His tank was surrounded, and his men emerged and surrendered. The last to leave the tank, Asser emerged bearing arms thus – Bion comments – forcing the Germans to shoot him. Bion refers to Asser's behaviour as bravery he would not himself have been capable of.

After their deaths, Sweeting and Asser stayed with Bion in a way that no one else from the war seems to have. Somehow it was deeply personal in relation to both of them, although so many he knew and had under his command had been killed before this. In locating the death of his soul now – at Amiens – he locates it at a time when he is not in a deadened state himself.

[24]   Get out

From *The Long Weekend*

"Where to? In, of course. We'll ride the rest of the way." They probably thought I was drunk [Bion had flu and had been passed some champagne to keep him going]. I told the tank commander to carry on as before when he had got it started again. Just then it *did* start, so suddenly that he was hurled against the sharp edge of the ammunition racks. The blow was on his temple and he lay there unconscious. I took over command of the tank; or perhaps it was the alcohol.

The scene was yellowish; not summer landscape, not autumn, not anything, but warm, and the tank was hot and stank of petrol. Nobody was about, certainly no enemy. Even the lack of mud gave a nightmare quality to the drive, for in real battles one did not travel fast and easily across rolling downland unopposed. Nor did one go for rides in tanks if one felt ill and bright-eyed.

I turned to shout to the driver. "Lots of sausage balloons up." I pointed to the long array of dark shapes looming almost overhead. Funny the way German observation balloons always looked so dark compared with our silvery shapes – obviously the Devil's Own.

I tried being jocular. "Do you know", I shouted, "I get the feeling we are being fired at!"

The driver looked tense and pale. He must be tired, I thought. "It's those balloons sir."

Of course – it had not occurred to me! We were under direct observation; they must be concentrating on us. But in that case why were there no shells bursting round us?

"Get out!" I shouted. "All of you! Walk close behind." They tumbled out. I took over driving the tank, meaning to drive a zig-zag course with the escape hatch over me open. Then I realized that with no crew I could not steer the tank and could not drive anywhere but straight ahead. I had no sense of fear. I opened the throttle so that the tank was at full speed.

Before I knew what I was doing I had left the driver's seat and joined the crew behind. It was difficult to keep up with the fast-moving driverless tank. Then, only then, panic overwhelmed me. Suppose they were not firing at us? Suppose they did not hit us? A fully equipped tank in complete working order would have been handed over to the enemy, abandoned on my orders by its crew.

I could not catch up with it; as I stumbled and tried to run to the door I fell. Then mercifully the shell hit, pierced and burst. The tank stopped, flames spurting everywhere. In a moment it was a total wreck.

(CWB I, pp. 292–293)

[25]   Leave

From *War Memoirs*

As soon as I got to camp, a leave warrant was handed to me, and I was told to meet a box-body Ford at a cross-roads just about 400 yards behind the front line from which the morning battle had started. I was very surprised and pleased, as I had not expected leave till very much later – for two or three months, at least. I dashed off down to the rendezvous and was surprised to find myself going down a road that was being quite heavily shelled. Imagine it if you can – a man with harassed nerves, a touch of flu, a leave warrant in his pocket and a beastly strife on a road he has to take. The leave warrant was the most demoralizing part of it. It makes you so careful when you feel you are so near safety as that.

I reached the rendezvous – a broken church – and waited. The car was late, of course. It was due at 6 p.m., and at 6.05 the enemy started to shell the village. What were they up to? Was it a counter-attack? And what was that fool of a driver doing? Of course they would shell the church. I'd put that fool of a man under arrest as soon as he appeared. At 6.10 I decided it would save unnecessary ceremony if I shot him off-hand. At 6.15 the church started going up, and I edged into the street and bit my nails and cursed the A.S.C. [Army Service Corps] and their works. Why couldn't they be punctual? A minute later there was a whirl of dust, a terrific screech of brakes – and there stood a dear little Ford box-body with a most impertinent look on its face. I shot into it like a rocket and bawled out, "Boulogne – and drive like hell." He did.

(*CWB III*, pp. 156–157)

After his leave, Bion returned to the front, and he remained there until the end of the war. He was offered the opportunity to return to England and set up a new battalion there, but he declined this.

[26] Refusal to parade

From *The Long Weekend*

"Sir!" saluted Sergeant Major Cannon, "Company refuses to come on parade."

"Tell them not to be so bloody silly." Off he went.

Here was a fine state of affairs. I had not the remotest idea what to do. All this stuff about the Guards – devilish awkward if it turned out to be true. Now my own company! I felt I would break out in a sweat at any moment. Suppose they still refused. They were nearly all new men, recently trained miners; they hated the army....

"Sir!"....

"Yes, Sergeant Major?" "They won't come out sir."

I knew it. What do I do now? No idea. It was with surprise and relief that I heard myself say, "Tell the Lewis gun crews to fall in with their guns at once. Post them to cover the huts."

"Sir!" ... He was back again in less than five minutes. "They are in position sir. Six guns facing the huts."

"With the hill behind the huts?"

"Yes sir."....

Sergeant Cannon again. "They've come out sir. They are on parade." I could have wept with relief. "I'll be out in a minute Sergeant Major. They can stand easy till I come." What was I talking about? Of course they could – there was nothing else for them to do.

Alone in the hut I wiped the sweat off my face and tried to stop my trembling. At last I couldn't stand it any more and walked onto the parade ground.

The guns were in position, glistening. The crews were looking at me intently; I could *feel* the penetrating curiosity. The company were fuming, angry. Wherever I let my eyes rest I fancied that the answering glance was angry, resentful, humiliated.

At last Sergeant Major Cannon reported, "All present and correct sir." I told him to stand at ease.

"Sergeant Major Cannon tells me you fellows didn't want to come on parade. You forget the wars not over – this is only an armistice. We'd have looked a bloody lot of fools if the Boches had come over there" – I pointed my stick at the hills behind – "and caught us while you were all stuck in there."

(*CWB I*, pp. 315–317)

The Armistice had been signed on the 11th day of the 11th month of 1918, but the order was to remain on battle-alert terms. Bion himself comments elsewhere that if the army were to stand down, it would be almost impossible to get it going again. Bion was in charge of a newly arrived company of Guards [Welsh miners], who were refusing to come out of their huts and parade. He ordered the guns to be turned on their huts. When he went to inspect the guns, Bion comments, "I chose not to remark that they were loaded with ball ammunition". "Ball ammunition", I discovered, leads to less severe wounding – the gunners believing he could actually order them to fire. After a tense interlude the Guards emerged to parade. Bion had had the guns turned to "cover the huts", "with the hill behind the huts". This meant that the guns were turned on the men, but also on the hill behind, from which the Boche could come, and against whom Bion and the men were united.

Although deeply critical of the authorities in the war, Bion did not dis-identify with authority. He never stopped holding authority himself.

Boche: Colloquial term for Germans in the First World War. Derived from the French word for cabbage, "caboche", it was a pejorative term essentially meaning a thickie.

Ball ammunition: A less lethal form of projectile.

[27] Bion, Myself and Asser

From *War Memoirs:* "Commentary"

Bion: . . . At Oxford, when I was writing the diary, I used to have a recurrent dream of clinging to the slimy bank of a torrent that rushed by some twenty feet below. As I was slipping, I tried to dig my fingernails into the mud. But as I became tired I moved to ease myself – and this meant a further slither. This vast raging torrent waiting for me below was the Steenbeck. I have described the trickle of dirty water that was the geographical fact. . . .

Myself: What upsets you most?

Bion: Your success, I think. I hesitate to say it, because it sounds ungrateful. I cannot imagine what was wrong, but I never recovered from the survival of the Battle of Amiens. Most of what I do not like about you seemed to start then. . . .

Bion: I remember. Asser was about to die – refusing to surrender. He could have been fighting for something of which I could not be aware. But his death killed me. At least, it made me feel I could never be a man with such intensity that I would knowingly embrace certain death.

(*CWB III*, pp. 209–211)

For ease of reference I repeat a note from the Introduction to this chapter.

In the late 1960s/early 1970s, the Bions, now in California, Francesca Bion made a typescript of the original War Memoir diaries, and Bion read it for the first time in 50 years. He wrote a "Commentary" – the conversation is between Bion, the inexperienced young man of 21, and Myself, the wise old man of 75.

[28] Who had gone mad?

From *Clinical Seminars,* "São Paulo 1978, Ten Talks"

Bion: There is always a chance that the opposed armies, on the strength of the shared emotion of terror, will fraternize. As for the individual, I remember one of my men, a young fellow of about nineteen, who began to smile in an extremely irritating manner. The senior N.C.O. wanted to have him punished for a crime which was called "dumb insolence". That smile was peculiarly irritating in the sense that neurologists talk about the nerve which is irritated and also in the sense in which socially we talk about being annoyed. The question was, who had gone mad? Who was in-sane? Un-healthy? We, who kept on fighting? Or this boy who had had a psychotic breakdown? Was it a burst of common sense which had broken out in him, while the rest of us went on with our shared psychosis, our continuous, murderous marriage with the enemy? Lots of people were frightened of breaking out; in the air force crews were afraid that they only had to go on flying combatant missions long enough and they would get killed. It is dangerous enough flying around anyway; it is insane to fly about when people are firing guns at you. What were these fighting pilots afraid of? Becoming ill? Or becoming sane? So far we seem capable of having a mass psychosis in which we all agree to go about in disciplined and organized gangs of murderers, dedicated to the destruction of people who wear different clothes. Sometimes we don't even bother with the uniform if we can say, "I am black; he is white; therefore he is wrong". Or, "I am white and he is black and therefore he is wrong". The colour of the skin saves us the trouble of going inside that skin.

(CWB VIII, p. 328)

Chapter 3

All My Sins Remembered:
Another Part of a Life

Introduction

Bion's autobiography continues with *All My Sins Remembered: Another Part of a Life*, the title of which is derived from the line, "The fair Ophelia! Nymph, in thy orisons / Be all my sins rememb'red", from Act 3, Scene 1, of Hamlet.

Francesca Bion

After demobilisation at the end of 1918, he went up to Oxford to read History at The Queen's College. Compared with undergraduates entering university from school, he and others were "old" war veterans and must have been in disturbed states of mind.

Nevertheless, his years there remained a cherished memory all his life, not least because he was a first-class athlete (playing rugger with the Oxford Harlequins and captaining the water polo team). He also remembered with gratitude conversations with Paton, the philosopher, and regretted not having studied philosophy.

On leaving Oxford, having disappointed his tutors by not achieving a First Class Honours degree (due, they said, to the strain of recent fighting) he tried school-mastering at his old school for two years and then embarked on medical studies at University College Hospital in London, already knowing that he was primarily interested in a strange, new subject called "psychoanalysis". He said he wisely avoided disclosing this at his initial interview; he mentioned instead, his athletic successes at Oxford and, lo and behold! he was offered a place.

As with his time at Oxford, the memories of these years from 1924 to 1930 were vivid and enduring. He was especially impressed by, and admired, Wilfred Trotter who was not only an outstanding brain surgeon, but also wrote *Instincts of the Herd in Peace and War*. This was to prove an important influence on Bion's interest in, and nascent theories about, group behaviour. It was first published in 1916 when the horrors of the First World War had already exposed the crass stupidity of leaders of nations and armies alike.

Bion had no copy of the book. It may have been among those he lost during air raids over London in the early thirties and by the fifties it was out of print. So I had not been able to read it until a few years ago when by, by chance, I came across a copy for 20p in an antiquarian bookshop in Oxford – a happy example of serendipity.

Trotter makes observations which remind one strongly of Bion's later views. He speaks of man's "resistiveness to new ideas, his submission to tradition and precedent"; of "governing power tending to pass into the hands of a class of members insensitive to experience, closed to the entry of new ideas and obsessed with the satisfactoriness of things as they are"; of "our willingness to take any risk other than endure the horrid pains of thought". Of the war, then in its second year, he wrote, "Western civilisation has recently lost ten millions of its best lives as a result of the exclusion of the intellect from the general direction of society . . . so terrific an object lesson has made it plain how easy it is for man . . . to sink to the irresponsible destructiveness of the monkey". And twenty years later, "man" was at it again.

After obtaining his medical qualification Bion spent seven years in psychotherapeutic training at the Tavistock Clinic, an experience he regarded, in retrospect, as having been of very doubtful benefit. In 1938 he began a training analysis with John Rickman, but this was brought to an end by the Second World War.

(Francesca Bion 1994, pp. 92–93)

Quotes

29 Oxford
30 Where do butterflies go when the climate becomes inclement?
31 Nightmare
32 A young woman
33 Studying medicine
34 Wilfred Trotter
35 And now this war (World War Two)
36 I am: therefore I question
37 Betty
38 Parthenope

[29]   Oxford

Oxford University, at which I found myself the next day – my mother having already returned to India by the earliest boat on which she could find a
passage – was a prospect that had aroused feelings of awe since the day I had
been granted an exhibition; so the reality of Oxford railway station came as
a shock. A hundred or so undergraduates milled around looking for their
luggage. Once it would have been porters they sought, but now there were
no porters and no wealthy golden youth to employ them. In army style we
went directly to the barrows, the trunks, and hopefully to the taxi queue.

Thus opened for me a period of unparalleled opportunities to which I
remained obstinately blind. I was overwhelmed before I started by the aura
of intellectual brilliance with which Oxford was surrounded. Actual contact with my contemporaries intensified my sense of inadequacy. They came
from schools with famous names; I did not. They came from homes with a
university tradition; I did not. "Here comes Bion with his non-conformist hat
on", was the kindly jest with which a fellow in my rugger team greeted my
arrival to board the bus for an "away" match. It embarrassed me, but it also
brought some relief – at least it was not that bloody "college cap". No one
said, "You there, you wearing that pious mug on your face, na poo! Finish!
"op it!" Oxford was very kind and tolerant.

(*CWB II*, p. 9)

[30]   Where do butterflies go when the climate becomes inclement?

One day in the High I saw a familiar figure, small, dapper, well-cut hacking jacket, finely polished boots, a disdainful sneer. I called out his name before I could stop myself. I knew he had seen me, but clearly had not heard me. For so small a man it was wonderful that he could command so great a height from which to look down upon Oxford and its dwarfs. ...

I'm sorry he cut me dead; at the time I felt I might have helped restore his wounds, ... In fact I could have done nothing for that terrible depth of misery and isolation. Where do butterflies go when the climate becomes inclement?

The poor Major. I see him now, dapper in the sunlight as he turned away from this figure from his past. . . .

Carter had come to see me a week or two before. I liked him and he liked me. He and Hauser and I had... lasted the war ... yet barrier there was. We could not reminisce about the war; and we had nothing else to talk about. Hauser and I never met again and we did not correspond. I could not imagine that we would write or meet even if the opportunity had come. It seemed impossible that our shared war could mean so little: yet that appeared to be the case. But I soon realized it was not so: the experience, however short the meeting, was not forgotten; I could forget names but I could not forget the people.

(CWB II, pp. 11–13)

[31]   Nightmare

Nevertheless, I did not see; I did not see that peacetime was no time for me. I did know, however many pretty ribbons I put on a wartime uniform, that wartime also was no time for me. I was twenty-four; no good for war, no good for peace, and too old to change. It was truly terrifying. Sometimes it burst out in sleep. Terrified. What about? Nothing, nothing. Oh well, yes. I had a dream. I dug my nails into the steep and slippery walls of mud that fell sheer into the waters of a raging, foaming Steenbeck. Ridiculous! That dirty little trickle? If blood is thicker than water, what price the thickness of dreams? Suppose broad daylight was not thick enough to keep out the terror. Suppose I was so terrified that I ran away when it was really a battle. I woke up. Was I going crazy? Perhaps I was crazy.

(*CWB II*, p. 15)

[32]   A young woman

At the end of that term I went to stay with a friend and on arriving at his home I was met by the most beautiful girl I had ever seen – his sister. She had just finished her last term at school. So had I, but I was not nineteen but twenty-six. I might excusably have been regarded as a mature man of experience and a war hero to boot. She was intelligent and, as I say, beautiful: I was immature and inexperienced except for a passion for a girl at my sister's school. She had been a year older than I, and I was then fourteen. Since then – nothing. My hand trembled when the holiday came to an end and I said goodbye.

"It's awful you must go", she said.

"Perfectly priceless", I blurted out.

"What?" she replied astonished.

I nodded speechlessly to her dress which she had worn particularly for me. Her dismay turned to a joyful laugh.

Later there came a box of wild roses, freshly gathered. Then she came to London to study massage. We met. Irresponsible to the end, I proposed and was accepted; she could not be expected to see through all the war-hero trapping. I could hardly discard the blessed gift of licensed bravery covering the nakedness of which the culture, the mental universe of which I was a part, seemed luckily unaware.

(*CWB II*, p. 17)

The young woman quickly ended the engagement – it seems because Bion had no financial security.

For many years I do not believe I thought of marriage at all. Of what is now recognized as "sex" I thought a great deal, but it was inseparable from ideas of temptation (nice feelings), madness, purity and high ideals. Having no contact of any kind with girls was easy – I thought they were a mean selection of selfish bitches mostly anxious to tell tales and get brothers into trouble – and contact with boys was restricted to those of unexceptionable morals and preferably athletically successful. However, there were the roses. At the time they were inseparable from "romance", innocence and love. Later I thought of them, and similarly provocative behaviour, as something that did not cost the donor much. Though it had been painful for me to contemplate any action which cost me thought, consideration and trouble – such as would be involved in finding a box, packing the flowers, taking them to a post office and buying stamps – I did not feel that this involved any such expense of spirit for the girl.

(*CWB II*, p. 23)

[33]   Studying medicine

"Why do you want to be a doctor?" the Dean of the medical school inquired. I was not going to say, "Because I want to be a psychoanalyst. . . .

Nevertheless I felt that here in this part of London I was more nearly in my class. I owed much of this to Elliot-Smith who lectured with consummate ease and mastery on the brain. Why I should obtain comfort from that I do not know, for I was fully aware that I could never see my subject so clearly that I could draw a section of the brain as if seen, say, through the sagittal plane, or any other that he chose to illustrate his point. My appreciation of his lectures was the more odd as I did not feel I would ever be able to pass an anatomy exam. . . .

Studying medicine was hard work. I knew what it felt like to be me and to have the feelings that I had, but I had no means of communicating them to a person not myself. I also knew what people not myself looked like; I could only see that they did not appear to be experiencing pain.

(*CWB II*, pp. 18–22)

[34]   Wilfred Trotter

Wilfred Trotter was small and neatly but powerfully built. His strong hands had a beauty which could not by any stretch of the imagination be regarded as the product of a manicurist's cosmetic skill. I remember the near horror with which I saw him enter a skull with powerful blows of a mallet on the chisel he held. Such was his control that he could and did penetrate the hard bone and arrest the chisel so that it in no way injured the soft tissue of the underlying brain.

Once a week he saw, with his attendant dressers of whom I was one, new and old patients who came up to the hospital from their homes and work. Julian Taylor also had his out-patient clinic and it was therefore possible to observe the contrast in styles of two brilliant, world-famous (at that time) technicians at work. . . .

J. T. could not tolerate the response to his enquiry "What is your trouble?", "It's my kidneys doctor." "Kidneys! What do you know about kidneys!" (or liver, or stomach, or whatever other anatomical structure or physiological function to which the patient chose to refer). It offended both his medical knowledge and his sense of propriety. The patient, frightened at having given offence to such an eminent authority, would close up and volunteer no further suggestions lest a further storm be evoked.

Trotter, on the other hand, listened with unassumed interest as if the patient's contributions flowed from the fount of knowledge itself. It took me years of experience before I learned that this was in fact the case. When a patient co-operates so far as actually to present himself for inspection, the doctor from whom help is being sought is being given the chance of seeing and hearing for himself the origin of the pain. No need to ask, "Where does it hurt?" – though it would clearly be a comfort to have his query answered in a language that he understands. The anger that is so easily aroused is the "helper's" reaction to an awareness that he does *not* understand the language, or that the language that he *does* understand is not the relevant one or is being employed in a manner with which he is unfamiliar. Trotter's undisturbed friendly interest had the effect of eliciting further evidence from the patient; the fount of knowledge did not dry up.

It was said that when Trotter did a skin graft it "took"; if Taylor did a skin graft – with equal or maybe even greater technical brilliance and accuracy – it did not take; the body rejected it; it was sloughed off. This I did not see, but that the story was told was itself significant of the impression that was created by the two men on their students.

(*CWB II*, pp. 37–38)

[35] And now this war (World War Two)

And now this war – with Germany of course. Ridiculous. Why is it that nobody did anything about it while I've been busy getting qualified? Well, thank goodness Mr Chamberlain had the sense to go and see Hitler and it has all been settled.

So I could go for two or three weeks to Church Farm, Happisburgh, in Norfolk, with a party of friends including actor John Glyn Jones and actress Betty Jardine. That at least was a success: Glyn Jones was extremely amusing; Betty Jardine, whom I had seen in *The Corn is Green* as Bessy Watty and also at the Players Theatre, was not so amusing, nor as attractive as I had expected, but was likeable. She was obviously a very fine actress. Nuisance about Hitler though.

I went on from Happisburgh to the south of France, passing through Monte Carlo which was on the route but otherwise uninteresting; nice petunias in the central square seemed to fill the neighbourhood with their glorious odour. But it was not sufficient to screen the less appealing stench of Hitler and Nazi Germany. It was easy to believe that the stink of the corpse of Imperial Germany mingled with the stink of decay from Imperial Britain was what the athletic perfume of post-war Oxford had failed to disguise in 1919. This was twenty years later and I still could not get the smell of Glory out of my hair. Roquebrune and its orange blossom, a walk to Monte Carlo, a good dinner and not very expensive vintage champagne, the soothing rhythm of the surf below my window – it was very agreeable. But I had no company except my thoughts, and twenty years had not been long enough to establish these with sturdy roots.

(*CWB II*, p. 45)

Bion went on to marry Betty Jardine.

Neville Chamberlain: Prime Minster in the years leading up to the Second World War. He is known for his appeasement foreign policy. In 1938 he went to see Hitler and signed an agreement to Hitler taking over the German-speaking Sudetenland region of Czechoslovakia. Hitler went on to invade Poland however, and the United Kingdom declared war on Germany on 3 September 1939.

[36]   I am: therefore I question

I am: therefore I question. It is the answer — the "yes, I know" — that is the disease which kills. It is the Tree of Knowledge which kills. Conversely, it is not the successful building of the Tower of Babel, but the *failure* that gives life, initiates and nourishes the energy to live, to grow, to flourish. The songs the sirens sing and have always sung is that the arrival at the inn — not the journey — is the reward, the prize, the heaven, the cure.

(*CWB II*, p. 55)

The Tree of Knowledge: One of the two trees in the Garden of Eden named in Genesis.

And the LORD God commanded the man, "You are free to eat from any tree in the garden; but you must not eat from the tree of the knowledge of good and evil, for when you eat from it you will certainly die."

(Genesis 2: 16–17)

The Tower of Babel: According to the Genesis myth, the Tower of Babel explains why humans speak many different languages.

Now the whole world had one language and a common speech. As people moved eastward, they found a plain in Shinar and settled there. They said to each other, "Come, let's make bricks and bake them thoroughly." They used brick instead of stone, and tar for mortar. Then they said, "Come, let us build ourselves a city, with a tower that reaches to the heavens, so that we may make a name for ourselves; otherwise we will be scattered over the face of the whole earth." But the Lord came down to see the city and the tower the people were building. The Lord said, "If as one people speaking the same language they have begun to do this, then nothing they plan to do will be impossible for them. Come, let us go down and confuse their language so they will not understand each other."

So the Lord scattered them from there over all the earth, and they stopped building the city. That is why it was called Babel – because there the Lord confused the language of the whole world.

(Genesis 11: 1–9)

The Sirens: In the Ancient Greek poem, The Odyssey, Odysseus manages to evade the death of many previous sailors by lashing himself to the mast of his ship so that he cannot fling himself into the sea, nor steer his ship to be wrecked on the rocky island from which the Sirens sing to lure men to their doom.

[37]   Betty

Betty had to make her last journey on her own, telling herself her last bed-time story about two nice men who were really being very brave and so considerate and kind. One of them was her husband, and I still cannot help hoping that she was not deprived of the comforting lie that he was really a man and a hero, and not just an artificial representation of a man stuck up in the show-case of a universe signifying nothing and tricked out with psycho-analytic dummies intended to fool the psychoanalytic church into believing that there are real souls that require to be humanized. What if there were thoughts and feelings and souls looking for a home? "For though the Body dies the Soul shall live for ever." "Summer suns are glowing" – Oh no! Not again Bion – "over land and sea. Happy light is flowing" – for you but not for me. "The bells of hell go ting-a-ling-a-ling" for her but not for me. The Body lives for ever.

(CWB II, pp. 63–64)

In 1945, while Bion was away on military duties in France, Betty Jardine tragi-cally died in childbirth. Of his experience in the First World War, Bion also says that his body lives – while he does not.

[38] Parthenope

Yet now I felt as never before; numbed and insensitive. That something was wrong, must be wrong, was brought home to me one week-end when I was sitting on the lawn near the house and the baby was crawling near a flower bed on the opposite side of the lawn. She began to call out to me; she wanted me to come to her.

I remained sitting. She now made to crawl towards me. But she called to me as if expecting me to come to fetch her.

I remained sitting.

She continued to crawl and now her calls became distressful.

I remained sitting.

I watched her continue on the painful journey across the vast expanse, as it must have appeared to her, that separated her from her Daddy.

I remained sitting but felt bitter, angry, resentful. Why did she do this to me? Not quite audible was the question, "Why do you do this to her?"

The nurse could not stand it and got up to fetch her. "No", I said, "let her crawl. It won't do her any harm." We watched the child crawl painfully. She was weeping bitterly now but sticking stoutly to her attempt to cover the distance.

I felt as if I were gripped in a vice. No. I would *not* go. At last the nurse, having glanced at me with astonishment, got up ignoring my prohibition, and fetched her. The spell snapped. I was released. The baby had stopped weeping and was being comforted by maternal arms. But I, I had lost my child.

I hope there is no future life.

I had begged Betty to agree to have a baby: her agreement to do so had cost her her life.

I had vowed to look after the child. It was not a promise to Betty; it was an unexpected vow to myself. It was a shock, a searing shock, to find such depth of cruelty in myself. I have since often recalled Shakespeare's words: "Nymph, in thy orisons be all my sins remembered." [*Hamlet*, III. i]

(*CWB II*, pp. 75–76)

After the death of his wife, Bion took on bringing up Parthenope – with a nanny. (Bion himself had been cared for by an Indian ayah as a child.) In the autobiography we hear of companionable times between father and daughter. The book ends, however, with the distressing incident described here by a man traumatised by war and loss.

Parthenope: Original name of the city of Naples.

Part II

Papers, books, notes, letters

Chapter 4

The 1930s and 1940s

Introduction

Bion does not give any details about when it first became clear to him that he wanted to be a psychoanalyst, but there are references to his interest from his days at Oxford. What is clear is that after some previous attempts at having psychotherapy for himself, it was his meeting in 1938 with the psychoanalyst John Rickman and his subsequent analysis with him that gave Bion an analytic setting strong enough to "contain" him. Three years earlier, in 1935, Bion himself was Samuel Beckett's psychotherapist.

Bion and Beckett

After qualifying as a psychiatrist, Bion worked at the Tavistock Clinic. It was during this time that he was Samuel Beckett's therapist and it is of note that on 14 October 1935 he took Beckett to hear one of Jung's Tavistock lectures. The Los Angeles psychoanalyst Annie Reiner (2013, p. 17) asked Bion about this time when she met him later in 1978 at UCLA. Reiner had just finished reading a new biography on Samuel Beckett, in which she discovered that Beckett had been in treatment with Bion. While this is well known now, it was a revelation to her then, although in her mind she had always connected the two remarkable men.

When she approached Bion and told him of her discovery, he was, she said, gracious as usual and took the time to stop to talk to her. "He looked at me with those penetrating wide eyes and said, 'Yes', and after a pause said, 'I don't believe I helped him much.'"

Reiner didn't think this could be totally accurate – it seemed to her that even if Bion was not yet developed as an analyst, two remarkable men spending time with each other was bound to have had some sort of an effect. It was after his treatment with Bion that Beckett wrote his groundbreaking plays *Waiting for Godot* ([1952] 1986), *Endgame* ([1961] 1986), and *Happy Days* ([1957] 1986). Reiner thought the plays contained images that may be construed as being informed by knowledge of the primitive unconscious. In *Endgame*, for instance, the two parents of the main character, Hamm, are on stage the whole time in trash cans.

Beckett's relationship with his mother was fraught with painful conflicts, and this seemed to be, like other symbols in his plays, physical representations of an inner life. In this case, the parental imagoes exist as garbage, undifferentiated and undigested. When Reiner spoke with Francesca Bion many years later, she mentioned to her Bion's comment about Beckett, to which Francesca replied, "I think they were very much alike."

Bion and Freud

In 1939 Freud arrived in London, but to my knowledge Bion did not meet him. At the same time in his papers on groups, written in the 1940s, we find extended debates with Freud's views. He was to continue in his internal dialogue with Freud throughout his life. The French analyst André Green has commented: "During my oral or written exchanges with him he [Bion] never tried to 'convert' me to his ideas or to those of Klein. We both agreed that our greatest debt was to Freud" (Green 1998, p. 649).

The Second World War (1939–1945)

The First World War had not been the end to war. Just over twenty years after Bion returned from the front, war had broken out again, Bion was now in his early 40s. He spent the Second World War years (1939–1945) working in the military psychiatric services – on a number of innovative projects. In response to a shortage of officers, for example, Bion initiated a way of determining who the "natural" leaders in a group were: a very different approach from the class-dominated system of selection in the First World War. He seems to have been unpopular with the military hierarchy, and he himself comments that he was the only person he knew who had received *no* promotion during the war years.

Experiences in Groups and Other Papers

The majority of the quotes in this chapter are from Bion's group work papers, written in the 1940s but not published until 1961. The book *Experiences in Groups and Other Papers* (1961) has since continued to be his best-selling book. The papers include both his work during the war and groups taken at the Tavistock from 1948 onwards.

Quotes

39   Bion and his first analyst John Rickman
40   Northfield: beginnings
41   Identification of the enemy
42   Northfield: now I can be frank
43   The most extraordinary experience

[39]   Bion and his first analyst, John Rickman

From a transcription of a tape recording, April 1979

However, when I was fortunate enough to come across John Rickman, I decided to launch out onto an analysis with him.

That I found to be extremely illuminating; to my surprise, psychoanalysis seemed to have a distinct relationship to what I thought was common sense. Then, alas, came the threat of war, and I found my analytic experience terminated.

(*CWB XI*, p. 346)

From *Bion in New York and São Paulo*

It was considered to be extraordinarily amusing that I had to recite this piece of verse [The Elephant's Child by Kipling]. I could not see the joke myself. I was told I was just like the Elephant's Child who asked these questions – and like a fool I asked another one. I said, "Who was the Elephant's Child's father?" That was not popular; it was not amusing. But I was not making a joke. I decided I had better be careful not to ask too many questions; it took me a long time to dare to start asking questions again. The person who made it easier for me was John Rickman who was the first psychoanalyst I ever met. I am still at it – I don't think it is any more popular now than it ever was.

(*CWB VIII*, p. 239)

Interview by Anthony G. Banet, Jr., 1976

...Yes, Melanie Klein has certainly influenced me. Before that, John Rickman, whom I liked very much, was also very influential, although it was clear later on that he had various personal difficulties. We have to use people who have these difficulties. They are the people who become our teachers; they are the people who make the advances. I certainly remember him with a great deal of affection.

(*CWB X*, pp. 152–153)

From *The Other Side of Genius*

18 July 1951

Luckily I have a great capacity for being lazy and I think this saves me from overwork. Rickman I don't think ever attached enough importance to this, perhaps by temperament, and I think he wasted himself very badly. He had a very good brain but I think for the last ten years there was a falling off. He did not himself realize it luckily. The surprising thing is that so few others noted it either though it was very marked....

(CWB II, p. 118)

John Rickman: In the First World War, Rickman was a conscientious objector. He did dangerous work for "war victim's relief" in Southern Russia and then worked with psychiatric patients in the United Kingdom. Rickman was analysed by Freud from 1919 to 1922 and qualified as a psychoanalyst in 1922. He was then in analysis with Ferenczi, travelling to Budapest in 1928. (Klein was also in analysis with Ferenczi.) In 1934 Rickman began an analysis with Melanie Klein that was to continue intermittently until 1941, and again for some sessions after the war.

[40]   Northfield: beginnings

No sooner was I seated before desk and papers than I was beset with urgent problems posed by importunate patients and others. Would I see the NCOs in charge of the training wing and explain to them what their duties were? Would I see Private A who had an urgent need for 48 hours" leave to see an old friend just back from the Middle East? Private B, on the other hand, would seek advice because an unfortunate delay on the railway had laid him open to misunderstanding as one who had overstayed his leave. And so on.

An hour or so of this kind of thing convinced me that what was required was discipline. Exasperated at what I felt to be a postponement of my work, I turned to consider this problem.

(CWB IV, pp. 105–106)

Bion has arrived at the Northfield hospital for soldiers invalided out of the war being fought in Europe. The quote is chosen particularly for the last line: "Exasperated at what I felt to be a postponement of my work, I turned to consider this problem." Inundated by demands, Bion is not taken over by them but, instead, sets to considering what the underlying problem is.

[41]   Identification of the enemy

I became convinced that what was required was the sort of discipline achieved in a theatre of war by an experienced officer in command of a rather scallywag battalion. But what sort of discipline is that? In face of the urgent need for action I sought, and found, a working hypothesis. It was, that the discipline required depends on two main factors: (i) the presence of the enemy, who provided a common danger and a common aim; and (ii) the presence of an officer who, being experienced, knows some of his own failings, respects the integrity of his men, and is not afraid of either their good-will or their hostility. . . .

There was no difficulty about detecting a common danger; neurotic extravagances of one sort and another perpetually endanger the work of the psychiatrist or of any institution set up to further treatment of neurotic disorders. The common danger in the training wing was the existence of neurosis as a disability of the community. I was now back at my starting-point – the need, in the treatment of a group, for displaying neurosis as a problem of the group. But, thanks to my excursion into the problem of discipline, I had come back with two additions. Neurosis needs to be displayed as a danger to the group; and its display must somehow be made the common aim of the group.

(*CWB IV*, pp. 106–107)

From "On Groups"

The common purpose to be substituted for the fighting soldier's aim to defeat the enemy had to be found, and it had to possess the same reality and urgency and importance for the survival of the society and the individuals composing it. Obviously, there was only one aim in a psychiatric hospital which could be comparable and in the event proved itself to be comparable – the determination to tackle neurotic disability as a problem, a social problem, of each man in the psychiatric centre.

(*CWB IV*, pp. 27–28)

The 'enemy' is neurosis. As part of his "displaying" the evidence of neurosis, Bion would walk around the wing and invite men to join him "just to see how the rest of the world lives" (*CWB II*, p. 110).

Bion goes on to say that an officer can function only if he takes as his task producing self-respecting men, not cannon fodder, nor a place to hide out the war; only in this way will the officer be free from the deep feelings of guilt that would make him ineffective.

John Rickman commented:

> The work of W.R. Bion seems to indicate that the thing a group most dreads is its impotence vis-à-vis an enemy, and its worst enemy is its own unfaced group-disruptiveness. He found that when the study of intra-group tension was made the task of the group, that group became more at peace with itself, its capacity for constructiveness rose and, also, its ability to work with other groups in friendly rivalry increased.
>
> (Rickman 2003, pp. 237–238)

However, the Northfield project was terminated suddenly, after six weeks. The military hierarchy was suspicious of the new method and Bion himself opposi- tional in the face of authority. It is striking that it was stopped so quickly, and that a project that ran for such a short period of time should have been so influential. The following quote is from his autobiography on his time at Northfield.

[42]   Northfield: now I can be frank

From *All My Sins Remembered: Another Part of a Life*

I asked them what they were doing. "Orderly duty, sir." I suggested they should wave goodbye to the windows and come with me to see what the rest of the hospital was doing.

I have already described the experience of Northfield Hospital elsewhere. Now that I write an autobiography I can be frank about how it feels to have been, once, a participant, and now a *laudator temporis acti*. Predominantly it is a matter of regret that an opportunity to achieve something valuable was precluded by being petty. Pearce could not have been expected to know any better and he needed help. So did Rees. It is therefore hardly surprising that they blundered. I could have helped them to avoid the worst blunders. But by stressing their blunders and indeed behaving in a way that made it clear that I would get them into further trouble, I deprived them of help and con-tributed to their making further blunders. About my Self I knew very little; about Pearce and Rees I knew nothing. It was like the relationship between my crew and myself and the forty tons of useless steel sinking fast below the mud of Hill 40; the Staff should have known about weather and ground conditions on Hill 40 in August....

So: what happened?

Rees had us posted off to where we could do no harm. So I shall never know what would have happened if privates in the Training Wing had caught the habit of asking questions or having opinions of their own which they might be able to hear in the silence of the sleep time when their fancies could become free to roam like the wind. In fact I think that some of the bees may have escaped from my bonnet.

I took the opportunity of meeting Betty on my way through London. She had by this time become more reconciled to the fact that I usually got the sack when my presence became obtrusive.

(*CWB II*, pp. 60–61)

Pearce and Rees were Bion's superiors: Pearce the Commander of Northfields.

"laudator temporis acti": One who praises past times.

[43] The most extraordinary experience

From *The Tavistock Seminars*

I remember John Rickman telling me about his experience at York railway station when a soldier came up to him and said, "Sir, weren't you at Northfield?" Rickman said he was. "It was the most extraordinary experience I ever had – just like being at university", said the soldier. That man hadn't a hope of ever getting to university – as far as we know. His educational and financial background, his cultural background, were all against him. So it was probably the only chance he had had. I don't know why, out of all the people at Northfield, that idea was transmitted to that particular person and changed his outlook – it certainly sounded as if it had. Whatever may have happened to all the pampered darlings of my generation at Oxford and Cambridge, they could pass through university without having the faintest idea of what a university was. But one man, who couldn't possibly know what a university was, almost certainly did.

(*CWB IX*, pp. 9–10)

[44]   Altered focus

I am reminded of looking through a microscope at an over thick section; with one focus I see, not very clearly perhaps, but with sufficient distinctness, one picture. If I alter the focus very slightly I see another. Using this as an analogy for what I am doing mentally, I shall now have another look at this group, and will then describe the pattern that I see with the altered focus.

The picture of hard-working individuals striving to solve their psychological problems is displaced by a picture of a group mobilized to express its hostility and contempt for neurotic patients and for all who may wish to approach neurotic problems seriously. This group at the moment seems to me to be led by the two absentees, who are indicating that there are better ways of spending their time than by engaging in the sort of experience with which the group is familiar when I am a member of it. At a previous session this group was led by one of the members now absent.

As I say, I am inclined to think that the present leaders of this group are not in the room; they are the two absentees, who are felt not only to be contemptuous of the group, but also to be expressing that contempt in action. The members of that group who are present are followers. I wonder as I listened to the discussion if I can make more precise the facts that give me this impression.

At first, I must confess, I see little to confirm me in my suspicions, but then I notice that one of the men who is asking the questions is employing a peculiarly supercilious tone. His response to the answers he receives appears to me, if I keep my mental microscope at the same focus, to express polite incredulity. A woman in the corner examines her fingernails with an air of faint distaste. When a silence occurs it is broken by a woman who, under the former focus, seemed to be doing her best to keep the work of the group going, with an interjection which expresses clearly her dissociation from participation in an essentially stupid game.

(*CWB IV*, pp. 136–137)

After the war Bion was invited by the Professional Committee of the Tavistock Clinic to take therapeutic groups. The groups were composed of around eight people, both patients and staff. In the quote Bion observes the group situation first one way and then another – seeing apparent cooperation on the one hand, but an underlying distaste and dismissiveness on the other.

[45]   A formidable task

I hope to show that in his contact with the complexities of life in a group the adult resorts, in what may be a massive regression, to mechanisms described by Melanie Klein as typical of the earliest phases of mental life. The adult must establish contact with the emotional life of the group in which he lives; this task would appear to be as formidable to the adult as the relationship with the breast appears to be to the infant, and the failure to meet the demands of this task is revealed in his regression.

(CWB IV, p. 207)

[46]   The enigmatic, brooding, and questioning Sphinx

In so far as I am felt to be leader of work-group function, and recognition of that fact is seldom absent, I, and the work-group function with which I am identified, am invested with feelings that would be quite appropriate to the enigmatic, brooding, and questioning Sphinx from whom disaster emanates.... This anxiety is not directed only towards the questioner but also to the object of the inquiry and is, I suspect, secondary to the latter. For the group, as being the object of inquiry, itself arouses fears of an extremely primitive kind. My impression is that the group approximates too closely, in the minds of the individuals composing it, to very primitive phantasies about the contents of the mother's body. The attempt to make a rational investigation of the dynamics of the group is therefore perturbed by fears, and mechanisms for dealing with them, that are characteristic of the paranoid-schizoid position. The investigation cannot be carried out without the stimulation and activation of these levels.

(CWB IV, p. 223)

Bion began his analysis with Klein in 1946. In the quote he puts aspects of his work on groups together with Klein's work on children's primitive phantasies about the contents of the mother's body.

[47]   "A kind of group deity": basic assumption Dependency (*ba*D)

The first assumption is that the group is meeting in order to be sustained by a leader on whom it depends for nourishment, material and spiritual, and protection....

Here is a description of a therapeutic group in which the dependent assumption, as I shall call it, is active.

Three women and two men were present. The group had on a previous occasion shown signs of work-group function directed towards curing the disability of its members; on this occasion they might be supposed to have reacted from this with despair, placing all their reliance on me to sort out their difficulties while they contented themselves with individually posing questions to which I was to provide the answers. One woman had brought some chocolate, which she diffidently invited her right-hand neighbour, another woman, to share. One man was eating a sandwich. A graduate in philosophy, who had in earlier sessions told the group he had no belief in God, and no religion, sat silent, as indeed he often did, until one of the women with a touch of acerbity in her tone, remarked that he had asked no questions. He replied, "I do not need to talk because I know that I only have to come here long enough and all my questions will be answered without my having to do anything."

I then said that I had become a kind of group deity; that the questions were directed to me as one who knew the answers without need to resort to work, that the eating was part of a manipulation of the group to give substance to a belief they wished to preserve about me, and that the philosopher's reply indicated a disbelief in the efficacy of prayer but seemed otherwise to belie earlier statements he had made about his disbelief in God. When I began my interpretation I was not only convinced of its truth but felt no doubt that I could convince the others by confrontation with the mass of material – only some of which I can convey in this printed account. By the time I had finished speaking I felt I had committed some kind of gaffe; I was surrounded by blank looks; the evidence had disappeared. After a time, the man, who had finished his sandwich and placed the carefully folded paper in his pocket, looked round the room, eyebrows slightly raised, interrogation in his glance. A woman looked tensely at me, another with hands folded gazed meditatively at the floor. In me a conviction began to harden that I had been guilty of blasphemy in a group of true believers. The second man, with elbow draped over the back of his chair, played with his fingers. The woman who was eating, hurriedly swallowed the last of her chocolate.

I now interpreted that I had become a very bad person, casting doubts on the group deity, but that this had been followed by an increase of anxiety and guilt as the group had failed to dissociate itself from the impiety.

(CWB IV, pp. 211–213)

For ease of reference I repeat a note from my Introduction. Working with groups, Bion sensed there to be underlying patterns operating in the themes that were presented on the surface. He came to think that there were three identifiable patterns; he called them basic assumption dependency (*baD*), basic assumption pairing (*baP*), and basic assumption fight/flight (*baF*). At any particular time, one assumption holds court, before being replaced by another. The change from one assumption to another is, in part, because none of the assumptions is satisfactory and when in the ascendency, its defects also start to press on the group. For example basic assumption dependency seems to offer the possibility of being wholly cared by the leader of the group, but at the same causes a reaction against being infantilised. Why there are "basic assumptions" at all is addressed in a later quote.

[48]   Of no interest or concern: basic assumption dependency (*baD*)

A woman is talking in a group consisting, on this occasion, of six people and myself. She complains of a difficulty about food, her fear of choking if she eats at a restaurant, and of her embarrassment at the presence, during a recent meal, of an attractive woman at her table. "I don't feel like that", says Mr A, and his remark is met by a murmur of sound from one or two others which could indicate that they were at one with him; could indicate it and does indicate it, but at the same time leaves them free to say, for this group had now become wily, if need arose, that they "hadn't said anything". The remainder looked as if the matter were of no interest or concern to them. . . .

In fact the interpretations I gave were concerned almost entirely with pointing out that the material that followed the woman's confidence to the group indicated the group's anxiety to repudiate that the woman's difficulty, whatever it was, was theirs, and furthermore that they were, in that respect, superior to the woman. I was then able to show that the reception the group had given to the woman's candour had now made it very difficult for any of the remainder of the group to speak, individually, of those other respects in which, in a burst of frankness, they were prepared to admit that they were "inferior". In short, it was not difficult to show that if a patient did go so far as to come to the group for help with a difficulty, what she got was an increase of feelings of inferiority, and a reinforcement of feelings of loneliness and lack of worth. . . .

Bion then thinks further about the woman and why it may be difficult for her to see that she is the recipient of other's projections:

Regarded in this light I would say that she felt that there was a single object, called the group, that had been split up into pieces (the individual members of the group) by her eating, and that the belief that this was so reinforced guilty feelings that the emotions associated with being the receptor of projective identifications were the fault of her behaviour. These feelings of guilt again made it difficult for her to understand the part played in her emotions by the actions of the other members of the group. . . .

And back to the group:

So far I have considered the "badness of the group" as it touches the patient trying to get treatment; we may now turn to consider this from the point of view of the members of the group who have been trying to achieve "cure" by the splitting and projective mechanisms described by Melanie Klein. Not only have they divested themselves of any of the troubles of the woman patient, but, if this mechanism is to be effective, they have laid them-selves open to the necessity for getting rid of any sense of responsibility towards the woman. This they do by splitting off good parts of their person-ality and placing them in the analyst. In this way the "treatment" that these individuals receive from the group is the achievement of a state of mind rec-ognizably akin to the "loss of individual distinctiveness", spoken of by Freud, on the one hand, and the depersonalization that we meet with in psychotics, on the other. At this point the group is in the state I have described as having the basic assumption of dependence dominant.

(CWB IV, pp. 238–240)

Why is this basic assumption Dependency? A key pointer is that the members of the group are "splitting off good parts of their personalities and placing them in the analyst". This can be surmised from their behaving as if only the analyst has good things to offer. In this way they hope to be rid of the responsibility for any troubles: the other woman's and their own.

[49]   The feeling of hope itself: basic assumption Pairing (*baP*)

I must return to consider the second basic assumption. Like the first, this also concerns the purpose for which the group has met. My attention was first aroused by a session in which the conversation was monopolized by a man and woman who appeared more or less to ignore the rest of the group. The occasional exchange of glances amongst the others seemed to suggest the view, not very seriously entertained, that the relationship was amatory, although one would hardly say that the overt content of the conversation was very different from other interchanges in the group. I was, however, impressed with the fact that individuals, who were usually sensitive to any exclusion from supposedly therapeutic activity, which at that time had come to mean talking and obtaining an "interpretation" from me or some other member of the group, seemed not to mind leaving the stage entirely to this pair. Later it became clear that the sex of the pair was of no particular conse-quence to the assumption that pairing was taking place. There was a peculiar air of hopefulness and expectation about these sessions which made them rather different from the usual run of hours of boredom and frustration....

I shall now turn to a consideration of the air of hopeful expectation that I have mentioned as a characteristic of the pairing group. It usually finds expres-sion verbally in ideas that marriage would put an end to neurotic disabilities; that group therapy would revolutionize society when it had spread sufficiently; that the coming season, spring, summer, autumn, or winter, as the case may be, will be more agreeable; that some new kind of community – an improved group – should be developed, and so on. These expressions tend to divert attention to some supposedly future event, but for the analyst the crux is not a future event but the immediate present – the feeling of hope itself. This feeling is char-acteristic of the pairing group and must be taken by itself as evidence that the pairing group is in existence, even when other evidence appears to be lacking. It is itself both a precursor of sexuality and a part of it. The optimistic ideas that are verbally expressed are rationalizations intended to effect a displacement in time and a compromise with feelings of guilt – the enjoyment of the feeling is justified by appeal to an outcome supposedly morally unexceptionable. The feelings thus associated in the pairing group are at the opposite pole to feelings of hatred, destructiveness, and despair. For the feelings of hope to be sustained it is essential that the "leader" of the group, unlike the leader of the dependent group and of the fight–flight group, should be unborn. It is a person or idea that will save the group – in fact from feelings of hatred, destructiveness, and despair, of its own or of another group – but in order to do this, obviously, the Messianic hope must never be fulfilled. Only by remaining a hope does hope persist.

(*CWB IV*, pp. 214–215)

[50] Sex: basic assumption Pairing (*baP*)

Since the pair relationship [analyst and patient] of psychoanalysis can be regarded as a part of the larger group situation, the transference relationship could be expected, for the reasons I have already given, to be coloured by the characteristics associated with the pairing group. If analysis is regarded as part of the total group situation, we should expect to find sexual elements prominent in the material there presented, and the suspicions and hostilities of psychoanalysis as a sexual activity active in that part of the group which is in fact excluded from the analysis.

(*CWB IV*, p. 227)

... psychoanalysis, in the light of my experience of groups, can be regarded as a work group likely to stimulate the basic assumption of pairing; that being so, psychoanalytic investigation, as itself a part of pairing group, is likely to reveal sexuality in a central position. Further, it is likely to be attacked as itself a sexual activity since, according to my view of the pairing group, the group must assume that if two people come together, they can only do so for sexual purposes. It is therefore natural that Freud should see the nature of the bond between individuals in a group as libidinous.

(*CWB IV*, p. 234)

Bion thought that Freud had overestimated the importance of sexuality, and that this came about because the very situation of psychoanalysis – analyst and patient – stimulates the basic assumption of pairing (*baP*), in which sexuality is in a central position.

[51]   Hatred or evasion of difficulty: basic assumption Fight/Flight (*baF*)

The third basic assumption is that the group has met to fight something or to run away from it. It is prepared to do either indifferently.

(*CWB IV*, p. 216)

Fight/Flight: Northfield Hospital

The existence of such a basic assumption helps to explain why groups show that I, who am felt to be pre-eminent as the leader of the group, am also felt to be shirking the job. The kind of leadership that is recognized as appropriate is the leadership of the man who mobilizes the group to attack somebody, or alternatively to lead it in flight. In this context I may mention that when with Dr Rickman I tried an experiment in the treatment of troops at Northfield Military Hospital it was assumed either that we were trying to get troops into battle [fight], or alternatively, that we were concerned to help a lot of scrimshankers to go on scrimshanking [flight]. The idea that treatment was contemplated was regarded as an elaborate, but easily penetrable deception. We learned that leaders who neither fight nor run away are not easily understood.

(*CWB IV*, pp. 149–150)

[52]   Panic: basic assumption Fight/ Flight (*baF*)

Panic does not arise in any situation unless it is one that might as easily have given rise to rage. The rage or fear are offered no readily available outlet: frustration, which is thus inescapable, cannot be tolerated because frustration requires awareness of the passage of time, and time is not a dimension of basic-assumption phenomena. Flight offers an immediately available opportunity for expression of the emotion in the fight-flight group and therefore meets the demand for instantaneous satisfaction – therefore the group will fly. Alternatively, attack offers a similarly immediate outlet – then the group will fight. The fight-flight group will follow any leader (and, contrary to views hitherto expressed, retains its coherence in doing so) who will give such orders as license instantaneous flight or instantaneous attack. Provided that an individual in the group conforms to the limitations of the fight-flight leader, he will have no difficulty in turning a group from headlong flight to attack or from headlong attack to panic.

(*CWB IV*, pp. 236–237)

In his seminar in São Paulo in 1978, Bion comments:

Using war as an example: An officer is not supposed to be unaware of a terrifying and dangerous situation; he is nevertheless supposed to be able to go on thinking if he finds himself in a position in which panic, panic fear arises – let me remind you of the god Pan. But he is not supposed to run away. He is supposed, in spite of being in the midst of this emotional storm, to go on thinking clearly. In that way he forms a focus from which the more disciplined reaction will build up; the troops will not run away, but will begin to stand fast.

I use that model deliberately because the situation in the consulting room appears to be so different. It is usually a comfortable room and apparently there is nothing to be frightened of. Yet patients can get up and leave the room and never come back again. The analyst is not supposed to find himself a prey to emotions which cause him to leave the room; he is not supposed to be unaware of these powerful feelings, nor is he supposed to stop thinking clearly. Nor is he supposed to be overwhelmed by desires, including sexual ones.

(*CWB VIII*, p. 318)

And in his *A Key to A Memoir of the Future,* also from the 1970s:

adrenals   What at a later stage in development can be described and felt as fear and aggression, "fighting" and "running away", are closely related to pharmacological reactions in the developing embryo. This statement cannot be supported as yet by what I call "scientific fact"; I only claim for it that it is a "rational conjecture". At some stage of post-natal development the personality will display strikingly powerful emotions and symptoms, as for example continuous crying of such a degree that the parents cannot tolerate it. When the patient is old enough, he will express the pressure of the intense feelings of which he is aware as a fear of going mad. Such expressions arouse, in the parents and doctors responsible for the care, reactions which are premature, inappropriate and liable to "blind" all intuition. In waking life this can emerge as the panic which afflicts even disciplined troops and their leaders in war.

(*CWB XIV*, p. 146)

The god Pan: Disturbed in his secluded afternoon nap, Pan's angry shout inspired panic in lonely places. Following the Titans' assault on Olympus, Pan claimed credit for the victory of the gods, because he had frightened the attackers. In the Battle of Marathon (490 BC), it is said that Pan favoured the Athenians and so inspired panic in the hearts of their enemies, the Persians.

[53] Proto-mental and psycho-somatic

The proto-mental system I visualize as one in which physical and psychological or mental are undifferentiated. It is a matrix from which spring the phenomena which at first appear – on a psychological level and in the light of psychological investigation – to be discrete feelings only loosely associated with one another. It is from this matrix that emotions proper to the basic assumption flow to reinforce, pervade, and, on occasion, to dominate the mental life of the group. Since it is a level in which physical and mental are undifferentiated, it stands to reason that, when distress from this source manifests itself, it can manifest itself just as well in physical forms as in psychological. The inoperative basic assumptions are confined within the proto-mental system....

(*CWB IV*, p. 177)

It must be borne in mind that the question whether a field is suitable for psychological investigation depends on other factors besides the nature of the field to be investigated, one being the potency of the investigating psychological technique. The recognition of a field of psychosomatic medicine illustrates the difficulty that attends any attempt at determination of the line that separates psychological from physical phenomena.

(*CWB IV*, p. 217)

[54]   Leaders Mad and Sane

In its search for a leader the group finds a paranoid schizophrenic or malignant hysteric if possible; failing either of these, a psychopathic personality with delinquent trends will do; failing a psychopathic personality it will pick on the verbally facile high-grade defective. I have at no time experienced a group of more than five people that could not provide a good specimen of one of these.

Once the leader is discovered the group treats him or her with some deference, and the occasional spicing of flattery – "Mr. So-and-so always keeps the discussion going so well" – serves to reinforce his position as leader. There is usually some tendency to test me for signs of jealousy, but this phase quickly passes. A comment that is often heard is that the group "could not do without" Miss X or Mr. Y, as the case might be. This comment is also made about myself. Though it appears to be insignificant enough, it is a matter to which we shall have to pay considerable attention later.

When the leadership of the individual concerned is well established in the eyes of all members of the group, difficulties arise. King Saul, the frogs, in Aesop, who would have a stork for king, the Pharaohs, all in varying degrees illustrate aspects of the group in its new situation. . . . Whenever a state exists that is likely to activate, or itself to have been activated by, the baD [basic assumption Dependency], there is a fear of dictatorship – a recent example is the often expressed fear that the Welfare State will lead to a tyrannical interference with liberty – the seizure of power by Communists, bureaucrats, etc. One of the most common calls in this situation is for a return to a belief in God, and indeed it will be surprising if in the small therapeutic group some member does not make this very plea. It expresses the desire to avoid the concrete embodiment of leadership in an actual member of the group. If I leave things to develop, many remedies will be proposed; revolt against the chosen leader, a claim that treatment should be available for all and that one person should not monopolize, and so on. In effect practically all the solutions adumbrated are recognizable as closely similar to procedures tried throughout history. What is not so easy to describe is what it is against which the group is seeking to protect itself.

Emotional oscillation in a group

My conclusion is that the situation derives from the stimulus produced by having, on the W [work group] level of the therapeutic group, leader and psychiatrist in one. The group is compelled to recognize that the spontaneously chosen leader is seriously disordered – as I mentioned earlier, it seems to be essential that in *baD* the leader should be "mad"; or – a description the group finds more flattering to itself and the individual concerned – a "genius". At the same time it is compelled to believe that he is the dependable leader. Now, this can only be done by a series of oscillations from one view to the other. If I refuse to intervene, and I have tested this situation several times by letting it go very far, even too far for safety, the oscillations become very rapid. And when, as in this situation, the distance separating the two beliefs is great – for it is hard to imagine two views more widely separated than a belief that the leader is mad and the belief that he is the dependable person on whom you rely for your welfare – then the oscillations have to be both rapid in time and large in excursion. The result is that the group can no longer contain the emotional situation, which thereupon spreads with explosive violence to other groups until enough groups have been drawn in to absorb the reaction.

(*CWB IV*, pp. 192–194)

Bion may well be describing a situation that he actually allowed to develop with a Tavistock group. I imagine that the "other groups" referred to could include the management of the Tavistock Centre.

King Saul: In the Book of Samuel in the Old Testament, when the Spirit of God came upon Saul, he stripped off his clothes and lay naked day and night.

The Frogs: Aesop's fable about a group of frogs who called on Zeus to give them a king, whereupon Zeus threw down a log, which fell into their pond with a terrific splash, terrifying them out of their wits. One brave frog peeped out from her hiding place, realized it wasn't moving, and hopped upon it. Joined by her froggie friends, they jumped up and down making fun of their "king". They asked again for a king and were sent a water snake, who proceeded to eat them. Supplicating Zeus to no avail, he told them simply to live with the consequences of their wishing. In other versions, the water snake is sometimes a stork or a heron – all frog-eating animals.

The Pharaohs: Kings of Ancient Egypt, were seen as god-kings, believed to mediate between man and gods and to have omnipotence, omniscience and powers over nature's fertility. After death, the pharaoh became divine, passing on his powers to his successor.

[55]   Counter-transference

. . . many interpretations, and amongst them the most important, have to be made on the strength of the analyst's own emotional reactions. It is my belief that these reactions are dependent on the fact that the analyst in the group is at the receiving end of what Melanie Klein has called projective identification, and that this mechanism plays a very important role in groups. Now the experience of counter-transference appears to me to have quite a distinct quality that should enable the analyst to differentiate the occasion when he is the object of a projective identification from the occasion when he is not. The analyst feels he is being manipulated so as to be playing a part, no matter how difficult to recognize, in somebody else's phantasy – or he would do if it were not for what in recollection I can only call a temporary loss of insight, a sense of experiencing strong feelings and at the same time a belief that their existence is quite adequately justified by the objective situation without recourse to recondite explanation of their causation. . . . I believe ability to shake oneself out of the numbing feeling of reality that is a concomitant of this state is the prime requisite of the analyst in the group: if he can do this he is in a position to give what I believe is the correct interpretation, and thereby to see its connection with the previous interpretation, the validity of which he has been caused to doubt.

(CWB IV, pp. 213–214)

The quote is from the last of the seven "Experiences in Groups" papers and was published originally in 1952. The seminal paper by Klein that Bion is referring to is "Notes on Some Schizoid Mechanisms", which was published six years earlier, in 1946. Bion was in analysis with Klein between 1946 and 1953.

Klein's focus is on what the person who "projects" is unconsciously doing. Bion draws attention to the effect on the receiver of the projection.

[56] To capture all that richness

Interview by Anthony G. Banet, Jr. (1976)

... I sometimes think that an analyst's feelings while taking a group – feelings while absorbing the basic assumptions of the group – are one of the few bits of what scientists might call evidence, because he can know what he is feeling. I attach great importance to feelings for that reason. You as an analyst can see for yourself what a shocking, poverty-stricken vocabulary it is for you – I'm frightened, I feel sexual, I feel hostile – and that's about it. But that's not what it's like in real life. In real life you have an orchestra: continuous movement and the constant slither of one feeling into another. You have to have a method to capture all that richness. In a group, you are in the unfortunate position of having very little evidence. The physician, the physical person, can get physical evidence, or so he thinks, anyway. When dealing with physical things, you can touch, you can feel, and you can smell, but we who use our minds are really up against it, because we don't know what the mind really is capable of perceiving. Even senses that were available to us at some stage in life we have lost.

(CWB X, p. 156)

This quote is from an interview in 1976. Bion had not taken any further groups since the beginning of the 1950s.

[57]   Emotions in the basic assumptions

...all the emotions of one basic assumption seemed to be welded together....
(*CWB IV*, p. 178)

Emotions associated with basic assumptions may be described by the usual terms, anxiety, fear, hate, love, and the like. But the emotions common to any basic assumption are subtly affected by each other as if they were held in a combination peculiar to the active basic assumption. That is to say, anxiety in the dependent group has a different quality from anxiety evident in the pairing group, and so on with other feelings.
(*CWB IV*, p. 217)

Anxiety, fear, hate, love, all, as I have said, exist in each basic-assumption group. The modification that feelings suffer in combination in the respective basic-assumption group may arise because the "cement" so to speak, that joined them to each other is guilt and depression in the dependent group, Messianic hope in the pairing group, anger and hate in the fight–flight group.
(*CWB IV*, p. 226)

Bion observes that while we may use the same words for the feelings in each basic assumption – i.e. love, anger . . . – the feelings are in fact "subtly affected" by their context. Individual emotions in a basic assumption cannot change independently of the other emotions. The "cement" is an inflexible link.

[58]   Is there something more fundamental underlying both the basic assumption and work groups?

We may now reconsider the three basic-assumption groups and the work group to see if they are not capable of resolution into something more fundamental. Granting that the postulate of basic assumptions helps to give form and meaning to the complex and chaotic emotional state that the group unfolds to the investigating participant, there is yet no reasonable explanation of why such assumptions should exist.

(*CWB IV*, pp. 221–222)

Is there something more fundamental underlying both the basic assumption and work groups? Do the basic assumptions have a positive function – a temporary management of something even more threatening or difficult for human functioning – psychotic anxiety? Shortly after reconsidering whether there is "something more fundamental", Bion makes the following comment:

A scrutiny of the facts seems to lead to a central difficulty in bringing together sexual love, equal parents, an infant like ourselves, the Messianic hope which I consider to be an essential component of the sexual love, and a compulsion to develop that in itself necessitates a capacity for understanding.

(*CWB IV*, p. 222)

This being all he says, we don't have much to go on. Might he be saying that a function of the assumptions is the prevention of the key elements for life and development, including sexual life, coming properly together? I think one model for this would be that of a chemical reaction. Did he think that the bringing together of the different elements would result in a "being alive" that may be experienced as too intense to bear?

A colleague commented that the "bringing together" of the different elements may be associated with infantile perceptions of the primal scene and the destructive and libidinal instincts around it. "If one thinks about it, the Dependency assumption is 'I am an infant and can hand over responsibility'. The second basic assumption of Pairing is that 'something is going on from which I'm excluded, but may or may not produce something helpful'. The third, Fight/Flight, is a reaction of basic aggression/or escape from aggression. In all these we can hear infantile phantasies around mother and parents."

[59]   The painful bringing together of the primitive and the sophisticated

The defence that schism affords against the development-threatening idea can be seen in the operation of the schismatic groups, ostensibly opposed but in fact promoting the same end. One group adheres to the dependent group, often in the form of the group "bible". This group popularizes the established ideas by denuding them of any quality that might demand painful effort and thereby secures a numerous adherence of those who oppose the pains of development. Thought thus becomes stabilized on a level that is platitudinous and dogmatic. The reciprocal group, supposedly supporting the new idea, becomes so exacting in its demands that it ceases to recruit itself. Thus both groups avoid the painful bringing together of the primitive and the sophisticated that is the essence of the developmental conflict.

(*CWB IV*, p. 221)

Chapter 5

The Other Side of Genius: Family Letters

Introduction: Francesca Bion

The first volume of Wilfred Bion's autobiography, *The Long Week-End*, covered the period up to 1919 when he was demobilized from the army and for the first time had to face civilian life as an adult, unqualified for any profession, or indeed for any occupation by which he might earn his living. Although incomplete and only in first draft, I wanted to publish the remainder of what he wrote [*All My Sins Remembered: Another Part of a Life*]; but it leaves us with a thirty-year blank and, even more unfortunately, an abiding impression of unrelieved gloom and profound dislike of himself.

This sad, self-searching testimony would on its own present a false picture of the life of a man who came to derive great happiness and reward from his marriage, family and work. The clearest evidence of this is provided by his letters to us, written with no audience in mind and no need to lay stress on his sins of omission, confident of our love and understanding. Almost all his creative thinking and writing were done during these years when he was at last released from the confines of war, bereavement and a sense of hopelessness.

We make public some of these private communications because they tell the reader so much – not about us, his wife and children, but about him, the husband and father. We are proud to have been his family and the recipients of his love.

Francesca Bion, Abingdon, Oxfordshire, 1984
(Francesca Bion, 1985, p. 7)

A number of quotes from *The Other Side of Genius* that refer to specific writings/ occasions have been included later in the book.

Quotes

60 Love
61 Different ball games
62 Bion and his children: Parthenope, Julian and Nicola
63 Queer job of mine
64 The strain of war

About Francesca Bion

Francesca Bion was born on 23 November 1922 and was in her early twenties when she met Bion, himself in his forties. The following is written by psychoanalyst Paulo C. Sandler.

> Francesca said: "Paulo, I choose my name. My parents called me Patricia Ivy, but I liked Francesca". Then she told me the name of her parents: Mrs Ivy and Mr Archibald Purnell. . . . It gradually became clear to me that Bion's texts, which I read avidly many times, were embedded, encircled and emanated the scent of Francesca. Since 1986, I published some works in English voicing the discovery that there was a mutual collaboration between Francesca and Dr Bion. Unfussy, she wrote in a letter: "This happens in married couples. I never thought about this before". She agreed with my idea and authorized me to write about the fact. This happened not only because she was who turned his handwritten texts into typewritten ones or because she was his editor. The sound of Francesca is visible in Bion's ideas and postures and vice-versa.
>
> I became aware that Francesca . . . had been a soprano singer in Thomas Beecham's orchestra – she won a scholarship to the Royal Academy of Music. She told me only after I confessed my love to classic music. "A gifted, but sarcastic man [Beecham]. He was rudely elitist . . . but what a conductor he was!" Francesca could not follow on, due to the obtrusion of war and financial reasons.

In 1983, when Paulo Sandler hoped to meet Francesca in person on a visit to London, she was ill with cancer. They met later, in 1993. On that occasion she asked Paulo what he would like to do.

> I am too interested in History and knew that the Churchill War Cabinets are now a Museum. I could not wait to visit it. My Dad once told me that England was a land of freedom: that I – and millions of people – were born because Churchill was a fighter for freedom". Francesca gently interrupted me: "I would like to go there too! I worked there during two years, as a statistician". . . . Francesca then told me that she had to sleep in King William Street's underground station as London endured the Blitzkrieg. In 1944, her services in the War Office, linked to the Secret Service, were needed abroad and she found herself in Cairo – the only woman on the staff. I know that her instant sympathy with André Green – a mutual friend – stemmed from this fact: both entertained the same

feelings about their Egyptian experience. "I was alone and met John, a rather cocky RAF Lieutenant specialized in fighter aircraft." . . . They married in Cairo Cathedral Church, "in March 1945. My Mother gave me the dress, made from silk – taken from a parachute!" . . . Lieutenant John McCallum was drawn as a test pilot and could not accompany his wife, who was ordered to return to England. He met his fate in 1949, testing a technological wonder: the first jet aircraft in the UK – the Gloster Meteor, already dubbed as "meatbox" and "widow's maker". Meanwhile Francesca tried to make music again. "I looked for The Glyndebourne Touring Company, which endured its worst financial shape. Of course all of us knew it, but what attracted me was that Beecham had made the one and only compliment I heard from him: he praised that company, which he conducted only one time! So I looked for it". . . . "I was the lead soprano in the first Edinburgh Festival (1947)". . . . When we later heard Mozart music in her home, in 2005, she told me, longingly, about her role in *Cosi fan Tutte*. Financial reasons made her abandon a promising career and taking a job at the Tavistock Clinic. You all know what happened after this: the widowed Francesca married with the widowed Dr Bion. . . .

(Paulo Cesar Sandler, personal communication, September 2015)

[60]   Love

Bion's first letter to Francesca

1951

The Homestead, Iver Heath

March 22

Francesca dear,

This does not seem to be a very sensible time in the morning to start writing you a letter but then I feel I cannot wait till tomorrow. Besides this is not *really* a letter but just a note and tomorrow I shall write a letter.

I walked back with a great wind blowing hazy clouds across a moon which was never visible but made all the trees stand out a deep grey against the silvery meadows and water. And all the time I could see you, and still see you, looking more ravishingly beautiful, as you did all the evening when I was with you, than anyone could believe possible. You were kind to be like that.

And here I shall have to stop for my thoughts will not flow freely when I feel that all I would say cannot be written – or certainly not when I keep thinking of mundane things such as whether I shall be in time to catch a morning post with this, or even whether there is a morning post on a Good Friday.

So, goodbye dear Francesca till tomorrow when I shall be writing you a letter. Remember me, please, to your Mother and give her my best Easter wishes.

Dear Francesca, bless you. With love from

Wilfred

(*CWB II*, p. 81)

May 3

Francesca darling,

. . . if this is a dream it is the longest and most marvellous dream I have ever had; if it is not a dream, then I don't know how to contain myself. My goodness, I think, how lovely, how lovely she is. And she has promised to marry me. How extraordinary!

(*CWB II*, p. 105)

Bion wrote the following letter when he had been admitted to hospital after fainting at Victoria station during an attack of influenza. Although ill, he had continued to see his patients. The irregularity shown by the ECG was never wholly accounted for.

4 February 1959

My darling,

It really did seem as if the sunshine had gone out of the ward when you went out just then, but thanks to letters I can start writing straight away. It is a queer thing about love that it teaches you that certain common phrases which seem never to have much meaning are really quite true. If it weren't for you I would not have found that out about the sunshine....

(*CWB II*, p. 144)

[61] Different ball games

July 9

My darling Wife,

The sound of your dear voice has really put some life into me in a most magical way . . . It has even had the effect of making me get out my own group paper and look at it. There really is a big difficulty about this. I think that to psychoanalyse patients properly – and I think I am doing this quite well at the moment – one has to keep one's touch concentrated on that sort of outlook; one should not do something too close to it – either analysis only or else something quite different, a complete change. They say you should never play a game with a stationary ball, like golf, when you are trying to play well in a game with a moving ball, like tennis. It is something of that sort. Anyhow I often feel after throwing myself into group work that I do very bad analysis just after it. Of course it may be illusory.

(*CWB II*, p. 115)

[62] Bion and his children: Parthenope, Julian and Nicola

1964

The Little Cottage

To Wells Rise, London December 29

My darling,

We are gathered in the lounge. Parthenope is writing, Julian and Nicola reading, and self writing while waiting for the phone to go. The room is beautifully warm because the snow has turned into rain and it is thawing, but it is blowing very hard. The roads have been awful – I fell down twice on the loop road on my way to the village shop, and on the second occasion the rescue team of Parthenope and Nicola likewise fell down. Julian rode his bike and did not come off but heaven know why not. Noises very life-like but not at all like Brands Hatch; quite outstandingly moderate in fact.

Our room was so cold I was jolly glad of the electric blanket. Unfortunately my ability to regulate it to maintain an equable temperature is impaired by sleep so I kept on waking up because I was either shivering with cold and stiff as I could well be while maintaining my ability to shiver, or else (having inadvertently switched on to "high") pouring with sweat and dreaming I was fighting my way through a tropical jungle. I awoke soon after 8.0 but all the others were still fast asleep. So I proceeded to get breakfast and relied on the resulting fracas to wake them, which gradually it did.

I constantly wonder how you are getting on – at this point you rang up. I forgot to ask you if you had the house properly warmed up. . . .

(*CWB II*, p. 155)

[63]   Queer job of mine

I never argue against other people's views. They (1) don't pay any attention, (2) use it to prove you are wrong, (3) get downright nasty about it and never forgive you, (4) pinch your idea when they have found out what it is, or (3) and (4). Only read the best – e.g. Freud and Klein: and acknowledge what you take. Acknowledging a bad writer is like becoming responsible for, and advertising him. You can see from the foregoing what a nasty character I have; alas, one does not improve with age.

I usually feel in this queer job of mine that I have hardly anything to say from the depths in other people's unconscious, and by the time I have emerged from that into the "glare" of other people's conscious I am too blindly bat-like to have anything to say.

(CWB II, pp. 236–237)

[64]   The strain of war

1973

I remember thinking Queen's dons were a bit soft in the head because they did not expect much from us; "they (us) couldn't be expected to do very well after the strain of war". Now I realize of course they were quite right. In the last war (Great, second lap) they didn't allow youngsters to get into fighting but I was only almost twenty-one at the *end* of my fighting career and I have since only very slowly come to realize what a *very* long time it took me to recover.

(*CWB II*, p. 239)

The *"Queen's dons:* Dons of Queen's College Oxford, where Bion attended immediately after the First World War.

Chapter 6

Papers of the 1950s

Introduction

In 1946 Bion wrote to John Rickman about his starting in analysis with Melanie Klein:

> I hope to start at the Institute on the 5th with the 1st year course; I'm just hoping to get the hang of it with Melanie a bit but at first she seemed to take the transference less thoroughly than you did. But maybe this is in part because it is a different stage. Anyway I believe I should profit.
>
> (Letter to Rickman, 28 January 1946, in Conci, 2011)

Bion resumed his psychoanalytic training after the war. Of Bion's training to be an analyst we don't hear much – a description of very tired people sitting in a seminar at the end of a long day, a caustic comment about having to recover from training – and analysis. He was older than many of his fellow students, including Betty Joseph, who trained at around the same time and became a close friend. Bion married Francesca in June 1951, and they had two children, Julian, born in July 1952 and Nicola, born in June 1955.

After qualification, Bion quickly progressed to membership. His membership paper, "The Imaginary Twin", was presented to the Society on 1 November 1950, and a quote from the published paper is included. Now in his fifties, Bion was working in private practice, and he no longer worked with groups. As mentioned in the Introduction, after the end of his analysis with Klein in 1953, he joined a small group of analysts who met regularly with her. The group included Hanna Segal, Betty Joseph, and Elliot Jacques. In their meetings they discussed clinical material, papers and the development of their pioneering work with psychotic patients (Segal, personal communication).

Bion's papers of the 1950s were presented to the International Psychoanalytical Congresses, and the Scientific Meetings of the British Psychoanalytical Society. I understand that Bion would often give a paper to the Societies' first meeting in September, after the long August analytic break. The papers were then published in the *International Journal of Psychoanalysis*. It is these papers that are the best known of his work in the United Kingdom.

While the papers are concise, the excerpts from his letters written during this period show that the process he went through in writing them was far from easy. He speaks of "complex subjects", "curiously elusive subjects" and not wanting to "rush into it prematurely". In his letters we also see that Bion is reading the work of writers from outside psychoanalysis in order to clarify and further his thinking.

The first three entries in this chapter are to do with his experience of training, analysis with Klein, and trying out an interpretation given to him by Klein on one of his own patients! The following quotes are from the papers of the 1950s, along with three quotes from letters he wrote to Francesca during this period.

Notes on concepts Bion is using and developing

The death instinct

Freud

Freud introduced his concept of the life and death instincts in his 1920 book, *Beyond the Pleasure Principle* – and from the beginning it has been controversial. Freud began with a problem that had emerged in the clinical setting of psycho-analytic treatment – one he believed he could not account for within his existing theory. The problem is that we appear compelled to repeat painful experiences. This, he thought, "astonishes people far too little".

French psychoanalysts Laplanche and Pontalis (1973) comment that psycho-analysis had been confronted from the very beginning by repetition phenomena: obsessional rituals, the repeating return of repressed material in current experi-ence. When Freud brought the notion of the compulsion to repeat to the fore in *Beyond the Pleasure Principle,* he grouped together a certain number of examples of repetition that had already been recognised, while further identifying other cases (fate neurosis and traumatic neurosis). He took into account the nature of masochism and the murderousness of the melancholic superego. These were the phenomena that, in Freud's view, warranted a new theoretical analysis. Laplanche and Pontalis also note that while compulsive repetition of what is painful is an irrefutable clinical fact, there is much disagreement among analysts as to the cor-rect theoretical explanation of it. Freud, however, concludes that:

> the whole ground is not covered by the operation of the familiar motive forces. Enough is left unexplained to justify the hypothesis of a compul-sion to repeat – something that seems more primitive, more elementary, more instinctual than the pleasure principle which it over-rides.

> (Freud 1920, p. 23)

It is far from clear why Freud thinks this. Laplanche and Pontalis note the contradictoriness of his own pronouncements on the matter. It has been suggested that personal factors – the war, his own illness, the death of his daughter Sophie – could have been preoccupying his thinking at this time. My own view is that Freud was faced by a scientific problem – that of repetition – but one that he thought could not be dealt with in the usual way, through clinical investigation. Instead, Freud goes outside psychoanalysis to the experimental natural sciences. He had, of course, come from neuroscience in the first place. James Strachey, in his introduction to *Beyond the Pleasure Principle*, comments that what is remarkable is the closeness with which some of the earlier chapters of the work follow the "Project for a Scientific Psychology" (1950 [1895]), drafted by Freud 25 years earlier, in 1895. Freud turns now to the experiments of the biologists, and in doing so, he not only goes outside psychoanalysis, but he is raising questions about the nature of life and death itself – why does anything come to life – what causes death? It seems he thought that he had to get a deeper or broader understanding than that provided by his psychoanalytic model of human functioning. This move has caused serious difficulties for psychoanalysis to do with the relation between theory and clinical practice, but it does seem that Freud thought he had to get a viewpoint that could not be obtained from inside the psychoanalytic field.

Freud concludes that instincts not only work "forwards", but also pull "backwards". He postulates that the death instinct aims at destructuralisation, dissolution, and death.

Klein

Klein took up Freud's view of there being a primary destructiveness in human beings, and she saw envy as a key instance of this. "I consider", she writes, "that envy is an oral-sadistic and anal-sadistic expression of destructive impulses, operative from the beginning of life, and that it has a constitutional basis" (Klein 1957, p. 176). A little later she describes it as "the angry feeling that another person possesses and enjoys something desirable – the envious impulse being to take it away or to spoil it". In her view, it is a manifestation of death instinct, which she thinks of as an instinctual internal destructive force felt as fear of annihilation (Spillius 1993, p. 1199).

Bion

Citing Freud's tentative suggestion in *Civilization and Its Discontents* (1930) of the importance of the conflict between life and death instincts, Bion thought that in relation to psychosis there is always a preponderance of innate destructiveness. Particularly in the earlier papers the reader will find the concept of the death instinct to be at the core of his thinking. My own impression is that the emphasis on destructiveness and hatred of reality, while always there, begins to make way for a more complex picture, in which Bion begins to draw attention to the significance of the object, of mental pain and of our experience of what we don't know.

Projective identification

Following Klein's introduction of the concept of projective identification, it was now being explored by Bion as well as by others. Bion recognised that projective identification can be a communication as well as a "getting rid of"/"controlling the world". He came to see projective identification as the most primitive of communications – one on which the very capacity to communicate is built – and the significance of the more mature mind of the mother (or analyst) in processing the projected unnameable stuff assailing the infant. Klein knew the environment to be important; Bion was to show how.

Hallucination

Hallucinations result from evacuation – instead of the senses being used to take something in, they are used to push it out – we see or hear things that are not actually there in the external world. Bion thinks that hallucination is more prevalent than we are aware of. He returns on a number of occasions to the difference between hallucinations and dreams and how we can mistake one for the other. He suggests, for example, that patients can want us to call hallucinations dreams in order to reassure them in their fears of madness.

The paranoid-schizoid (Ps) and depressive (D) positions

Melanie Klein identified mental constellations that occur in everyone in infancy and then throughout life. The paranoid-schizoid position is the most primitive. It is characteristic of the earliest months of life and of states of unintegration throughout life. Anxieties of a primitive nature swamp the immature ego in infancy and are associated with the primitive defences of splitting into good and bad (both of the self and of the object). The self feels under attack and preoccupied with its own survival.

The paranoid-schizoid position is gradually superseded by the depressive position. Instead of splitting the object the mother comes to be seen as a whole – both hated and loved. The fact that destructive impulses are aimed at loved ones augers in the experiences of guilt and concern.

In later quotes we hear Bion imagining the experience of an infant who is discovering a reliable good object and beginning to realise that attacks on itself are not caused by a present persecutor, but are feeling stirred up by the absence of the good and reliable object. There is relief in this discovery, but the realisation that the mother who is loved is the same object as the mother who is hated augurs in new anxiety that one's own destructiveness will damage the object. If these anxieties can be borne, along with guilt and loss, then primitive "thinking" can develop and reparative capacities emerge. The infant or adult can remain more "within" themselves without having to project their destructiveness outwards.

Unbeknownst to Hanna Segal, a quote by her describing the "depressive position" experience of believing that everything has been destroyed was used after the destruction of the World Trade Center as a rallying call for the World Trade Center Mural Project:

> It is when the world within us is destroyed, when it is dead and loveless, when our loved ones are in fragments, and we ourselves in helpless despair – it is then that we must recreate our world anew, reassemble the pieces, infuse life into dead fragments, recreate life.
>
> (Segal 1952, p. 199)

Britton has commented on Bion's use of the concepts thus:

> The paranoid-schizoid position was seen as a natural precursor of the depressive position in infancy. It was described as a state where time did not exist, part objects were perceived as whole objects, identification rather than object-relating was the mode, and absolutes ruled even though other contrary absolutes coexisted. The transition to the depressive position meant integration, the perception of whole objects consisting of parts instead of part objects being seen as whole objects, a sense of time, cause, and effect, and the existence of necessity. Bion later suggested that what he called Ps and D, roughly meaning unintegration and integration, were alternating states he called Ps $\rightleftharpoons$ D.
>
> (Britton 2015, pp. 65–57)

Quotes

[65]   On training

My experiences of psychoanalytic training were, in fact, very depressing. Like the first railway coaches which were made to look as much like horse-drawn vehicles as possible, I found the whole apparatus of training was just a copy of the methods suitable for conventional training in conventional experience. But as I became more and more acquainted with psychoanalysis, the more utterly unsuitable this seemed. Some of it was due to the fact that we were all tired people, listening to people who were even more tired at the end of a day's hard work, who then fell back on doing what everybody else did. As I sat in small, over-crowded, uncomfortable rooms I thought that this was more suitable as a penitential exercise than anything connected with a cultural activity.

(CWB VII, p. 192)

It took me a very long time to realize that the actual experience of being psychoanalysed was a traumatic one, and it takes a long while before one recovers from it.

(CWB IX, p. 7)

Both quotes are from later years, when Bion was in his seventies. The second quote is from a seminar he gave at the Tavistock Centre on 28 June 1976.

Bion was asked by Los Angeles psychoanalyst James Gooch what he would recommend for a training course. He responded that it should be made clear which core concepts the trainee was required to understand before qualification, but that the trainee should be able to choose which courses to attend. Those teaching should teach only what they were interested in. A seminar should not be more than four weeks long, with a four-week break between seminars. He was "cagey" about the question of training analysts, placing an emphasis on people being able to choose whom they want among those who had graduated in the institution. Graduation was to involve presenting one's work to a committee or to the whole society, who would then vote. Gooch thought the latter point to be "kind of brutal" and asked about the possibility that the group or committee might be prejudiced. Bion responded: "Well that would be too bad, but such a group shouldn't survive anyhow" (from Culbert-Koehn 2011, pp. 86–87).

[66]   Analysis with Klein

From the transcription of a tape recording made in April 1979

After the war, Rickman did not feel that it was possible to continue with me because we had had plenty of experience together during the war. However, I took the plunge and went to see Melanie Klein. I found that what she said, while seeming very often to be rather extraordinary stuff, had a kind of common sense about it – not altogether what I would have regarded as obvious or clear to me, but on the other hand not divorced from what I knew about myself or other people, or even about my war experience.

(CWB XI, pp. 346–347)

From *All My Sins Remembered*

Melanie Klein, of whom I had heard and had had some chance of observing from a distance on one or two occasions, was a handsome, dignified and somewhat intimidating woman. My experience of association with women had not been encouraging or conducive to the growth of any belief in a successful outcome. However, I went to see her. I tried to indicate that I was worthy of her consideration, but she did not understand, or chose not to know – I don't know which – the enormous significance of the DSO [Distinguished Service Order]. As I had not succeeded in believing that it was more than a cosmetic cover for my cowardice, the reality of which was never in the least doubt since I knew what it felt like to have *my* feelings, I thought that her ignorance might be reinforced by her disbelief in my masculine excellence. I had, in short, no evidence to support my application. She nevertheless agreed to accept me. How I was to pay my fees and read the psychoanalytic theories of Melanie Klein – I had looked at them and could not make head or tail of what I read – I had no idea.

My analysis pursued what I am inclined to think was a normal course: I retailed a variety of preoccupations; worries about the child, the household, financial anxieties – particularly how I was to find the money for such psychoanalytic fees *and* provide a home and care for the baby. Looking back on it I think my gifts as a sponger might have qualified me as a mendicant friar – unless of course that profession has some method of collecting from the friar such money as he collects or secretes. Mrs Klein remained unmoved and unmoving. I was very glad that she did, but that did not lead to the abandonment of my grievance. I suppose, reconsidering the matter, I expected to be supported in what I considered to be very moderate affluence. Why and on what grounds I thought the community required my continued existence is a puzzle, especially as I am now not likely to be eligible or desirable in any society – socially or militarily. Melanie Klein, however, was not easily led away from her awareness of a universe that is not subject to the needs and wishes of human beings, even when they came to her for analysis. . . .

She tried to pass on to me her interpretations of the material of which her senses made her aware. But to become efficacious her methods were dependent on my receptivity. This is in no way different from any other form of human assistance – there must be someone or something willing to receive.

How banal is this conclusion! How obvious! And how perpetually that fact becomes clear and how frequently ignored. Yet a willing cooperation in teacher and taught is difficult to achieve when the participants are human. This banal observation seemed to be more than usually bitterly resisted when it was I who had to listen to what my senses told me, even with the assistance of Melanie Klein. But as time passed I became more reconciled to the fact that not even she could be a substitute for my own senses, interpretations of what my senses told me, and choice between contradictories. I did not become more amenable to her views but more aware of my disagreement. None the less there was something about that series of experiences with her that made me feel gratitude to her and a wish to be independent of the burden of time and expense of money and effort involved.

At last, after some years, we parted. She, I think, felt I still had a lot to learn from her but she agreed to the termination – partly no doubt through the realization that enough of WRB was enough.

I was, however, mistaken in thinking that we had seen the last of each other and that I was free to go. But I shall not anticipate that part of the story.

(*CWB II*, pp. 71–73)

From "São Paulo 1978"

... before we know what has happened we have become "Kleinians" or –
Interpreter: – I would like to know what "Kleinian" means.
Bion: You are optimistic. Even Mrs Klein didn't know what it meant –
                she protested at being called a "Kleinian". But, as Betty Joseph
                told her, "You are too late – you are Kleinian whether you like
                it or not". There was nothing she could do about it.

(*CWB VIII*, pp. 328–329)

From *A Memoir of the Future*

Melanie Klein's interpretations began to have a vaguely but truly illuminating quality. It was as if, literally as well as metaphorically, light began to grow, night was replaced by dawn.

(*CWB XIV*, p. 122)

James Gooch

JoAnn: Did he ever talk to you about his own analysis with Klein, or did he ever say anything to you about Freud or about Jung?

Jim [Gooch] He made references that gave me the impression that he gave Klein a very hard time. And that . . . she wasn't easy. He said something like, "well, you can have some idea what it must have been like for Mrs. Klein to have me as an analysand" or something like that. He could be very ornery and very tenacious and stubborn at times. . . .

(Culbert-Koehn 2011, p. 82)

James Gooch: A patient of Bion's in California in the 1970s.

[67]   Trying out an interpretation from Klein on one of his own patients

From "São Paulo 1978"

Melanie Klein gave me an interpretation which puzzled me for a long time. She said, "You feel mutilated, castrated, as you emerge from the womb". That sounded like pure nonsense to me. By that time I was also seeing a patient, so I thought I would try it out on him too.

(CWB VIII, p. 325)

[68]   "The Imaginary Twin" (1950)

From *The Other Side of Genius*

July 9 [1951]

This is I believe a really good paper and it very badly needs expansion and publication. Probably I had better concentrate on that at least till the summer holiday.

(*CWB II*, p. 115)

The above quote is from a letter to his wife Francesca. The one that follows is from the paper itself:

There was plenty of oedipal material, produced on a most superficial level, which I duly interpreted, to meet with a perfunctory response or none at all.

My awareness of a change in the analysis developed over a period of some three months. At first it seemed as if my interpretations were only meeting with more than usually stubborn indifference, and then as if I was a parent who was issuing ineffectual exhortations and warnings to a refractory child. In due course I pointed this out to him and a change, not easily formulated, occurred. There was still the dreary monotone of associations but there was now a quality which derived from what I can best describe as the rhythm of his associations. It was as if two quite separate co-existent scansions of his material were possible. One imparted an overpowering sense of boredom and depression; the other, dependent on the fact that he introduced regularly spaced pauses in the stream of his associations, an almost jocular effect as if he were saying "Go on; it's your turn".

Examining the matter still further, I noticed that the associations were all stale associations inviting a stale response. If I broke the rhythm, he showed signs of anxiety or irritability; if I continued to give the interpretations, which it now became clear he both invited and expected, there emerged a sense of having reached a dead-end.

...I drew his attention to peculiarities in his behaviour, notably the rhythm of "association–interpretation association", which indicated that I was a twin of himself who supported him in a jocular evasion of my complaints and thus softened his resentment....

His response was striking. His voice changed and he said, in a depressed tone, that he felt tired and unclean. It was as if, in a moment, I had in front of me, unchanged in every respect the patient as I had seen him at the first interview. The change was so sudden as to be disconcerting.

(*CWB VI*, pp. 56–59)

Bion presented his paper "The Imaginary Twin" to the Society on 1 November 1950, to qualify for membership. For ease of reference I include the following note from the Introduction. We hear that he has been duly interpreting the Oedipal content, to little effect. He then describes his observation of the interaction happening between the patient and himself. This is an early example of what was to go on to become a substantial shift in psychoanalytic technique, from paying attention to content to paying more attention to the "actions" (enactments) between patient and analyst.

Scansion: The rhythm of a line of verse.

[69]   Appreciative parents

From *The Other Side of Genius:* "Letters to Francesca"

August 13 1952

Redcourt [The Bions' home]

My darling wife,

... I had a pleasant surprise and relief to-day as my patient – "the" one – turned up and was not quite so virulent as before; but what was better, when his father arrived, he started off by saying that both he and his wife were *amazed* at the change in the boy. He said he was kind, considerate and with a marked sense of responsibility, and that they had never known him like that before. I told him I was very glad to hear it because of course what I saw was all the anxiety and conflict and hate, and that although I could *deduce* progress that was not the same as an independent witness. Now aren't you pleased? I am. It is one of the things that goes towards making one feel that all the sweat and blood of this business is well worth it – not that one always has such appreciative parents. It is a great load off my mind and it is very gratifying to me because it makes me feel, *What* a *clever* husband you've got!....

(*CWB II*, p. 121)

[70]   Language

From "Notes on the Theory of Schizophrenia"

Language is employed by the schizophrenic in three ways; as a mode of action, as a method of communication, and as a mode of thought....

(CWB VI, p. 74)

Since verbal thought depends on the ability to integrate, it is not surprising to find that its emergence is intimately associated with the depressive position which, as Melanie Klein has pointed out, is a phase of active synthesis and integration. Verbal thought sharpens awareness of psychic reality and therefore of the depression which is linked with destruction and loss of good objects. The presence of internal persecutors, as another aspect of psychic reality, is similarly unconsciously more recognized. The patient feels that the association between the depressive position and verbal thought is one of cause and effect – itself a belief based on his capacity to integrate – and this adds one more to the many causes of his hatred of analysis, already well in evidence, which is, after all, a treatment which employs verbal thought in the solution of mental problems....

(CWB IV, pp. 81–82)

The experiences I have described to you compel me to conclude that at the onset of the infantile depressive position, elements of verbal thought increase in intensity and depth. In consequence the pains of psychic reality are exacerbated by it and the patient who regresses to the paranoid-schizoid position will, as he does so, turn destructively on his embryonic capacity for verbal thought as one of the elements which have led to his pain.

(CWB IV, p. 93)

[71]   Realisations of insanity

From "Notes on the Theory of Schizophrenia"

I wish to take up the story at the point at which the splits are brought together, the patient escapes from his state of mind and the depressive position is ushered in. In particular I wish to draw attention to this concatenation of events when it is suffused by the illumination achieved through the development of a capacity for verbal thought. I have made it clear that this is a most important turning-point in the whole analysis. You may therefore have formed the impression that at this point the analysis enters into calm waters. It is necessary therefore that I should leave you with no illusions about this.

What takes place, if the analyst has been reasonably successful, is a realization by the patient of psychic reality; he realizes that he has hallucinations and delusions, may feel unable to take food, and have difficulty with sleep. The patient will direct powerful feelings of hatred towards the analyst. He [the patient] will state categorically that he is insane and will express with intense conviction and hatred that it is the analyst who has driven him to this pass. The analyst ought to expect concern for the patient's welfare to drive the family to intervene and he must be prepared to explain an alarming situation to them. He should strive to keep at bay surgeons and shock therapists alike while concentrating on not allowing the patient for a single moment to retreat either from his realization that he is insane or from his hatred of the analyst who has succeeded, after so many years, in bringing him to an emotional realization of the facts that he has spent his whole life trying to evade. This may be the more difficult because, when the first panic begins to subside, the patient himself will begin to suggest that he feels better. Due weight must be given to this, but care must be taken to prevent its being used to delay investigation in detail of the ramifications in the analytic situation of the changes brought about in the patient's object relationships by the realization of his insanity....

(CWB VI, pp. 82–83)

In 1953 the International Psychoanalytical Congress was held in London and Bion gave this paper there. Klein's paper on schizoid mechanisms had been published in 1946, and there was great interest in the analysis of psychotic patients. His analysis with Klein had ended in the same year.

Bion, as well as Hanna Segal and others, speak with some urgency about how to work with psychotic patients who are beginning to give up some of their psychotic defences and become more in touch with the reality of their "madness".

[72]   Importance of phantasies and dreams

From "Language and the Schizophrenic"

"I have a problem I am trying to work out."

"As a child I never had phantasies."

"I knew they weren't facts so I stopped them."

"I don't dream nowadays."

Then after a pause the patient went on in a bewildered voice, "I don't know what to do now."

I said, "About a year ago you told me you were no good at thinking. Just now you said you were working out a problem – obviously something you were thinking about."

Patient: "Yes."

Analyst: "But you went on with the thought that you had no phantasies in childhood; and then that you had no dreams; you then said that you did not know what to do. It must mean that without phantasies and without dreams you have not the means with which to think out your problem." The patient agreed and began to talk with marked freedom and coherence.

(CWB IV, p. 81)

The quote shows Bion's thinking about the meaning and consequences of the psychotic person's incapacity to dream. Experiences such as this may have contributed to his further enquiries into the nature of dreaming.

[73]   Congress in Geneva

From *The Other Side of Genius:* "Letters to Francesca"

July 24

Francesca darling,

...As soon as I went down to post the letter to you, there at the barrier was Elliott Jaques, and there by his side Melanie [Klein]. So we had lunch. And very good too: an artichoke, a mixed grill consisting of sweetbreads, veal, chop, pork sausage, fennel, kidney and tournedos excellently cooked. Then raspberries and a coffee ice cream. And the sun blazed and a cool breeze blew and the Rhone dashed along in front of us.

We then had a drive for some miles along Lake Geneva, beautiful in the sun with all the families out in their chic. The most amazing sight is a fountain which throws the water 270 feet into the sky – a remarkable feat of hydraulic engineering. And so back to an afternoon rest....

Then the reception. In a very big hall in the best hotel. There must have been about a thousand people. Masses of all sorts and my reeling brain saw Argentinians and Brazilians and one Mexican and – some talking broken English and some broken French but all, I gather, had been greatly stimulated by my articles, my "sporadic" articles one of them said. I felt like a stuffed cod served with hot butter sauce and looked it. I *had* to drink, and the more I drank the more of course I sweated. Many friends say what a pity you aren't here. Of course. And so do I, many times....

(CWB II, p. 134)

July 26

My darling,

I'm starting this before breakfast partly as I may not have time later and partly to let Elliott and Melanie get off to the Congress without me. I feel a bit battered at the moment. To be a bit irreverent, it all reminds me of stories a friend of mine told me about Marlene Dietrich who, said he, was surrounded by a squad of the most beautiful – teutonically beautiful that is – young men, who leapt – that was the only movement permitted I gather – to fulfil her slightest wish, and to beat off any would-be intruder. If Melanie had her way, and she has a lot of it, she would make the whole Klein group quite ridiculous in every-one's eyes. I have an excuse in my "nervousness" so mean to arrive by myself on foot. I may be wrong, of course. But I don't think so....

(CWB II, pp. 136–137)

The afternoon was a success but I feel a bit flat partly because it was pretty evident that no one understood a word I was talking about. M. K. says they will do later: perhaps. First B., who is a rogue, spoke for 29 minutes instead of 20 allotted; then Segal for 27 minutes instead of 20 allotted; then I, who spoke for 19 – a bit fast. In the discussion B. attacked me quite rightly for the clinical material, but it gave me the chance to explain what my paper was about and to explain a part of a part of an interpretation, and I gather from one or two people that it made an enormous difference to those who previously had been puzzled.

(CWB II, p. 137)

[74] On why schizophrenic disturbance occurs

From "The Development of Schizophrenic Thought"

Schizophrenic disturbance springs from an interaction between (i) the environment, and (ii) the personality. In this paper I ignore the environment and focus attention on four essential features of schizophrenic personality. First is a preponderance of destructive impulses so great that even the impulses to love are suffused by them and turned to sadism. Second is a hatred of reality which, as Freud pointed out, is extended to all aspects of the psyche that make for awareness of it. I add hatred of internal reality and all that makes for awareness of it. Third, derived from these two, is an unremitting dread of imminent annihilation. Fourth is a precipitate and premature formation of object relations, foremost amongst which is the transference, whose thinness is in marked contrast to the tenacity with which it is maintained. The prematurity, thinness, and tenacity are pathognomic and are alike derived from dread of annihilation by the death instincts. The schizophrenic is preoccupied with the conflict, never finally resolved, between destructiveness on the one hand and sadism on the other.

(*CWB VI*, p. 86)

The Nineteenth International Psychoanalytical Association Congress took place in Geneva, Switzerland (Sunday, 24 July to Thursday, 28 July, 1955). Bion read his paper – "Development of Schizophrenic Thought". It was published the following year in the *International Journal of Psychoanalysis*. The next quote is from the paper.

[75]   Main theories drawn on

From "The Development of Schizophrenic Thought"

The conclusions I arrive at were forged in analytic contact with schizophrenic patients and have been tested by me in practice. That I arrived at some degree of clarification, I owe mainly to three pieces of work. As they occupy a key position in this paper I shall remind you of them.

First: Freud's description, which I referred to in my paper at the London Congress of 1953, of the mental apparatus called into activity by the demands of the reality principle and in particular of that part of it which is concerned with conscious awareness of sense impressions. Second: Freud's tentative suggestion, in *Civilization and its Discontents*, of the importance of the conflict between Life and Death instincts. The point was taken up and developed by Melanie Klein, but Freud seemed to recede from it. Melanie Klein believes that this conflict persists throughout life, and this view I believe to be of great importance to an understanding of the schizophrenic. Third: Melanie Klein's description of the phantasied sadistic attacks that the infant makes on the breast during the paranoid-schizoid phase, and her discovery of Projective Identification. Projective Identification is a splitting off by the patient of a part of his personality and a projection of it into the object where it becomes installed, sometimes as a persecutor, leaving the psyche from which it has been split off correspondingly impoverished.

(*CWB VI*, pp. 85–86)

Bion is committed to being as clear as possible about which theories he is drawing on. He is of the view that a few good theories, well understood, are what is needed. Later he would comment that six or seven good theories should be sufficient.

[76]　Bion and Winnicott

From "The Differentiation of the Psychotic from the Non-Psychotic Personalities"

On this morning he [the patient] arrived a quarter of an hour late and lay on the couch. He spent some time turning from one side to another, ostensibly making himself comfortable. At length he said, "I don't suppose I shall do anything today. I ought to have rung up my mother." He paused and then said: "No; I thought it would be like this." A more prolonged pause followed; then, "Nothing but filthy things and smells", he said. "I think I've lost my sight". Some twenty-five minutes of our time had now passed....

(CWB VI, p. 101)

The patient jerked convulsively and I saw him cautiously scanning what seemed to be the air around him. I accordingly said that he felt surrounded by bad and smelly bits of himself including his eyes which he felt he had expelled from his anus. He replied: "I can't see." I then told him he felt he had lost his sight and his ability to talk to his mother, or to me, when he had got rid of these abilities so as to avoid pain.

In this last interpretation I was making use of a session, many months earlier, in which the patient complained that analysis was torture, memory torture. I showed him then that when he felt pain, as evidenced in this session by the convulsive jerks, he achieved anaesthesia by getting rid of his memory and anything that could make him realize pain.

(CWB VI, p. 104)

Following Bion's presentation of this paper to a Scientific meeting of the British Psychoanalytical Society, Winnicott wrote to him about it. This means that we fortuitously have a record of the two men's thinking about the same piece of clinical material.

Bion's emphasis is on the patient's attack on his abilities "so as to avoid pain". He comments that he, Bion, is in the dark about the patient's actual mother. Here is Winnicott talking about the same material:

Winnicott

It is true that the interpretations you made were very likely right at the moment but if one violates the reported scene by taking it in abstract, always a dangerous thing to do, I would say that if a patient of mine lay on the couch moving to and fro in the way your patient did and then said: "I ought to have telephoned my mother" I would know that he was talking about communication and his incapacity for making communication.

Should it interest you to know, I will say what I would have interpreted: I would have said: "A mother properly oriented to her baby would know from your movements what you need. There would be a communication because of this knowledge which belongs to her devotion and she would do something which would show that the communication had taken place. I am not sensitive enough or orientated in that way to be able to act well enough and therefore I in this present analytic situation fall into the category of the mother who failed to make communication possible. In the present relationship therefore there is given a sample of the original failure from the environment which contributed to your difficulty in communication. Of course you could always cry and so draw attention to need. In the same way you could telephone your mother and get a reply but this represents a failure of the more subtle communication which is the only basis for communication that does not violate the fact of the essential isolation of each individual. . . .

You will see that from my point of view you were talking about the environment although you said you were not going to do so and you were indicating by this clinical material that this man has a relative lack of capacity for communicating because of some experiences in which his mother or whoever was there failed in the original maternal task at the stage when the mother is closely identified with her baby, i.e. at the very beginning.

I know that there is a tremendous amount other than this sort of thing in the psychotic illness and that all the other things that you and others bring in are important, notably the parking out of personal elements in the environment. You happen to give clinical material, however, which screamed out for an interpretation about communication and this is why I want to make this comment.

(Winnicott 1987, pp. 91–92)

Discussion

Winnicott's emphasis is on a failure "in the original maternal task", while Bion's emphasis is on the consequences of an excessive innate destructiveness (death instinct) in the patient and the preponderance of this factor in the psychotic part of the personality. In a debate with the Winnicotian scholar, psychoanalyst Jan Abram, on the question of the difference between "holding" (Winnicott) and "containing" (Bion), I was struck by Abram's comment that she does not think of infants as having a fear of dying. I, by contrast, had the notion of an infant's fear of dying in my "analytic blood", as it were. The most cited Bionian example of the mother's containment of the infant is of the infant's fear of dying. How come the hypothesised Bionian infant has a fear of dying, and the hypothesised Winnicotian infant does not? It hinges, I think, on whether one is of the view that infants are born with an inherent destructiveness. The Kleinian/Bionian model of the infant is that it is born containing a drive (death instinct) that is dangerous to it. This inherent destructiveness has to be projected outwards into the mother, for the safety of the infant. One of the key tasks of the infant/mother in this model is to manage the infant's normal inborn destructiveness. Winnicott does not share the view that there is an innate destructive factor that has to be "parked out" and contained by the mother. From this point of view, "containing" and "holding" are not being expected to do the same job. Bion is "containing" the patient's attack and breaking of links; Winnicott's focus is on the mother's "holding" the communication of the infant (Winnicott 1987, pp. 91–92).

[77]   Projective identification as communication

From "On Arrogance"

[I]n so far as I, as analyst, was insisting on verbal communication as a method of making the patient's problems explicit, I was felt to be directly attacking the patient's methods of communication. From this it became clear that when I was identified with the obstructive force, what I could not stand was the patient's methods of communication. In this phase my employment of verbal communication was felt by the patient to be a mutilating attack on *his* methods of communication. From this point onwards, it was only a matter of time to demonstrate that the patient's link with me was his ability to employ the mechanism of projective identification. That is to say, his relationship with me and his ability to profit by the association lay in the opportunity to split off parts of his psyche and project them into me.

On this depended a variety of procedures which were felt to ensure emotionally rewarding experiences such as, to mention two, the ability to put bad feelings in me and leave them there long enough for them to be modified by their sojourn in my psyche, and the ability to put good parts of himself into me, thereby feeling that he was dealing with an ideal object as a result. Associated with these experiences was a sense of being in contact with me, which I am inclined to believe is a primitive form of communication that provides a foundation on which, ultimately, verbal communication depends.

(*CWB VI*, p. 136)

Bion makes what is a mutative shift in perspective, from focusing solely on the level of disturbance in the patient to focusing on the analyst's capacity to take in the patient's projections. His recognition that allowing the patient's projection to "sojourn in my psyche" could result in some modification of the patient's "bad feelings" anticipated his soon-to-arrive thoughts about the container, the contained, and the relation between the two. Bion does not talk about the effect on him of doing this for the patient. In later years he emphasises the importance of the analyst's emotional experience, but he is mostly private about his own.

From *A Key to A Memoir of the Future*

sojourn   *Milton* describes a period during which he was "detained in that obscure sojourn". He refers to a state of mind from which he emerged, but into which many analysands fear to enter – usually described as "a breakdown".

(*CWB XIV*, p. 220)

Money-Kyrle

But how do these theories help the ordinary analyst? I think he [Bion] has already learnt from Melanie Klein's work to recognize when his patient is projecting into him. And Bion's work has made it easier for us to distinguish between a desperate projective-identification and a destructive one, or, as possibly both forms were there, to see which was the predominant one.

I say this because I believe (though not with certainty) it both easy and terrible to mistake a desperate projection for a destructive one. For by this means, I think, the beginnings of a constructive link between patient and analyst may be destroyed. Of course, it is also a mistake to fail to interpret a destructive projection; but, if it is missed, the chance to see it again is sure to recur.

(Money-Kyrle 1978, pp. 462–463)

John Milton (1608–1674)

II. *Light: Day: Night*

Invocation to Light
The rising world of waters dark and deep,
Won from the void and formless infinite.
Thee I re-visit now with bolder wing,
Escap't the Stygian Pool, though long detain'd
In that obscure sojourn, while in my flight
Through utter and through middle darkness borne
With other notes then to th' Orphean Lyre
I sung of Chaos and Eternal Night.

(Milton, *Paradise Lost, Book III*)

[78] Writing the paper "Attacks on Linking"

On 2 February 1959, Bion spent some time in hospital after having fainted. As noted in *The Other Side of Genius*: irregularities shown by his ECG were never fully explained.

From *The Other Side of Genius:* "Letters to Francesca"

St George's Hospital, London

Wednesday morning. Feb. 4th. [1959]

After a rackety sort of night I feel like unburdening some more to you. The House Physician came round last night and asked after me. He said I should stay in "a few days" even if the ECG was OK. This does not surprise me, but I would like to know how far the "few days" is going to extend. He said my weight was too much and suggested, for my height, twelve stone.

I cannot help thinking, as I read the book I have here on Scientific Method [Braithwaite], what a terrible lot of bilge I have read in my time. There has always been a certain amount, too much I think, of gullibility about me, and it makes me swallow a lot of nonsense – not only in books I think – that I could do without. I wish I could feel more confident that I wouldn't add to the flood of rot but of course if I did I would probably lack the necessary self-criticism....

February 4

...If I could only mobilize some thoughts before I came out I might get a paper done. Unfortunately it is a most complex subject [Attacks on Linking] and I don't want to rush into it prematurely. However, I can go on churning and I shan't complain. if it is two weeks and not six off work....

February 5

...I continue to cogitate on my paper but it is a curiously elusive subject and comes and goes. At the moment I am feeling there is nothing in it, but I am used to this....

February 9

I had a very good night after I had persuaded them to get rid of two of my three blankets. This morning I have done a bit more writing and checked the reading with it – a quite considerable amount of work though it does not look it on the paper. But I think it is clearly expressed and that is a big problem with this stuff....

February 11

My darling,

Here I am – sitting in a chair in a gale of wind. So I am obviously coming on, but what I shall be when the draught is finished is nobody's business....

I am at the moment feeling a bit depressed about my paper, wondering if it's all just working round stalking a most majestic mare's nest; a horrid feeling. The fact that there are correlations between scientific hypotheses and interpretations is at first reassuring, but then I begin to wonder if it is only an appearance caused by my saying commonplaces, that everyone knows, in a high-falutin' way. Ending up with a blinding flash of the obvious....

February 13

Another morning, my darling, after a good night's rest. I sometimes feel I ought to have been a recluse, some kind of Oxford don, only then we should not have enough money – we don't have enough apparently anyway, but that is a detail which afflicts anyone who would like to go on Hellenic tours or read good books or go to Glyndebourne. But the serious and disturbing thing is the awful sense of frustration I get because I feel I have something I must write but cannot get at it because of the pressure of the stark need to live at all. I can see from my stay here, where it is obvious that sheer force of circumstances makes it impossible to do anything but write and read the appropriate books, how absolutely uninterested I am in anything else except to see and be near you and the family. After that, but really mixed up with the reading and writing, is my work with the patients which I want to do for its own sake. I know I can't shuffle off all these damned financial worries and responsibilities but I certainly feel they are killing my capacity for work – destructive demands for some accursed Trust meeting, group meeting, attendance at a Society meeting, or *anything* almost that will destroy another evening I might have at home....

February 15

...I feel momentarily stuck with my paper. It is curious; when this happens I often find I have some other idea, but I am reluctant to pursue it for fear of just leaving a lot of loose ends and never coming to any point. And yet it is also true that taking up the new thread can turn out to have quite an important connection with what I have said before and may indeed be a way round the deadlock....

Later. In the upshot I did a lot more thinking but hardly any writing and what there is of it feels as if I had only partially got a grasp of what I wanted to say. Still, I feel if I have learnt nothing else I have begun to learn that to write something you must write – anything, anyhow, somehow, so long as you write. Only this way is any meaning likely to come of it.

(CWB II, pp. 142–152)

[79] I don't know what the matter is with the child

From "Attacks on Linking"

The analytic situation built up in my mind a sense of witnessing an extremely early scene. I felt that the patient had experienced in infancy a mother who dutifully responded to the infant's emotional displays. The dutiful response had in it an element of impatient "I don't know what the matter is with the child." My deduction was that in order to understand what the child wanted, the mother should have treated the infant's cry as more than a demand for her presence. From the infant's point of view she should have taken into her, and thus experienced, the fear that the child was dying. It was this fear that the child could not contain. He strove to split it off together with the part of the personality in which it lay and project it into the mother. An understanding mother is able to experience the feeling of dread, that this baby was striving to deal with by projective identification, and yet retain a balanced outlook. This patient had had to deal with a mother who could not tolerate experiencing such feelings and reacted either by denying them ingress, or alternatively becoming a prey to the anxiety which resulted from the introjection of the infant's feelings. The latter reaction must, I think, have been rare: denial was dominant.

(CWB VI, p. 148)

The above quote is from "Attacks on Linking", the paper he discusses in his letters from hospital.

This is the same patient as was discussed in the quote "Projective identification as communication" (1958) written the year before. In the above quote we see a further clarification of Bion's nascent thoughts about the infant's projection of unbearable primitive anxieties and the mother's "containment" of these. In this instance it is the mother who refuses the link between herself and the infant. In the following quote, also from "Attacks on Linking", we hear of a patient who attacks his own linking capacities.

[80]   Main conclusions

From "Attacks on Linking"

The prototype for all the links of which I wish to speak is the primitive breast or penis. . . .

(*CWB VI*, p. 138)

Observation of the patient's disposition to attack the link between two objects is simplified because the analyst has to establish a link with the patient and does this by verbal communication and his equipment of psychoanalytic experience. Upon this the creative relationship depends and therefore we should be able to see attacks being made upon it. . . .

(*CWB VI*, p. 139)

The main conclusions of this paper relate to that state of mind in which the patient's psyche contains an internal object which is opposed to, and destructive of, all links whatsoever from the most primitive (which I have suggested is a normal degree of projective identification) to the most sophisticated forms of verbal communication and the arts.

In this state of mind emotion is hated; it is felt to be too powerful to be contained by the immature psyche, it is felt to link objects and it gives reality to objects which are not self and therefore inimical to primary narcissism.

The internal object which in its origin was an external breast that refused to introject, harbour, and so modify the baneful force of emotion, is felt, paradoxically, to intensify, relative to the strength of the ego, the emotions against which it initiates the attacks. These attacks on the linking function of emotion lead to an over-prominence in the psychotic part of the personality of links which appear to be logical, almost mathematical, but never emotionally reasonable. Consequently the links surviving are perverse, cruel, and sterile.

The external object which is internalized, its nature, and the effect when so established on the methods of communication within the psyche and with the environment, are left for further elaboration later.

(*CWB VI*, p. 152)

L. Pistiner de Cortiñas

. . . let us call her D − , a pretty woman of about 35 who was single and had experienced a series of failures in her attempts to start a love relationship. On the one hand she wrote poetry, while on the other she showed in her analysis a cynical and envious part of her personality, which she also feared to a certain extent. She was rude / inconsiderate and intolerant and if I happened to be a few minutes late in seeing her she was absolutely intransigent in her attitude. While all of those character- istics were egosyntonic, there didn't seem to be any conflict with either those aspects of her personality or with her analysis as she considered that, whenever something didn't go according to plan, it was her ana- lyst's fault. She was then able to turn the perspective around as when, at a given moment, she started to relate a number of dreams, without associa- tions, so much so that I finally realised the dreams were being used as a screen behind which she was hiding the most authentic of herself. After a lot of work in her analysis, she had a dream in which the analyst was considered as a chocolate of a second quality. At one point in the analy- sis, when she had gained more insight into her state of envy, she said that it looked to her as if her analyst had put on weight and, with a certain unease / awkwardness, finally said that she feared that her analyst was pregnant. The deepest motive for this was the envy that this supposed pregnancy produced in her. The analyst was definitely not pregnant, but D's analysis had started to bear fruit and she was much more committed to it, at least in part. At that time, she was coming to sessions four times a week and for different reasons – most of them apparently economic – she started to cancel until it became evident that the cynical and envious side of her could not tolerate her development or that of the analysis. Devel- opment in the analysis meant pregnancy and her envious part could not tolerate it. She also had some acting out in which she was exposed to a sexual violation. Envy was channelled through the supposed pregnancy of the analyst, which meant that something creative was developing in her analysis, and eventually she stopped coming for analysis altogether. She said it was just for a time, but she never came back. I have always wondered about how her life unfolded from that time. . . .

(Pistiner de Cortiñas 2016, pp. 10–11)

Betty Joseph

On the struggle against dependency

During this and the next few sessions we gained further understanding of the importance of this aspect of her struggle against dependence. A. described her growing insight very clearly at the end of the same week, when she told me that she had decided to join her husband for the week- end and had been thinking how very enjoyable the few days might be; then this idea became connected with the work we had been doing in the sessions and suddenly, as she described it, all "the pleasure drained away like sand running through my fingers". We could see that when she was thinking happily of the weekend, this became a good experience like a good feed, then she saw that the experience, feed, was connected with my work, as if milk was seen to come from a breast which was mine and attached to my body – so she drained it away, could not use it and turned it into sand, like faeces or urine. Here then we could see that the link that she could not tolerate and had to destroy was that between the good work – feed – and myself (this whole problem is discussed in detail by Dr. Bion [Attacks on linking] and that indeed it was her rivalry with me, standing for her mother, her envy, resentment, and anger that were stimulated when she was dependent on me and I was felt to be helpful, that was the real problem we were up against. Thus, A., in avoiding the unhappiness and difficulties which she associated with needing her mother, lost also the happiness and good experiences of her babyhood.

(Joseph 1959, pp. 216–217)

[81]   *Second Thoughts*

The papers of the 1950s and early 1960s were originally published in the *International Journal of Psycho-Analysis*. Then in 1967, nearly ten years later, the papers were collected together in a book, *Second Thoughts*. This is also the year that Bion went to Los Angeles as a visiting speaker and talked to them about working with psychotic patients. The title is derived from the lengthy new commentary added to the papers.

From the Introduction

> For those who want the papers as they were originally printed, here the papers are, but I have added a commentary which involves an evolutionary change of opinion. I do not regard any narrative purporting to be a report of fact, either of what the patient said or of what I said, as worth consideration as a "factual account" of what happened.
>
> (*CWB VI*, p. 53)

The "Commentary" at the end of the book contains his "second thoughts". Here is an example:

> The "desire" for cure is one example of precisely the desire that must, in common with all desires, not be entertained by a psychoanalyst. The reader will find evidence in these papers [the papers of the 1950s] that though I had suspected, I had not grasped the importance of this point.
>
> (*CWB VI*, p. 189)

Chapter 7

Cogitations

Introduction

Francesca Bion

"Cogitations" was the name Bion gave to his thoughts transferred to paper. The physical act of writing was, he found, an aid to his thinking – typing would have been too noisy and "fidgety". He wrote slowly, neatly, with very few alterations, on loose sheets, most of which he subsequently fastened together in two lots (unfortunately not in chronological order). Many are undated, but I believe that the order in which I have arranged them is not grossly in error. They cover the period from February 1958 to April 1979. In addition to relating the subject matter to his published papers and books, I have applied some Holmesian detective work to variations in the colour of ink and paper, and to the style of handwriting, which he changed from time to time as he tried to improve his hand.

These occasional writings were his attempt to discipline, clarify, and evaluate complex ideas – both his own and those of others – by setting them out visually and by often addressing them to an imaginary audience. He never re-read them, but he must have thought them worth preserving because they escaped consignment to the waste-paper basket during gleeful paper-tearing sessions, especially before leaving Los Angeles in 1979. They will be of particular interest to those already familiar with Bion's work as an illustration of his doubts, his arguments with himself, and of how his initial ideas developed. They should not be read in isolation by newcomers, but as an adjunct to his published works, especially those of the 1960s.

The compilation of this book affirms my belief that it forms an essential part of Bion's work and that it would be a considerable loss to psychoanalysis if its contents were to remain imprisoned in filing cabinets.

(Francesca Bion 1990, p. 7)

André Green

"Cogitations" is the name given by Bion to his thoughts transferred to paper. These reflections had been left behind in Bion's filing cabinets, and, unearthed by his wife Francesca, are now available for us to read. It is all very well to desist from publishing what is deemed unworthy of publication, but it must be admitted that Bion's sketches and cast-offs are much more valuable than the common run of material that finds its way into print. These day-to-day jottings are like a breath of fresh air from the open sea.

Compared with Bion's published works, the *Cogitations* are thrilling to read and often less difficult to assimilate, because the author's formulations are less condensed and because he makes us witnesses to the process of the unfolding of his thought. We literally *follow* him. . . .

(Green 1992, p. 585)

Green also comments:

Bion is the only Kleinian for whom the model of the dream is more important than the model of the baby. Such an option presumably reflects the renunciation of the empiricist or pragmatic position so often embraced by the protagonists of a psychoanalytic constructivism based on a naive conception of development.

(Green 1992, p. 587)

Notes on concepts Bion is using and developing

Dreaming and alpha-function

In *Cogitations* we see Bion's growing interest in dreaming and his gradual departure from Freud's theory of dreaming (dreams as the protector of sleep, wish-fulfilment) to ideas about the function of dreams in the "digestion" and "suffering" of emotional experiences. In early 1960 he would go on to draw a distinction between Freud's dream-work and what he calls dream-work-α. This was then replaced by simply "alpha-function". He then tended to use alpha-function and "dreaming" somewhat interchangeably. In his advocacy of "awake dreaming", we see his radical view that we also dream when awake and dreaming is a core way in which the mind works. The idea that we dream while awake is the subject of a number of further quotes in later chapters of the book. It has had far-reaching consequences in the development not only of theory, but of psychoanalytic technique.

Quotes

82 What does the psychotic patient think analysis is?
83 Unconscious oedipal anxiety

[82] What does the psychotic patient think analysis is?

February 1958

Psychotic mechanisms

At last I think I see daylight on a point that has baffled me for a long time: what does the psychotic patient think analysis is? Partly an activity that is followed by consequences such as those that attend on events in the realm of physical fact; partly a mental event in which consequences (as they exist in the world of physical reality) do not exist – there are only sequences. In a dream an act *appears* to have consequences; it has only sequences. What is needed is a spatial model to represent a dream. The verbal description would then be seen as an artefact in which certain elements, in an agglomeration that has no time component and no events that are consequent on other events, are highlighted by the imposition on them of causality and temporality. The capacity to impose on these elements both causality and temporality depends on the existence of a non-psychotic personality. This non-psychotic personality must be capable of (a) frustration, and hence awareness of temporality, (b) guilt and depression, and hence an ability to contemplate causality (since contemplating causes involves the possibility of having to contemplate one's own responsibility for certain events in the chain of causes). The capacity for verbalization is, as I have shown already, itself a function of the depressive position [see "Notes on the Theory of Schizophrenia"].

One result is that verbal reporting of a dream is only possible when enough work has been done for the patient to be able to tolerate temporality and causality, i.e. frustration and guilt-depression, and the patient is therefore able to produce the artefact we call "a dream" from the "agglomeration" of mental urine and faeces [see "Attacks on Linking"].

(*CWB XI*, p. 9)

[83]   Unconscious oedipal anxiety

10 January 1959

> . . . Let us approach it clinically: a patient enters the consulting room, notices that the couch is in some disorder but, making only a minor adjustment, lies on it and proceeds with his associations. In due course evidence from his associations indicates that at this particular juncture, and taken with sundry other facts not germane to this discussion, he is experiencing an increase in anxiety and, furthermore, that the anxiety has as its ideational content the disordered couch as part of the furniture of a scene of parental intercourse. This conclusion, and the interpretation that is the psychoanalytic act by which it is expressed, is arrived at on the basis of observed facts seen in the light of a psychoanalytic hypothesis. But common sense tells this patient that he is lying on an ordinary couch and that ordinary people, as he himself might say, would know that that is what it is and that its disorder was due to the movements of the previous patient upon it.

(CWB XI, p. 17)

Two points of view – or what Bion calls "vertices" – are described: one in which the disordered couch is the scene of "parental intercourse", and the "common-sense" view in which it has just been ruffled by the previous patient. In health we might register both the "common-sense" view and, unconsciously, the reference to "parental intercourse". Unconscious references can give depth to our experience of external reality without overwhelming our conscious minds with unconscious material. In the case of Bion's patient, there may not be a flexible or permeable barrier between the conscious and unconscious mind, but an "either-or" – either only a ruffled couch or only a scene of "parental intercourse".

[84]   A bad obstructive object

15 July 1959 (4.30 a.m. Blast it!)

X said ... well, what? He used words in such a way that they seemed to indicate that his mother or relatives had cut off supplies; that he could sell out £500 of shares and go to the cottage, in which case there would only be £50 and that just could not buy food. "That's all there is to it." I attempted to draw attention to the fact that even while there was an opportunity for analysis, he could make no use of it. He defends by taking this as an accusation in which he is to blame and thus denies the existence of a very bad obstructive object.

(*CWB XI*, p. 35)

Bion attempts to show the patient that in his (the patient's) internal world is an internal obstructive object that is getting in the way of him making use of his analysis. Bion describes the patient as defensively turning this into Bion doing something to him – the patient unable to look at what he is doing to himself. A search on the PEP Web (Psychoanalytic Electronic Publishing website) for "internal object" produced entries from 1932 onwards, primarily from papers by Klein, her followers or those critiquing her concept. The model of internal objects is in Bion's "analytic blood".

Definition of internal objects

The concept of the internal object was most distinctly used by Melanie Klein in her description of the depressive position (Klein 1935). It is distinct from that of a mental representation used more frequently by other groups of psychoanalysts. She stated: "[An internal object] is felt to be a physical being, or rather a multitude of beings, which with all their activities, friendly and hostile, lodge inside one's body, particularly inside the abdomen, a conception to which physiological processes and sensations of all kinds, in the past and in the present, have contributed (D16, Melanie Klein Trust papers, Wellcome Library; published in Hinshelwood 1997, p. 885).

Klein wrote these notes probably in the early 1940s, when dispute with other groups of psychoanalysts was especially strong. Her intention was to convey an imaginative unconscious phantasy of internal persons with their own experiences and motivations. This was not easily understood at the time (see Hinshelwood 1997). But with the expansion of the idea in the paper by Heimann in 1943 [1952], we have an approximation to Klein's thinking.

When the organs of distance perception, for instance sight, begin to be comprehended in early infancy, a field of vision is built up, comprising objects that the ego/self relates to. In a comparable manner, Klein was suggesting that inner perception from all the other internal senses, such as hunger, colic, temperature and so on, are similarly represented as objects located within the body at the site where the sensations arise. It is an apperception that is quickly superseded in the course of development but remains as a continuing awareness at a "deep" layer of the unconscious.

The conception of internal objects therefore represents the experience of internal agents, similar to Freud's superego, but multiplied to include a belief that important external objects, primarily the early caregivers, have been internalised and remain in a continuing relationship with the ego. The personality, at this unconscious level, is a kind of internal society, "the internal group with which the solitary individual is in a dynamic relationship" (Menzies 1981, p. 663).

(R. D. Hinshelwood, personal communication, 2018)

[85] Loved by the group

15 July 1959 (4.30 a.m. Blast it!)

This digression brings me back to the psychotic defence against inter-pretation. . . . which constitutes, or is felt to constitute, an attack on the patient's narcissism. In practice this means evading the elucidation of illusory, delusory, or hallucinatory mechanisms for making the patient feel loved, lest such elucidation should show him that such love as he wishes to feel that he receives does not in fact exist. This in turn means that the analyst has to convey by various means that he loves the patient, and that in this respect he is a representative of the common sense of the patient's social group which loves the patient more than it loves itself. This latter belief can of course be supported by the patient by his believing that analysis itself is an expression of such group love for him. Or, in early infant terms, that the breast is a gift to him from the family group.

In so far as the patient is successful in evading the attacks on his narcis-sism, he experiences a hallucinatory gratification of his craving for love. This, like all hallucinatory gratification, leaves the patient unsatisfied. He therefore greedily resorts to a strengthening of his capacity for hallucination, but there is naturally no corresponding increase in satisfaction.

(CWB XI, p. 36)

Bion suggests that the very fact of analysis can be taken by the patient as evidence that he is loved by the "group", and a pressure can be exerted on the analyst to not disrupt this view. The analyst might then evade interpreting the patient's narcissism.

Clinical note

The patient returned to her Monday session with much to tell me about the week-end. I had the familiar sense that I was to provide an admiring, loving audience, and also that she had no awareness of my having had a weekend or any feelings she might have about it. In the past, when I talked to her about these matters, she would become angrily upset, and the upset would contain within it a silencing mechanism to prevent us going any further. We have managed to go further, how-ever, and it has become somewhat more possible to talk about what is happening.

The following day the patient arrived in rather high mood. She told me she had – immediately before the session – arranged to change an appointment with X. (The changed appointment concerned what she would be doing after her ses-sion on the approaching Friday – the last session before the summer break.) She was anxious that she would be accused by me of an acting out and said that she hadn't meant to do anything, she hadn't known what she was doing. It is hard to fully convey the way in which this is said. Her voice becomes different and loses any variety or depth. She is "innocent", and I am put in the role of a harsh super-ego. I asked her whether she was aware of what she may have been feeling when she made the change of appointment. "Triumph" she said unequivocally. Then she added an illuminating comment: "Getting X to say yes (to the change) was the same as if you would be saying "yes you can have an extra session on Monday", because finishing on Friday would be too difficult for me."

Here we see that the patient's "innocence" and naivety are linked to a trans-gression of boundaries – getting an extra Monday session, not having to accept an ending on the Friday. She is blissfully (but blindly) "the one". She is going to triumph over the group (get a special session, unlike the other patients).

It does seem that as a young child the patient's family group may have been "too much in her face". The parental relationship overly exposed in front of her, and too many other babies too quickly to be taken in – contributing to a retreat to day-dream world in which she is the centre of the group's attention.

[86] I do not understand

25 July 1959

"I do not understand", or, "do not know why", or "do not know how", etc. may be taken either as a *positive* statement of *inability* to dream, or a defiant assertion of a capacity for *not* dreaming.

(CWB XI, p. 42)

By "a defiant assertion of a capacity for *not* dreaming" Bion means the triumphant rejection of dreaming by a patient who believes themselves to have a superior system based on evacuation and hallucination, rather than the digestion of experience involved in dreaming.

[87]   Awake dreaming

27 July 1959

Anxiety in the analyst is a sign that the analyst is refusing to "dream" the patient's material: not (dream) = resist = not (introject). . . . *Freud* meant by dream-work that unconscious material, which would otherwise be perfectly comprehensible, was transformed into a dream, and that the dream-work needed to be undone to make the now incomprehensible dream comprehensible. I mean that the conscious material has to be subjected to dream-work to render it fit for storing, selection, and suitable for transformation from paranoid-schizoid position to depressive position, and that unconscious pre-verbal material has to be subjected to reciprocal dream-work for the same purpose. *Freud* says Aristotle states that a dream is the way the mind works in sleep: *I* say it is the way it works when awake.

(*CWB XI*, p. 47 [emphasis added])

Clinical note: on the difference between daydreams and "waking dreams"

The patient was taken up with the Royal Wedding. This was seen as the perfect wedding – the wedding that she was waiting to happen to her. She complained about her own life – it was useless – not what she wanted – nor had expected to have – and she was trapped in it.

Then she told me that she'd had a dream. In the dream she was serving someone in a shop. A complaint expressed in the dream was that she was in a lowly position. She should be being served. Work we had been doing prior to this led me to think about an attitude she held in which life was treated as if it was a commodity. Friends (probably in response to this) tried to give her things/commodities to make her life better, concrete solutions, advice on jobs, timetable adjustments, food. I was aware of a pull to a similar response in myself. When I spoke to her about this, she replied that what I said about her friends' behaviour was right; she added that their behaviour caused her to feel interfered with.

It is difficult to convey what a breakthrough this was. Instead of the repetitive complaint about her life and the inadequacy of people's attempts to help, I was hearing something new about her experience. I knew myself in the transference the pressure to try to "do something", now I could see more clearly her anxiety that I would intrude.

After a silence, she added that it had sounded like I was talking "French psychoanalysis".

I said that what I was saying might sound foreign to her, but she seemed to feel that it was psychoanalysis.

She laughed.

There was another silence.

Then she told me that a strange thing had just happened to her. "She had just been – well dreaming – almost asleep and dreaming." The dream was of herself and her brother playing a game in childhood – one that involved putting a pen nib in a hole to move the pieces around.

I think that between us in this session we had got hold of the existence of a two-way relationship in her life, and this then opened into a space in which she could dream/play about a two-way relationship (a nib in a hole). The Royal Wedding was a daydream; we then hear about a night dream in which she is serving someone in a shop, and then of an experience that may be described as "dreaming whilst awake".

[88] Nameless dread

28 July 1959

If the dream-work capacity is destroyed, the patient feels dread which is peculiarly terrifying because it is nameless, and because the namelessness itself springs from the destruction of the patient's capacity for dream-work which is the mechanism responsible for naming.

(*CWB XI*, p. 49)

Clinical note

A middle-aged woman patient in analysis described to her analyst how she woke up every morning filled with terror. She had no dreams or thoughts accompanying this, just a sense of imminent catastrophe and disintegration, which seemed more formless and anxiety-inducing than the reality of dying. Her analyst thought this was a manifestation of infantile nameless dread, as described by Bion (Susan Lawrence, personal communication).

[89]   2 + 2 = 4

6 August 1959

That 2 + 2 = 4 is sometimes said to be self-evident, an axiom. But it is by no means clear that this is or always has been so, any more than it has always been obvious that if I want something in my room which is out of reach I shall have to leave my chair, walk over to it and fetch it. At some point even the process of walking required thought, probably conscious thought. My suggestion is that it still requires thought, but that it is now waking unconscious thought which has been made possible by α [alpha-function]. And it is similarly thanks to the operation of α that it seems obvious that 2 + 2 = 4. If α has not operated, it is probable that it would not be "obvious" at all....

Let us then transfer the statement, 1 + 1 = 2, to the field of biological science by considering what happens if 1 rabbit (male) is added to 1 rabbit (female), all enclosed in a suitable hutch. In this instance 1 + 1 may easily be found to make quite a considerably larger number than 2 rabbits.

(CWB *XI*, pp. 59–60)

I am reminded of a video of Bion at the Tavistock. He is with a group of professionals who are all very concerned about a boy they have been assessing. They tell Bion that, although intelligent, the boy does not know that 2 + 2 equals 4. Bion responds by asking what the boy does think 2 + 2 equals. No one had asked the boy this. One possibility is that the 2 + 2 may relate – emotionally and unconsciously – to his phantasy of his parents.

[90]   5 from 3

The following quote is from Bion's novel *A Memoir of the Future*, written over ten years later.

> MEMORY I dreamed I was taking thirty oranges away from five. In the dream I didn't see anything extraordinary about taking thirty oranges away from five. The five were very fat, big and greedy and had lots of oranges. I was angry that they should have such masses of oranges when they *were* oranges themselves already! So I suppose I did not see why they should not have thirty taken from them. It was really rather funny – really! What's so funny about it, said one of the big ones. I felt frightened. . . .
>
> Well, as I was saying, of course you can't take thirty from five – not in reality; not with real numbers. If someone invents negative numbers and you add them to natural numbers, *then* you can take five from three and get minus two! . . . Well, if you have a new kind of space, call it mental space, then you may have to invent a new addition to go with it. Or, if you invent new numbers you have to invent new mathematics. They have: they have invented negative numbers . . . If you weren't so proud of being sane, someone would be sure to notice how frightened you were of "insanity". You wear your "bravery" as a cloak for your cowardice and things you are afraid of – it must be terrible to have a para-sympathetic and a "voluntary" nervous system so close to each other! What dreams, what thoughts, the other system has!
>
> (*CWB XI*, pp. 63–64)

[91]   A projectively identified dream

10 August 1959

But do not visual images symbolize or represent in some way? And if so, has no dream-work-α taken place? Probably it has; it seems likely that certain feelings have been ideogrammaticized, but *not* for purposes of digestion mentally – only as receptacles to contain, to imprison the idea or feeling and then to eject it. In that case the visual image itself is used as the target for projective identification and then is used as a missile container for further projective identification. If so, perhaps the visual element in dreams is significant because it is felt that the feeling can be excreted further and more effectively if it is put into an object *seen*, perhaps in a hallucinatory manner, because such an object does not need, as with other senses, to be at close quarters for contact. Therefore, in a projectively identified dream, the dream itself is felt to be analogous to a hallucinated object, not for hallucinatory gratification of ingestion, but for hallucinatory excretion. . . .

(*CWB XI*, p. 69)

In Bion's view "dreams" can be used for evacuation as well as mental digestion. In fact, he says, the visualness of images may make them particularly suited for evacuation, because of the distances involved in seeing, compared, for example, to touching.

[92] Certitude

21 August 1959

It is very important that the analyst knows not what *is* happening, but that he *thinks* it is happening. That is the only certitude to which he lays claim. If he does not know that he thinks such-and-such is happening, he has no grounds for making the interpretation. This may help to bridge the gap. The theory that is being subjected to empirical test must be related to its power to enable the analyst to feel certain that he *thinks* that *x* is the case – not to its power to make it certain that *x* is the case. The fact susceptible of empirical test is the certainty, or the degree of certainty, that the analyst can achieve about what he thinks is going on. He could say, "I quite realize that my view may be entirely wrong, but I do know that I am certain at any rate that *this* is my view".

(*CWB XI*, p. 72)

Bion, more than most, has explored what we do not know and cannot know. He does not, however, believe that this should result in our qualifying what we say – that is, "it may be the case" or "perhaps you are. . . ." In his view, conviction is needed for interpretation: not bravado or arrogance, but confidence. Some question whether Bion was arrogant!

[93] Improvised personality: who is the improviser?

13 September 1959

The contact with a psychotic patient is an emotional experience, presenting some precise features that differentiate it from the experience of contact of a more usual kind; the analyst does not meet a personality, but a hastily organized improvisation of a personality, or perhaps of a mood. It is an improvisation of fragments; if the impression is predominantly of friendliness, there will nevertheless be easily discernible fragments of hostility embedded in the conglomerate that has been assembled to do service, for the occasion, as a personality. If the impression is predominantly of depression, the mosaic of fragments will reveal incongruous bits of a smile without context other than a kind of contiguity with surrounding fragments; tears without depth, jocosity without friendliness, bits of hate – all these and many more fragmentary emotions or ideas jostle each other to present a labile façade.

But at once the question arises: is it a façade? If so, what lies behind it? Or, if it means that this improvised personality is all, or nearly all, there is, who or what is responsible for the improvisation? If it is a façade, what does it conceal, and to what end?

The encounter is not unlike the more everyday event of a face-to-face conversation with someone who has a marked squint: at which eye does one look? For the analyst the problem is central, not peripheral. He must decide whether he is speaking to the apparently improvised personality, to the improviser who has had the improvisation forced upon him so as to effect a meeting with the analyst, or to an improviser whose improvisation is one behind which he wishes to remain concealed.

Suppose the patient to be, or to have been, capable of normality: the conglomerate of fragments of personality which serves the patient for a personality can only be regarded as evidence of a disaster. The discussion of such a case is difficult because we are concerned not with the ordinary structures of the human personality for which terms such as ego, id, superego have been made available by Freud, but with the shattered fragments of these which have now been reassembled but not rearticulated.

(*CWB XI*, pp. 76–77)

[94]   Narcissism ↔ Social-ism

Undated

(previous dated entry 30 October 1959)

The conflict in the individual between socialism and narcissism

In his paper, "Instincts and Their Vicissitudes" [1915c], Freud makes the suggestion that the relation between the ego and sexuality may be regarded in two apparently equally well justified ways. In the one, the individual is regarded as of prime importance; in the other, as a transitory appendage to the germ plasm bequeathed to him by the race. He postulates, expressly disavowing any greater authority for his statement than that appertaining to a postulate, that the conflict is between sexuality and the ego instincts. He suggests that study, particularly of the schizophrenias, might require modification of the theory.

I agree that one side of the conflict is associated with the ego, but it seems to me that difficulties are caused by making a division between ego instincts on the one hand and the sexual instincts on the other. A more fruitful division is one between narcissism on the one hand, and what I shall call socialism on the other. By these two terms I wish to indicate the two poles of all instincts. This bi-polarity of the instincts refers to their operation as elements in the fulfilment of the individual's life as an individual, and as elements in his life as a social or, as Aristotle would describe it, as a "political" animal. The exclusive mention of sexuality ignores the striking fact that the individual has an even more dangerous problem to solve in the operation of his aggressive impulses, which, thanks to this bi-polarity, may impose on him the need to fight for his group with the essential possibility of his death, while it also imposes on him the need for action in the interests of his survival. There need be no conflict, but experience shows that in fact there is such a conflict – not between sexuality and ego instincts, but rather between his narcissism and his socialism, and this conflict may manifest itself no matter what the instincts are that are dominant at the time.

(CWB XI, p. 103)

Another quote, this time from his earlier group papers:

The individual is a group animal which is at war, not simply with the group, but with himself for being a group animal, and with those aspects of his personality that constitute his "groupishness".

(CWB IV, p. 199)

Narcissism ⇌ social-ism is one of only two pairs of concepts linked by a double arrow in Bion's work, the other being the much better known Ps ⇌ D (paranoid-schizoid functioning ⇌ depressive position functioning). The double arrow indicates the possibility and the necessity of movement in both directions. We see the concept narcissism ⇌ social-ism in use for six years, from 1959 to 1965.

In relation to pairs of concepts, we are prone to take sides – in the psycho-analytic world, for example, seeing the paranoid-schizoid position as bad and the depressive position as good, the death instinct as bad and the life instinct as good. By contrast, Bion attends to the movement in both directions between the two different states (neither being good or bad). With regard to narcissism ⇌ social-ism, we are more familiar in the Kleinian tradition with viewing narcissism as involving the pathological turning away from the object – that is, narcissism is 'bad' – rather than as coexisting and interacting with the containment provided by the object. Bion's discussion of narcissism challenges this view. For example, he states: "If narcissistic love is unsatisfied the development of love is disturbed and cannot extend to love of objects" (*CWB V*, p. 191).

By "social-ism" Bion does not, I think, mean the individual's relation with the group, but "those aspects of his personality that constitute his 'groupishness'". Bion did not see the individual as predating the group and then coming together with other individuals for reasons of protection and efficiency but, rather, that the "groupishness" in the personality finds expression through group life. I think that one way to conceive of the task of our internal groupishness is to do with the capacity to "leave ourselves out" as individuals. We know a dimension where we do not count as individuals, and it is this that is in conflict with the aspect of the self that is most preoccupied with being individual.

[95]   Search for procedures by which error is made to declare itself

6 February 1960

Beset as he is by the examples in history of the many occasions on which men of great ability and integrity have been unable to maintain a grasp of the truth about the phenomena that they wish to investigate, and made further aware of the pitfalls attending his search by the fact that his study is itself an investigation of a most serious source of errors in human judgement, the analyst's problem is to find a method – if there is one – by which he can be aware that he is falling into error, and even (if possible) of what kind of error he has become the victim. The search for this method constitutes for the psychoanalyst the search for a scientific method. For him the scientific method is that procedure, or series of procedures, by which error is made to declare itself.

(*CWB XI*, p. 121)

One method Bion arrives at is the use of his Grid (see Chapter 10).

[96]   Compassion and truth

11 February 1960

Compassion and truth

1   Compassion and Truth are both senses of man.
2   Compassion is a feeling that he needs to express; it is an impulse he must experience in his feelings for others.
3   Compassion is likewise something that he needs to feel in the attitude of others towards him.
4   Truth is something man needs to express; it is something he needs to seek and to find; it is essential for fulfilment of his curiosity.
5   Truth is something he needs to feel in the attitude of others towards him.
6   Truth and compassion are also qualities pertaining to the relationship that a man establishes with people and things.
7   A man may feel he lacks a capacity for love.
8   A man may lack capacity for love.
9   Similarly, he may feel he lacks a capacity for truth, either to hear it, or to seek it, or to find it, or to communicate it, or to desire it.
10   He may in fact lack such a capacity.
11   The lack may be primary or secondary, and may diminish truth or love, or both.
12   Primary lack is inborn and cannot be remedied; yet some of the consequences may be modified analytically.
13   Secondary lack may be due to fear or hate or envy or love. Even love can inhibit love.
14   Applying (8) and (10) to the Oedipus myth, the death of the Sphinx is a consequence of such lack, as the question posed was not intended to elicit truth, and consideration for itself could not exist to erect a barrier against self-destruction. Tiresias may be said to lack compassion less than regard for truth. Oedipus lacked compassion for himself more than he lacked regard for truth.

(*CWB XI*, p. 123)

There is little compassion in the story of the Sphinx – it kills those who get the riddle wrong, and itself dies when Oedipus gets the riddle right. Tiresias has some compassion in his warning against Oedipus's pursuit of the truth, but he has less regard for the truth. Oedipus cannot be compassionate to himself for what he has done.

Bion's list may be assumed to be obvious, but the clinical situation throws light on the relevance of putting truth and compassion together. It can happen that compassion and truth are out of sync with each other. A person may apply themselves to facing up to the "truth" – although painful and guilt inducing. This, however, can get ahead of the compassion needed to properly support the new insight in the ego. Instead, the new insight gets taken up by an accusing superego as ammunition. Some patients look down on compassion as a fudge to falsely feeling better. One reason for this, I think, is that compassion challenges the superior part of the personality and is treated dismissively as a consequence.

Clinical note

The patient dreamed that she was on a wooden ship. There were two toilets – which wasn't enough. She saw a third toilet – which she was not really supposed to use – and she quickly dived into it. Her poo and the toilet paper were not flushed away, but left as a pile on the side of the hole. She went back to clear it away, but someone else already had.

The patient has two siblings – the two toilets were perhaps theirs. She hadn't felt there to be space for her, and so grabbed what she could to put together a picture of herself. Her wanting to be special had been exposed and had shamed her, but in the dream compassion entered the picture in the understanding of not having had straightforward access to the necessary equipment for growing up.

[97]   Displacement

February 1960

Displacement

Painful feelings related to a situation that has immediately arisen are displaced – for example, feelings of rejection, i.e. of rejecting and being rejected.
The true self is felt not to be wanted nor yet to want the other true self;
something must be done with these feelings. They are entertained, but the
subject of the thoughts is no longer felt to be the person, someone in the
past, who has immediately stimulated them, and around that person there is
spun out a web of hostile reverie. Such past objects are carefully preserved;
maybe they are specifically created for that purpose in the first instance.
Note that the painfulness of the feeling is largely increased by the feeling
that the rejection is of a true self and cannot therefore be assumed to be
capable of resolution.

What seems to have happened is that the immediate cause is suppressed,
perhaps before it has become clear to the patient that he has been stimulated at all. And at once the old "memory" is substituted for the awareness of the current event. The subject of the early story becomes the main
character, after the patient, in the current day-dream, which has been drawn
across to shut out the thinking proper to the immediate reality situation. Is
not this account sufficient?

Another version: the feelings of rejection and hate are split off from the
personality and are felt about someone absent in time and space.

To what extent are the mechanisms of dream-work evident elsewhere?
For example, can all cruel and hostile feelings be displaced into a stammer?
Or are they all condensed? In short, is it not possible that the mechanisms
that Freud describes as peculiar to dream-work are in reality found to be
operating over a wide area of the psyche and in a great number of different
functional fields?

(CWB XI, p. 133)

22 February 1960

1   I have just displaced this [his work] by thinking I was giving a paper to
     the Society.
2   I have emotionalized it by making it an occasion where I am loved and
     admired.

3   I have replied to a hostile criticism from X with a moderation that does me credit.
4   In short, my mind is wandering, and I am transforming the task, which I have already put off for an hour, into an event that is pleasing and successful.

Is this not very like a dream, wish-fulfilment and frustration-evasion and all? (And may not all this be "digestion", a way of fixing an experience in mind?)

(CWB XI, p. 135)

[98] Regression

[Undated – 1960]

Analytic technique

More than one patient has said my technique is not Kleinian. I think there is substance in this. I would put it as follows: I consider that the behaviour of the patient is a palimpsest in which I can detect a number of layers of conduct. Since all those I detect must, by that very fact, be operating, conflicts are bound to occur through the conflicting views obtaining contemporaneous expression. . . .

Winnicott says patients *need* to regress: Melanie Klein says they *must not*: I say they *are* regressed, and the regression should be observed and interpreted by the analyst without any need to compel the patient to become totally regressed before he can make the analyst observe and interpret the regression.

(*CWB XI*, p. 161)

In the quote above the different layers detected by Bion have "contemporaneous expression". I am reminded of how one can see moments of all the ages of a person in their face. In Bion's view, the analyst should be able to see the younger and more primitive layers of conduct in the present without the patient needing to "become" younger.

Winnicott and Klein on regression

Masud Khan highlights Winnicott's distinction between the role of wishes and needs in the clinical process:

It is proper to speak of the patient's wishes, the wish (for instance) to be quiet. With the regressed patient the word wish is incorrect; instead we use the word need. If a regressed patient needs quiet, then without it nothing can be done at all. If the need is not met the result is not anger, only a reproduction of the environmental failure situation which stopped the processes of self growth. The individual's capacity to "wish" has become interfered with, and we witness the reappearance of the original cause of a sense of futility. . . .

Those among his colleagues who have imputed that Winnicott fostered regression in his patients have not kept this distinction in mind. Furthermore Winnicott was referring to an area of incapacity in the patient from early environmental failure which can be realised by the patient through this very specialised type of "acting out" in the analytic situation.

(Khan 1975, p. xxiv)

Klein, by contrast, disagrees with the idea of the reliving of infantile experiences in the consulting room through non-interpretative activities (Spillius 1983, p. 324). Heimann and Isaacs in the *Freud-Klein Controversies 1941–45* comment:

> The work of Melanie Klein, in her much more extensive observations and analytic studies of very young children, has amplified the well-known facts of regression and thrown new light upon their interconnections. . . .
>
> (King and Steiner 1991, p. 689)

> As Freud showed, it is frustration which initiates regression. But, in our view, it does so not only by a simple "damming-up" of libido, but also by evoking hate and aggression and consequent anxiety. The newly evoked hate and aggression reactivate the hardly overcome pre-genital sadism, and this in its turn pulls back the libido to its earlier forms, in order to neutralize the destructive forces once again at work in the mind. Freud himself classed regression as a defence. We understand more fully now what it is a defence against. . . .
>
> (King and Steiner 1991, p. 693)

> Genitality breaks down and regression comes about when the reparative tendencies are disturbed (through frustration and the ensuing hatred and aggression), since the genital is then felt to be proved destructive and dangerous. This brings into operation not only the fear of hurting and damaging the external loved object, but also the dread of the "bad" internal object, the superego.
>
> (King and Steiner 1991, p. 697)

Palimpsest: A text on which earlier writing has been rubbed off and written over, but where the original text is still just visible. It can be more broadly defined as anything that has been reused and altered but still bears the visible traces of its earlier form, such that different layers of time can be discerned: for example, a house can be a palimpsest of the taste of successive owners if elements of their choices are still visible.

[99] Bird-watching

27 March 1960

…The patient says, "I went on Hampstead Heath yesterday and did some bird-watching".

Taking the meaning first:

1 Does he mean he was scrutinizing their sex life?
2 Or is it an attempt to describe getting into the hands of the police by behaving in a suspicious way?
3 Or does he mean he has at last taken some exercise?

And so on with other speculations. Then, having decided that point, what is the interpretation?

(*CWB XI*, p. 162)

[100]   Narcissus

Written between 1961 and 1967.

> The youth who seeks a mirror in which to observe his beauty is punished
> by God. This last choice is made in the hope that it will serve to elucidate
> problems of curiosity and learning associated with the personality of the
> investigator himself – his need to find a mirror, that is to say a tool, which
> will help him to satisfy his curiosity, his *loving* curiosity, about himself. The
> curiosity, one might say, is not disinterested. (The lack of integrity vitiates it
> if one is expecting scientific curiosity.) The punishment seems peculiar....
>
> (*CWB XI*, p. 228)

In the Kleinian tradition Narcissus is understood to be trapped gazing at what he
believes is a lost love-object, but which objectively is the idealised aspect of his
own self. He believes himself to be in love; but he dies of starvation, because he
cannot turn to a real object who might have satisfied his real needs. In short, the
narcissist destroys the perception of the need of a real object and replaces that
object with a projected part of the idealised self and is trapped, unable to seek
further. Bion's version of Narcissus above is more sympathetic.

   We see a further aspect of his understanding of narcissism in the following
quote in which he describes his recognition that he is to be the mirror to his
patient's Narcissus.

> I would say that, listening to the free associations, one would think some-
> thing like this: the patient is wanting me to agree with him; it is obvious from
> the way he is putting forward a suggestion that he has a beautiful personality.
> It appears to me that it is a morally beautiful personality; my personality is
> likewise beautiful; in fact I am to be a mirror of his excellence....
>
> (*CWB XI*, p. 229)

Narcissus: A hunter, renowned for his beauty in Ancient Greek myth, showed
contempt for all who loved him, especially the nymph Echo, who was besotted
by him. When Nemesis, the goddess of revenge, learned of his behaviour, she
led Narcissus to a pool, where he saw his own reflection in the water and fell
in love with it, not realizing that it was merely an image. Unable to leave his true
love even for a moment, he starved to death, or, in other versions of the story,
he drowned, committed suicide, or, as Ovid has it in Book 3 of *Metamorphoses*
(completed in 8 AD), he became the white Narcissus flower.

[101]   Closed system

Written between 1961 and 1967.

> The patient who has no regard for truth, for himself, or for his analyst
> achieves a kind of freedom arising from the fact that so much destructive
> activity is open to him for so long. He can behave in a way that destroys
> his respect for himself and his analyst, provided he always retains enough
> contact with reality to feel that there is some respect to destroy; and this he
> can always assume if his analyst continues to see him. If his analyst does not
> continue, then he has destroyed the analysis. But destruction of the analysis
> is to be avoided, for it entails loss of freedom – at least till a new object is
> found – thus introducing a need for moderation that is apparent at other
> points in the closed system that the patient strives to produce. An obvious
> instance of this is the need to avoid successful suicide or murder. In brief, it
> is necessary for the patient to avoid any step calculated to effect change, and
> yet to change enough to ensure more analysis either for the reason that he
> has temporarily become a greater liability and needs more care, or because
> he shows such promise that it would be wrong to stop just when affairs
> have reached so happy a posture.
>
> (*CWB XI*, pp. 239–240)

[102]   Substitutes

Undated – 1968

> Drugs are substitutes employed by those who cannot wait.
>
> The substitute is that which cannot satisfy without destroying the capacity for discrimination of the real from the false.
>
> Whatever is falsely employed as a substitute for the real, is transformed thereby into a poison for the mind.
>
> The substitution of that which is peripheral to action instead of that which is central must cause imbalance.
>
> Imbalance is betrayed by the resort of the helpless to an assumption of omnipotence.
>
> Immaturity, confusion, helplessness and impotence are replaced, in those who are intolerant of frustration, by prematurity, order, omnipotence and power.
>
> That which should be a prelude to action is replaced by action; action is replaced by what should have preceded it.
>
> Hubris is the sin of Oedipus, the planners of the Tower of Babel, Adam and Eve, the animal that uses action as a substitute for thought, and thought as a substitute for action (not a prelude to it)....
>
> (CWB XI, p. 287)

The reader may recall a quote from Bion's time at boarding school:

> "Sublimation", not yet a Freudian term, was used by some for what in fact was a substitution. Games were substituted for sex; even religion was thought of by the more advanced as if it were some harmless substitute. No one thought that sublimation could mean the reaching for, yearning for games which were sublime, a religion that was sublime and not a stopper that could dam back the noxious matter till it stank, or bury the growth of personality till it turned cancerous.
>
> (CWB I, p. 108)

[103]   Scarcity

August 1975

There is a scarcity of time; a scarcity of knowledge; scarcity of ability. Therefore choice becomes of fundamental importance – choice of time, theories, and facts observed.

(*CWB XI*, p. 334)

Chapter 8

"The Theory of Thinking"

Introduction

Originally published in the *International Journal* under the title "The Psycho-Analytic Study of Thinking", this 1962 paper, just nine pages long, is still one of the ten most frequently accessed articles in the psychoanalytic literature. I have included much of the paper in the quotes (as well as quotes from elsewhere in Bion's work).

Oliver Lyth

> . . . Bion, during the sixties, showed immense literary productivity. In 1961 he gave at the 22nd International Congress in Edinburgh, his paper "A theory of thinking". This paper represents a distinct change in his writing and thinking about psychoanalysis. His previous papers had been extremely astute and sensitive observations on clinical material. He starts this paper by saying "it is a theoretical system", albeit a theoretical system to be empirically verified by practising analysts.
>
> (Lyth 1980, p. 271)

Edna O'Shaughnessy

> What does Bion mean by "thinking"? He does not mean some abstract mental process. His concern is with thinking as a human link – the endeavour to understand, comprehend the reality of, get insight into the nature of, etc., oneself or another. Thinking is an emotional experience of trying to know oneself or someone else. Bion designates this funda- mental type of thinking – thinking in the sense of trying to know – by the symbol K. If xKy, then "x is in the state of getting to know y and y is in a state of getting to be known by x".
>
> (O'Shaughnessy 1981, p. 181)

Quotes

[104]   Thoughts and thinking

> 101. It is convenient to regard thinking as dependent on the successful out-
> come of two main mental developments. The first is the development of
> thoughts. They require an apparatus to cope with them. The second devel-
> opment, therefore, is of this apparatus that I shall provisionally call thinking.
> I repeat – thinking has to be called into existence to cope with thoughts.
>
> It will be noted that this differs from any theory of thought as a product of
> thinking, in that thinking is a development forced on the psyche by the pressure
> of thoughts and not the other way round. Psychopathological developments
> may be associated with either phase or both, that is, they may be related to a
> breakdown in the development of thoughts, or a breakdown in the develop-
> ment of the apparatus for "thinking" or dealing with thoughts, or both.
>
> (CWB VI, p. 154)

On thoughts

The way the above quote is most often understood is that Bion is referring to
primitive "stuff" not yet at the level of thought. He may, however, also be referring to "unthinkable" thoughts. In his 2008 paper on "Bion's Four Principles of
Mental Functioning", Thomas Ogden quotes the writer and poet Edgar Allan Poe:
"those unthoughtlike thoughts that are the souls of thought" (Poe 1848, p. 80).

On the apparatus for thinking

In Bion's view the human mind has been brought into being by the need/demand
for it. Secondly, the primordial mind is understood to have developed by learning
from the way the body works, in particular the digestive system, which provides a
model enabling the organisation of mental processes. Initially to provide restraint
from action (as discussed originally by Freud), the mind also takes on the task "of
self knowledge" for which it is "ill suited". Rather than seeing humans as having superior thinking capacities, the picture Bion gives is of our struggling with
rudimentary equipment.

> I suggest that thinking is something forced on an apparatus, not suited for
> the purpose, by the demands of reality, and is contemporary with, as Freud
> said, the dominance of the reality principle. A modern analogy is provided
> by the fact that the demands of reality not only forced the discovery of
> psychoanalysis, but have led to the deflection of verbal thought from its
> original function of providing restraint for motor discharge to the tasks of
> self-knowledge for which it is ill-suited and for the purpose of which it has
> to undergo drastic changes.
>
> (CWB IV, p. 324)

[105]   The developmental history of thoughts

Psychoanalytically the theory that the infant has an inborn disposition corresponding to an expectation of a breast may be used to supply a model.... the
pre-conception (the inborn expectation of a breast, the a priori knowledge
of a breast, the "empty thought") when the infant is brought in contact with
the breast itself, mates with awareness of the realization and is synchronous
with the development of a conception. This model will serve for the theory
that every junction of a pre-conception with its realization produces a conception. Conceptions therefore will be expected to be constantly conjoined
with an emotional experience of satisfaction.

(*CWB VI*, p. 154)

The infant enters the world with one side of a puzzle (the pre-conception of the
breast), which is then fitted together through actual experience with the other
side (the actual breast) – giving an "emotional experience of satisfaction". Bion
thought the infant also to be born with a pre-conception of the parental couple.

[106] All-aloneness

From *A Key to A Memoir of the Future*

…Dependence and being all-alone are both unpleasant states of mind. Even an infant seems to be aware of being alone and being dependent on the assistance of something which is not its Self. The early awareness of these feelings is linked with vulnerability and cruelty.

(*CWB XIV*, p. 164)

How does an infant become aware of being alone? Is it all "learning from experience", or is there some inborn capacity to recognise "all-alone" also involved? This matters because the capacity to "recognise" the absence of the object is conjectured to lie at the base of primitive "thinking" (see following quote). Eigen speaks of capacities that "run deeper" than internalisation. The quote is from a paper on "Faith" and so more to do with Bion's later work, but I thought might raise interesting questions at this point.

Michael Eigen

The sources of creative experiencing run deeper than internalization and go beyond it. If one reads these authors [Winnicott, Lacan and Bion] carefully, one discovers that *the primary object of creative experiencing is not mother or father but the unknowable ground of creativeness as such.* Winnicott, for example, emphasizes that what is at stake in transitional experiencing is not mainly a self or object (mother) substitute, but the creation of a symbol, of symbolizing experiencing itself. The subject lives through and towards creative immersion (including phases of chaos, unintegration, waiting). What he symbolizes and seeks more and more of is the absorption of creative experiencing and the way this latter makes use of objects through successive waves of self-other awareness. Maternal or paternal object relations may subserve or thwart this experiencing but must not be simply identified with it.

(Eigen 1981, p. 431)

[107] "Thought" in the absence of the breast

I shall limit the term "thought" to the mating of a pre-conception with a frustration. The model I propose is that of an infant whose expectation of a breast is mated with a realization of no breast available for satisfaction. This mating is experienced as a no-breast, or "absent" breast inside. The next step depends on the infant's capacity for frustration: in particular it depends on whether the decision is to evade frustration or to modify it.

If the capacity for toleration of frustration is sufficient the "no-breast" inside becomes a thought, and an apparatus for "thinking" it develops. This initiates the state, described by Freud in his "Two Principles of Mental Functioning", in which dominance by the reality principle is synchronous with the development of an ability to think and so to bridge the gulf of frustration between the moment when a want is felt and the moment when action appropriate to satisfying the want culminates in its satisfaction. A capacity for tolerating frustration thus enables the psyche to develop thought as a means by which the frustration that is tolerated is itself made more tolerable.

(CWB VI, pp. 154–155)

Bion has already begun to formulate his concept of container–contained in which he explores how the infant's "thinking" develops through the *presence* of the more mature mind of the mother. In the above quote he draws attention to the experience of the *absence* of the mother. Freud and Klein were aware that the experience of frustration is significant, but it is Bion who puts tolerance of frustration and the experience of absence at the centre of development.

Clinical note

The patient had asked her ex-partner about what to do with some writings and photographs she had left behind when they had separated some years previously. The ex-partner had sent a polite reply saying to get rid of them. The patient hastily took the items out and deposited them in the communal bins – and then set out to her analysis. In the session she became anxious about what was in the bags (she had been through them previously), and what she might have lost by throwing them out. She would look on her return. One bag was at the bottom of a bin and might now be covered by other rubbish. The second bag, however, was on top of other rubbish at the top of a bin and should still be available. As the session proceeded, the patient was able to become aware of how she had felt upset and rejected by the polite message. She described how clear and clean it had made her feel when she threw away the ex-partner's belongings. It became clearer that she found being left unbearable and the "clearness" and "cleanness" had come about through a throwing away/evacuating her feelings about the ex-partner's absence. Her anxiety about what she had thrown away had in it a potential realisation that she had thrown away something important from her own mind that she needed to get back. When she could experience her upset at being left, she became more able to think again.

[108]   Frustration

From *Cogitations*

The entry is undated but would have been written between 1961 and 1967. "A Theory of Thinking" was published in 1962.

Frustration

A sense of frustration engenders feelings that are hard to tolerate. Intolerance varies with the individual and may be pronounced, according to the age and character of the person who experiences it. The baby experiences frustration, does not like it and makes, or is forced to make, a decision: it must decide whether to deny frustration or to modify it.

This bald statement can hardly be said to represent a fact. As with all psychoanalytic theories, it is necessary to make statements, as Freud pointed out, which are sufficiently exaggerated accounts of the facts they represent to make the facts themselves stand out unmistakably and yet not fall into caricature, which induces an opposite error. But it is true that early frustration presents the baby with a problem that has to be solved, and one on the solution of which much depends. Suppose the child to be extremely intolerant of frustration: the danger is that it will strive to deny frustration and to continue to deny it until its appreciation of the world of reality is itself impaired. In the extreme case of such denial the foundations for psychosis are being laid, for an awareness of the real world is an essential part of contact with reality. The hatred of frustration is easily extended to embrace reality itself in a way that is typical of the psychotic; it may then be extended to that part of the mental apparatus on which the awareness of reality and frustration depends.

There are degrees of intolerance of frustration, and there are degrees of intensity with which it is denied, until we reach that moderate degree of denial that passes over into the state of mind, typical of the development of the domination of what Freud called the reality principle, in which frustration and its associated feelings, painful though they are, are tolerated sufficiently to enable the personality to entertain the possibility of modification of frustration rather than denial.

(*CWB XI*, pp. 236–238)

Clinical note

A clinical example illustrates this difficulty to tolerate frustration and the pull towards the destruction of the capacity to perceive reality. A young male patient dreamt of building a rocket and taking off in it, and then dying in it. He told the analyst he wanted to get rid of everyone, including all his ordinary life, such as going to the supermarket, his work, and his analysis. When he thought of the chaos at home when he was growing up and how he just wanted everything to be perfect, peaceful, he needed to go somewhere like a planet of his own (Susan Lawrence, personal communication).

Clinical note

A patient, more intolerant of frustration than was obvious because it was well hidden, became silent after our having done some useful work together. When I asked him about it, he reported having become very annoyed over some small detail that wasn't right and had then lost contact with what we had been addressing. Frustration cannot be borne sufficiently for the achievement of the work to sink in.

I have found that patients who are intolerant of frustration often hold a belief that they *should not have to* experience frustration and pain and that it is really very helpful to draw their attention to this. An example – a patient told me about a dream she'd had the night before. In the dream she was climbing a hill. She realised there were holes in the hill; how deep, she didn't know, but she could fall into them. She wound the cord of her binoculars carefully around her hand so that she didn't drop them. Was there something in her life that she wasn't seeing? In her associations to the dream, her anxiety about making a payment, later that day, to a company she didn't recognise came to the fore. She did not want the agitation that came with that recognition. She wanted either to put the matter from her mind, or to embark on a sort of hyper-action to immediately rid herself of the problem. She commented that she had always believed that agitation was something one *shouldn't have to feel* – but without being able to experience the agitation, there was in fact no possibility of being able to think. That the patient can now hold on to her binoculars is an achievement. Earlier in the analysis she would put herself in considerable danger through not seeing. This was graphically illustrated when she stepped out onto a large road believing the traffic to be one way – the way she was looking – and was almost hit by a bus coming the other way. When I asked about her experience of looking "her way", she sounded to have been in quite a high state, believing the world to be at her feet – the way she wanted it to be, rather than the way it actually is (with all the frustration involved in that).

[109]   Bad object

If the capacity for toleration of frustration is inadequate, the bad internal "no-breast", that a personality capable of maturity ultimately recognizes as a thought, confronts the psyche with the need to decide between evasion of frustration and its modification.

Incapacity for tolerating frustration tips the scale in the direction of evasion of frustration. The result is a significant departure from the events that Freud describes as characteristic of thought in the phase of dominance of the reality principle. What should be a thought, a product of the juxtaposition of pre-conception and negative realization, becomes a bad object, indistinguishable from a thing-in-itself, fit only for evacuation. Consequently the development of an apparatus for thinking is disturbed, and instead there takes place a hypertrophic development of the apparatus of projective identification. The model I propose for this development is a psyche that operates on the principle that evacuation of a bad breast is synonymous with obtaining sustenance from a good breast. The end result is that all thoughts are treated as if they were indistinguishable from bad internal objects; the appropriate machinery is felt to be, not an apparatus for thinking the thoughts, but an apparatus for ridding the psyche of accumulations of bad internal objects. The crux lies in the decision between modification and evasion of frustration.

(*CWB VI*, p. 155)

Ignês Sodré

In "A Theory of Thinking" Bion . . . states: "Thinking has to be called into existence to cope with thoughts." In psychotic states, "What should be a thought . . . becomes a bad object, indistinguishable from a thing-in-itself, fit only for evacuation". I am suggesting that in severe obsessional states, even though the individual is not psychotic, and maintains some contact with reality, a part of the personality gets involved in such powerful defensive manoeuvres that a form of thought disorder occurs in which thinking becomes ineffectual in relation to thoughts.

Freud's famous obsessional neurotic, the Rat Man, presents us with a striking example of obsessional thinking. The Rat Man tells Freud that he heard from "the cruel Captain" a story about a horrible torture: a pot containing rats would be inverted onto a criminal's buttocks, and the rats would then burrow their way into the person's anus. The patient's "great obsessional fear" takes over at this point, as he has the horrible thought that the rat torture will happen to his two love objects, his father and "the lady"; he has both thoughts "simultaneously" which I think implies that the rats attack the parents together, in intercourse. This triangularity becomes even more explicit in the episode that precipitates the onset of the full-blown obsessional neurosis.

The cruel Captain tells the Rat Man that Lieutenant A paid the post-office girl the money he (the patient) owed her for the delivery of his pince-nez; and even though the Rat Man knew this to be a mistake (he knew the girl had paid for it herself), he immediately abandons what he knows to be the true version of events, and adopts the captain's version. This new, false version changes a dyadic relationship (Rat Man/girl) into a triadic one (Rat Man/Lieutenant A/girl). Paying Lieutenant A back now becomes the central point of his tormenting situation: the rat torture will happen to his father and "the lady" if he does not pay the money to A.

From this point onward he is totally in the grip of obsessional thinking. The phantasy is of attacking sadistically, and also of excitedly participating in the parents' intercourse through the omnipotence of his thoughts, yet the words of the cruel Captain (who clearly represents a sadistic father) intrude violently into his mind (against his will, as it were, through the backside of his mind) and become these concrete ratlike thoughts that torture him. Against rat-thoughts, rational thinking is powerless; only obsessional rituals can be used to try to control these torturer-thoughts. So, while the phantasy is of a sadistic attack that destroys the link between the parents and corrupts their intercourse, a sadistic attack is being perpetrated by rat-thoughts in his mind, attacking his thinking process so that mental links are destroyed. Ultimately, the Rat Man's thinking is the real victim of the rat torture. Thinking is attacked to destroy the knowledge – the absolute certainty – that the parents' intercourse excludes him.

(Sodré 1994, pp. 381–382)

[110]   Time

The relationship with time [of intolerance of frustration] was graphically brought home to me by a patient who said over and over again that he was wasting time – and continued to waste it. The patient's aim is to destroy time by wasting it. The consequences are illustrated in the description in Alice in Wonderland of the Mad Hatter's tea-party – it is always four o'clock.

(CWB VI, p. 156)

Clinical note

We had recently agreed that a patient would end her analysis eighteen months hence. In the following weeks the patient angrily described her analysis as a relentless demand on her to get to her sessions day after day, always the same, like the film "Ground Hog Day". She was extremely impatient to finish and have the time and money this would free up for her – she wanted the ending to be NOW, while also believing the situation would go on for ever – without end. In both the scenario of "end now" and of "never end", time and the sense of a process have been destroyed.

Dana Birksted-Breen

Time is first in the mother's psyche in what Bion . . . describes in the notion of "reverie", the time of sojourn in the mother's mind of the inchoate Beta elements and their transformation into elements which the infant is able to assimilate. For the infant, therefore, the time which can be tolerated will be, at first, the time of transformation within the mother's psyche, if the mother is able herself to tolerate the time factor. I call "reverberation time" the time it takes for disturbing elements to be assimilated, digested and transformed. It is the infant's introjection of that process and the creation of a reverberation time which enables the development of the infant's own capacity to develop and tolerate a sense of time. In the analytic interchange, the reverberation time may be of long duration with the analyst having to contain for months or even years the projections before transformation can take place. . . . It is the ana- lyst's own capacity to wait, to tolerate remaining in discomfort, which can be introjected by the patient enabling him/her eventually to remain with his/her own state of mind. As the patient becomes more able to tol- erate the feeling, one can see how the time lag before the expulsion of the unwanted feeling becomes longer until, eventually, the patient can stay with the previously intolerable feeling. The word "work", which is used in connection with the psychoanalytic process as in "working through" (Durcharbeitung) or Klein's "working through the depressive position" and Green's "work of the negative", suggests a different relation to time emphasising the aspect of process, as does the notion of integration to which it leads. This contrasts with the instantaneity of the hallucinatory wish-fulfilment, the immediate gratification or the instant expulsion of the unwanted emotion.

(Birksted-Breen 2003, pp. 1505–1506)

Alice in Wonderland – *Lewis Carroll*

A Mad Tea-Party

There was a table set out under a tree in front of the house, and the March Hare and the Hatter were having tea at it: a Dormouse was sitting between them, fast asleep, and the other two were using it as a cushion, resting their elbows on it, and talking over its head. "Very uncomfortable for the Dormouse", thought Alice; "only, as it's asleep, I suppose it doesn't mind.". . . .

The Hatter was the first to break the silence. "What day of the month is it?" he said, turning to Alice: he had taken his watch out of his pocket, and was looking at it uneasily, shaking it every now and then, and holding it to his ear.

Alice considered a little, and then said "The fourth."

"Two days wrong!" sighed the Hatter. "I told you butter wouldn't suit the works!" he added looking angrily at the March Hare. . . .

Alice had been looking over his shoulder with some curiosity. "What a funny watch!" she remarked. "It tells the day of the month, and doesn't tell what o'clock it is!"

"Why should it?" muttered the Hatter. "Does your watch tell you what year it is?"

"Of course not", Alice replied very readily: "but that's because it stays the same year for such a long time together."

"Which is just the case with mine", said the Hatter.

Alice felt dreadfully puzzled. The Hatter's remark seemed to have no sort of meaning in it, and yet it was certainly English. "I don't quite understand you", she said, as politely as she could. . . .

Alice sighed wearily. "I think you might do something better with the time", she said, "than waste it in asking riddles that have no answers."

"If you knew Time as well as I do", said the Hatter, "you wouldn't talk about wasting it. It's him."

"I don't know what you mean", said Alice.

"Of course you don't!" the Hatter said, tossing his head contemptuously. "I dare say you never even spoke to Time!"

"Perhaps not", Alice cautiously replied: "but I know I have to beat time when I learn music."

"Ah! that accounts for it", said the Hatter. "He won't stand beating. Now, if you only kept on good terms with him, he'd do almost anything you liked with the clock. For instance, suppose it were nine o'clock in the morning, just time to begin lessons: you'd only have to whisper a hint to Time, and round goes the clock in a twinkling! Half-past one, time for dinner!"

("I only wish it was", the March Hare said to itself in a whisper.)

"That would be grand, certainly", said Alice thoughtfully: "but then – I shouldn't be hungry for it, you know."

"Not at first, perhaps", said the Hatter: "but you could keep it to half-past one as long as you liked."

"Is that the way you manage?" Alice asked.

The Hatter shook his head mournfully. "Not I!" he replied. "We quarrelled last March – just before he went mad, you know – " (pointing with his tea spoon at the March Hare,) " – it was at the great concert given by the Queen of Hearts, and I had to sing. . . .

"Well, I'd hardly finished the first verse", said the Hatter, "when the Queen jumped up and bawled out, 'He's murdering the time! Off with his head!'"

"How dreadfully savage!" exclaimed Alice.

"And ever since that", the Hatter went on in a mournful tone, "he won't do a thing I ask! It's always six o'clock now."

[111]   Omnipotence and omniscience

If intolerance of frustration is not so great as to activate the mechanisms of evasion and yet is too great to bear dominance of the reality principle, the personality develops omnipotence as a substitute for the mating of the pre-conception, or conception, with the negative realization. This involves the assumption of omniscience as a substitute for learning from experience by aid of thoughts and thinking. There is therefore no psychic activity to discriminate between true and false. Omniscience substitutes for the discrimination between true and false a dictatorial affirmation that one thing is morally right and the other wrong. The assumption of omniscience that denies reality ensures that the morality thus engendered is a function of psychosis. Discrimination between true and false is a function of the non-psychotic part of the personality and its factors. There is thus potentially a conflict between assertion of truth and assertion of moral ascendancy.

(*CWB VI*, pp. 156–157)

In the assumption of omnipotence and omniscience we are in a black-and-white world that lacks complexity – and compassion. Bion locates this state of mind on the boundary between psychosis and the world of reality-principle functioning. The patient who holds rigidly to this position may be trying to protect themselves from psychosis, as well as wishing to powerfully reject the vulnerabilities of ordinary life.

Clinical note: a retreat to omniscience

A male patient told a colleague he had two dreams, but the second one was unimportant. In the first dream he was in a tall building, maybe like a school, and there were many people, mostly his peers, there. He was sleeping on the ground floor. A man arrived, and the patient was now not in the dream. The man could control everybody's minds. The patient thought this was important, as it was perhaps a part of himself, his "super" mind, but he didn't think this was a good thing.

The analyst commented that the building was like the session, where the patient takes control, deciding for both of them that the other dream was not important (Susan Lawrence, personal communication).

[112]   A greedy vagina-like "breast"

If mother and child are adjusted to each other projective identification plays a role in the management through the operation of a rudimentary and fragile reality sense; usually an omnipotent phantasy, it operates realistically. This, I am inclined to believe, is its normal condition. When Melanie Klein (1946, p. 102) speaks of "excessive projective identification", I think the term *excessive* should be understood to apply not only to the frequency with which projective identification is employed, but to excess of belief in omnipotence. As a realistic activity it shows itself as behaviour reasonably calculated to arouse in the mother feelings of which the infant wishes to be rid; if the infant feels it is dying it can arouse fears in the mother that it is dying. A well-balanced mother can accept these and respond therapeutically: that is to say in a manner that makes the infant feel it is receiving its frightened personality back again but in a form that it can tolerate – the fears are manageable by the infant personality. If the mother cannot tolerate these projections, the infant is reduced to continued projective identification carried out with increasing force and frequency. The increased force seems to denude the projection of its penumbra of meaning. Reintrojection is effected with similar force and frequency. Deducing the patient's feelings from his behaviour in the consulting room, and using the deductions to form a model, the infant of my model does not behave in a way I ordinarily expect of an adult who is thinking: it behaves as if it felt an internal object with the characteristics of a greedy vagina-like 'breast' has been built-up, stripping of its goodness all that the infant receives or gives, leaving only degenerate objects. This internal object starves its host of all understanding that is made available. In analysis such a patient seems unable to gain from his environment and therefore from his analyst.

(*CWB VI*, pp. 157–158)

Bion is talking about what happens when containment by the mother fails and the person re-introjects a failed container. A somewhat milder version of what Bion describes is actually quite common. Patients describe how in frightening new situations (such as a new job) they critically attack themselves as failures. It doesn't occur to them that they might expect to find the internal capacity to understand their fears and support themselves (in the same way that they may have lacked the understanding of others in infancy). Instead, the understandability of how they are feeling is stripped away and replaced by superior self castigation. Offers of help are disparaged.

Clinical note

This is an example of a dream in which projective identification left a patient feeling attacked and in pieces.

Patient: For no particular reason I couldn't leave the house . . . Last night I had a weird dream, it was like a James Bond film, in fact James Bond was in it, and it was like on an oil platform, I don't know what it was, but there was a conveyor belt, as if for some machinery, and he kept getting caught up in it, and getting his fingers caught. So when he got to the top he was in a state, you know those beggars who are missing limbs, he had to join a band of those, and every time they went out, they were so savage, they would loose more bits of their bodies. One guy was leading the gang, most of his torso was missing and was saying they wouldn't let James Bond go until he has lost every bit of his body. But then James Bond comes up with a ruse to get away. Oh there was doctor who came in, and he managed to make a deal with her so that he can leave.

But it's not clear whether he gets away or not.

Analyst: It sounds very frightening.

Patient: Yes it was pretty appalling and intense. I woke up before he got away and felt I should go back to sleep to give it a happy ending.

At the start of her analysis this patient and her analyst recognised that she had managed internally by projectively identifying herself with people around her, from her earliest years . This situation had lead to her sustaining a lively entertaining "James Bond" persona, but underneath this she felt she was being consumed and left in a severely depleted and violently impoverished state, where she was missing pieces, like the beggars' missing organs in the dream. (Susan Lawrence, personal communication.)

A colleague's female patient was quite infatuated with a man whom she had met through work; she spent her days thinking how she could look after him. In her sessions she was preoccupied with looking after the analyst, advising her on curtain choices, consoling her on her husband's illness. After the weekend, she complained to the analyst that it felt like she had a giant hole inside her, that she felt left with absolutely nothing, and that this made her quite desperate.

The analyst and her patient understood that she projectively identified with those to whom she provided care. Her unconscious assumption was that this would be a means to get care for herself . When this failed, as at the weekend, she was left distraught, feeling hollowed out and missing parts of herself. (Susan Lawrence, personal communication.)

[113] Alpha-function: the self is able to know itself

It is a logical necessity to suppose that such a function [alpha-function] exists if we are to assume that the self is able to be conscious of itself in the sense of knowing itself from experience of itself.

(*CWB VI*, p. 158)

From *"A Key to A Memoir of the Future"*

Alpha a communicable shorthand for something which is not, and is not like, but is becoming.

(*CWB XIV* 1.14, p. 147)

[114]   Nameless dread

> Normal development follows if the relationship between infant and breast permits the infant to project a feeling, say, that it is dying, into the mother and to reintroject it after its sojourn in the breast has made it tolerable to the infant psyche. If the projection is not accepted by the mother the infant feels that its feeling that it is dying is stripped of such meaning as it has. It therefore reintrojects, not a fear of dying made tolerable, but a nameless dread.
>
> (*CWB VI*, p. 159)

Monica Horovitz

"Nameless dread", is a sort of negative of the Kabbalistic "*Ein Sof*" (infinite unknown, infinite of infinities), which is destructive and not life-bearing. The dream work is damaged, short-circuited, or has failed. Even if contact with external/internal reality is possible, it remains unexploitable.

Primo Levi (1963) ends his book *The Truce* with a horrific recurrent dream which, after his return, visited him at regular intervals: "It is a dream within a dream, varied in detail, one in substance. I am sitting at a table with my family, or with friends, or at work, or in the green countryside; in short, in a peaceful relaxed environment, apparently without tension or affliction; yet I feel a deep and subtle anguish, the definite sensation of an impending threat. And, in fact, as the dream proceeds, slowly or brutally, each time in a different way, everything collapses and disintegrates around me, the scenery, the walls, the people, while the anguish becomes more intense and more precise. Now everything has changed to chaos; I am alone in the centre of a grey and turbid nothingness, and now, I know what this thing means, and I also know that I have always known it; I am in the Lager once more, and nothing is true outside the Lager. All the rest was a brief pause, a deception of the senses, a dream; my family, nature in flower, my home. Now this inner dream, this dream of peace, is over, and in the outer dream, which continues, gelid, a well-known voice resounds: a single word, not imperious, but brief and subdued. It is the dawn command of Auschwitz, a foreign word, feared and expected: get up, "*Wstawać*".

This word means to get up in Polish. Its sense is not so much brutal as imperative. But it is the contrary that is true, for the imperative, however violent it may be, is addressed to someone, whereas the infinitive does not imply any particular address.

All that remains is the anonymous and murderous message that comes in this "peaceful relaxed environment, apparently without tension or affliction".

Traumatic dreams, nightmares, repeat themselves and are there by way of an attempt to elaborate the signifier of the traumatic which is as close as possible to the real (le réel). In order to link the scream with speech. To search for a paternal function which restores thought to dreams. If something is necessary which allows us to dream our dreams (♀), something is also necessary to permit us to understand them (♂) (Grotstein 1981).

And for this reason nightmares are dreams which, paradoxically, make one feel things as if they are real. They try to represent and to contain what hurts us and wounds us, to limit the pain and to generate new possibilities. They offer a space for the work of transformation in the depth of the wounds.

Could it be said that an analysis is precisely the encounter of the movement of the emotions towards the narrative of a subject who, with the support of another, leads us to go round " id/it" (ça) several times in order to emerge from this process as Other. There remains a place from which, I venture to affirm after others, it is possible to transmit the essence of what is human.

"Pensar entre dos, como si hacer el pensamiento fuera igual a hacer el amor", Roberto Juarroz

Roughly translated: "To think needs two, As if to make thought would be the same as making love"

(Horovitz 2015, pp. 87–88)

[115]   Correlation

The tasks that the breakdown in the mother's capacity for reverie have left unfinished are imposed on the rudimentary consciousness; they are all in different degrees related to the function of correlation.

(*CWB VI*, p. 159)

Denis Flynn

Correlation: a clinical illustration

In all this period I would say bit by bit . . . the work of correlating his [the patient's] thinking and feeling, and his knowledge about himself, is going on, sometimes forwards or backwards, but going on. He is relatively well defended; so in ordinary terms he has a "bolshie attitude" to psychoanalysis, he enjoys working out his frustrations and negative feelings on his male analyst (largely in line with an already interpreted paternal transference), then he is largely passive, sometimes resistant and sometimes mute and disabled, unable to react (as I am beginning to discover largely in line with an emerging maternal transference). But positively also he can be sensitive and honest about his internal states. Yet overall I think the analysis is not fully personal for him. . . .

Then shortly after the long break the setting and normal sessions were interrupted by my cancelling some sessions. At first he was upfront hurt and stunned, and felt I had "wiped him out of my mind". After I was away he associated to his experience of having his mother walk out of his life, so he could never trust her mother "and her distortions" again. He remained silent seeming fearful about me, then could only say something vague and opaque, that he was "feeling something about his mother". I understood that he did not have access to what he was feeling and thinking, i.e. he felt something but as yet he had no further realisation about what he knew, his evolving self-knowledge. . . .

When there followed shortly a second interruption of sessions he was then more shocked and hurt, sensing I was doing something cruel to him. As he struggled to think he now told me about his experience as a small baby when his slightly older brother severely injured himself in a fall. The image was of him – the baby – being utterly passive and unable to do a thing while something terrible was going on. This connected for me with other similar experiences throughout his childhood and adolescence. I sensed in him a questioning mixture of anger, blame and unconscious guilt – what had he done to make this happen? He then also voiced a worry about him always "doing his own thing", without purpose or agreement with others, and "doing mad things". Andrew feels the analyst like his parents is dumping him and cutting off, but he also is linking this with him knowing about, i.e. acknowledging, his own unpredictability and instability. So although it is disturbed the work of "correlation" is still going on to a degree, and he is learning more about himself.

When there was a third (and final) interruption of the sessions it was the last straw. Andrew became totally cut off and cold. Then after a long silence he blasted out like an angry expletive, "It's "bizarre". A little later he said he felt I was "playing with him." I interpreted that he was shocked and stunned, "now", and his capacity to think and know was broken into. Yet as I reflected I thought to myself that indeed what he was experiencing was concrete and "bizarre" for him, as he said. In some ways I as the analyst was felt to be not just lax or neglectful, but I had become for him a version of a "bizarre object" (in Bion's sense) – morally superior, attacking and aloof, just disappearing without reason. I needed to accept this was his view of me, and think what it must mean for him to be at this impasse and how the reality that to him I was bizarre. It took a long time over many sessions for him to recover, to resurface, at all.

So after a considerable time Andrew began to recover his capacity to think and to create links of thinking, so that the work of correlation of his experience, including this experience, could occur. He began over time to make sense of the loss of his analyst in terms of the sudden loss of his mother, and brought the following dream: "I was in . . . London with a friend, but the way was barred. I was coming home, to here, and crossing the threshold into the house. There was a wreathe for my mother, which had her maiden name on it. I felt it was bizarre like I did not know anything about her." Many links could now be made by him, which previously seemed impossible: to the blocking and breaking up of the analysis; to being more in touch with painful memories and thoughts about his mother's death; to his surmise that with these cancellations we were both thinking about death; to coming "here" – back to the analysis and some other very personal links to "here" from his past; to finding a link in the dream between his loss of his mother and his experience of loss here in the analysis. The "bizarreness" now had changed (-through painful uncertainty and doubt, internal persecutory suffering and his work, and mine, of α-function and correlation of many aspects of his experience) from something impersonal and irrational, to awareness of his "not knowing" and from a painful jolt of reality of loss. His dream now included some integration of his awareness there was a lot that was "bizarre" that he did not know.

(Flynn 2014, pp. 6–8)

[116]   Wilfully misunderstanding object

The rudimentary consciousness cannot carry the burden placed on it. The establishment internally of a projective-identification-rejecting-object means that instead of an understanding object the infant has a wilfully misunderstanding object – with which it is identified. Further its psychic qualities are perceived by a precocious and fragile consciousness.

(*CWB VI*, p. 159)

[117]   Fourfold apparatus

The apparatus available to the psyche may be regarded as fourfold:

1   *Thinking*, associated with modification and evasion.
2   *Projective identification*, associated with evasion by evacuation and not to be confused with normal projective identification. . . .
3   *Omniscience* (on the principle of *tout savoir tout condamner* [everything known everything condemned]).
4   *Communication*.

(CWB VI, p. 159)

[118]   Translation into action

In other words just as sense-data have to be modified and worked on by alpha-function to make them available for dream thoughts, etc., so the thoughts have to be worked on to make them available for translation into action.

Translation into action involves publication, communication, and commonsense.

(*CWB VI*, p. 160)

The last point is addressed in the following three quotes.

We might assume that analysis is to do with thinking not "action". Later on, in the "Key" to his novel *A Memoir of the Future*, we find the following comment:

. . . "doing something" Confusion is created by the failure to distinguish between thought that is a prelude to action, and thought used as a substitute for action. This leads to an inability to distinguish between someone who is only "talking" and somebody who is "saying something". This distinction is of vital importance in psychoanalysis.

(*CWB XVIII*, p. 166)

(This quote is also included in the discussion of Column 6 in the Grid.)

[119] Publication

Publication in its origin may be regarded as little more than one function of thoughts, namely making sense-data available to consciousness. I wish to reserve the term for operations that are necessary to make private awareness, that is awareness that is private to the individual, public. The problems involved may be regarded as technical and emotional. The emotional problems are associated with the fact that the human individual is a political animal and cannot find fulfilment outside a group, and cannot satisfy any emotional drive without expression of its social component. His impulses, and I mean all impulses and not merely his sexual ones, are at the same time narcissistic. The problem is the resolution of the conflict between narcissism and social-ism. The technical problem is that concerned with expression of thought or conception in language, or its counterpart in signs.

(CWB VI, p. 160)

Ron Britton

Too ready to publish

. . . I refer here to more than inadequacy of material, ideas, or presentation, but specifically to a blind sort of over-confident belief that what is said or written by the author deserves and will receive widespread approval; usually it is associated with banality. In the cases I am thinking of, the phenomenon itself is a contributing cause to the poverty of the text rather than lack of ability in the author. It can therefore afflict previously successful writers or potentially talented authors.

It is, I suggest, a form of intellectual complacency that can arise as part of a manic defence. It results from the unconscious phantasy of being the special representative of a superior power. This superior power is itself derived by the attributive projective identification of the phantasised omniscient self into an actual object, which might be a person or a school of thought. Such projective identification gives a sense of having a special connection with this power without having to claim omnipotence or omniscience for the self, thus preserving reality sense and avoiding psychosis. It may take the form of an orthodoxy in which the individual author has *a priestly function*; or it may take an iconoclastic form in which the spirit of the new is felt to emanate from some intellectually respectable version of divine revelation. This then forms the basis for *a prophetic function*.

In other cases the complacency is derived from an incorporative identification, in which the authority of an earlier author has been imbibed together with his ideas and absorbed into the thinking of the author, not by intellectual assimilation but by an acquisitive identification, which results in the disappearance of the intellectual debt to the original author and an illusion of originality. There is always an underlying precariousness in this structure because the derivation of the ideas is lacking and the sense of authority is only achieved by assertion, and therefore any challenge leads simply to more assertiveness.

Publication anxiety

I think that a profound *fear of rejection by the primary intended listener* in its most serious form leads to an inability to conceptualise or, in lesser states of inhibition, produces an inability to write. . . .

I think it emanates from a fear of criticism by third parties who are regarded as authoritative, and a *fear of disaffiliation* from colleagues with whom the author feels the need to be *affiliated*. . . . The conflict is between the urge to communicate a novel idea to a receptive audience, thus winning their allegiance, and the conflicting wish to say something to bind the author to his affiliates and ancestors by the utterance, in a shared language, of shared beliefs – the recital of a creed as a means of unification. . . .

Britton then discusses Thomas Kuhn's seminal work of on scientific paradigms. He concludes that when the prevailing paradigm is "authoritative", publication is easier for those who

are happy adding "facts" to expand, exemplify, and refine the paradigm. This is the phase of "normal science". For more restless, ambitious, or determinedly original spirits, the fear in this phase is that they will not find creative space for themselves – the latter being more at home in times of paradigm change.

(Britton 1994, pp. 1214–1215)

[120]   Communication

> This brings me to communication. In its origin communication is effected
> by realistic projective identification. . . . It may develop, if the relationship
> with the breast is good, into a capacity for toleration by the self of its own
> psychic qualities, and so pave the way for alpha-function and normal thought.
> But it does also develop as a part of the social capacity of the individual. This
> development, of great importance in group dynamics, has received virtually
> no attention; its absence would make even scientific communication impos-
> sible. Yet its presence may arouse feelings of persecution in the receptors of
> the communication. The need to diminish feelings of persecution contrib-
> utes to the drive to abstraction in the formulation of scientific communica-
> tions. The function of the elements of communication, words and signs, is
> to convey either by single substantives or in verbal groupings, that certain
> phenomena are constantly conjoined in the pattern of their relatedness.
>
> (*CWB VI*, pp. 160–161)

In the quote we see his view that "abstraction" can diminish feelings of persecution. Why should this be? Abstraction may protect somewhat from the unconscious meaning and feelings involved. It can also put knowledge into a shared
social realm, without people feeling that they are being forced to accept someone
else's thoughts.

[121]   The common emotional view

An important function of communication is to achieve correlation. . . . The failure to bring about this conjunction of sense-data, and therefore of a commonplace view, induces a mental state of debility in the patient as if starvation of truth was somehow analogous to alimentary starvation. . . .

The emotions fulfil for the psyche a function similar to that of the senses in relation to objects in space and time: that is to say, the counterpart of the commonsense view in private knowledge is the common emotional view; a sense of truth is experienced if the view of an object which is hated can be conjoined to a view of the same object when it is loved, and the conjunction confirms that the object experienced by different emotions is the same object. A correlation is established.

A similar correlation, made possible by bringing conscious and unconscious to bear on the phenomena of the consulting room, gives to psychoanalytic objects a reality that is quite unmistakable even though their very existence has been disputed.

(CWB VI, p. 161)

Denis Flynn

In places Bion argues in a Kantian way, . . . that "the emotions fulfil a similar function for the psyche to that of the senses in relation to objects in time and space". In effect Bion is saying that the emotions are "conditions of experience", like in Kant's sense "space" and "time" are conditions of experience of our knowledge of the external world (Kant 1929: pp. 63–82, and *passim*): it is through such conditions of experience that we create our perception of the external world. So similarly for Bion an ongoing emotional awareness must underlie anything we can know, and indeed it creates what we can know, "K".

"The function of correlation" is an essential part of or tool of observation, so we would say in ordinary terms that without such correlation our observations would lack emotional depth or truth. Or we would say that such observations were "flat" or "two-dimensional" – both analogies about space; or that they had no emotional "context" for the individual in terms of how they live their lives or in terms of their developmental patterns and progress – this time analogies about the continuity of time.

(Flynn 2014, p. 2)

Chapter 9

Learning from Experience

Introduction

> In spite of his deep dislike of evening meetings – two or three a week at
> the end of an already very long day's work – he accepted these positions
> [Director of the London Clinic of Psychoanalysis from 1956–62, Presi-
> dent of the British Psychoanalytical Society from 1962–1965. Chairman
> of the Melanie Klein Trust from 1960].
>
> Looking back, it surprises me that in the midst of so much work and
> so many commitments, we had any time for a private life. However,
> weekends were sacrosanct times for relaxing with the family, conver-
> sation, listening to music (our tastes were catholic but favourites were
> Bach, Mozart, Haydn, Britten and Stravinsky), reading, contemplating
> and writing. He once said, "I want to be a psychoanalyst. But I do not
> want that experience to make it impossible for me to have a life worth
> living where I could never go to the theatre or a picture gallery or paint
> or swim.
>
> (Francesca Bion 1994, p. 97)

Prior to *Learning from Experience*, Bion had written papers; this was his first
book. During the 1960s, Bion, himself in his sixties, was to write four short
books – *Learning from Experience* (1962), *Elements of Psycho-Analysis* (1963),
Transformations (1965), and *Attention and Interpretation* (published 1970). At
the beginning of *Learning from Experience*, Bion makes the following comment
about the publication of a book on the "attempt to understand our understanding":

> I have experience to record, but how to communicate this experience to
> others I am in doubt; this book explains why. For a time I thought of concen-
> trating on analysis of trainees. I am confident that psychoanalysts are right
> in thinking that this is the only really effective method of passing on analytic
> experience that we have at present; but to limit one's energies to this activ-
> ity smacks of the esoteric cult. On the other hand, publication of a book,

such as this, may seem premature. Nevertheless I believe it may be possible to give some idea of the world that is revealed by *the attempt to understand our understanding*. If the reader is tempted to go further the object of the book is achieved.

(*CWB IV*, p. 263; emphasis added)

The themes treated briefly in Bion's paper, "A Theory of Thinking", are explored in *Learning from Experience* in their complexity and clinical relevance. Bion also talks about the experience of the infant – from the "inside". He is clear that it is a hypothetical infant, and we cannot know its experience, but he has an extraordinary capacity to imagine himself into the baby's experience.

Notes on concepts Bion is using and developing

Alpha-function

Bion gives a name "alpha-function" to the process by which something that was not thought at all comes to be thought. There must be such a process, he says, because we can observe the before (unthought stuff) and the after (thinking/dreaming/understanding). The term alpha-function allows him to designate what he wants to explore without having to stipulate what the process is composed of. Bion wants to turn our attention to the "process" rather than the objects on either side. We are to look, not at the bud and the rose, but the process of unfurling that occurs between the two.

Container–contained

Container–contained ($♀♂$) – the concept that was to become so well known – is an aspect of alpha-function; it is discussed in the penultimate chapter of the book. Bion had used the term "contained" for the first time in his 1956 paper, "The Development of Schizophrenic Thought" in which he describes a psychotic patient's projection of "expelled particles of ego" into objects that are then experienced as "containing"/being taken over by the projection. Then, in his 1958 paper "On Arrogance", he described how allowing the patient's projection to "'sojourn in my psyche" could result in some modification of the patient's "bad feelings".

Freud himself had been well aware that without the care of the mother, self-regulation through the pleasure principle could not operate; this, however, is different from Bion's model in which not only does the environment provide the conditions for an individual's self-regulation, but the regulation of the self is provided by the object. A question he leaves us with is whether there can be any transformation of infantile experience without the containment provided by an object. André Green (1998, p. 656) has commented that Bion excludes the spontaneous transformation from beta-elements to alpha-elements without the help of the object.

Quotes

122 Cannot dream, cannot go to sleep, and cannot wake up
123 Destruction of contact with alive objects
124 Enforced splitting
125 A man talking to his friend
126 Contact barrier
127 Beta-screen: "Purposiveness of the unthought"
128 What receives the love?
129 A difference in psychical quality
130 Reverie
131 Infants have different capacities for toleration of frustration
132 Need for precise formulation of theory
133 L H K
134 The K link
135 Hypochondriacal symptoms
136 Poincaré
137 Observation and interpretation: avoiding a harsh break in observation
138 Less than six theories enough
139 Container–contained
140 Minus container–contained (−♀♂) "Without-ness"
141 "Super" ego

[122]   Cannot dream, cannot go to sleep, and cannot wake up

... the patient who cannot dream cannot go to sleep and cannot wake up.

(*CWB IV*, p. 275)

Thomas Ogden

. . . Bion offers a reconceptualisation of the role of dreaming in human life. Dreaming occurs continuously day and night, though we are aware of it in waking states only in derivative form, for example, in reverie states occurring in an analytic session. . . . If a person is unable to transform raw sensory data into unconscious elements of experience that can be stored and made accessible for linking, he is incapable of dreaming (which involves making emotional linkages in the creation of dream-thoughts).[2]

Instead of having a dream (experienced as a dream), the individual incapable of alpha-function registers only raw sensory data. For such a person, the raw sensory data (beta-elements) experienced in sleep are indistinguishable from those occurring in waking life.[3] Unable to differentiate waking and sleeping states, the patient "cannot go to sleep and cannot wake up" (Bion 1962, p. 7 [see quote above]). Such states are regularly observed in psychotic patients who do not know if they are awake or dreaming because what might have become a dream (were the patient capable of alpha-function) becomes, instead, an hallucination in sleep or waking life. Hallucinations are the opposite of dreaming and of unconscious thinking in a waking state.

Conversely, not all psychic events occurring in sleep (even those events in visual imagistic form that we remember on waking) merit the name "dream". Psychological events occurring in sleep that appear to be dreams but are not dreams include "dreams" to which no associations can be made, hallucinations in sleep, the repetitive (unchanging) "dreams" of those suffering from traumatic neuroses, imageless "dreaming" consisting only of an intense feeling state or a muscular action in sleep. Though these phenomena occurring in sleep may appear to be dreams, they involve no unconscious psychological work – the work of dreaming – which results in psychological growth. One can hallucinate for a lifetime without the slightest bit of psychological work being done. For (my interpretation of) Bion, dreaming, if it is to merit the name, must involve unconscious psychological work achieved through the linking of elements of experience (which have been stored as memory) in the creation of dream-thought. This work of making unconscious linkages – as opposed to forms of psychic evacuation, such as hallucination, excessive projective identification, manic defence and paranoid delusion – allows one unconsciously and consciously to think about and make psychological use of experience. A person unable to learn from (make use of) experience is imprisoned in the hell of an endless, unchanging world of what is.

(2) Bion uses the word "thoughts" to include both thoughts and feelings.

(3) For Bion (1957 [*CWB VI*]), there are always co-existing psychotic and non-psychotic parts of the personality. Consequently, a patient's inability to dream (which is a reflection of the psychotic part of the personality) is, in every instance, to some degree accompanied by a non-psychotic part of the personality capable of alpha-function and consequently able to produce conscious thought, dream-thought and unconscious thinking while the individual is awake

(Ogden 2003, pp. 18–19)

[123]   Destruction of contact with live objects

Attacks on alpha-function, stimulated by hate or envy, destroy the possibility of the patient's conscious contact either with himself or another as live objects. Accordingly we hear of inanimate objects, and even of places, when we would normally expect to hear of people. These, though described verbally, are felt by the patient to be present materially and not merely to be represented by their names. This state contrasts with animism in that live objects are endowed with the qualities of death.

(*CWB IV*, pp. 276–277)

Bion draws a parallel between the patients described above and scientists. He argues that we tend to think in terms of inanimate objects and mechanisms because of an inherent difficulty in the human mind to think about animate processes.

The scientist whose investigations include the stuff of life finds himself in a situation that has a parallel in such patients. The breakdown in the patient's equipment for thinking leads to dominance by a mental life in which his universe is populated by inanimate objects. The inability of even the most advanced human beings to make use of their thoughts, because the capacity to think is rudimentary in all of us, means that the field for investigation, all investigation being ultimately scientific, is limited, by human inadequacy, to those phenomena that have the characteristics of the inanimate. We assume that the psychotic limitation is due to illness; but that that of scientist is not. . . . It appears that our rudimentary equipment for "thinking" thoughts is adequate when the problems are associated with the inanimate, but not when the object for investigation is the phenomenon of life itself. Confronted with the complexities of the human mind the analyst must be circumspect in following even accepted scientific method; its weakness may be closer to the weakness of psychotic thinking than superficial scrutiny would admit.

(*CWB IV*, p. 282)

To talk of "mechanism" suggests that, whatever the phenomenon is that is thus described, it is likely that the implied model is more suitable to the inanimate machine than to a living organism. It is likely to emphasize those aspects of the living organism which it shares with the inanimate. This defect is serious because we require models when the problem is most complex, that is when the characteristics of growth are central; and that is most of the time. The term mechanism implies the model of a machine which is precisely what the realization is not.

(CWB IV, pp. 346–347)

Harry Guntrip

Physical scientists do not usually regard psychic phenomena as having the same material trust-worthiness for investigation as material facts. In whatever way we acquire our knowledge of our thoughts, feelings and volitions, we do not get to know them by seeing, hearing, touching, tasting or smelling them, but by a *wholly subjective inner process which we call recognition or realization of our immediate experience.* . . . Of course, sensory perception is also a subjective experience, but it has an objective reference which is entirely absent from our experiencing of ourselves. . . . Have we got a "Mental" Science? . . . there are only two possible solutions:

i   To limit science to the study of material phenomena. . . .
ii   To expand the meaning of science to include the study of "mental" phenomena in its own and not in physical terms.

(Guntrip 1967, pp. 33–34)

Bion's intention is the second. In addition, he thought that psychoanalysis had a contribution to make to our understanding of the physical sciences.

Harry Guntrip: An analyst in the British Independent Tradition, writing at around the same time as Bion.

Animism: (1) a living soul is attributed to inanimate objects and natural phenomena; (2) the belief in a supernatural power that animates the material world.

Libidinal: Libido, a Latin term meaning desire. In Freud's model of the mind it designates the instinctual sexual energy underlying all mental activity.

[124]   Enforced splitting

> We must now examine enforced splitting associated with a disturbed rela-
> tionship with the breast or its substitutes. The infant receives milk and other
> creature comforts from the breast; also love, understanding, solace. Sup-
> pose his initiative is obstructed by fear of aggression, his own or another's.
> If the emotion is strong enough it inhibits the infant's impulse to obtain
> sustenance.
>
> Love in infant or mother or both increases rather than decreases the
> obstruction partly because love is inseparable from envy of the object so
> loved, partly because it is felt to arouse envy and jealousy in a third object
> that is excluded. The part played by love may escape notice because envy,
> rivalry and hate obscure it, although hate would not exist if love were not
> present. Violence of emotion compels reinforcement of the obstruction
> because violence is not distinguished from destructiveness and subsequent
> guilt and depression. Fear of death through starvation of essentials compels
> resumption of sucking. A split between material and psychical satisfaction
> develops. . . . its object and effect is to enable the infant to obtain what later
> in life would be called material comforts without acknowledging the exis-
> tence of a live object on which these benefits depend.
>
> (CWB IV, pp. 278–279)

Bion goes on to describe a patient who demanded more and more material comforts in the consulting room, as well as more and more interpretations, but these
were treated as if they were inanimate objects, like the number of pillows.

Clinical note

The previous day I had let the patient know that I needed to cancel a session in
three weeks' time. When she arrived for her session, she said that the "not knowing where she was thing" had happened on her way to today's session. It is a state
of mind in which she is very disorientated, doesn't know where she is or what she
is doing, even what her name is. Just prior to this happening to her, she had been
making arrangements for what she would do on the morning of the cancelled session. We came to see more just how much she relied on the material fact of her
sessions, knowledge of her relationship to me being split off. The material fact
of the sessions was, I think, like the milk in Bion's discussion of enforced splitting, the relationship between us the "love" that is split off. She was treating my
cancellation like a "thing" and was disorientated by her cancelling out what she
might feel.

[125]   A man talking to his friend

The chapter in which Freud sums up his metapsychology in the *Interpretation of Dreams* is Chapter 7 – as is Bion's!

Chapter Seven

If a man has an emotional experience when asleep or awake and is able to convert it into alpha-elements he can either remain unconscious of that emotional experience or become conscious of it. The sleeping man has an emotional experience, converts it into alpha-elements and so becomes capable of dream thoughts. Thus he is free to become conscious (that is wake up) and describe the emotional experience by a narrative usually known as a dream.

A man talking to a friend converts the sense impressions of this emotional experience into alpha-elements, thus becoming capable of dream thoughts and therefore of undisturbed consciousness of the facts whether the facts are the events in which he participates or his feelings about those events or both. He is able to remain "asleep" or unconscious of certain elements that cannot penetrate the barrier presented by his "dream". Thanks to the "dream" he can continue uninterruptedly to be awake, that is, awake to the fact that he is talking to his friend, but asleep to elements which, if they could penetrate the barrier of his "dreams", would lead to domination of his mind by what are ordinarily unconscious ideas and emotions.

The dream makes a barrier against mental phenomena which might overwhelm the patient's awareness that he is talking to a friend, and, at the same time, makes it impossible for awareness that he is talking to a friend to overwhelm his phantasies. The psychotic's attempt to discriminate one from the other leads to rational thought characterized by a peculiar lack of "resonance". What he says clearly and in articulated speech is one dimensional. It has no overtones or undertones of meaning. It makes the listener inclined to say "So what?" It has no capacity to evoke a train of thought. . . .

In this theory the ability to "dream" preserves the personality from what is virtually a psychotic state. It therefore helps to explain the tenacity with which the dream, as represented in classical theory, defends itself against the attempt to make the unconscious conscious. Such an attempt must appear indistinguishable from destruction of the capacity to dream in so far as that capacity is related to differentiating conscious from unconscious and maintaining the difference so established.

(*CWB IV*, pp. 283–284)

Bion also raises the possibility that night dreams may be a consequence of "awake dreaming" not having fully processed the emotional experiences during the day:

> I wonder if dreams, i.e. the actual emotional experiences are not the emotional experiences I do not have, or cannot allow myself to have, during wakefulness.
>
> (*CWB XI*, p. 144)

Awake dreaming?

The subject has come up at various points already. It seemed better to hold on to the question until the subject was somewhat established. My question is not about the process Bion is describing, which happens when we are awake, but why he calls this dreaming? What does the awake process have in common with night dreams?

1   Freud thought that night dreams protect sleep. Dreaming while awake also has a protective function – in this instance it protects our conscious functioning. Alpha-function is responsible for the continuing differentiation of conscious and unconscious elements.
2   Night dreams show an extraordinary capacity for selecting what is key. In dreaming while awake do we see a somewhat analogous capacity in our being able to arrive at what Poincaré calls a selected fact – a "condensed" fact that profoundly orientates us in relation to the myriad of things happening.
3   What, however, of visual images in night dreams – is there an equivalent of this in dreaming while awake?

[126] Contact barrier

I shall now transfer all that I have said about the establishment of conscious and unconscious and a barrier between them to a supposed entity, that I designate a "contact-barrier"; Freud used this term to describe the neuro-physiological entity subsequently known as a synapse. In conformity with this my statement that the man has to "dream" a current emotional experience whether it occurs in sleep or in waking life is re-formulated thus: The man's alpha-function whether in sleeping or waking transforms the sense-impressions related to an emotional experience, into alpha-elements, which cohere as they proliferate to form the contact-barrier. This contact-barrier, thus continuously in process of formation, marks the point of contact and separation between conscious and unconscious elements and originates the distinction between them. The nature of the contact-barrier will depend on the nature of the supply of alpha-elements and on the manner of their relationship to each other. They may cohere. They may be agglomerated. They may be ordered sequentially to give the appearance of narrative (at least in the form in which the contact-barrier may reveal itself in a dream). They may be ordered logically. They may be ordered geometrically.

(*CWB IV*, p. 285)

Freud's concept of repression is largely replaced in Bion's model of the mind by the idea of a "contact barrier" made up of alpha-elements, which constantly maintains a differentiation between conscious and unconscious elements.

Bion suggests that night dreams may reveal some representation of the contact barrier. What, however, does he mean by "ordered logically" and "ordered geometrically"?

Sean Watson

A whirlpool appears in a turbulent flow of water. The whirlpool is an island of order in an apparently chaotic environment. It has a definite structure, but its component parts are constantly changing, there is a flow of matter through the system, and it is sustained by a flow of energy. The molecules making up organic cells are constantly being replaced, the cells of the body are constantly being replaced, thousands per minute. The body is not a static structure, like a building or a machine, it is a structured process. This is true for any complex dissipative system. The "contact-barrier", which Bion describes as "continuously in process of formation", is a dissipative structure precisely in the sense described by Prigogine and others. Alpha- and beta-elements are themselves dissipative-structures. They are sub-systems of the process of transmutation which is the contact-barrier. These elements are always coming from somewhere and going somewhere else, always becoming transformed versions of themselves, or something else entirely.

(Watson 2002, p. 251)

M. Teising

Whereas for Freud the contact-barrier regulates the quantity of energy and founds a topographical structure, Bion understands the contact-barrier as a psychic function that simultaneously regulates boundary demarcation and making contact. In the psychoanalytic process, the contact-barrier created by patient and analyst regulates the events in the transference and countertransference. . . .

My starting point for the reflections in this paper was a comment made by a patient whom I had heard about during the supervision of a psychiatric team. She had said, "Help, I'm not completely watertight." This image has since enabled me to gain a better understanding of psychotic phenomena. When psychotic patients have difficulty in differentiating whether the voices they are hearing come from inside or outside and whether their thinking is being controlled by themselves or from outside when they hear spoken thoughts or commenting voices, the boundaries conceived are just as porous as they are in uncontrolled affective outbursts that infringe other people's boundaries and sometimes indicate primary process material. These patients are incapable of securely fulfilling the lifelong task of differentiating between private and external reality while also holding them in mutual connection. They express fears of dissolving, melting away, losing themselves and so on. The autistic safeguarding of boundaries can be understood as a reaction to a porous boundary experience. Many people with psychotic symptoms experience a central relational conflict between their wish for (fusional) proximity and their inability to tolerate it. They are afraid of being scorched by it. Psychotic symptoms then create the necessary distance and protect them from close proximity. Moreover, not being completely "watertight" and its definition not only depend on the individual's condition and the nature of his existence with an other but are also influenced by third parties in his environment.

I also then considered the concepts of being "not completely watertight" in the sense of being too open and "too watertight" in the sense of being too closed in my psychoanalytic work in the classical treatment setting and went on to investigate our ideas concerning the frontier between self and object.

(Teising 2005, pp. 1627–1628)

[127]   Beta-screen: "Purposiveness of the unthought"

... the beta-element screen [is] coherent and purposive. An interpretation that the patient was pouring out a stream of material intended to destroy the analyst's psychoanalytic potency would not seem out of place. Equally apt would be an interpretation that the patient was concerned to withhold rather than to impart information. One peculiarity of the situation is the plethora of interpretations that would occur to anyone with any common sense. Yet they do not occur to the patient. These common-sense interpretations have a common characteristic in that all are accusatory, or, alternatively, laudatory as if far-fetched with intent to reassure the patient of his goodness in the teeth of the evidence. This is not fortuitous; it would be difficult in face of the evidence to maintain that it was. One is forced to a conclusion that is unexpected and surprising, namely, that the beta-element screen – I shall call it beta-screen for short in future – has a quality enabling it to evoke the kind of response the patient desires, or, alternatively, a response from the analyst which is heavily charged with counter-transference.

(CWB IV, pp. 290–291)

If the evasion of frustration dominates, this affects not only how the mind behaves, but how it develops. This is important to note because the "unthought" (beta-element) is not only raw experience yet to be processed, it can also be highly sophisticated manipulations produced by a mind that has become expert at "regulating" itself by evacuation.

Larry Brown notes Bion's view that an envious attack is a primary factor in the reversal of alpha-function, but he suggests that the reversal can also be caused by the destructive effects of massive trauma. The beta screen is then understood to be an agglomeration of the "shards of a shattered psyche":

Larry Brown

The beta-screen and trauma

Bion states that the beta screen is "coherent and purposive", but is also rigidly organized and impermeable to learning from experience. . . .

(Brown 2005, p. 402)

My main thesis is that massive traumatic experiences affect the psyche by bringing about an impairment in the capacity for symbolic thinking (what Bion calls the alpha-function), which results in the formation of a rigidly structured traumatic organization (the beta screen, comprised of beta elements, in Bionian terms) that dooms the traumatized patient to seemingly endless patterns of enactment, thereby precluding the ability to learn from experience. . . .

(pp. 399–402)

[128]   What receives the love?

The milk, we may assume with a degree of conviction we cannot feel about love, is received and dealt with by the alimentary canal; what receives and deals with the love? The question may be a formulation based on inadequate thinking, and therefore liable to lead to error, unless we consider what the situation is with the mother. As the infant receives the milk and deals with it by the alimentary system, so the mother provides it by the glandular system, yet milk has been known to fail and the failure has been attributed to emotional upsets. The infant likewise has been supposed to suffer digestive disturbances originating in an emotional upset. It may be useful to suppose that there exists in reality a psycho-somatic breast and an infantile psycho-somatic alimentary canal corresponding to the breast.

(*CWB IV*, p. 301)

We are more familiar with thinking about psycho-somatic phenomena from the point of view of emotional upset being located in the body, but the question "what receives and deals with the love" indicates a view of the body healthily involved in emotional life.

[129] A difference in psychic quality

Suppose the infant is fed; the taking in of milk, warmth, love, may be felt as taking in a good breast. Under dominance of the, at first unopposed, bad breast, "taking in" food may be felt as indistinguishable from evacuating a bad breast. Both good and bad breasts are felt as possessing the same degree of concreteness and reality as milk. Sooner or later the "wanted" breast is felt as an "idea of a breast missing" and not as a bad breast present. We can see that the bad, that is to say wanted but absent, breast is much more likely to become recognized as an idea than the good breast which is associated with what a philosopher would call a thing-in-itself or a thing-in-actuality, in that the sense of a good breast depends on the existence of milk the infant has in fact taken. The good breast and the bad breast, the one being associated with the actual milk that satisfies hunger and the other with the non-existence of that milk, must have a difference in psychical quality. "Thoughts are a nuisance" said one of my patients, "I don't want them." Is a "thought" the same as an absence of a thing? If there is no "thing", is "no thing" a thought and is it by virtue of the fact that there is "no thing" that one recognizes that "it" must be thought?

(*CWB IV*, pp. 301–302)

One might be inclined to wonder why this has to be put in such a complicated way. My impression is that Bion may be trying to imagine himself in the baby's "shoes". From his imagined position inside the baby's experience, one can see how the repeated movement backwards and forwards gradually leads to noticing a difference in psychic quality between the present good breast and not-present bad breast – the difference that lies at the base of being able to begin to think. The patients Bion was writing about in the 1950s had not been able to recognise this difference.

[130]   Reverie

For example, when the mother loves the infant what does she do it with? Leaving aside the physical channels of communication my impression is that her love is expressed by reverie.

Though the difficulties of penetrating the adult mind in analysis are great they are less so than attempting to penetrate the infant's by speculative hypothesis; investigation of reverie in the adult may afford us an entry into this problem. We may deduce from reverie, as the psychological source of supply of the infant's needs for love and understanding, what kind of psychological receptor organ is required if the infant is to be able to profit from reverie as it is able, thanks to the digestive capacities of the alimentary canal, to profit from the breast and the milk it supplies. Put in another way, assuming alpha-function as that which makes available to the infant what would otherwise remain unavailable for any purpose other than evacuation as beta-elements, what are the *factors* of this function that relate directly to the mother's capacity for reverie?

The mother's capacity for reverie is here considered as inseparable from the content for clearly one depends on the other. If the feeding mother cannot allow reverie or if the reverie is allowed but is not associated with love for the child or its father this fact will be communicated to the infant even though incomprehensible to the infant. Psychical quality will be imparted to the channels of communication, the links with the child. What happens will depend on the nature of these maternal psychical qualities and their impact on the psychical qualities of the infant, for the impact of the one upon the other is an emotional experience subject from the point of view of the development of the couple and the individuals composing it, to transformation by alpha-function. The term reverie may be applied to almost any content. I wish to reserve it only for such content as is suffused with love or hate. Using it in this restricted sense reverie is that state of mind which is open to the reception of any "objects" from the loved object and is therefore capable of reception of the infant's projective identifications whether they are felt by the infant to be good or bad. In short, reverie is a factor of the mother's alpha-function.

(*CWB IV*, p. 303)

Neville Symington points out how the powerful projections of a new born baby can be met by either a reactive chain or a responsive scenario.

Neville Symington

The infant is born radiating unseen particles that rip into the very fabric of the mother's emotional structure. All the mother knows is that she is overcome with unbearable feelings. . . . The baby, we suppose, is bombarded from within by the nameless dread and he or she has no structure to withstand it so it ricochets off at the mother. What the mother consciously feels is that she feels awful, finds herself lonely all day, wishes she could be at work again. Then she sees her husband out at work all day and she resents him and what is in her ricochets off into her husband. The husband does not know what has happened. He begins to feel that his wife does not understand him. He begins to remember his parents' attempts to discourage him from marrying her; "She's not your class, dear, she won't understand the way you are brought up". These thoughts grow in him and he begins to pay attention to his secretary at work and is soon having an affair with her. The wife finds out and is bitter, feels an outrage of unsupport and the spiral of bitterness and resentment increases. . . .

It is not to our purpose to pursue this scenario any further but what occurs is a *reactive* chain and its source is the birth of a new baby. It is that with the birth of the new-born baby there arrives into the human community a huge quantum of primeval dread in a configurative pattern that does not have the structure to support it. Therefore this newly arrived bundle of radiating particles has to be met with a structure to support it. In a *responsive* scenario rather than a *reactive* chain the mother absorbs these particles and is probably helped to do it because her husband is in *responsive* intercourse with her. The emotional relationship between husband and wife provides a third force to contend with the unwelcome amount of primeval anxiety that is suddenly thrust into their midst.

(Symington 1990, p. 100)

[131]   Infants have different capacities for toleration of frustration

An infant endowed with marked capacity for toleration of frustration might survive the ordeal of a mother incapable of reverie and therefore incapable of supplying its mental needs. At the other extreme an infant markedly incapable of tolerating frustration cannot survive without breakdown even the experience of projective identification with a mother capable of reverie; nothing less than unceasing breast feeding would serve and that is not possible through lack of appetite if for no other reason.

(*CWB IV*, p. 305)

[132] Need for precise formulation of theory

As an example of an attempt at precise formulation I take alpha-function and two factors, excessive projective identification and excess of bad objects. Suppose that in the course of the analysis these two factors are obtrusive to the exclusion of other factors that the analyst has observed. If psycho-analytic theory were rationally organized it should be possible to refer to both these factors by symbols which were part of a system of reference that was applied uniformly and universally. The Kleinian theory of projective identification would be referred to by initials and a page and paragraph reference. Similarly, Freud's view of attention would be replaced by a reference. This can in fact be done, though clumsily, by reference to page and line of a standard edition even now. Such a statement could lend itself to mere manipulation, more or less ingenious, of symbols according to apparently arbitrary rules. Provided that the analyst preserves a sense of the factual background to which such a formulation refers, there are advantages in the exercise in precision and rigour of thought that is exacted by an attempt to concentrate actual clinical experience so that it may be expressed in such abstract notation. Further the analyst can see from an inspection of his formalizations which theories he is using and which he neglects. From evidence of neglect he could deduce either that his psychoanalytic armoury was becoming impoverished or that certain psychoanalytic theories were not in his experience standing up well to the test of clinical usefulness.

(*CWB IV*, pp. 306–307)

For example, if reference to transference is made by specific quotation it can be seen that the writer is claiming to use the term with meanings already established. If conscious anxiety about the analyst is said to be a factor in the transference it would be apparent that the writer had in mind some phenomenon not the same as that described by Freud in the passage to which reference is made.

(*CWB IV*, p. 308)

If the individual analyst built up for himself an anthology of working psycho-analytic theory on a foundation of a few good basic theories well understood and capable, individually and in combination, of covering a great many of the situations he might expect to meet, it might help the creation of a notation.

(*CWB IV*, p. 309)

The next quote repeats the last sentence and follows on from there.

[133]   L H K

If the individual analyst built up for himself an anthology of working psycho-analytic theory on a foundation of a few good basic theories well under-stood and capable, individually and in combination, of covering a great many of the situations he might expect to meet, it might help the creation of a notation. What follows is a sketch to indicate the lines along which progress could be made and which I have found helpful.

The feelings we know by the names "love" and "hate" would seem to be obvious choices if the criterion is basic emotion. Envy and Gratitude, Depression, Guilt, Anxiety, all occupy a dominant place in psychoanalytic theory and would seem with Sex to be choices to place with love and hate. In fact I prefer three factors I regard as intrinsic to the link between objects considered to be in relationship with each other. An emotional experience cannot be conceived of in isolation from a relationship. The basic relation-ships that I postulate are (1) X loves Y; (2) X hates Y; and (3) X knows Y. These links will be expressed by the signs L, H and K....

(CWB IV, p. 309)

Bion's example

Suppose an imaginary situation of a type with which an analyst is familiar; the patient Smith is talking freely and is co-operative and friendly; in the course of his associations he mentions that he knows a certain psycho-therapist, Jones, who is a very stupid man and knows virtually nothing about psychoanalysis. The patient knows him well and has good reason, he says, to dislike him. He once treated a friend of his, Mr May, with shocking results. His friend's marriage, which had always been harmonious until his friend took up treatment. . . . etc. Obviously this is a complex communication. There is a link between the patient and the analyst; there are various links between the patient and the psychotherapist, between patient and his friend, between the patient and his friend's analyst. For the link between the patient and analyst there is direct evidence. With regard to the patient's report of the other links the evidence is mostly indirect although the direct evidence which the session affords could be used, if thought desirable, to supplement the patient's own statements. The patient says he knows Jones. Is this to be recorded as Smith K Jones? He says he dislikes Jones. Should it be Smith H Jones? The patient says "his friend" Mr May. Should this then be Smith L May? Or is there some previous material in the analysis, or some manner or intonation that suggests a link, Smith L Mrs May? But perhaps there is some material that suggests there is a homosexual relationship between Smith and Mr May? There need be no end to the questions stimulated by an imaginary episode or limit to the number of answers for each question. But it is hardly less true to say just that about a real session. Yet on the answers to the questions, which the analyst begins to entertain, will depend his interpretation of the direct evidence of the nature of the transference....

(*CWB IV*, p. 310)

The analyst must allow himself to appreciate the complexity of the emotional experience he is required to illuminate and yet restrict his choice to these three links....

It will be seen that the use of HKL, to force the analyst to establish the "key" of the session is not the same as using it to record an emotional experience; that is to say it is a usage that provides a less than full account of what is known to have happened. But it introduces an element that must be an essential part of any recording system before that system can be regarded as satisfactory, namely the working tool.

(*CWB IV*, p. 311)

[134] The K link

As I propose to use it, it does not convey a sense of finality, a meaning that x is in possession of a piece of knowledge called y, but rather that x is in the state of getting to know y, and y is in a state of getting to be known by x.

(CWB IV, p. 314)

The question "How can x know anything?" expresses a feeling; it appears to be painful and to inhere in the emotional experience that I represent by x K y. An emotional experience that is felt to be painful may initiate an attempt either to evade or to modify the pain according to the capacity of the personality to tolerate frustration.

(CWB IV, p. 315)

K represents the link I have adumbrated: –K [minus K] represents the link constituted by NOT understanding, i.e. mis-understanding. The implications of this can best be grasped by noting that –L [minus love] is not the same as H, nor –H [minus hate] the same as L.

(CWB IV, p. 319)

Edna O'Shaughnessy

What does Bion mean by "thinking"? He does not mean some abstract mental process. His concern is with thinking as a human link – the endeavour to understand, comprehend the reality of, get insight into the nature of, etc., oneself or another. Thinking is an emotional experience of trying to know oneself or someone else. Bion designates this fundamental type of thinking – thinking in the sense of trying to know – by the symbol K. If xKy, then "x is in the state of getting to know y and y is in a state of getting to be known by x".

(O'Shaughnessy 1981, p. 181)

[135]   Hypochondriacal symptoms

Hypochondriacal symptoms may ... be signs of an attempt to establish contact with psychic quality by substituting physical sensation for the missing sense data of psychic quality.

(*CWB IV*, p. 320)

[136]   Poincaré

Bion: Poincaré describes the process of creation of a mathematical
             formulation thus:

Poincaré: "If a new result is to have any value, it must unite elements long
             since known, but till then scattered and seemingly foreign to
             each other, and suddenly introduce order where the appear-
             ance of disorder reigned. Then it enables us to see at a glance
             each of these elements in the place it occupies in the whole.
             Not only is the new fact valuable on its own account, but it
             alone gives a value to the old facts it unites. Our mind is frail
             as our senses are; it would lose itself in the complexity of the
             world if that complexity were not harmonious; like the short-
             sighted, it would only see the details, and would be obliged to
             forget each of these details before examining the next, because
             it would be incapable of taking in the whole. The only facts
             worthy of our attention are those which introduce order into
             this complexity and so make it accessible to us."

Bion: This description closely resembles the psychoanalytic theory
             of paranoid-schizoid and depressive positions adumbrated by
             Mrs. Klein. I have used the term "selected fact" to describe
             that which the psychoanalyst must experience in the process
             of synthesis.

1   H. Poincaré. *Science and Method* (Dover Publications), 1914.

(CWB IV, p. 339)

David Taylor

A sense of the complexity of Bion's evolving position regarding psychoanalysis as a scientific style of enterprise can be seen by looking at the
use he made of the ideas of the great French mathematician and philosopher of science, Henri Poincaré (1854–1912). Poincaré's influence upon
Bion's formulation of the idea of the selected fact is well known, and
this is repeatedly acknowledged by Bion. . . . However, the full extent
of Poincaré's influence upon Bion is less well appreciated and also less
clearly acknowledged. In Poincaré's approach to the nature of science,
Bion found a view which was sympathetic to his own sense of the matter. In addition to the notion that the scientific quality of a theory is to
be judged by the extent to which it unifies, simplifies and illuminates
otherwise disparate or incoherent facts, Poincaré specified the principles
to be used in the selection of facts. He thought that these must permit a

scientific description to go beyond brute facts to what he called the soul of the fact. By this he simply meant our understanding of the principle, the physical law, of the way that the thing in question might work. Poincaré also considered that the thing itself can never be known, that scientific theories can only ever be approximations, and that they can never be fully proven. The reader will realise how much versions of each of these positions can be found to run through Bion's thinking.

However, Poincaré argued strongly that these considerations do not imply that scientific truth is unascertainable. He reasoned that scientific truth, while always an approximation, aims to be as close an approximation as possible. It is established by the application of two complementary procedures. One of these is the testing of the predictions which a scientific theory makes possible and of the extrapolations that may follow from them. The other is the working out of a proof which involves the production and publication of an assessable line of reasoning – mathematical, logical, symbolic, semantic and so on – with a form and content appropriate to the discipline.

(Taylor 2011, pp. 1102–1103)

David Taylor goes on to argue that this rigour is no longer present in Bion's later work. This needs to be set, I think, against the fact that Bion is increasingly interested in his later work in the quality, depth and breadth of the clinical observations made by psychoanalysts - the basic building blocks of our scientific endeavour.

[137]   Observation and Interpretation: avoiding a harsh break in observation

The first requisite for the use of a theory is proper conditions for observation. The most important of these is psychoanalysis of the observer to ensure that he has reduced to a minimum his own inner tensions and resistances which otherwise obstruct his view of facts by making correlation by conscious and unconscious impossible. The next step is for the analyst to bring his attention to bear. Darwin pointed out that judgment obstructs observation. The psychoanalyst however must intervene with interpretations and this involves the exercise of judgment. A state of reverie conducive to alpha-function, obtrusion of the selected fact, and model-making together with an armoury limited to a few essential theories ensure that a harsh break in observation of the kind Darwin had in mind becomes less likely; interpretations can occur to the analyst with the minimum disturbance of observation.

(*CWB IV*, p. 352)

[138]   Less than six theories enough

If every analyst set himself the task of producing a handbook of psychoanalytic theories to provide a foundation of the minimum number of premises from which a wide range of subsidiary theories could be deduced, I believe it would be possible with less than six major theories. Psychoanalytic virtue lies not in the number of theories the analyst can command but the minimum number with which he can meet any contingency he is likely to meet.

(*CWB IV*, pp. 353–354)

In a later book, *Transformations*, we find the following list:

(1) The theory of projective identification and splitting; mechanisms by which the breast provides what the patient later takes over as his own apparatus for α-function.

(2) The theory that some personalities cannot tolerate frustration.

(3) The theory that a personality with a powerful endowment of envy tends to denude its objects by both stripping and exhaustion.

(4) The theory that at an early stage (or on a primitive level of mind) the oedipal situation is represented by part objects.

(5) The Kleinian theory of envy and greed.

(6) The theory that primitive thought springs from experience of a non-existent object, or, in other terms, of the *place* where the object is expected to be, but is not.

(7) The theory of violence in primitive functions.

... [T]hese theories, as extensions of the oedipal situation, must be present in the analyst's mind in a form that enables them to be represented in a wide range of grid categories.

(*CWB V*, pp. 171–172)

And from the International Seminars in his seventies:

There are plenty of people who will say "Don't you know the theories of psychoanalysis?", and I could say, "No I don't, although I have read them over and over again. I now feel that I only have the time to read the very, very best psychoanalytic theories – if only I knew what they were." However, that is what I would try to limit myself to.

(*CWB VII*, p. 131)

[139] Container–contained

5. Melanie Klein has described an aspect of projective identification concerned with the modification of infantile fears; the infant projects a part of its psyche, namely its bad feelings, into a good breast. Thence in due course they are removed and re-introjected. During their sojourn in the good breast they are felt to have been modified in such a way that the object that is re-introjected has become tolerable to the infant's psyche.

6. From the above theory I shall abstract for use as a model the idea of a container into which an object is projected and the object that can be projected into the container: the latter I shall designate by the term contained. The unsatisfactory nature of both terms points the need for further abstraction.

7. Container and contained are susceptible of conjunction and permeation by emotion. Thus conjoined or permeated or both they change in a manner usually described as growth. When disjoined or denuded of emotion they diminish in vitality, that is, approximate to inanimate objects. Both container and contained are models of abstract representations of psychoanalytic realizations.

(*CWB VI*, p. 356)

John Steiner

Another central issue, which I have always thought Bion glosses over, is the question of how it comes about that containment leads to psychic change. Caper uses Bion's model, which assumes that when patients feel understood and contained they not only gain relief from anxiety but also develop, in some unspecified way, a capacity for self-containment and understanding. Now, I think containment is necessary for this development, but it is not sufficient. A further stage is needed for patients to acquire or reacquire such a capacity. Indeed, it is a common clinical experience for patients to feel contained only as long as they believe they control and possess the analyst as an anxiety-relieving object. The additional stage must surely involve the relinquishing of omnipotent control over the object; in the ensuing process of mourning, lost elements and capacities are regained that previously had been projected.

(Steiner 2000, p. 642)

[140]   Minus container–contained (−♀♂) "Without-ness"

... it is necessary to consider −♀ [minus container] and −♂ [minus contained] and −(♀ ♂) [minus container–contained] in more detail. There are a number of peculiar features that are difficult to reconcile in a coherent theory. I shall accordingly describe them first without any attempt at explanation.

In the first place its predominant characteristic I can only describe as "without-ness". It is an internal object without an exterior. It is an alimentary canal without a body.

(CWB IV, p. 363)

Container–contained has the characteristic of "within-ness": something is put in to something else, something is taken in to something else. By contrast, "an alimentary canal without a body" is not *in* anything. Is "without-ness" an object that wishes to put itself in the position of being everything – not needing a body to be in, not having a body to feed?

Clinical note

An adolescent boy describes states of mind in which he is not asleep, not dreaming, and experiences "hallucinations". In some of the "hallucinations" he believes himself to have murdered someone, in others that someone is there to murder him. He is a highly functioning boy in his daily life.

A second patient is unusually afraid of violent horror films. She finds herself unable to differentiate between fiction and reality. At the same time, in actual reality she fails to spot potential dangers to herself and her loved objects and inadvertently places herself and her objects in danger. She is rather blind to the actual risk of violence, while overwhelmed by its fictional presentation in films. In relation to the analyst, she is not aware of having any feelings, while experiencing violent feelings towards others outside the analysis.

The third patient told me that while he had been knowingly riding too fast on his bike, he "imagined" that someone might open a car door unthinkingly, and he would crash into it and be hurled through the air across the road and then run over. Very badly injured, he would be in hospital. Would I come to see him?

The three clinical vignettes are examples in which violent feelings are not held "within" a container: in the first example not held within dream and sleep, in the second example not held within phantasy and the transference relation, in the third example not held within the patient's internal world and the mind of the analyst – possibly in an analogous way to what Bion is describing as "an alimentary canal without a body".

[141]   "Super" ego

The object that I described as being re-introjected as ♀♂ in K was one in which the relationship of the elements ♀ and ♂ was commensal. In –K it is envious and therefore it is necessary to consider –♀ and –♂ and – (♀♂) in more detail. There are a number of peculiar features that are difficult to reconcile in a coherent theory. I shall accordingly describe them first without any attempt at explanation. . . .

It is a super-ego that has hardly any of the characteristics of the super-ego as understood in psychoanalysis: it is "super" ego. It is an envious assertion of moral superiority without any morals. In short it is the resultant of an envious stripping or denudation of all good and is itself destined to continue the process of stripping. . . . The process of denudation continues till –♂ [minus contained] –♀ [minus container] represent hardly more than an empty superiority-inferiority that in turn degenerates to nullity.

In so far as its resemblance to the super-ego is concerned –(♀ ♂) [minus container–contained] shows itself as a superior object asserting its superiority by finding fault with everything. The most important characteristic is its hatred of any new development in the personality as if the new development were a rival to be destroyed.

(*CWB IV*, p. 363)

Edna O'Shaughnessy

The pathological superego also watches the ego from a "higher" place, but it is dissociated from ego functions like attention, enquiry, remembering, understanding. Mrs A's "O God", for example, is not trying to know; it is denuding and condemning me, and with violent projective identifications establishes a transference situation where she and I are relating as abnormal superego to abnormal superego – both extractors of worth and pointers at failure. Nor does Mr B's Sceptic of the Renaissance remember that a living development, a "renaissance" between patient and analyst occurred in the analysis, or enquire how it was that this renaissance came to be destroyed by a rush of erotised fantasies. It is full of hate and prejudice, sceptical of all renaissance; its aim is to destroy links within the self and between the self and its objects.

(O'Shaughnessy 1999, p. 868)

Clinical note

The patient had a high level of organisational skills and could draw people together to work as a group. What caused her much more anxiety was allowing herself to "think". Her thoughts were kept well back in the corners of her mind.

Her mother had been violent, as well as caring for her. As a child the patient was very "good", but this was not sufficient for her own protection. If a child's face showed anything that might cause the mother guilt when she was beating another child, that child would also be beaten. My patient seems to have stopped herself knowing what she thought so that nothing would show on her face. The learning problems this caused her were disguised by her becoming adept at memorising what she needed to know. The internalised threatening mother was joined together in her internal world with a threatening superego. She was painfully (but healthily) angry about how much time she had spent throughout her life appeasing this critical voice, which constantly intruded into her mind.

Chapter 10

The Grid

Introduction

Unlike most of the rest of the book, the quotes in this chapter are not presented chronologically but follow the layout of the Grid. The chapter includes quotes on the Grid from the whole of Bion's writings.

My colleague, Susan Lawrence, who read a first draft for me, described the book as being like a sandwich. It begins with biography and ends with Bion's novel. Both give a strong sense of Bion as a person and are accessible. Moving into the sandwich, she could grasp what was being said until she got to *The Grid* and *Elements of Psycho-Analysis*. Here was the meat in the sandwich, but it was not very understandable. Perhaps this area of Bion's work was intrinsically less suited to the format of quotes. Curiouser and curiouser, I realised that I had actually myself put in longer quotes, with less commentary where, in fact, they were needed most. When preparing the other quotes in the book, I had had my imaginary readers in mind in deciding what commentary was needed. In relation to the Grid, I had not done this and had to address myself to rectifying it.

It is possible, I think, that Bion may have been abstracting from the way his own mind actually worked in his design of the Grid – "gridifying" his own thinking. In his clinical accounts one can see him determining the level of development of the patient's communication and the use to which it is being put; his own openness (or defensiveness); and the way the patient and he "move" in relation to each other.

Bion in his later work expresses doubts about the Grid, and it has not been taken up to date in any substantial way except as a teaching tool for Bion's model of the mind: it may still be early days to know.

Ron Britton

I have often been asked whether it is worth pursuing an understanding of the grid. A detailed knowledge of the grid is certainly not necessary to understand Bion's major conceptual contributions such as the theories of thinking, containment and preconceptions, his development of Ps ⇌ D or his description of the nature of psychotic thinking, nor to grasp his ideas on psychoanalytic technique. However it is indispensable for a serious study of the development of his thinking just as it is necessary to know Freud's abandoned "Project for a scientific psychology" (1950 [1895]) if one wants to understand in depth his later theorising.

(Britton 1998, p. 818)

Introduction to the detail of the Grid

The Grid has a horizontal and a vertical axis. The vertical axis – the *rows* – are to do with the level of symbolic development of the analytic material being communicated between patient and analyst. I start the chapter with quotes about this as it contains the more familiar terms – beta-elements, alpha-function, alpha-elements, dreams and myths, pre-conceptions. Most primitive or rudimentary are the beta-elements (Row A) going through to the most abstract: algebraic calculus (Row H). I focus on the first three rows.

The horizontal axis – the *columns* – are to do with how something is being used: that is, is the material concerned designating an area to be explored (Column 1); or is it being used defensively (Column 2); is it to record (Column 3); is it attention (Column 4); or inquiry (Column 5); or is it an action (Column 6). I have been asked whether the uses are arranged along any particular continuum. I think they are, and this can be seen most clearly when Bion experiments with "mapping" the Oedipus myth onto the Grid. This, he thought, should be possible because the Oedipus myth and the Grid are both models of the human mind. Column 1 Bion links to the Oedipal oracle – "the description of the criminal who is wanted"; the middle columns are the to and fro of the ensuing story; Column 6 is where Bion locates the interpretation of what has been discovered.

The rows and the columns together divide up the area into small squares – for example, Dreams (Row C) crosses paths with all the columns. Dreams being used defensively would be located in C2: Row C (Dreams) and Column 2 (material used defensively). Hanna Segal gave a vivid example of such a situation in her description of a patient who brought her many dreams. On one occasion he brought a dream that threw light on the way he was using the dreams in the session. In the dream he was on a sledge crossing the frozen wastes. He was throwing chunks of meat off the back of the sledge to keep the chasing wolves at bay. Segal saw that he had been throwing his dreams at her – like the chunks of meat – to keep her at bay. I will end the Introduction with a comment from Bion, made in Los Angeles (1967).

After one's gotten fed up with feeling a perfect fool, and feeling that one really ought to do something about the patient, the tendency will be to reach for the nearest interpretation available to put an end to an intolerable situation and to what are really quite nasty feelings which have got a great deal of substance in them. Now this is the kind of thing which makes me feel we really need to consider the category of what is going on. (This is what I've tried to express in a book about the Grid.) What is a patient saying this for? What is he saying? What does he mean? If possible, what is the interpretation and why?

(LASS, pp. 63–64)

Quotes

The Rows:

142   Row A: Beta-elements
143   On the line between beta- and alpha-elements: "the blood spoke in her cheek"
144   Row B: Alpha elements
145   Row C: Dream thoughts, dreams, myths – dream thoughts
146   Row C: Dream thoughts, dreams, myths – dreaming along
147   Row C: Dream thoughts, dreams, myths – Myths
148   Row D: Pre-conception

The Columns:

149   Column 1: The description of the criminal who is wanted
150   Column 1: The infant cannot tolerate weaning because dominated by loss of the breast
151   Column 2: Tiresias
152   Column 2: No-emotion
153   Columns 3, 4, 5: Notation, Attention, Inquiry
154   Column 6: Action
155   Uses of the Grid

THE GRID

	Defini-tory Hypo-theses 1	ψ 2	Nota-tion 3	Atten-tion 4	Inquiry 5	Action 6	...n
A β-elements	A1	A2				A6	
B α-elements	B1	B2	B3	B4	B5	B6	...Bn
C Dream Thoughts Dreams, Myths	C1	C2	C3	C4	C5	C6	...Cn
D Pre-conception	D1	D2	D3	D4	D5	D6	...Dn
E Conception	E1	E2	E3	E4	E5	E6	...En
F Concept	F1	F2	F3	F4	F5	F6	...Fn
G Scientific Deductive System		G2					
H Algebraic Calculus							

[142]   Row A: Beta-elements

From *Elements of Psycho-Analysis*

1. β-elements. This term represents the earliest matrix from which thoughts can be supposed to arise. It partakes of the quality of inanimate object and psychic object without any form of distinction between the two. Thoughts are things, things are thoughts; and they have personality.

(*CWB V*, p. 23)

We go first to the rows, labelled down the side of the Grid and to do with levels of development. The first row contain the beta-elements. To reiterate, the term "beta-element" is used by Bion to designate the raw stuff of experience before it has been digested. Beta-elements can also result from an attack on alpha-function – or a regression from alpha-function. Bion goes on to say that at the level of beta-elements we don't differentiate between inanimate and animate objects. One example he gives is a psychotic patient's replacement of references to people, by references to places. Another example is the hallucination of voices from material objects.

A key point about beta-elements is that they cannot be used in thought until transformed into alpha-elements. They can only be used in projection. On them we also depend for our "emergency" system of evacuating unbearable affect.

Larry Brown

Larry Brown has drawn attention to an example from Bion himself in the war.

Bion felt sick. He wanted to time think. . . . He tried to think. (*War Memoirs*, "Amiens" [*CWB III*, pp. 252–253])

This "bombardment" by sensory fragments reduced Bion to vomiting in order to evacuate the sensory overload and must also have taught him, in retrospect, how the desperate mind madly discharges experience that cannot be abstracted.

(Brown 2012, p. 1200)

Thomas Ogden: A clinical example of beta-element functioning

Ms C spoke rapidly, jumping from topic to topic, each of which concerned a specific aspect of the "organisation of her life" (a term she and I used to refer to her operational thinking and behaviour). She told me how long she had jogged that morning, whom she had met in the elevator of her apartment building on the way to and from the run, and so on. Early on, I had interpreted both the content and the process – so far as I thought I understood them – of such recountings of the seemingly inexhaustible minutiae of her life.

Ms C's unceasing verbiage – seemingly impervious to interpretation – had engendered in me, during the first years of the analysis, feelings of helplessness, anger and claustrophobic fear (for example, feelings of being suffocated or of drowning). . . . Ms C's non-stop verbiage had had the effect of disrupting my capacity to make use of my reverie experience (which is central to my being able to do the psychological work necessary to "catch the drift" (Freud 1923, p. 239) of what is happening at an unconscious level in the analytic relationship). . . . In a sense, in the analysis with Ms C, I was experiencing chronic reverie-deprivation which, like sleep deprivation, can precipitate a psychosis. The countertransference psychosis allowed me to experience first-hand something like the patient's psychotic experience of not being able to dream (either while asleep or unconsciously while awake).

(Ogden 2003, pp. 24–28)

[143]   On the line between beta- and alpha-elements: "the blood spoke in her cheek"

From *Brazilian Lectures: "1973 São Paulo"*

> The poet Donne has written "the blood spoke in her cheek ... as if her body thought". This expresses exactly that intervening stage which in the Grid is portrayed on paper as a line separating beta-elements from alpha-elements. Note that I am not saying that it is either beta or alpha but the line *separating the two* which is represented by the poet's words. The practising analyst has to be sensitive while the conversation is taking place to what is taking place ... a situation of change from something which is not thought at all to something which is thought.
>
> (*CWB VII*, p. 44)

We might assume that anything physical is a beta-element. My own view is that the body – like the mind – has both beta- and alpha-functioning. The sexuality of the body, for example, may deepen through experience (alpha-function) or, conversely, may be used evacuatively in the avoidance of pain (beta).

On Bion's reference to Donne's poem, see also:

> "Her pure and eloquent blood
> Spoke in her cheeks, and so distinctly wrought,
> That one might almost say, her body thought."

> Or, putting it differently, the analyst needs to be able to listen not only to the words but also to the music, so that he can hear a remark which is not easily translated into black marks on paper, which has a different meaning when it is made in tones of sarcasm, or in terms of affection or understanding, or by a person who has actual experience of authority – though the words might be the same in each instance.
>
> (*CWB X*, p. 140)

And in his later *A Key to A Memoir of the Future*:

> **blush** "Her pure and eloquent blood spoke in her cheeks . . .", John Donne, The Second Anniversary; *his description of a physical reaction suggesting that the body itself might think cannot be bettered.* Similarly, "unscientific" traces can be discerned in the survival of terms like "rhinencephalon". These "survivals" should be regarded with respect by psychoanalysts concerned with patients who are sensitive about their noses and their watery productions.

Even physiologically there are traces in the "extra-cellular fluid" unpolluted by salt and other chemicals, as are the oceans. Only psychoanalytic observation is likely to unveil the relationship between post-natal and pre-natal mentation.

(*CWB XIV*, p. 154; emphasis added)

Bion and poetry

On hearing of the central importance poetry held in Bion's life and his plan to compile an anthology of poems, Annie Reiner recalled an incident in Beverly Hills in the 1970s. There was a bookshop in the area where both she and Bion had their consulting rooms. It was small and dusty and had an equally dusty-looking proprietor, who never looked up and rarely spoke. She bought from him all of Bion's books, including first editions of the slender hardbound copies of *Learning From Experience* and *Elements of Psycho-Analysis*. As she paid, the usually curmudgeonly proprietor commented on her interest in Bion's work. He was obviously impressed by Bion, and, perhaps with a bit of pride, he added: "He comes in here all the time, mostly to buy poetry" (Reiner 2013).

Clinical note

When the patient first walked in to my room, I was struck by the rigid way she moved. In our early meetings I could see that she was preoccupied with regulating her physical state – always worried about whether she going to be too hot or too cold, too tired, too hungry or too full. She was also worried – frightened – about any physical ailment or even blemish. Her body had to be perfect. She spoke of sex as something that she wished she were very good at, but didn't really enjoy. Over time, we began to see the emergence of a more libidinal body. A man at work was paying her attention, and she began to look more alive and trendily glamorous. She went on a date with him and woke feeling hot in the night. She didn't associate the heat with her date, but I thought it was a rudimentary excited sensation, which could be linked with a rudimentary psychic representation. A "meeting place between something which is not thought at all to something which is thought".

John Donne: Although his dates are 1572–1631, the poet John Donne's prose began to be noticed around the same time that Bion was fighting in the First World War. Donne became "a cult figure" in the 1920s and 1930s when T. S. Eliot and others took up his poetry.

[144]   Row B: Alpha-elements

From *Elements of Psycho-Analysis*

2. α-elements. This term represents the outcome of work done by α-function on sense impressions. They are not objects in the world of external reality but are products of work done on the sensa believed to relate to such realities. They make possible the formation and use of dream thoughts.

(*CWB V*, p. 23)

Alpha-function transforms beta-elements into alpha-elements. One example Bion gives is that of Vermeer:

24 February 1960
    ... the artist helps the non-artist to digest, say, the Little Street in Delft by doing α-work on his sense impressions and "publishing" the result so that others who could not "dream" the Little Street itself can now digest the published α-work of someone who could digest it. Vermeer was able to digest the facts in a particular way, or perhaps they were particular facts. The same presumably is true of the scientist. But why did the work done by Aristarchus not have any impact for close on two thousand years? And why did Kepler's work succeed relatively quickly? It may be that it was less a matter of concern at the time of Aristarchus. Is opposition necessary? Must the reality view be opposed before it can flourish?

(*CWB XI*, pp. 139–140)

And again, on Vermeer:

If Vermeer can paint the little street in Delft, and if people can look at it, then they will never see a street in the same way again. The painter has brought about a change in the individual which makes it possible for him to see a truth that he has never seen before.

(*CWB VII*, p. 62)

Jan Vermeer (1632–1675): Dutch painter of extraordinary virtuosity in the degree of detail and precision he employed to render the scenes of middle-class life he was commissioned to paint. He was not much appreciated, however, in his own lifetime, leaving just over 30 paintings to posterity when he died, and his family destitute. The painting to which Bion refers, *The Little Street*, is a depiction of a seventeenth-century gabled red-brick house in Delft, seen from the street. A woman sits in the doorway, doing her sewing; two figures kneel on the street outside, and another woman, seen side-on, leans over a barrel of washing in the alleyway next door.

Aristarchus of Samos (c. 310 – c. 230 BC): Ancient Greek mathematician and astronomer, was the first person to declare himself for the heliocentric world view – that is, to argue that the Earth goes around the Sun (and not the other way round). He also theorised that the other stars he could see were suns just like ours, but much further away. He could not be proved right until the invention of the telescope.

Johannes Kepler (1571–1630): German mathematician and astronomer whose work on the planetary laws of motion provided an important plank in Isaac Newton's discoveries of the laws of gravity. He also contributed to the early science of optics, inventing an improved version of the refracting telescope, which his contemporary, Galileo Galilei, employed. His ideas on astronomy paved the way for the subject to be seen as part of a universal mathematical physics, as he improved on Nicolaus Copernicus's heliocentric theory by explaining how the planets' speeds varied due to their elliptical rather than circular orbits.

[145]   Row C: Dream thoughts, dreams, myths – dream thoughts

From *Elements of Psycho-Analysis*

3.   Dream thoughts. These depend on the prior existence of β- and α-elements: otherwise they require no elaboration beyond that which they have received in classical psychoanalytic theory. They are communicated by the manifest content of the dream but remain latent unless the manifest content is translated into more sophisticated terms.

With dreams one reaches a realm in which there is direct evidence of the phenomena with which one has to deal.

(CWB V, pp. 23–24)

In a recent collection of papers on Bion (Mawson 2011), "Section III – Mainly Clinical" begins with two authoritative papers: the first, by the Italian analyst Antonio Ferro, on the "Clinical Implications of Bion's Thought" and the second by the British analyst Edna O'Shaughnessy, "Relating to the Superego". Ferro describes Bion's psychoanalytic approach thus:

> The focus is no longer on a psychoanalysis that aims to remove the veil of repression or to promote integration of split-off objects, but on a psychoanalysis interested in the development of the tools that allow the development and creation of thought – that is, the mental apparatus for dreaming, feeling and thinking.
>
> (Ferro 2011, p. 156)

The O'Shaughnessy paper is a classic paper in the Kleinian tradition of taking up the omnipotent aspect of the patient's functioning in the detail of the here and now. The difference between the two papers is striking. It cannot be wholly accounted for in terms of different kinds of patients, nor only in terms of a differentiation between earlier and later Bion. A principal foundation of Bion's thought is the distinction between the procedures designed to evade frustration and those designed to modify it. Do Ferro and O'Shaughnessy focus, respectively, on these opposite poles: O'Shaughnessy on her patient's evasion of reality and Ferro on the modification of his patient's contact with reality through the development of the patient's capacity to "dream"?

Antonino Ferro

I see that my technique is very close to row C of the grid. . . .
    If one is somewhere along row C, there is always the possibility of "dreaming" or "visualizing other possibilities with the eyes of the mind or the alpha-function". . . .

Luigi and the rifle: dreaming the symptom

Luigi is a severely obsessional librarian. At our very first interview, he says he has a father with an aortic aneurysm and a paralysed uncle. (This suggests to me two different forms of functioning in the patient, one incontinent and the other that immobilizes him, as in his obsessive rituals.) He goes on to tell me how he spends ages "cleaning", "sweeping", and tidying up the garden lawn, where animals sometimes dig "holes".

In this ritual-filled world (the rituals being practised both at work and at bedtime) he seems to have one area of freedom: his hobby of hunting. He has to look after two dogs, clean his guns, and organize the various hunts. He goes on to describe his grandfather's terrible experience during the war when he found that his house had been destroyed by a bomber, killing his entire family. He then returns to the subject of his highly complex cleaning rituals (meanwhile I cannot help associating the hunting with the bomber [the Italian word caccia means both] and the death of his whole family).

In the next session he refers to Mario Tobino's famous book *Le libere donne di Magliano*, about women patients in a mental hospital (introducing the subject of madness?), and then mentions an inexplicable tic: whenever he feels tense, he raises his right shoulder and moves it backwards. A friend tells him it looks like he is "signalling a jack to his partner in [the card game of] *briscola*". He then launches into a long account in which the words "funeral" and "hunting [*caccia*] rifle" constantly recur.

At this point everything comes together in my mind, like a jigsaw with the pieces previously scattered higgledy-piggledy. The raising and backward movement of the right shoulder is precisely the effect of the "recoil" of a rifle: Luigi is a kind of killer, who constantly eliminates anyone who makes him feel tense. We cannot see the rifle, but what remains is the recoil, the cleaning rituals after every crime, the holes dug in the garden so as not to leave any trace of the buried bodies. When the rage is at fever pitch, he takes off in his bomber (*caccia*) and kills everyone in sight.

So here we have the dream that I was able to dream on his behalf. We now need to observe the development of these themes together: we shall see the Quentin Tarantino function and shall then have to decide what to do with this Django Unchained, dressed as a well brought-up librarian.

(Ferro 2015, pp. 192–195)

[146]   Row C: Dream thoughts, dreams, myths – dreaming along

From *Cogitations*

29 September 1959

Drowsiness is coming to me; it is part of the relaxation I have to achieve if my ideas are to be accessible. I must *dream* along, but then I risk going fast asleep. I have had to shut my eyes because they sting. Then I nearly went to sleep. "Watch the wall my darling, while the Gentlemen go by." [Rudyard Kipling, "A Smuggler's Song".] A smuggling process I must not know anything about. A wrapping up and packing of the goods I wish to remove from the environment. Does this mean that   [alpha-function] is to *hide* things from the conscious? If so, it is nearer to Freud's view of dream-work. The conscious is the servant of the unconscious. It is the conscious whose job it is to lie and deceive and protect the unconscious in its activities.

(*CWB XI*, p. 83)

Rudyard Kipling (1865–1936)

"A Smuggler's Song"

IF you wake at midnight, and hear a horse's feet,
Don't go drawing back the blind, or looking in the street,
Them that ask no questions isn't told a lie.
Watch the wall my darling while the Gentlemen go by.

Five and twenty ponies,
Trotting through the dark –
Brandy for the Parson,
"Baccy for the Clerk.
Laces for a lady; letters for a spy,
Watch the wall my darling while the Gentlemen go by!
Running round the woodlump if you chance to find
Little barrels, roped and tarred, all full of brandy-wine,
Don't you shout to come and look, nor use "em for your play.
Put the brishwood back again – and they'll be gone next day!

If you see the stable-door setting open wide;
If you see a tired horse lying down inside;
If your mother mends a coat cut about and tore;
If the lining's wet and warm – don't you ask no more!

If you meet King George's men, dressed in blue and red,
You be careful what you say, and mindful what is said.
If they call you " pretty maid", and chuck you "neath the chin,
Don't you tell where no one is, nor yet where no one's been!
Knocks and footsteps round the house – whistles after dark –
You've no call for running out till the house-dogs bark.
Trusty's here, and Pincher's here, and see how dumb they lie
They don't fret to follow when the Gentlemen go by!

"If You do as you've been told, "likely there's a chance,
You'll be give a dainty doll, all the way from France,
With a cap of Valenciennes, and a velvet hood –
A present from the Gentlemen, along "o being good!

Five and twenty ponies, Trotting through the dark –
Brandy for the Parson, "Baccy for the Clerk.
Them that asks no questions isn't told a lie –
Watch the wall my darling while the Gentlemen go by!
                                        (Kipling 1906)

Kipling's son Jack also fought in the First World War. Jack was killed.

[147]   Row C: Dream thoughts, dreams, myths – myths

From *Elements of Psycho-Analysis*

The myths (Row C of the Grid) provide a succinct statement of psycho-analytic theories which are relevant in aiding the analyst both to perceive growth and to achieve interpretations that illuminate aspects of the patient's problems that belong to growth.

(*CWB V*, p. 54)

Clinical note: an example of associating to myth in a clinical context

The patient (P) presented a view of herself as positively opening up her curiosity and her sexuality to new experiences. It seemed the analyst was either to be encouraging or to be experienced as a repressive force.

P had a dream (of which only a skeleton report was given). In the dream P was out having a meal with the analyst. The atmosphere was one of excitement and sexual involvement. They decided to go on somewhere else to have coffee/drinks, not wanting the evening to end. P said the dream was about her erotic transference to the analyst, which she believed the analyst did not want to know about.

She said she didn't have any associations and moved on quickly to another topic, as if there were nothing more to be known. The analyst drew attention to this, and an unexpected thought then came to P. If her analyst was having a sexual relationship with her, it would bring the analyst into disrepute. At the time of the dream, there was other material that gave weight to a wish to bring the analyst into disrepute.

Further to this, in the dream there is to be no experience of an absence – the analyst does not have a separate personal life – nor is there to be an end to the evening.

The patient's view has been that the analyst has not allowed the emergence of the erotic transference. The patient experiences the analyst as being like a vengeful god crushing her emerging sexuality. The analyst considers that the patient may wish to locate herself in – even destroy – the analyst's private world. The two views have some analogy to the two views of the Tower of Babel presented by Bion. In the first view the destruction of the tower is caused by a jealous and vengeful god (the patient's view of an analyst jealous of the patient's emerging sexuality). In the second version the tower of Babel is understood to be the people's omnisciently putting themselves in the place of god.

[148]   Row D: Pre-conception

From *Elements of Psycho-Analysis*

4.   The pre-conception. This corresponds to a state of expectation. It is a state of mind adapted to receive a restricted range of phenomena. An early occurrence might be an infant's expectation of the breast. The mating of pre-conception and realization brings into being the conception.

(CWB V, p. 24)

Bion also differentiates between:

Preconception and Pre-conception

Lest it seems confusing to use the term preconception as something to be distinguished from a scientific deductive system and then speak of an analytic theory as an analyst's preconception I shall use the term pre-conception to distinguish it from a preconception. Pre-conception, as I have placed it in row D of the grid, is a term representing a stage in the development of thinking; preconception, in the sense of the analyst's theoretical preconceptions refers to the use of a theory and so belongs to columns 3 and 4 of the grid.

(CWB V, p. 64)

The following rows in the Grid are:

5.   The conception. The conception may be regarded as a variable that has been replaced by a constant. If we represent the pre-conception by $\psi(\xi)$ with (ξ) as the unsaturated element, then from the realization with which the pre-conception mates there is derived that which replaces (ξ) by a constant. The conception can however then be employed as a preconception in that it can express an expectation. The mating of $\psi(\xi)$ with the with the realization satisfies the expectation but enlarges the capacity of $\psi(\xi)$ for further saturation.

6.   The concept is derived from the conception by a process designed to render it free of those elements that would unfit it to be a tool in the elucidation or expression of truth. ....

7.   The scientific deductive system. In this context the term "scientific deductive system" means a combination of concepts in hypotheses and systems of hypotheses so that they are logically related to each other. ....

8.   Calculi. The scientific deductive system may be represented by an algebraic calculus. ....

(CWB V, pp. 24–25)

[149]   Column 1: The description of the criminal who is wanted

From *Elements of Psycho-Analysis*

1.   The pronouncement of the oracle defines the theme of the story and can be regarded as a definition, or definitory hypothesis. It resembles a preconception, or an algebraic calculus, in that it is an "unsaturated statement" that is "saturated" by the unfolding of the story; or an "unknown", in the mathematical sense, that is "satisfied" by the story. It is the statement of the theme of the story that is to unfold; the description of the criminal who is wanted.

(*CWB V*, p. 44)

We turn now to the columns of the Grid, named along the horizontal axis.

Bion tried mapping the characters in the Oedipus myth onto the columns of the Grid. He thought that the Oedipus myth was more than a content of the mind (a story remembered in the mind), and carried essential information about the nature of the mind itself. If both the myth and the Grid are understood to carry essential information about how the mind works, it makes sense to see whether the myth can be "mapped" onto the Grid. I am going to use what he says about the characters in the Oedipus myth to present the columns of the Grid, as it is perhaps a more vivid way to approach it.

Col. 1 is Definitory Hypothesis. We might expect a definition to be the end of a process and to be saturated (full) in the sense of being the final word about what something is. Bion, however, wants to put it at the beginning. The definitory hypothesis is the pronouncement of the oracle . . . the description of the criminal who is wanted. The key point is that anything belonging in this column is "unsaturated": the oracle has yet to be fulfilled. The baby's scream gives the mother the chance of finding "the criminal who is wanted" – finding what is actually making the baby scream.

I was surprised to come across references to Col. 1 in Bion's work on "eschewing memory and desire". The discipline of "memory and desire" is looked at in detail in the chapters on Bion's later work; suffice it to say here that it includes actively recognising and attempting to put aside preconceived ideas that could colour one's observations. Would this not include "oracles"? Betty Joseph said that this column was the one aspect of the Grid that did not make sense to her (personal communication).

A second surprise is that Bion describes the activity of Col. 1 as painful. Why should having a definition be painful? – One might expect it to be a comfortable state of mind in which we know where we are. This, however, would be the holding of definitions as possessions one can accumulate. Bion, by contrast, emphasises how the definitory hypothesis exposes us to what we do not know and the loss of what is not named by it. He describes a state of mind that is not comfortably adding to its store of definitions but is painfully aware of what he calls "the negative dimension". Talking about "not knowing" and "being in ignorance" can become rather a cliché. By contrast, I think Bion's state of mind when seeing patients was more aware of "not knowing" than we usually are.

From *Transformations*

> I use these formulations to express, in exaggerated form, the pain which is involved in achieving the state of naivety inseparable from binding or definition (col. 1). Any naming of a constant conjunction involves admission of the negative dimension and is opposed by the fear of ignorance. Therefore at the outset there is a tendency to precocious advance, that is, to a formulation which is a col. 2 formulation intended to deny ignorance – the dark night of the senses.
>
> (*CWBV*, p. 269)

The oracle in the Oedipus myth

From the oracle at Delphi, Oedipus learns of the prophecy that he will end up killing his father and marrying his mother. Believing he is fated to murder his adoptive father, Polybus, and marry his adoptive mother, Merope, he tries to avoid the inevitable and flees to Thebes. During the journey, at a crossroads, he has a quarrel with a stranger, an older man, and kills him (this was his father Laius). On reaching Thebes, he discovers that the city is being ravaged by a monster, the Sphinx, and he discovers that the person who can solve the Sphinx's riddle and lay it to rest will inherit the throne of Thebes and the hand of the Queen, who is, unbeknownst to him, his own mother Jocasta.

Some years later, a plague has cast its pall over Thebes, which can only be lifted if the culprit responsible for killing its former king, Laius, can be found. Oedipus discovers to his horror that it was he. When Jocasta realizes that she has married (and had children with) her own son, she hangs herself. Oedipus then seizes two pins from her dress and blinds himself with them.

The oracle is of something that has not yet happened (Bion calls it "unsaturated"). When Oedipus kills his father and marries his mother, it becomes saturated – the prediction has been matched with the actual experience of it happening.

[150]   Column 1: The infant cannot tolerate weaning because dominated by loss of the breast

From *Attention and Interpretation*

Any definitory hypothesis, be it exclamation, name, theoretical system, or extended statement such as a book, has, and has always been recognized to have a negative function. It must always imply that something *is*; equally it implies that something is *not*. It is therefore open to the recipient to infer one or other according to his temper. . . . A model would be the infant who cannot tolerate weaning because it is dominated by the *loss* of the breast and who therefore cannot accept what it might have instead. The patient cannot tolerate the definitory hypothesis and therefore does not achieve the pre-conception.

(*CWB VI*, pp. 233–234)

[151]   Column 2: Tiresias

From *Elements of Psycho-Analysis*

> Tiresias may be regarded as representing the hypothesis, known to be false, that is maintained to act as a barrier against the anxiety anticipated as a concomitant of any hypothesis or theory that might take its place.
>
> (*CWB V*, p. 44)

Bion includes in Col. 2 all the defensive manoeuvres (of patient or analyst) that are aimed at preventing the emergence of a more accurate but more frightening idea (*CWB V*, p. 67), including:

> Statements representing the realization in such a way that the analyst's anxiety that the situation is unknown and correspondingly dangerous to him, is denied by an interpretation intended to prove to himself and the patient that this is not so. Any practising analyst appreciates that this state of affairs belongs to the domain of counter-transference and indicates analysis for the analyst. But as even analysts cannot have all the analysis they may consider desirable the theory used as a barrier against the unknown will remain in the armoury of analyst as well as patient.
>
> (*CWB V*, p. 20)

In what he calls a psychoanalytic game, Bion suggests that the analyst might take an interpretation he has been satisfied with, and put it into Col. 2.

> and then ask himself what the interpretation, correct though it may be, would be excluding. The analyst can set himself similar exercises not as a mere tax on his ingenuity but as a method of exercising and developing his capacity for intuition.
>
> (*CWB V*, p. 114)

Bion is concerned that unacknowledged fear or anxiety in the analyst stemming from archaic areas in himself and possibly induced by the patient may lead the analyst to interpret in a defensive way – including interpretations that make the patient responsible or blame him.

Parthenope Bion Talamo

"Stop it" interpretations

In my early days as an analyst, I coined the phrase (in my own private language for thinking about my work in): "stop it" interpretations. This referred to those which made the patient suddenly "dry up", in an unpleasant fashion as though they had been shamed or bullied into silence, and I think that they had a lot to do with my own unconscious counter-transference. Analytical practice and attempts at putting into practice the discipline advocated by Bion "without memory and desire" have greatly improved this slight tendency on my part, which was certainly an attack on both the patient's and my own curiosity.

(Bion Talamo 2011, pp. 577–578)

Some questions about Column 2

1   Bion names the column with the 23rd letter of the Greek alphabet Ψ. This letter is used in various different disciplines, including physics, but also stands for psychology or psychiatry. It is not clear why it is used here.
2   As a newly qualified analyst, I presented some clinical material for André Green's "Masterclass" for the British Psychoanalytical Society. In my introduction to the patient, I said I thought she had a feel for the truth. André Green stood up and said, "We all lie all the time." Taken aback, I wondered if having "truth" and Col. 2 as turning a blind eye to the "truth" as main categories in how I thought about the mind was possibly a very British affair.
3   Tiresias is a more complex character than he is given credit for!

Tiresias

Tiresias in "Oedipus Rex"

In Sophocles' play "Oedipus Rex", King Oedipus asks Tiresias, the blind seer, to help him to end a plague destroying his city of Thebes by finding Laius' killer. (Laius was the former king of Thebes who turned out to be Oedipus' estranged father). Tiresias does not want to tell Oedipus the truth, for obvious reasons, and asks to be sent home. Experiencing Tiresias' reticence as deliberate thwarting, he insults the seer and eventually accuses him of plotting to kill Laius. At this, Tiresias loses his temper and declares Oedipus need look no further than the mirror to find Laius' killer, and that he is guilty of even worse than parricide. Oedipus mocks Tiresias's blindness and calls him a false prophet. But Tiresias retorts that Oedipus is the blind one: blind to the corrupt details of his own life. As the men continue to argue, Tiresias prophesies that Oedipus will know who his parents are by the end of the day, and that this knowledge will destroy him. He leaves with a riddle: the killer of Laius is a native Theban who many think is a foreigner; he will soon be blind; he is both brother and father to his children; he killed his own father. The criminal being described (Column 1) will turn out to be Oedipus himself.

His rather unexpected background given his reputation for **not** *wanting to see.*

As a young man, Tiresias had come upon two snakes mating. Rather than turning away, he had attacked them. The goddess Hera punished him by turning him into a woman (he was later changed back). In one story he was blinded when he came upon Athene bathing in a lake and found himself unable to turn away. Athene later attempted, but was unable to restore, his sight, and she gave him the gift of prophecy instead. In a second story Zeus and Hera are debating whether men or women have the most pleasure during sex. Given that Tiresias has been both man and woman, they consult him. Tiresias says it is the woman. This gets him attacked by Hera, who blinds him, but he is given the gift of prophesy by Zeus.

[152]   Column 2: No-emotion

From *Attention and Interpretation*

The patient feels the pain of an absence of fulfilment of his desires. The absent fulfilment is experienced as a "no-thing". The emotion aroused by the "no-thing" is felt as indistinguishable from the "no-thing". The emotion is replaced by a "no-emotion". In practice this can mean no feeling at all, or an emotion, such as rage, which is a column 2 emotion, that is, an emotion of which the fundamental function is denial of another emotion.

(*CWB VI*, pp. 236–237)

Clinical note

As a young child the patient had felt utterly unbearably oedipally enraged and betrayed and had never recovered from this. This event seemed to have vanquished all other feelings, including love, and the patient was left overly reliant on his mind in place of his feelings. The only feeling he was aware of was a constant underlying irritability, from which he had no rest. He said that the only feeling he had was anger. I think this can be helpfully understood as a Col. 2 emotion fending off a greater complexity of more vulnerable feelings.

[153]   Columns 3, 4, 5: Notation, Attention, Inquiry

From *Elements of Psycho-Analysis*

3. The myth as a whole may be taken as the record of a realization and therefore to fulfil the function Freud attributed to notation.
4. The Sphinx stimulates curiosity and threatens death as the penalty for failure to satisfy it. It can represent the function Freud attributed to attention, but it implies a threat against the curiosity it stimulates.
5. Oedipus represents the triumph of determined curiosity over intimidation and may thus be used as a symbol for scientific integrity – the investigatory tool.

(*CWB V*, p. 44)

Col. 5 was originally called the "Oedipus" column, this then being changed to "Inquiry". Bion's Col. 3, "Notation" and Col. 4, "Attention", take up Freud's "Formulations on the Two Principles of Mental Functioning" (1911) (the most quoted of Freud's papers by Kleinian analysts).

Sigmund Freud

I shall be returning to lines of thought which I have developed elsewhere when I suggest that the state of psychical rest was originally disturbed by the peremptory demands of internal needs. When this happened, whatever was thought of (wished for) was simply presented in a hallucinatory manner, just as still happens to-day with our dream-thoughts every night. It was only the non-occurrence of the expected satisfaction, the disappointment experienced, that led to the abandonment of this attempt at satisfaction by means of hallucination. Instead of it, the psychical apparatus had to decide to form a conception of the real circumstances in the external world and to endeavour to make a real alteration in them. A new principle of mental functioning was thus introduced; what was presented in the mind was no longer what was agreeable but what was real, even if it happened to be disagreeable. This setting-up of the reality principle proved to be a momentous step.

In the first place, the new demands made a succession of adaptations necessary in the psychical apparatus, which; owing to our insufficient or uncertain knowledge, we can only retail very cursorily.

The increased significance of external reality heightened the importance, too, of the sense-organs that are directed towards that external world, and of the consciousness attached to them. Consciousness now learned to comprehend sensory qualities in addition to the qualities of pleasure and unpleasure which hitherto had alone been of interest to it. A special function was instituted which had periodically to search the external world, in order that its data might be familiar already if an urgent internal need should arise – the function of *attention (1)*. Its activity meets the sense-impressions half way, instead of awaiting their appearance. At the same time, probably, a system of *notation* was introduced, whose task it was to lay down the results of this periodical activity of consciousness – a part of what we call memory.

The place of repression, which excluded from cathexis as productive of unpleasure some of the emerging ideas, was taken by an impartial passing of judgement, which had to decide whether a given idea was true or false – that is, whether it was in agreement with reality or not – the decision being determined by making a comparison with the memory-traces of reality.

A new function was now allotted to motor discharge, which, under the dominance of the pleasure principle, had served as a means of unburdening the mental apparatus of accretions of stimuli, and which had carried out this task by sending innervations into the interior of the body (leading to expressive movements and the play of features and to manifestations of affect). Motor discharge was now employed in the appropriate alteration of reality; it was converted into action.

Restraint upon motor discharge (upon action), which then became necessary, was provided by means of the process of thinking, which was developed from the presentation of ideas. Thinking was endowed with characteristics which made it possible for the mental apparatus to tolerate an increased tension of stimulus while the process of discharge was postponed. It is essentially an experimental kind of acting, accompanied by displacement of relatively small quantities of cathexis together with less expenditure (discharge) of them. For this purpose the conversion of freely displaceable cathexes into "bound" cathexes was necessary, and this was brought about by means of raising the level of the whole cathectic process. It is probable that thinking was originally unconscious, in so far as it went beyond mere ideational presentations and was directed to the relations between impressions of objects, and that it did not acquire further qualities, perceptible to consciousness, until it became bound to verbal residues.

(Freud 1911, pp. 219–221; emphasis added)

[154]   Column 6: Action

From *Elements of Psycho-Analysis*

In this, the last category that I propose to distinguish, the statement, though still embodied in a representation identical with those employed in all the other statements, is used as an operator. The intention is primarily that the communication will enable the patient to effect solutions of his problems of development. (The patient of course can use it to effect solutions of his problems rather than solutions of his problems of development, that is, he can use the interpretation as advice not interpretation, but it is not here my intention to discuss these and other responses of the patient.) Functions of interpretations that fall in this category, and therefore the interpretations in this one of their aspects, are analogous to *actions* in other forms of human endeavour. For the analyst the transition that comes nearest to that of deci-sion and translation of thought into action is the transition from thought to verbal formulations of category 6.... it is clear that activities of this category are those in which the sense of loneliness and isolation are most likely to be in evidence.

(*CWB V*, p. 21)

[155]   Uses of the Grid

From *Elements of Psycho-Analysis*

I turn now to uses of the grid. The summary is not intended to be exhaustive.

A. Meditative Review

1.   Suppose that at the end of the day's work the analyst wishes to review some aspect of his work about which he is doubtful. Assume further that the preoccupation centres on some phrase of the patient's. Recalling the session, the context of the statement, the patient's intonation, the analyst can place the statement in a category which, in the light of after knowledge, he thinks is correct. Such meditation is related to notation and memory. It is akin to recording what took place and is an example of using the grid and the theories it represents for the purposes of notation. Even if he does not commit his work to paper the analyst is doing something that will stamp the episode in his memory.

2.   The analyst may place it speculatively in any grid category he chooses. He can then give direction to his speculations by considering what the implications would be if in fact the statement belonged to the category in which he had provisionally and speculatively placed it. This means that he has "bound" a number of elements and can proceed to discover the meaning of their supposed conjunction. The grid assists in giving direction to his speculations.

3.   In the course of 1 and 2 he will be considering the possibility of other categories in which the statement might with propriety have been placed. Such activity is a stimulant to the analyst's capacity for attention.

4.   The analyst can scrutinize his interpretations by subjecting them to the same procedure as that to which he has submitted the patient's associations in 1, 3, and 4.

5.   The analyst can place the association and its actual, or proposed interpretation, in the appropriate categories and thus examine the *couple*, association and interpretation. Thus he can compare and examine the relationship not of the association to the interpretation but of the category of the association to the category of the interpretation. Thus a basis can be provided for investigation of the developmental value of interpretation and association according to the nature of the relationship of their categories.

6.   The analyst can take conflicting statements in the patient's associations, place them according to their respective grid categories, and then scrutinize the nature of the conflict by a comparison of the *categories* of

the conflicting statements. It should then be possible to see what is contributed to conflict by the nature of the categories of the conflicting statements.

B.The psychoanalytic game

In A I have proposed uses for the Grid closely associated with actual analytic experiences. The Grid may, however, be profitably used in a kind of analytic make-believe in which the experiential element is far less dominant. Such an imaginative exercise is closer to the activity of the musician who practises scales and exercises, not directly related to any piece of music but to the *elements* of which any piece of music is composed.

(CWB V, pp. 83–84)

Chapter 11

Elements of Psycho-Analysis

Introduction

Following chapter 10 on the Grid, in which quotes from different books were collected together, we now return to taking each book in turn. *Elements of Psycho-Analysis* (1963) follows *Learning from Experience* (1962).

What is an element? It is a key term for Bion (alpha-element, beta-element, elements of psychoanalysis)

Some chemical elements, like gold, silver and copper, have been known for thousands of years. Some, like the radioactive meitnerium, have been created in laboratories. These are all substances that cannot be separated into simpler elements. Bion wants to identify the equivalent "non-reducible" elements in psychoanalysis. Another meaning of element may also be relevant. Water is the element of a fish – it is its natural habitat. I am reminded of a joke told by the then President of the British Society, David Bell. Two fish are swimming along. One says to the other, "the water's nice today"; the other fish replies, "what's water?" In his attention to the "elements", Bion wants us to see what is most essential and often most taken for granted.

Which elements does Bion arrive at in the book?

Bion's intention in the book is to delineate the key elements of psychoanalysis. As is so often the case, Bion's discussions of the elements are alive with observations and complexities and mostly not at all list-like.

The two fundamental ways in which thinking develops are the first two of his elements:

Container–contained

$Ps \rightleftharpoons D$

From here on, matters become more complicated, and it quickly becomes clear that my initial intention to give a list of elements is not going to be easy and is perhaps not going to be possible.

LHK (Loving, Hating, Knowing): briefly referred to at the beginning of the book, the links provided by L, H and K are confirmed as being included as an element later in the book.

A further element is decision:

> Since the analyst is constantly called upon to decide whether to intervene with an interpretation, decision, and its components of loneliness and introspection, should be regarded as an element of psychoanalysis at least from the point of view of the analyst and therefore probably from the point of view of both patient and analyst.
>
> (*CWB V*, p. 19)

Pain is an element.

> The lesson to be drawn from this discussion [reversible perspective] is the need to deduce the presence of intense pain and the threat that it represents to mental integration. I shall therefore consider pain as one of the elements of psychoanalysis.
>
> (*CWB V*, p. 53)

In Chapter 16, Bion considers "instinct" and "emotion" for inclusion among the elements. His view about the inclusion of "sex" – a key element in Freud's model of the mind – is that it is a complexity derived from more elemental substances.

Towards the end of the book we find the following comment. I include it for consideration.

> I define the elements of psychoanalysis as being those phenomena whose various aspects can be seen to fall within the grid categories even though some categories must for the time being remain empty. Such phenomena are:
>
> (a) Ideas as described in Chapters 1–18.
> (b) Feelings as described in Chapter 19, including pain.
> (c) Association and Interpretation.
> (d) The couple (association and interpretation).
> (e) Conflicting pairs (I use the term "pair" so as to leave the term "couple" free for the phenomena of (d) above).
> (f) The two axes of the grid (as special cases).
>
> (*CWB V*, pp. 84–85)

Psychoanalytic objects

As well as elements, the book addresses the question of "psychoanalytic objects". The psychoanalytic object is different from the more familiar "internal object". The psychoanalytic object is specific to psychoanalysis.

Ron Britton

What he was seeking to do was to disentangle the elements of psycho-analysis in order to define them and to delineate what he called psy-choanalytic objects. His purpose was to abstract these sufficiently to free them from the particularities of their clinical narrative and mythic context to give them more precision and utility. A psychoanalytic object would be something formed by the discourse and behaviour of the patient and found by the use of the analyst's mind from his observa-tion and emotional experience of the situation, aided by his theories. The psychoanalytic object would have particular qualities of current sensory experience; it would acquire a narrative derived from the patient's per-sonal myth and it would include one or more of the passions, L, H or K, love, hate or knowledge. It might, for example, be an oedipal situation evident in the transference of the moment, shaped by the patient's per-sonal oedipal myth and driven by one or more of the passions.

Bion saw the activities of an analysis as the detection and location of these "psychoanalytic objects" leading to the analyst making interpreta-tions based on them. He expected the trained analyst to do this in large part intuitively and unselfconsciously using his knowledge and expe-rience. Bion's description of elements, functions and psychoanalytic objects was an attempt to define systematically what already took place in psychoanalysis and not to prescribe a method.

(Britton 1998, p. 818)

To balance the complexities above, here is a quote from one of Bion's London patients:

Francis Tustin

I have often been asked whether Dr. Bion talked in the somewhat inscru-table, oracular way in which he sometimes wrote. I can say very firmly that this was not so. He was always brief, to the point and extremely simple and clear. . . .

Dr. Bion aroused in me the courage to see things from a different per-spective from the current and accepted ones, and also different from his. He provoked me to think for myself – to have a mind of my own. He did this by asking challenging questions and by making unexpected remarks rather than by imposing a rigid interpretive scheme on what I said and did. In so doing, he made me think about what was happening to me in my own terms.

(Tustin 1981, p. 175)

Quotes

[156]   Elements to be like letters of the alphabet

> The defect of the existing psychoanalytic theory is not unlike that of the ideogram as compared with a word formed alphabetically; the ideogram represents one word only but relatively few letters are required for the formation of many thousands of words. Similarly the elements I seek are to be such that relatively few are required to express, by changes in combination, nearly all the theories essential to the working psychoanalyst. . . .
>
> The task is to abstract such elements by releasing them from the combination in which they are held and from the particularity that adheres to them from the realization which they were originally designed to represent.
>
> (CWB V, p. 8)

Both theories and myths take the form of narratives. Bion is interested in whether these can be broken down into their elements. In this endeavour Bion is attempting something not dissimilar to Freud's approach to dreams. Freud came to the view that as we wake our dreams go through a secondary revision to make them palatable for our waking minds to remember – the dream is turned into a narrative. Analysis of the dream involves determining the elements that are being held in combination in the narrative, and then each element is addressed in its own right.

Bion hopes that the identification of the separate elements in any particular narrative will clarify whether apparently different conditions are essentially the same: see, for example, the quote on agoraphobia and claustrophobia.

Ideogram. Character symbolizing the idea of a thing. Examples include numerals and Chinese characters.

[157]   IN

> If a patient says he cannot take something in, or the analyst feels he cannot take something in, he implies a container and something to put in it. . . . The patient is "in" analysis, or "in" a family or "in" the consulting room; or he may say he has a pain "in" his leg.
>
> (CWBV, p. 11)

The first of the elements that Bion identifies is that of container–contained (♀♂). He points out the ubiquity of its occurrence in the way we think and talk. He is recommending that one listens for references from the patient that are about "something being put into something else" in order to see what kind of relation between the container and the contained may be characteristic for a particular person.

Chris Mawson

> Bion emphasized that he was not putting forward a new theory but was describing and exploring an observable pattern, a configuration, that keeps on cropping up, both inside and outside the consulting room. Bion reiterated that detecting the underlying pattern was only the beginning of theorizing about it and its relationships to other phenomena, and that the status of the ♀♂ configuration, and ideas associated with it, were provisional: a model rather than a theory.
>
> (Chris Mawson, personal communication)

[158]   Dimensions of sense, myth and passion

Psychoanalytic elements and the objects derived from them have the following dimensions.

1.   Extension in the domain of sense.
2.   Extension in the domain of myth.
3.   Extension In the domain of passion.

(CWBV, p. 15)

James Gooch, an American psychoanalyst who was in analysis with Bion in Los Angeles, gave the following example of one of Bion's interpretations to him:

> I remember an interpretation for instance. He had cited the evidence as he usually did, and I remember saying well, "I can see why you say that, and believe that it's probably true, but I just can't feel it". And he said, "Well it may be the sort of thing you experienced with [your] aunt". And, (snap of fingers), there it was.
>
> (Culbert-Koehn 2011, p. 84).

The evidence would, I think, belong to the domain of sense. The domain of myth is Bion's reference to "the sort of thing experienced with your aunt", and there is evidence of the domain of passion in the snap of Gooch's fingers recalling the exchange.

[159] Constructions

From *Brazilian Lectures:* "1974 São Paulo"

The view, expressed by Freud, which I found has a great deal of meaning for me is that many of these interpretations are almost meaningless, but these constructions are not. I remain unexcited by being told that I am omnipotent, or that I am helpless. I do, however, feel slightly more interested if somebody says that I think I am God; if it means nothing else, at least it means that somebody is being rude. To that extent it is an improvement on being told that one is omnipotent. But I would go further; I would like the individual concerned to tell me what sort of god I was behaving like. There is a large variety of gods which one's behaviour could resemble. If the individual, instead of being rude or hostile, would tell me which kind of god I resembled, I would find that construction much more meaningful and comprehensible. There is much to be said for a short story which I can understand and which, therefore, is a vehicle which communicates meaning. For example, if somebody said that I am like the god of Babel, that I am so jealous and envious that I would not like anyone to climb up a higher tower than the pedestal on which I was happening to sit myself, that I would like to make them so confused and on such bad terms with one another that they would not be able to construct a better and higher and more glorious tower – if I were given that sort of interpretation I would feel that I had a clearer idea (although I might not like it) of how I appeared to somebody else. That is why I am more in favour of the construction than some word that I could look up in the dictionary leaving me no better for the expenditure of time.

(*CWB II*, p. 195)

I have included this quote here as a possible illustration of the domain of myth and its link to Freud's "constructions".

[160]   Detachment at the cost of loneliness

The dictum that an analysis must be conducted in an atmosphere of deprivation is usually understood to mean that the analyst must resist any impulse
in himself to gratify the desires of his analysands or to crave gratification
for his own. To narrow the expression of this statement without contracting
the area covered by it; at no time must either analyst or analysand lose the
sense of isolation within the intimate relationship of analysis.

No matter how good or bad the co-operation may turn out to be the
analyst should not lose, or deprive his patient of, the sense of isolation that
belongs to the knowledge that the circumstances that have led to analysis
and the consequences that may in future arise from it are a responsibility
that can be shared with nobody. Discussions of technical or other matters
with colleagues or relatives must never obscure this essential isolation.

Opposed to the establishment of a relationship yielding experiences of a
sense of responsibility is the drive to be mean and greedy. The sense of loneliness seems to relate to a feeling, in the object of scrutiny, that it is being
abandoned and, in the scrutinizing subject, that it is cutting itself off from the
source or base on which it depends for its existence.

To summarize: Detachment can only be achieved at the cost of painful
feelings of loneliness and abandonment experienced (1) by the primitive
animal mental inheritance from which detachment is effected and (2) by the
aspects of the personality that succeed in detaching themselves from the
object of scrutiny which is felt to be indistinguishable from the source of its
viability. The apparently abandoned object of scrutiny is the primitive mind
and the primitive social capacity of the individual as a political or group animal. The "detached" personality is in a sense new to its job and has to turn
to tasks which differ from those to which its components are more usually
adapted, namely scrutiny of the environment excluding the self, part of the
price paid is in feelings of insecurity.

(CWB V, p. 18)

Freud reports that when he was young and was learning how to use his mind
differently, he experienced a loneliness. Some have questioned whether, in his
psychoanalytically formative years, Freud was as lonely as he claimed. It is
sometimes implied that he was exaggerating his loneliness to augment a picture of the heroic nature of the task. It is possible, however, that there was a
loneliness caused by his repositioning himself internally, in a way that allowed
a new kind of attention to be directed externally. I quote Freud from one of his
early letters to Fliess:

Every now and then ideas dart through my head which promise to realize everything, apparently connecting the normal and the pathological, the sexual and the psychological problem, and then they are gone again and I make no effort to hold onto them because I indeed know that neither their disappearance nor their appearance in consciousness is the real expression of their fate. On such quiet days as yesterday and today, however, everything in me is very quiet, terribly lonely. I cannot talk about it to anyone, nor can I force myself to work, deliberately and voluntarily as other workers can. I must wait until something stirs in me and I become aware of it. And so I often dream whole days away. . . .

(Freud to Fliess, 3 December 1897; in Masson, 1985, p. 284)

Is psychoanalytic alpha-function the same as maternal reverie?

Towards the end of the quote, Bion comments that the "'detached' personality is in a sense new to its job". As analysts, we are trained to do a particular kind of work – arguably this is a new kind of work for the mind. By contrast, maternal "reverie" is an old kind of work, as old as the species, and perhaps not even correctly described as work at all.

Bion provides us with a visual image of the process of containing through his reference to a reticulum (a network of intercellular fibres). Of the reticulum, he says the gaps are the sleeves, and the threads forming the meshes are emotions. The gaps are made available by the meshes of emotion, and from this point of view, the emotional capacity of the mother to be available to her baby and the emotional capacity of the analyst to be available to the patient have much in common.

There is, however, another aspect of how mental space comes into being, in relation to which the analyst and the mother are quite different. In his later work, *Attention and Interpretation,* Bion comments that mental space comes into being through the experience of the absence or loss of what was there before. This idea is also in his "Theory of Thinking" paper (1962), in which he states that the first thought comes about in the space created by the experience of the absence of the breast. Both mother and analyst consent to feel, think and share the emotions contained in projections, as if they were a part of themselves, but is there a difference in the loss they may experience in order to make this space available? The mother has to bear putting her own needs somewhat out of the picture, but this is somewhat ameliorated by her identification with her baby and her meeting of her own infantile needs through her care of the baby. In a good-enough situation she is also cared for by the father, and there is some analogy to this in the analyst being cared for within her analytic identity/community. The key difference is that the analyst is not to forget that she or he is alone. The analyst is intended to *not* identify his or her own infantile needs with the patient. I think Bion is saying that in order to be available to the patient, we as analysts have to learn how to turn away from our own primitive animal self. As a result of this "new job" the primitive animal part of the self feels abandoned, and even the part looking out towards the patient is unsure of its viability.

[161]   Infant: meanness and generosity

... the infant, filled with painful lumps of faeces, guilt, fears of impending death, chunks of greed, meanness and urine, evacuates these bad objects into the breast that is not there. As it does so the good object turns the no-breast (mouth) into a breast, the faeces and urine into milk, the fears of impending death and anxiety into vitality and confidence, the greed and meanness into feelings of love and generosity and the infant sucks its bad property, now translated into goodness, back again.

(*CWB V*, p. 30)

This is a key, often cited, quote: Bion has an unusual capacity to think himself into the place of what experience may be like for the baby.

Why does he say "into the breast that is not there"? I think he is describing the moment before the mother comes. On other occasions he describes what he imagines to happen if the mother doesn't come.

[162] Frustrated and outraged masters

> We have therefore to consider . . . reason, which in its embryonic form under the dominance of the pleasure principle is designed to serve as the slave of the passions, has forced it to assume a function resembling that of a master of the passions and the parent of logic. For the search for satisfaction of incompatible desires would lead to frustration. Successful surmounting of the problem of frustration involves being reasonable and a phrase such as the "dictates of reason" may enshrine the expression of primitive emotional reaction to a function intended to satisfy not frustrate. The axioms of logic therefore have their roots in the experience of a reason that fails in its primary function to satisfy the passions just as the existence of a powerful reason may reflect a capacity in that function to resist the assaults of its frustrated and outraged masters. These matters will have to be considered in so far as dominance of the reality principle stimulates the development of thought and thinking, reason, and awareness of psychic and environmental reality.
>
> (*CWB V*, p. 34)

We tend to think of "reason" as acting in the service of the "reality principle" and very different from the pursuit of pleasure. Bion is suggesting, however, that there is a being "reasonable" that is under the dominance of the pleasure principle and is a way of avoiding the problem of frustration. People who are overly "reasonable" can be too pliant – like trees that are grown indoors and need supports, unlike those growing outside and strengthened by the wind blowing against them. "A powerful reason", Bion says, can resist "the assaults of its frustrated and outraged masters" and be stimulated by them.

Clinical note

A patient began a session saying that I would be bored with him. The feared "boredom" included both an anxiety that I would not be interested in him, but also a denial or denigration of my analytic attention. It occurred to me that if I am denigrated in this way, the patient is angry with a denigrated object rather than with a loved object. He avoids being angry with a loved object and the conflict of feelings – the challenge this would involve.

282 Papers, books, notes, letters

[163] Persecuted by feelings of depression and depressed by feelings of persecution

I shall suppose the existence of a mixed state in which the patient is persecuted by feelings of depression and depressed by feelings of persecution. These feelings are indistinguishable from bodily sensations and what might, in the light of later capacity for discrimination, be described as things-in-themselves. In short β-elements [beta-elements] are objects compounded of things-in-themselves, feelings of depression-persecution and guilt and therefore aspects of personality linked by a sense of catastrophe: fuller elaboration will have to wait on clinical discovery.

(*CWB V*, p. 37)

Norma Tracey

Bion sees it as an innate part of the self's rhythm to fall apart and to come together again. Out of this perception I conceive that the problem of the depressed mother is that she has no faith that if she falls apart she will come together again, indeed she has proof in her past of being unheld and of not coming together again. She is frozen in terror and dare not go into catastrophe so there is no resolution, no arrival at her own identity. She is left at the mercy of raw unprocessed emotions, which Bion describes as *beta elements*, "a mixed state in which the patient is persecuted by feelings of depression and depressed by feelings of persecution". This, he says, all points to catastrophe (Bion 1963 [*CWB V*]). I would suggest that, at some early stage in the depressed mother's life, the "holder of the faith", the mother, has failed her and has failed to hold her through catastrophe. The catastrophe, being in consequence too much to tolerate, has caused disassociation and deadness. The movement between faith and catastrophe is frozen. The problem of the depressed mother is that she dare not go mad and therefore cannot reach sanity. She has lost faith. The place where faith and catastrophe meet, where self is born, where knowing can occur, is not accessible to her.

(Tracey 2000, pp. 187–188)

[164]   The sexual component in the Oedipus myth

Freud's use of the Oedipus myth illuminated more than the nature of the sexual facets of the human personality. Thanks to his discoveries it is possible by reviewing the myth to see that it contains elements that were not stressed in the early investigations because they were overshadowed by the sexual component in the drama. The developments of psychoanalysis make it possible to give more weight to other features.

(*CWB V*, p. 41)

As has been discussed in relation to *baP* (basic assumption Pairing), Bion thought that Freud had overestimated the importance of the sexual instinct. This view continued throughout his work. The Oedipus myth, which was found by Freud to shed light on L (love) and H (hate), is found by Bion to be "equally illuminating for the K (knowledge) link" (*CWB V*, p. 45). Bion then makes the following intriguing, although not easily understandable, point about the sexual element:

No element, such as the sexual element, can be comprehended save in its relationship with other elements; for example with the determination with which Oedipus pursues his inquiry into the crime despite the warnings of Tiresias. It is consequently not possible to isolate the sexual component, or any other, without distortion. Sex, in the Oedipal situation, has a quality that can only be described by the implications conferred on it by its inclusion in the story. If it is removed from the story it loses its quality unless its meaning is preserved by an express reservation that "sex" is a term used to represent sex as it is experienced in the context of the myth.

(*CWB V*, pp. 41–42)

[165]   The patient reports, but does NOT believe, that he has had a dream

The patient reports, but does NOT believe, that he has had a dream. The dream, an experience of great emotional intensity, is felt by the patient to be a straightforward recital of the facts of a horrifying experience. He expects that the analyst, by treating it as a dream requiring interpretation, will give substance to his day dream that it was only a dream. In short, the patient is mobilizing his resources, and these include the facts of the analysis, to keep at bay his conviction that the dream not only was but is the reality and the reality, as the analyst understands it, is something to be appreciated only for those elements that are suited to refutation of the "dream".

This account is not of a new theory of dreams, but is a description of a state, seen in an extremely disturbed patient, but probably of fairly common recurrence.

(CWB V, p. 45)

Michael Feldman

Bion has given a vivid illustration of the complexity of the relationship that may exist. He described a patient who reported a dream, which led the analyst to believe that the patient had had a dream. The patient, however, did not believe that he had had a dream but that he was giving a straightforward recital of a horrifying experience. He expected that, if he reported it as a dream requiring interpretation the analyst would confirm his daydream that it was only a dream, thus keeping at bay his conviction that the dream not only had been, but was still the reality of his experience.

The pressure on the analyst to make these distinctions derives not only from his own interest and curiosity and his more theoretical views of the requirements of the analytic process; it may also reflect the anxieties, uncertainty, or confusion aroused by the material the patient has brought, and the emotional impact of the unconscious currents present in the session, such as the one just described.

There will of course often be conscious or unconscious demands from the patient to attend to the "reality" of the situation, and it is vital for the patient to have a sense that the analyst is open to the realities of his current life, or his history, and the ways he is affected by the analytic setting. It is inevitable that the analyst will become drawn into having opinions, making judgments, apportioning responsibility or blame, basing these on his own experience and bias and on what he judges to be the "reality" of the situations with which he is presented. These forces may result in both patient and analyst becoming apparently quite reasonably concerned with facts, and history, with what the mother or father or partner was *actually* like, how they interacted with the patient, and with what effect. There will be similar concerns about the analyst's personality, technique, and conduct, and how these affect the patient.

The focus of the analyst's attention often *does* become drawn toward making judgments about either material reality or the patient's psychic reality – trying to assess, for example whether the patient's mother was *actually* cruel, whether she behaved in a seductive or intrusive fashion on a particular occasion. In that frame of mind, it is often difficult to attend closely to the reality of what is being enacted between the analyst and patient: the way the patient might be using the communication about his mother to subtly draw the analyst into an alliance with him against the mother or drive the analyst into an alliance with the mother against him, thus seeking to re-create important aspects of the oedipal configuration that exist in his internal world.

(Feldman 1993, pp. 275–276)

[166]   Modification of archaic phantasies and mental development

The common-sense view of mental development is that it consists in an increase of capacity to grasp reality and a decrease in the obstructive force of illusions. Psychoanalysts suppose that the exposure of archaic phantasies to modification by a sophisticated capacity for approximation to a series of theories, that are consistent and compatible with the reception and integration of further experience, is therapeutic in its effects.

(*CWB V*, p. 46)

Ron Britton

I am persuaded by Klein's theory of phantasies that they are the mental representation of all impulses, anxieties, and somatic experiences. Klein's view was that in addition to the active unconscious phantasies interweaving within the events of everyday life, there were quiescent archaic phantasies in the "deep unconscious" that under disadvantageous circumstances might intrude on the ego (Klein 1958, p. 241). I do not know where or what the "deep unconscious" is, but it sounds like a repository for phantasies that under normal circumstances in everyday waking life are not given credibility. They may find a place in dreams, where they may or may not trouble us. If they are "believed" in dreams we have a "nightmare." However, such phantasies have a license to intrude on us when disbelief is suspended, as at a horror movie. One could argue that they also find a place in religious belief systems. For the sophisticated, such "superstitious" beliefs do not extend into the natural world except, according to Freud, as the "uncanny" (*unheimlich*) experiences that he described in his paper of that name (1919).

Freud's explanation for the *unheimlich* experience is that one encounters something in the world that appears to reinstate a primitive belief. He distinguishes between a mind in which such beliefs have been *surmounted* and remain latent, and one where they have been *abolished*, and sees surmounted archaic beliefs as capable of reemerging if given apparent support by the external world. "Conversely", he wrote, "anyone who has completely and finally rid himself of animistic beliefs will be insensible to this type of the *Unheimlich*" (1919, p. 248). I think this distinction is a most important one in analysis. I would make the distinction between beliefs that have been surmounted or apparently outgrown, and those that have been worked through and relinquished. It is relinquishment that is necessary for psychic change, and it takes time to work through and mourn a lost belief, as it does to mourn a lost object. A belief that has been surmounted I regard as one simply overcome by another belief – one that remains dependent on the prevailing context. It is like believing one thing when in company and in daylight, and another when alone in the dark. I think that one of our tasks in analysis is to sniff out such latent beliefs, and that the place they can usually be found is in the unconscious aspects of the transference.

(Britton 2003, pp. 1336–1337)

[167]   Reversible perspective

Chapter Twelve

The model of reversible perspective, when applied to the analysis, reveals a complex situation. The patient detects a note of satisfaction in the analyst's voice and responds in a tone conveying dejection. (What was said is irrelevant to our immediate concern.) The patient detects a moral supposition in an interpretation: his response is significant for its silent rejection of the moral supposition. That which makes one person see two faces and the other a vase remains insensible, but in the domain of sense impressions there is agreement. The interpretation is accepted, but the premises have been rejected and others silently substituted.

In any interpretation there is a significant assumption, one being that the analyst is the analyst: this assumption may be denied silently by the patient. Although he appears to accept the interpretation he denies its force by having substituted another assumption. Further associations may show what *his* assumption is.

The debate between analysand and analyst is therefore unspoken; what the analyst says is shown to be agreed by both parties to the analysis, but – it is insignificant. The conflict is therefore kept out of discussion because it is confined to a domain which is not regarded as an issue between the analyst and analysand. The supposition that the analyst is the analyst and the analysand the analysand is but one of these domains of disagreement that is passed by silently....

The [patient's] pause may seem indistinguishable from one that a neurotic patient will make in order to digest the interpretation he has heard. I doubt whether the true nature of the pause can be clinically observed; it may be that an ability to differentiate depends always on long experience of the patient's pauses and the discovery, later rather than sooner, that after many months of apparently successful analysis the patient has gained an extensive knowledge of the analyst's theories but no insight. The pause is not being employed to absorb fully the implications of the interpretation, but rather to establish a point of view, not expressed to the analyst, from which the analyst's interpretation, though verbally unchanged and unchallenged, has a meaning other than the one the analyst intended to convey....

Chapter Thirteen

Reversible perspective is evidence of pain; the patient reverses perspective to make a dynamic situation static....

(CWB V, pp. 48–52)

[168] Pain

Pain cannot be absent from the personality. An analysis must be painful, not because there is necessarily any value in pain, but because an analysis in which pain is not observed and discussed cannot be regarded as dealing with one of the central reasons for the patient's presence. The importance of pain can be dismissed as a secondary quality, something that is to disappear when conflicts are resolved; indeed most patients would take this view. Furthermore it can be supported by the fact that successful analysis does lead to diminution of suffering; nevertheless it obscures the need, more obvious in some cases than in others, for the analytic experience to increase the patient's *capacity* for suffering even though patient and analyst may hope to decrease pain itself. The analogy with physical medicine is exact; to destroy a capacity for physical pain would be a disaster in any situation other than one in which an even greater disaster – namely death itself – is certain.

(*CWB V*, p. 53)

[169]   Growth

Growth is a phenomenon that appears to present peculiar difficulties to perception either by the growing object or the object that stimulates it, for its relationship with precedent phenomena is obscure and separated in time. Difficulty in observing it contributes to the anxiety to establish "results", e.g. of analysis.

(CWB V, p. 54)

[170] Transference

The elements of the transference are to be found in that aspect of the patient's behaviour that betrays his awareness of the presence of an object that is not himself. No aspect of his behaviour can be disregarded; its relevance to the central fact must be assessed. His greeting, or neglect of it, references to couch, or furniture, or weather, all must be seen in that aspect of them that relates to the presence of an object not himself; the evidence must be regarded afresh each session and nothing taken for granted for the order in which aspects of the patient's mind present themselves for observation are not decided by the length of time for which the analysis has endured. For example, the patient may regard the analyst as a person to be treated as if he were a thing; or as a thing towards which his attitude is animistic.

(*CWB V*, p. 59)

[171]   Communication within the self obscure

The processes by which private knowledge is communicated within the individual is obscure and elucidation waits on advances that psychoanalysts have yet to make. The dream has fresh significance if it is regarded as a private myth.

(CWB V, p. 77)

[172]   Pre-conception of the parental couple

I am postulating a precursor of the Oedipal situation not in the sense that such a term might have in Melanie Klein's discussion of Early Phases of the Oedipus Complex, but as something that belongs to the ego as part of its apparatus for contact with reality. In short I postulate an α-element version of a private Oedipus myth which is the means, the pre-conception, by virtue of which the infant is able to establish contact with the parents as they exist in the world of reality. The mating of this α-element Oedipal pre-conception with the realization of the actual parents gives rise to the conception of parents.

If, through envy, greed, sadism or other cause, the infant cannot tolerate the parental relationship and attacks it destructively, according to Melanie Klein the attacking personality is itself fragmented through the violence of the splitting attacks. Restating this theory in terms of the Oedipal pre-conception: the emotional load carried by the private α-element Oedipal pre-conception is such that the Oedipal pre-conception is itself destroyed. As a result the infant loses the apparatus essential for gaining a conception of the parental relationship and consequently for resolution of Oedipal problems: it does not fail to solve those problems – it never reaches them.

(*CWB V*, pp. 77–78)

[173]   The analyst's Ps ⇌ D and Beckett

The patient may be describing a dream, followed by a memory of an incident that occurred on the previous day, followed by an account of some difficulty in his parents' family. The recital may take three or four minutes or longer. The coherence that these facts have in the patient's mind is not relevant to the analyst's problem. His problem – I describe it in stages – is to ignore that coherence so that he is confronted by the incoherence and experiences incomprehension of what is presented to him. His own analysis should have made it possible for him to tolerate this emotional experience though it involves feelings of doubt and perhaps even persecution. This state must endure, possibly for a short period but probably longer, until a new coherence emerges; at this point he has reached g D, the stage analogous to nomination or "binding" as I have described it. From this point his own processes can be represented by ♀♂ – the development of meaning.

(*CWB* V, p. 85)

Container–contained or Ps ⇌ D first?

It is tempting to suppose that the transformation of β-element to α-element depends on ♀♂ and the operation of Ps ⇌ D depends on the prior operation of ♀♂. Unfortunately this relatively simple solution does not adequately explain events in the consulting room; before ♀♂ can operate, ♀ has to be found and the discovery of ♀ depends on the operation of Ps ⇌ D. It is obvious that to consider which of the two ♀♂ or Ps ⇌ D is prior distracts from the main problem.

(*CWB* V, p. 37)

From *Cogitations*

If psychoanalysts can abandon themselves to analysis in the psychoanalytic sessions, they are in a position when recollecting the experience in tranquillity to discern their experience as part of a greater whole. Once that is achieved, the way is open for the discovery of configurations revealing yet other and deeper groups of theory. But the discoverer must be prepared to find that he has started another round of group oscillations. Persecution ⇌ Depression.

(*CWB* XI, p. 273)

Chris Mawson

In 1945 Beckett returned to Dublin for a brief visit, during which a sudden insight occurred to him, standing in his mother's room, where he had been feeling depressed and demoralized. Beckett had, for a long time, felt inadequate and inferior, fearing that he would never equal his hero James Joyce, whom he admired much too much – the Joyce who was never stuck for a word or an idea. What Beckett wrote about this epiphany is relevant to our topic.

Beckett wrote:

"I realized that Joyce had gone as far as one could in the direction of knowing more, [being] in control of one's material. He was always adding to it; you only have to look at his proofs to see that. I realized that my own way was in impoverishment, in lack of knowledge and in taking away, in subtracting rather than in adding."

The creative thinkers . . . , Freud, Beckett, Bion – developed methods which were based on the bracketing, the sequestration, of narrative order, cohesion, established knowledge, and used a purposeful suppression of them in order to allow the emergence of an underlying pattern to experience. . . .

Intuition and the experience of incoherence

Behind all that I say is the idea that the observer's experience of incoherence is primary and essential to the task. As Bion wrote, in *Elements of Psycho-Analysis*:

To the analytic observer the material must appear as a number of discrete particles unrelated and incoherent (Ps $\rightleftharpoons$ D). The patient may be describing a dream, followed by a memory of an incident that occurred on the previous day, followed by an account of some difficulty in his parents' family. The recital may take three or four minutes or longer. The coherence that these facts have in the patient's mind is not relevant to the analyst's problem. His problem – I describe it in stages – is to ignore that coherence so that he is confronted by the incoherence and experiences incomprehension of what is presented to him. His own analysis should have made it possible for him to tolerate this emotional experience though it involves feelings of doubt and perhaps even persecution. This state must endure, possibly for a short period but probably longer, until a new coherence emerges. . . .

For Bion, it is at this point that a process of intuition has precipitated an unexpected coherence in the emotional elements of the total transference situation, which includes the emotional state of the analyst/observer. He calls such a moment, g D.

296 Papers, books, notes, letters

What Bion means by this is that the moment of intuition, of the "selected fact", is likely to precipitate an emotional shift in the mind of the observer, an emotional movement which is towards depression – but in the sense meant by Melanie Klein in her description of the depressive position, as a counterpart to it. The preceding phase, of incoherence, Bion treated as an analogue of Klein's other emotional configuration, which Bion denoted as Ps.

Once a moment of receptive psychoanalytic attention has allowed this mechanism to fluctuate productively, which Bion called Ps ⇌ D, Bion thought that the intuited clinical fact was, potentially at least, available to the faculties of clinical imagination and later theoretical reasoning: all aided by a process he referred to as container–contained ($♀♂$).

(Mawson 2015, pp. 4–6)

Chapter 12

Transformations: Change from Learning to Growth

Introduction

In the middle stages of doing *Bion: 365 Quotes*, I worked through the quotes consecutively from beginning to end for the first time. As I worked through the *Transformation* quotes, I became quite unsettled, even rather disturbed. It was like swimming along and then being thrown around in a rougher sea. On closer scrutiny, one disturbing factor is the depth to which Bion conveys the psychotic experience. A second is his questioning of his own categories/organisation of his perception and thought. There is also the effect of quite simply not understanding.

There are very different views of *Transformations* and Bion's later works – very strong views. The psychoanalyst David Taylor makes the important comment: "Bion's heavyweight ingredients can make for a strong inclination to take shortcuts . . ." (Taylor 2011 p. 1102).

I hope the quotes in this chapter will make the detail of what he says more available and mitigate against shortcuts.

In a letter to his children we hear of Bion's own struggles with this book.

> 1963
>
> I have almost finished all the writing I want to do for my book [*Transformations*] But the last chapter is important and therefore tricky. And then comes all the correction and excision which I find a bit tiresome.
>
> (*CWB II*, p. 197)

The last two quotes in this chapter are from the final chapter – "St John of the Cross" and "Fear of megalomania".

Notes on concepts Bion is using and developing

(I include material from the Introduction for ease of reference.)

Transformation and invariance

Bion states that the book is devoted to transformation and invariance. He differentiates between different modes of transformation, in particular between "transference" and "transformations in hallucinosis". In transference we "transfer" as a current experience what is repressed, but in a way that allows of some "intercourse" with the actual reality. By contrast, "Transformation in hallucinosis" is evacuative rather than explorative, and rivalrous rather than in "intercourse" with the world.

On invariance, one of the most compelling clinical examples is of his identification of "invariants" through the breakdown of a psychotic patient in analysis (*CWB V*, p. 132). "Things" that appeared as psychosomatic symptoms suddenly become externalised. Having an understanding of the invariant elements supports the analyst's maintenance of the analytic setting through the patient's breakdown.

Specificity and abstraction

Two related challenges to psychoanalytic theory and practice in the book are, first, the need to be more specific. It is not enough, for example, to say that a patient is hallucinating. Bion wants to interest us in the world of the patient's hallucination in its varied and detailed nature – through being with the patient, not standing off observing the action. The second challenge is the need for greater abstraction. Bion impatiently comments on the multitude of psychoanalytic theories. His view is that if we became more capable of observing underlying configurations, we would see that a lot of things being described as different are actually the same.

Scientific thinking and religious thought & language

In order to facilitate the quality of his observations and his capacity to *be* with the patient, Bion also explores his own deeply embedded assumptions. He wants to broaden his observations beyond the model provided by the senses or embedded in the culture (i.e. our model of cause and effect). He draws on the experience of the mystics in his analysis of the prevalence of pleasure-principle functioning in what we assume to be our scientific thinking and in the increasing attention he pays to "being" rather than "knowing". As psychoanalytic discourse, his religious language can be quite shocking. In this book, he does not civilise either psychosis or religion.

Quotes

[174]   Transformation and invariance

Two concepts [will be] introduced, transformation and invariance. The book will be devoted to these concepts and their application to the problems of psychoanalytic practice.

(CWBV, p. 131)

To forestall misgivings and criticisms which may have an insidious appeal for the psychoanalyst: a book on psychoanalysis in which the first chapters contain no substantial reference to sexuality, conflict, anxiety, or Oedipus situation, may seem irrelevant, or of specialized interest and minor consequence. In fact, if the matters I am discussing are regarded as seriously as I think they should be, it becomes possible for the analyst to have a firm and durable grasp of the reality of the analytic experience and the theories to which it approximates. The theory of transformations and its development does not relate to the main body of psychoanalytic theory, but to the practice of psychoanalytic *observation*. Psychoanalytic theories, patient's or analyst's statements are representations of an emotional experience. If we can understand the process of representation it helps us to understand the representation and what is being represented. The theory of transformations is intended to illuminate a chain of phenomena in which the understanding of one link, or aspect of it, helps in the understanding of others. The emphasis of this inquiry is on the nature of the transformation in a psychoanalytic session.

(CWBV, p. 156)

Bion wants *Transformations* to illuminate the practice of psychoanalytic observation.

[175]   A field sown with poppies

Chapter One

Suppose a painter sees a path through a field sown with poppies and paints it: at one end of the chain of events is the field of poppies, at the other a canvas with pigment disposed on its surface. We can recognize that the latter represents the former, so I shall suppose that despite the differences between a field of poppies and a piece of canvas, despite the transformation that the artist has effected in what he saw to make it take the form of a picture, *something* has remained unaltered and on this *something* recognition depends. The elements that go to make up the unaltered aspect of the transformation I shall call invariants.

(*CWBV*, pp. 127–128)

Within this usage of the term "transformation" there are three ways that need to be distinguished from each other. These are related to: (i) the total operation which includes the act of transforming and the end product (sign T); (ii) the process of transformation (sign T α) and (iii) the end product (sign T β).

(*CWBV*, p. 135)

Bion here differentiates between the process of transformation and the end product. This is not the first time he has made an explorative differentiation: in his "Theory of Thinking", for example, he differentiated "thoughts" from "thinking".

[176]   Invariants

The task is to find what are the invariants under psychoanalysis and what the nature of their relationship to one another.

(CWB V, p. 128)

The recognition of an invariant relationship also lies at the heart of Freud's work. Freud made a link between the relationship between the nipple and the mouth, the penis and the vagina, and the anus and faeces. This lay at the base of his radical rethinking of sexuality to include infantile sexuality, as well as adult genital sexuality.

[177]   Parallel lines

What is the relationship of the point at which parallel lines meet to the points at which lines that are not parallel meet? The railway lines ... can be seen to meet; the surveyor would not confirm the finding and nor would the neurologist. Though this problem is not of consequence to the psycho-analyst it may resemble problems which are.

(CWB V, pp. 128–129)

And a further quote from his next book *Attention and Interpretation* published five years later.

The analytic situation requires greater width and depth than can be provided by a model from Euclidean space.

(CWB VI, pp. 114–115)

To put it colloquially, one is to learn to think "outside the box". The box being reality based on our senses and mathematically represented by the model of Euclidean space. Analysts are already somewhat familiar with thinking outside these boxes. We know, for example, that a person's personality is not confined within their physical body. The patient may be physically in the session but mentally and emotionally absent, or the patient may project themselves into the analyst.

[178]   Interpretation is a transformation

The original experience, the realization – in the instance of the painter the subject that he paints, and in the instance of the psychoanalyst the experience of analysing his patient, is *transformed* by painting in the one and analysis in the other into a painting and a psychoanalytic description respectively. . . . An interpretation is a transformation; to display the invariants, an experience, felt and described in one way, is described in another.

(*CWB V*, p. 129)

[179]   Invariants: a clinical example

The man could be regarded, in view of the predominance of psychotic mechanisms and bizarre behaviour, as a borderline psychotic. Analysis seems to proceed slowly and there may be little evidence open to observers or members of the family that his behaviour is different from what it has been.

Then a change: friends or relations who have been denying that there is anything the matter cannot ignore his illness. He has been strange: he spends hours seated morosely in a chair; he appears to be hearing voices and seeing things. On this latter point there is some doubt; in the consulting room it is difficult to say if the patient is describing a delusion or indulging his fancy. In analysis he is hostile and confused. There is sudden deterioration. The alarm of relatives is evident in letters and other communications from them or the family doctor. There appears to be reason for the analyst to be alarmed, or, if he is not, to lay himself open to grave miscalculation and consequent blame.

In such a situation the common view is so pervasive that it is difficult to suppose that the analyst's anxieties and those of the relatives could be regarded profitably as anything other than rational and appropriate to the facts. Preservation of an analytic view, of what is taking place, is made difficult because it can fit so easily into a pattern of denial, by the analyst, of the seriousness of his predicament. In such a situation the analyst will take such steps as his experience in the management of analytic cases dictates. He will try to assess the contribution that his own psychopathology may be making. I mention these points without discussion save for their bearing on transformation and invariance. In the material I wish to include the analyst's anxieties and, in so far as he has access to them, those of the patient's relatives and friends. The analyst's main concern must be with the material of which he has direct evidence, namely, the emotional experience of the analytic sessions themselves. It is in his approach to this that the concepts of transformation and invariance can play an illuminating role.

Change from an analytical experience, confined to the consulting room, to a crisis that involves more people than the pair is remarkable for a number of features. It is catastrophic in the restricted sense of an event producing a subversion of the order or system of things; it is catastrophic in the sense that it is accompanied by feelings of disaster in the participants; it is catastrophic in the sense that it is sudden and violent in an almost physical way. This last will depend on the degree to which analytical procedure has produced a controlled breakdown. Since, for the purposes of this description, it is easier to deal with phenomena whose characteristics are exaggerated I shall rely on the description of events pertaining to the less analytically controlled episode. It must be borne in mind, however, that the analytically controlled event is more difficult to deal with in that the reactions being more restrained the elements in the situation are correspondingly unobtrusive and difficult to detect. Furthermore, in the analytically controlled event the catastrophic elements bear the same relationships to other elements as katabolic features bear to anabolic features in metabolism. I shall therefore ignore complications which I do not for the present wish to introduce.

To return to my illustration: there are three features to which I wish to draw attention: subversion of the system, invariance, and violence. Analysis in the pre-catastrophic stage is to be distinguished from the post-catastrophic stage by the following superficial characteristics: it is unemotional, theoretical, and devoid of any marked outward change. Hypochondriacal symptoms are prominent. The material lends itself to interpretations based on Kleinian theories of projective identification and internal and external objects. Violence is confined to phenomena experienced by psychoanalytical insight: it is, as it were, *theoretical* violence. The patient talks as if his behaviour, outwardly amenable, was causing great destruction because of its violence. The analyst gives interpretations, when they appear to be appropriate to the material, drawing attention to the features that are supposed by the patient to be violent.

In the post-catastrophic stage, by contrast, the violence is patent, but the ideational counterpart, previously evident, appears to be lacking. Emotion is obvious and is aroused in the analyst. Hypochondriacal elements are less obtrusive. The emotional experience does not have to be conjectured because it is apparent.

In this situation the analyst must search the material for invariants to the pre- and post-catastrophic stages. These will be found in the domain represented by the theories of projective identification, internal and external objects. Restating this in terms of clinical material, he must see, and demonstrate, that certain apparently external emotionally-charged events are in fact the same events as those which appeared in the pre-catastrophic stage under the names, bestowed by the patient, of pains in the knee, legs, abdomen, ears, etc., and, by the analyst, of internal objects. In brief, what present themselves to the outward sense of analyst and patient as anxious relatives, impending law-suits, mental hospitals, certification, and other contingencies apparently appropriate to the change in circumstances, are really hypochondriacal pains and other evidences of internal objects in a guise appropriate to their new status as external objects. These then are the invariants or the objects in which invariance is to be detected.

(*CWB V*, pp. 132–134)

"Things" that appeared as psychosomatic symptoms suddenly become externalised. Having an understanding of the invariant elements can support the analyst's maintenance of the analytic setting.

[180]   Violent externalisation of internal objects

I shall turn now to the relationship of violence to the change that has taken place from pre- to post-catastrophic.

The change is violent change and the new phase is one in which violent feelings are violently expressed. By analogy with an explosion, the patient's state of violent emotion sets up reactions in the analyst and others related to the patient in such a way that they also tend to be dominated by their over-stimulated internal objects thus producing a wide externalization of internal objects. In practice in the precatastrophic stage, the violence of the emotions has to be deduced and this is true even of the post-catastrophic stage if the breakdown is analytically controlled. Though adequate as a theory there is advantage in using an explosion and its expanding pressure-waves as a model. I shall do so.

(CWBV, p. 134)

This quote is a continuation of the previous one. I have separated it out to draw attention to his comment that violent over-stimulation can produce a wide externalisation of internal objects. One way of picturing this is of circular ripples going out from a stone thrown into water. The crisis may only be possible to absorb and modify at the outer ring first – that is, not by the person themselves. I am reminded of the Symington quote that accompanies Bion's quote on reverie in *Learning from Experience,* when he speaks of the infant being "born radiating unseen particles that rip into the very fabric of the mother's emotional structure" (Symington 1990, p. 100).

The knowledge in the British Society about psychotic patients derived from the work of Bion, Segal, Rosenfeld and others is further developed today by those working with psychotic mechanisms including Feldman, Britton and Steiner. Recognising the dynamic Bion is describing helps mitigate against the analyst getting caught up in the externality of the situation.

[181] Transference "a rigid motion transformation"

The aspect of transference important in transformation is that which Freud [1920, p. 18] described as a tendency "to repeat as a current experience what is repressed" instead of recollecting it as a fragment of the past. He goes on to say, "This reproduction appearing with un-welcome fidelity always contains a fragment of the infantile sex life, therefore of the Oedipus complex and its off-shoots, and is played regularly in the sphere of transference, i.e. the relationship to the physician." It is this "unwelcome fidelity" that helps to make the term "transference" so appropriate. At its worst the fidelity of the reproduction tends to betray the analyst into interpretations that have a repetitive quality seeming to suggest that what the patient says about someone else applies almost unchanged to what he thinks and feels about the analyst. Though such interpretations are a parody of what transference interpretations should be they contain a germ of truth. The feelings and ideas appropriate to infantile sexuality and the Oedipus complex and its off-shoots are *transferred*, with a wholeness and coherence that is characteristic, to the relationship with the analyst. This transformation involves little deformation: the term "transference", as Freud used it, implies a model of movement of feelings and ideas from one sphere of applicability to another. I propose therefore to describe this set of transformations as "rigid motions".

1   Freud, S.: *Beyond the Pleasure Principle* (1920), p. 18.

(*CWBV*, p. 143)

Although the transference ("rigid motion transformation") has a "repetitive quality", it contains a crucial element of enquiry and discovery. A core way in which we learn is the comparison of external reality with our unconscious phantasy of it—the comparison of the actual mother's loving behaviour with the unconscious phantasy of the mother as an attacking witch. This is mostly not a conscious activity. Hanna Segal was one of Bion's contemporaries (and one of the few analysts he makes reference to). She has commented that in the process of making such comparisons between internal phantasy and external reality, we not only correct unconscious phantasy, but unconscious phantasy enables and deepens exploration of the world. With transference we have both a repetition and an alive engagement with the world.

We know that the reality principle is but a modification of the pleasure principle, a modification brought about by reality testing. I would suggest that thinking is a modification of unconscious fantasy, a modification similarly brought about by reality testing. The richness, depth, and accuracy of a person's thinking will depend on the quality and malleability of the unconscious fantasy life and the capacity to subject it to reality testing.

(Segal 1964, p. 194)

[182] Superego takeover

In practice the problem arises with schizoid personalities in whom the super-ego appears to be developmentally prior to the ego and to deny development and existence itself to the ego. The usurpation by the super-ego of the position that should be occupied by the ego involves imperfect development of the reality principle, exaltation of a "moral" outlook and lack of respect for the truth. The result is starvation of the psyche and stunted growth.

(*CWB V*, p. 160)

Ron Britton

Freud's ideas on the superego changed and became increasingly complex in the development of new ideas. That the id is more primitive than the ego, however, is undoubted. Indeed Freud said, "It may be said of the id that it is totally non-moral, of the ego, that it strives to be moral, and of superego that can be super-moral and can then become as cruel as only the id can be." In other words, the only agency that is truly moral, in Freud's view, is the ego.

Klein's rather different view of the early superego was that it was formed at the beginning by splitting off the hostile averse impulses from the loving, seeking, and attaching desires of what would normally be the central self. In other words, it derives from an anti-object part of the self. Fairbairn called it first the "internal saboteur" and later the "anti-libidinal ego." In Klein's account, this limited precursor is modified by the incorporation of the goodness of parental care and the superego becomes a complex structure. This emphasizes, of course, how much we need a good object. But in complex structures, there is always a hint of cruelty at its core. At its best, it is a rather severe moralizing parental organization, at its worst it is ego-destructive, self-destructive monster.

I suggested (and I used the Book of Job as a literary source to suggest this) that development should include emancipation of the ego from the superego, and that that should come about by the reclamation of the role of judge by the individual making a judgment on their own superego. It is a process that I believe psychoanalysis in particular can promote. In other words, I am suggesting that we should emancipate ourselves from the judgments of our rulers and we should do so by forming a judgment on them.

(Britton, Chused, Ellman, & Likierman 2006, p. 291)

I do think there is something about that which has to do with wanting to get away from the terrible struggle of dealing with the world as it actually is. I'm very struck by the fact that complexity itself is something which is regarded as a terrible strain. Therefore simplifications are very attractive. . . .

This takes me back to Freud's comment that the ego *strives to be moral*. I love that phrase. He doesn't say the ego is moral. The ego strives to be moral. The id is amoral and the superego is only super-moral and cruel. Therefore there is a form of gratification in moral superiority. You might call it the Moral principle, a sort of up-market version of the pleasure principle. And it's constantly endorsed through the news media.

Indignation is the mode. When people are indignant, I find it very difficult to take them seriously. You can be very, very angry about something; you can be enraged. Being outraged is something else. Outrage is indignation, and outrage is to do with entitlement. The more that society feels entitled to have a very happy life, to have no misfortunes, to live forever – the more opportunity for indignation it has. It's outraged daily.

(Britton, Feldman, Stein, & Tucker, S. 2010, p. 319)

[183]   Problems analysts have

What psychoanalytic thinking requires is a method of notation and rules for its employment that will enable work to be done in the absence of the object, to facilitate further work in the presence of the object. The barrier to this that is presented by unfettered play of an analyst's phantasies has long been recognized: pedantic statement on the one hand and verbalization loaded with unobserved implications on the other mean that the potential for misunderstanding and erroneous deduction is so high as to vitiate the value of the work done with such defective tools.

(*CWB V*, p. 165)

This is a rather caustic, pithy allusion to analyst's minds being cluttered with their own phantasies, and assumptions not based on observation. The "absent object" is, I think, the patient. Bion refers to the need for analysts to have tools with which to review their work outside the session. His Grid is one such tool.

[184]   Projective transformations

The analytic situation requires greater width and depth than can be provided by a model from Euclidean space. A patient who, in my view, is displaying projective transformations and requires the use of Kleinian theories for
comprehension, also uses a field which is not simply the analyst, or his own
personality, or even the relationship between himself and the analyst, but
all those and more. He will say "... this woman" "... this dream" and use
other similarly undefined (to the analyst) expressions. As this vagueness is
an expression of β-element [beta-element] "thinking" the vagueness is not
due to loss of definition but can obtrude because the analyst is in a position
analogous to that of a listener to the description of a work of art that has
been implemented in materials and on a scale that is not known to him.
It is as if he heard the description of a painting, was searching on a canvas
for the details represented to him, whereas the object had been executed
in a material with which he is unfamiliar. Such a patient can talk of a "penis
black with rage" or an "eye green with envy" as being visible in a painting.
These objects may not be visible to the analyst: he may think the patient is
hallucinating them. But such an idea, perhaps sound to the view of a psychiatrist, is not penetrating enough for his work as an analyst. Hallucination may
be more profitably seen as a dimension of the analytic situation in which,
together with the remaining "dimensions", these objects are sense-able (if
we include analytic intuition or consciousness, taking a lead from Freud, as a
sense-organ of psychic quality).

(CWB V, pp. 228–229)

This is one of the quotes I particularly had in my mind when writing the introduction to this chapter. Bion is saying that one has got to go into the patient's world,
"a work of art that has been implemented in materials and on a scale that is not
known to him [the analyst]". One is not simply to say that the patient is hallucinating. One can hear Bion's respectful engagement in his patient's world. He
comments elsewhere that the world of hallucination is as various and interesting
as the world of dreams.

[185]   The unconscious and the infinite

The differentiating factor that I wish to introduce is not between conscious and unconscious, but between finite and infinite.

(CWBV, p. 167)

Infinity?

Bion is writing about this kind of thing quite a bit by now. The idea of infinity may seem paradoxical. It is like zero in the sense that it is a very important "number", yet it is no number at all. Zero comes before numerical reality, and infinity where numerical reality runs out. This may be helpful in understanding what Bion means by it – he wants to refer to what is beyond our existing categories and capacities. In a later quote, for example, he says the following:

> Confronted with the unknown, «the void and formless infinite», the personality of whatever age fills the void (saturates the element), provides a form (names and binds a constant conjunction) and gives boundaries to the infinite (number and position). Pascal's phrase "*Le silence de ces espaces infinies m'effraie*" can serve as the expression of intolerance and fear of the "unknowable" and hence of the unconscious in the sense of the undiscovered or the unevolved.
>
> *(CWBV, p. 279)*

> (*Le silence eternel des ces espaces infinis m'effraie* – *The eternal silence of these infinite spaces frightens me.*)

If we take eternity to mean not infinite temporal duration but timelessness, then eternal life belongs to those who live in the present.

(Wittgenstein 1922, 6.4311)

[186]   A technique of interpretation

I find I have constantly to give interpretations in the form that some impulse "leads to" a particular defect (or characteristic) of the mode of thought; or that some characteristic of the mode of thought "gives rise" to a particular impulse, as, for example, that frustration, engendered by failure to solve a problem, "leads to" a destructive attack on the analytic approach.

(CWB V, pp. 179–180)

Bion is not just saying to the patient that he or she is being attacking, he is saying *why* it is happening.

[187] Thought feared to destroy perfect object

[The] complications arising through the existence of an extremely under-standing mother, particularly understanding by virtue of ability to *accept* projective identification. A reaction associated with this resembles character disorder, an unwillingness to face loss of an idyllic state for a new phase and suppression of the new phase because it involves pain. It is against this background of hallucinosis, projective identification, splitting and persecu-tion, accepted as if it were the ideally happy state, that I want to consider the domain of verbal communication. The sense of well-being engendered by a belief in the existence of the perfectly understanding mother (or analyst) adds force to the fear and hatred of thoughts which are closely associated with, and may therefore be felt to be indistinguishable from, the "no-breast". A painful state of mind is clung to, including depression, because the alterna-tive is felt to be worse, namely that thought and thinking mean that a near perfect breast has been destroyed.

(*CWBV*, pp. 181–182)

Clinical note

Following a helpful session, the patient had a dream in which she was dancing. This was new. The dance, however, took place in an ordinary setting that was not the "perfect" setting she felt she was entitled to and would approve of. Her anxiety about failing to have an idyllic state of affairs constrained the dance in the dream and obstructed our being able to think in the session.

[188]   "Concentration of emotion ⇌ widening the spectrum of emotions"

I shall suppose that the increase of intensity in narcissism is accompanied by a narrowing or concentration of emotion till it can be said to be one emotion such as love or hate or fear or sex or any other. Similarly the intensity of social-ism is accompanied by a widening of the spectrum of emotions.

(*CWBV*, pp. 197–198)

Bion is not linking narcissism to splitting and idealisation but something closer to what Freud calls "primary narcissism". He saw "narcissism ⇌ social-ism" as describing the two "poles" of all instincts, emotions and ways of thinking. Two poems illustrate what Bion may mean by a "concentration of emotion" and "a widening of the spectrum of emotion". The first to illustrate an instance of a state of mind in which there is a moment of being drawn into a "concentration of emotion" – into the "dark and deep" of the woods in snow. The second poem is to illustrate a "widening of the spectrum of emotions" in the "the drunkenness of things being various".

A concentration of emotion: Robert Frost

"Stopping by Woods on a Snowy Evening"

Whose woods these are I think I know.
His house is in the village, though;
He will not see me stopping here
To watch his woods fill up with snow.
My little horse must think it queer
To stop without a farmhouse near
Between the woods and frozen lake
The darkest evening of the year.
He gives his harness bells a shake
To ask if there is some mistake.
The only other sound's the sweep
Of easy wind and downy flake.
The woods are lovely, dark and deep,
But I have promises to keep,
And miles to go before I sleep,
And miles to go before I sleep.

(Frost 1923)

A widening of the spectrum of emotion: Louis MacNeice

Snow

The room was suddenly rich and the great bay-window was
Spawning snow and pink roses against it
Soundlessly collateral and incompatible:
World is suddener than we fancy it.
World is crazier and more of it than we think,
Incorrigibly plural. I peel and portion
A tangerine and spit the pips and feel
The drunkenness of things being various.
And the fire flames with a bubbling sound for world
Is more spiteful and gay than one supposes –
On the tongue on the eyes on the ears in the palms of one's hands –
There is more than glass between the snow and the huge roses.

(MacNeice 1936)

We might assume that a "widening" would be less intense than a "concentration". Bion thinks not: there is intensity in narcissism and intensity in social-ism. There is intensity in the "dark and deep of the woods" in the first poem and in the "drunkenness of things being various" in the second poem.

Clinical illustration

Patient A: a difficulty with "oneness"

From the point of view of the poem, "Stopping by Woods on a Snowy Evening", Patient A might be seen as like the horse that shakes its bells. She might say, "Why are we pausing here, when I have lists of tasks to do". A's life has been dominated by lists of things that have to be done. One can feel under great pressure in sessions to suggest practical solutions. In her first meeting with me she described her sense of living on the surface.

As the analysis proceeded, we saw how she longed to feel one intense emotion – one emotion so "concentrated" that it would be beyond doubt and would put her doubts to rest. Was this a wish for a magical solution to her difficulties? While this seemed partially right, I had also been moved and struck by how A suffered from a profound anxiety that she was not wanted. She believed herself never to be "the one": I was believed to want another one, a different kind of patient instead of her. Might it be that, to be able to deeply recognise and understand what "one" emotion is, the person needs to have experienced themselves as having been the "one"?

Patient B: a difficulty with "a spectrum of emotions"

In B's illusory phantasy world she is the "one" – never one of a group. She moves in the world as if she were the central character in a movie. She has a difficulty being one of the group. It does seem that as a young child B's "family group" may have been "too much in her face". The parental relationship was overly exposed in front of her, and there were too many other babies, too quickly, to be taken in. She may not have been as helped with her narcissism as she needed, and it became a refuge from a world that would involve her in a "spectrum of emotions" more "various" and "more spiteful and gay than one supposes" (MacNeice 1936).

[189]   Antidote rather than solution

The infant's experience of the breast as the source of emotional experiences (later represented by terms such as love, understanding, meaning) means that disturbances in relationship with the breast involve disturbance over a wide range of adult relationships. The function of the breast in supplying meaning is important for the development of a capacity to learn. In an extreme instance, namely the fear of the total destruction of the breast, not only does this involve fears that he has ceased to exist (since without the breast he is not viable) but fears that meaning itself, as if it were matter, had ceased to exist. In some contingencies the breast is not regarded as the source of meaning so much as meaning itself. This anxiety is often screened by the fact that the analyst gives interpretations and thus seems to provide evidence that meaning exists. If this is not observed the patient's intolerance of meaninglessness is not interpreted: he will pour out a flood of words so that he can evoke a response indicating that meaning exists either in his own behaviour or in that of the analyst. Since the first requisite for the discovery of the meaning of any conjunction depends on the ability to admit that the phenomena may have no meaning, an inability to admit that they have no meaning stifles the possibility of curiosity at the outset. ... Since the patient's attention is directed to finding evidence of meaning, but not to finding what the meaning is, interpretations have little effect in producing change until the patient sees that he is tapping a source of reassurance to provide an *antidote* to his problem and not a *solution* of it.

(*CWB V*, pp. 198–199)

The patient is so frightened about having destroyed the object that he or she just wants the object (the analyst) to keep reassuring them – this would be to provide an antidote rather than a solution.

[190]   Agoraphobia/claustrophobia and the "place where the thing was"

Patients and analysts are constantly using different terms to describe situations that appear to have the same configuration. I want to find invariants, under psychoanalysis, to all of them. This condition is almost filled by the term "place where the thing was" or "space". Almost, but not quite. Its virtue can be seen in the fact that it will do equally well for agoraphobia or claustrophobia, and to that extent avoids two terms for configurations that are only apparently different. What is needed is a solution that will dispose finally of the diversity of terms, at present required to describe the experience called "claustro- or agoraphobia", and the far more serious defect associated with it, namely, the elaboration of as many theories as there are sufferers, matched by almost as many theories as there are therapists, when it is acknowledged that the configurations are probably the same.

(*CWB* V, p. 237)

Claustrophobia and agoraphobia are related to "the place where something was". If the infant cannot bear loss, instead of having an experience of absence (while retaining an internal connection to the absent object), the individual is either trapped in a present torturing object (claustrophobia) or lost without an object at all (agoraphobia).

Clinical note

The patient said that something had suddenly clicked. She had noticed that whenever there was a loss – like my cancelling a session or even when one of her own customers cancelled – she immediately dealt with it by organising something to do as an alternative. She could never rest. She was always filling up her space. On the one hand, she would feel "got at" by all the tasks she had to do – an enactment of a present torturing object? On the other hand, she could feel that she didn't have a life at all – that there was nothing she had that she could live "in".

[191]   Rivalry in hallucinosis

(i)   Hallucination is seen as a method of achieving independence which the patient considers to be superior to psychoanalysis.

(ii)   Its failure, in so far as it is seen as a failure, is attributed to the rivalry, envy and thieving propensities of the analyst.

(iii)   Rivalry, envy, greed, thieving, together with his sense of being blameless, deserve consideration as invariants under hallucinosis.

(iv)   The concept of hallucinosis needs to be widened to fit a number of configurations which are at present not recognized as being the same. . . .

(*CWBV*, p. 245)

Transformation in hallucinosis

When the presenting problem in analysis is the hallucinations of the patient a crux has been reached. In addition to the problem that the patient is attempting to solve by transformation in hallucinosis is the secondary problem presented by his method of solution. This secondary problem appears in analysis as a conflict between the method employed by the analyst and the method employed by the patient. The conflict can be described as a disagreement on the respective virtues of a transformation in hallucinosis and a transformation in psychoanalysis. The disagreement is coloured by the patient's feeling that the disagreement between patient and analyst is a disagreement between rivals and that it concerns rival methods of approach. Unless this point is made clear no progress can be made. When it has been made clear the disagreement still continues but it becomes endo-psychic: the rival methods struggle for supremacy within the patient. The characteristics of the conflict are easier to discern when externalized as a conflict between analyst and patient and this can lead to a collusion between the two for the patient finds it more tolerable and the analyst easier.

(*CWBV*, pp. 253–254).

Clinical note

The patient convincingly presented her difficulties as lying in the outside world. Putting it overly simply, she wanted to believe that her problems would be solved by finding a man who would both sweep her off her feet and provide her with the financial means to be freed from work. What gave me pause for thought was that I noticed I was unable to think about her internal reality – in fact, I found I was having difficulty thinking at all.

I noticed that she and I could end up in a kind of argument about whether what mattered was her internal or her external reality, with me sounding like I was on a "high horse" about truth and reality-principle functioning – these having a moral ascendency over functioning by hallucinosis. I now had "reality-principle functioning" as a "superior" system!

[192]   A baffling situation

It is common to find some feature, such as the cruelty of the super-ego, and to suppose that one has discovered the key to a baffling situation only to find that the same feature occurs in other situations which bear no marked resemblance to the situation to which one hoped the key had been discovered. In my experience this difficulty arises because the *key* has been detected in the elements of a second, third or subsequent cycle of psychoanalytic (that is, analyst's) transformations when it should be sought in the nature of the transformations effected by the analysand.

(*CWB V*, pp. 248–249)

Clinical note

Although intending to be vigilant about assumptions I might be making, I have on occasion realised myself to be making an assumption so ego-syntonic that it had previously passed unnoticed. At one such moment of realisation I think the change in me – without saying anything explicitly to the patient – may have contributed to a change in her and her willingness to come towards me – in what was otherwise a rather stuck situation. I realised that I was assuming that it was only her difficulties that meant she did not enjoy and value symbolisation as I did. In fact, I had chosen a profession that prioritised processes of symbolisation. I enjoyed listening to dreams. I found it an achievement when a previously unknown influence on the personality came to be symbolised in dream. The patient didn't necessarily share this. Certainly her profession was a very different one. When I realised this about myself and was informed by it in what I said, I think we gained some helpful separateness. I found that the patient was then able to tell me something of great importance to her that she hadn't been able to say before.

[193]   Hyperbole

It is a commonplace that any attempt at scientific inquiry involves distortion through the exaggeration of certain elements in order to display their significance....

(*CWB V*, p. 252)

Just as exaggeration is helpful in clarifying a problem so it can be felt to be important to exaggerate in order to gain the attention necessary to have a problem clarified. Now the "clarification" of a primitive emotion depends on its being contained by a container which will detoxicate it. In order to enlist the aid of the container the emotion must be exaggerated. The "container" may be a "good breast", internal or external, which is able to detoxicate the emotion. Or the container may not be able to tolerate the emotion and the contained emotion may not be able to tolerate neglect. The result is hyperbole. That is to say, the emotion that cannot tolerate neglect grows in intensity, is exaggerated to ensure attention and the container reacts by more, and still more, violent evacuation. By using the term "hyperbole" I mean to bind the constant conjunction of increasing force of emotion with increasing force of evacuation. It is immaterial to hyperbole what the emotion is; but on the emotion will depend whether the hyperbolic expression is idealizing or denigrating.

(*CWB V*, p. 253)

Later in the book Bion makes a related point regarding hyperbole used by the analyst:

The abstruse interpretation relates to desire in the analyst, a wish to feel that he can see further than his analysand or some other who serves as a rival. It belongs to the domain of hyperbole.

(*CWB V*, p. 276)

[194] Vitality from the same characteristics

[The patient believes] that their well-being and vitality spring from the same characteristics which give trouble. The sense that loss of the bad parts of his personality is inseparable from loss of that part in which all his mental health resides, contributes to the acuity of the patient's fears. This acute fear is inseparable from any attempt to resolve the crux. Is the patient going to repeat the former error by becoming confirmed in his adherence to transformation in hallucinosis or will he turn to transformation in psychoanalysis?

(*CWB V*, p. 255)

Perfectionism is one place this can be seen. Patients can hear the analyst to be suggesting that they lower their standards and settle for their current unsatisfactory situation. The analyst is being heard through the patient's system (which is dominated by rivalry), rather than as working in a different system – that of "transformation in psycho-analysis".

Clinical note

A patient dreamt that he was in his parents' house: they were absent, but his best uncle was around. The patient thinks his uncle is smart but not nice. In the dream the patient remembered carrying a pile of papers upstairs, he put it on his desk, and his brother pushed it over; he became enraged, and the world went "all black". He woke up enraged at his partner.

He told his analyst that he was afraid that the papers represented all his capacity to think and his abilities. He thought he was the good person in the dream.

It seemed to the analyst that as the patient became aware of the more furious destructive brother aspects of himself, he was terrified that all his abilities in his split-off "good person side" would be overwhelmed in the blackness and would collapse (Susan Lawrence, personal communication).

[195]   Impossible to sing potatoes

It is not knowledge of reality that is at stake, nor yet the human equipment for knowing. The belief that reality is or could be known is mistaken because reality is not something which lends itself to being known. It is impossible to know reality for the same reason that makes it impossible to sing potatoes; they may be grown, or pulled, or eaten, but not sung. Reality has to be "been": there should be a transitive verb "to be" expressly for use with the term "reality".

(*CWB* V, p. 259)

[196]   Transformation in "O"

> To rigid motion transformations, projective transformations, transforma-
> tions in hallucinosis, I shall now add transformations in O.
>
> > (*CWB V*, p. 266)

> The point at issue is how to pass from "knowing" "phenomena" to "being"
> that which is "real".
>
> > (*CWB V*, p. 259)

"O"

> ... acceptance in O means that acceptance of an interpretation enabling the
> patient to "know" the part of himself to which attention has been drawn is
> felt to involve "being" or "becoming" that person. For many interpretations
> this price is paid. But some are felt to involve too high a price, notably, those
> which the patient regards as involving him in "going mad" or committing
> murder of himself or someone else, or becoming "responsible" and there-
> fore guilty.
>
> > (*CWB V*, p. 273)

Clinical note

On her return from the summer break, the patient told me about an incident in which a "very nice, supportive woman" had talked her into purchasing a ticket for an excursion in a small boat – although she is terrified of water. The patient assumed the woman would be on the boat. In the event, it was a young man who drove the boat. The patient thought he responded to her fear of being on the water by going faster and further out, into deeper water, sadistically controlling her and enjoying her fear. As we talked further about the incident, the patient considered that she herself could feel sadistic, and that she could fear I would be sadistic, but she hastened to establish that we both knew neither (her or my sadism) was real. With horror she said she would never let herself actually be sadistic. I thought that she was so anxious about *becoming* the person who could really feel sadistic (and have an analyst who might really have to grapple with her own sadism) that she was vulnerable to remaining in the nice world represented by the woman selling her the ticket.

[197]   St John of the Cross

From the last chapter of the book:

> My term "psychological turbulence" needs elucidation. By it I mean a state of mind the painful quality of which may be expressed in terms borrowed from St John of the Cross. I quote:
>
> "The first (night of the soul) has to do with the point from which the soul goes forth, for it has gradually to deprive itself of desire for all the worldly things which it possessed, by denying them to itself; the which denial and deprivation are, as it were, night to all the senses of man. The second reason has to do with the mean, or the road along which the soul must travel to this union – that is, faith, which is likewise as dark as night to the understanding. The third has to do with the point to which it travels – namely, God, Who, equally, is dark night to the soul in this life."
>
> I use these formulations to express, in exaggerated form, the pain which is involved in achieving the state of naivety inseparable from binding or definition (col. 1). Any naming of a constant conjunction involves admission of the negative dimension and is opposed by the fear of ignorance. Therefore at the outset there is a tendency to precocious advance, that is, to a formulation which is a col. 2 formulation intended to deny ignorance – the dark the night of the senses. The relevance of this to psychological phenomena springs from the fact that they are not amenable to apprehension by the senses. . . .
>
> (CWB V, pp. 268–269)

The unexpectedness of an analyst referring to the work of St John of the Cross may get in the way of looking at what is being said. Three points struck me particularly:

1   The process described involves a giving up of possessions. While the quote refers to "worldly things", Bion draws on it in exploring ideas about "mental possessions", and how these are different from thoughts.
2   There is an emphasis on our fear of ignorance and how we can advance "precociously" to avoid the experience of ignorance.
3   The Grid is very much a part of the thinking that is going to lead to what he later says about memory, desire and understanding. It is not surprising that Col. 2 (the prevention of "the emergence of a more accurate but more frightening idea" (CWB V, p. 67) is referred to. What surprised me is Bion's reference to Col. 1 – "achieving the state of naivety inseparable from binding or definition". With Col. 1 Bion is drawing attention to the possibility of observing patterns or constant conjunctions before going on to explore

their meaning. This is important, because it facilitates observation before the application of our psychoanalytic metapsychology – it helps us to see what is there, rather than what our theory would lead us to expect to see.

St John of the Cross (Spanish: San Juan de la Cruz; 1542–14 December 1591): A major figure of the Counter-Reformation, a Spanish mystic, a Roman Catholic saint, a Carmelite friar and a priest who was born at Fontiveros, Old Castile.

[198] Fear of megalomania

From the last chapter of the book:

> The third "dark night" is associated with the transformations in O, that is from K g O. The transformation that involves "becoming" is felt as inseparable from becoming God, ultimate reality, the First Cause. The "dark night" pain is fear of megalomania. This fear inhibits acceptance of being responsible, that is mature, because it appears to involve *being* God, being the First Cause, being ultimate reality with a pain that can be, though inadequately, expressed by "megalomania".

> (*CWB V*, p. 269)

Bion again surprises. He seems to be saying that infantile omnipotence is never wholly overcome, and that to get to the place of mature responsibility, we may have to pass close by to indigestible infantile megalomania. We may limit ourselves defensively, because we are frightened of our megalomania.

Chapter 13

On memory and desire

Introduction

"Notes on Memory and Desire" was originally given without notes on Wednesday 16 June 1965, at a Scientific meeting at the British Psychoanalytical Society; it was summarised subsequently in a highly abridged form by Bion in 1967 as "Notes on Memory and Desire". It was also given in Los Angeles.

The paper was written between *Transformations* (1965) and *Attention and Interpretation* (1970) and, apart from two book reviews, is the only thing that Bion published during those years – years that also saw the move to California and the beginning of his teaching trips to South America.

Note: In some of his writings Bion includes "understanding" along with memory and desire. By this he means a defensive saturated understanding.

Parthenope Bion Talamo: Laying low and saying (almost) nothing (1998)

The Tar-baby said nothing, and Brer Fox, he lay low.

The . . . quotation comes from one of the Uncle Remus stories (Pritchard 1925), The Wonderful Tar-Baby Story, which is part of the saga of the unending struggle between Brer Rabbit and Brer Fox, who was his sworn enemy. In this particular story, Brer Fox makes a sort of statue of tar mixed with turpentine and sets it in the road along which the rabbit will be passing. The tar-baby, of course, does not reply to Brer Rabbit's polite greeting – so Brer rabbit, punches, kicks, and butts it with his head, to teach it a lesson in good manners, getting completely stuck in it, all four paws and his head too, while Brer Fox lies low, and the tar-baby goes on saying nothing. As a matter of fact, the two lively characters in the story must also have "run" together somewhat in my mind, as I remember my father misquoting it as "Brer Fox, he lay low and he said . . . Nothing". Naturally, I may be wrong about its being his misquotation (although he frequently did so, just slightly, adopting and adapting phrases to his own need) and it may simply be mine. The pertinent aspect of this, in any case, is that I now tend to think of Bion as an analyst partaking a little of the characteristics of all three figures, the fox, the tar-baby, and the rabbit. (This might be said to be a sub-set of his internal group!)

For example, his comments on α-elements in *Cogitations* make it quite clear that there really were moments when he felt "stuck", like the rabbit, and that he was only able to get clear of the morass by thinking very deeply about his own emotional reactions to the atmosphere in the consulting room. (Not to be confused with the idea of using one's countertransference, which he liquidates rather scathingly in *Bion in New York and São Paulo*, 1977–1978.) Furthermore, one gets the impression from several people who had been in analysis with him that he must, at times, have seemed rather like the tar-baby, too, saying almost nothing, or perhaps nothing at all. And as for the fox? Well, from my childhood memories of him, I can imagine my father "laying back" in the rocking-chair in his consulting room and just waiting to see and to feel his way through what was about to happen – although not with the malicious intentions of the story-tale fox.

The complex concept of working without memory or desire links up, in fact, with the idea of trying to purify your mind, letting what is inessential sediment somewhere and drain away, so that you could have the "laying low" without the sneaky or violent element.

(Bion Talamo 2011, pp. 597–599)

Quotes

199 Constant conjunction
200 Desire and covetousness
201 Memory
202 A clock that shouts at you
203 Analysts to make up own minds about what they would call "memory" and "desire"

[199]   Constant conjunction

> By a constant conjunction I mean that in certain circumstances you might notice that certain elements kept on turning up constantly conjoined; that you think, for example, that there is fur, claws, whiskers – and you bind the lot by saying "Cat"; the object of that being that once you have bound this constant conjunction you can then set about researching as superficially or as deeply as you choose, into what you mean by this term. It is rather different from the ordinary view – about the ordinary views which are held philosophically about abstraction. I am really suggesting that you start with the unknown, that you note a constant conjunction, that you bind it by a term which is vitally meaningless, and then proceed to investigate what you mean by that term, for the rest of your life if you are so inclined.
>
> (*CWB VI*, p. 7)

Bion's recommendation to work with discipline of memory, desire and understanding is important in order to observe, not the flux of moment to moment material, but constant conjunctions that can become observable if one puts aside "the peculiarities that make us creatures of circumstance". The conjunction of elements is to be observed before its meaning is then enquired in to. This affords the possibility – highlighted in Hinshelwood's work "Research on the Couch" (2013) – of some degree of separation between observation, and then the understanding of the material observed with the use of analytic theory.

[200]   Desire and covetousness

[By desire] I mean … something rather positively covetous, as it were; something one wants to have. It has a certain similarity to memory, in that one could say about memory that you tend to remember various things which you like to possess and in this sense memory itself is very often used as if it were a container in which one keeps these objects that one desires.

(CWB VI, p. 8)

From *Los Angeles Seminars and Supervision*, also 1967.

Now the next point that I want to come to is such a simple one that I almost hesitate to mention it. It is to do with, if you feel so disposed, carrying out a sort of minor experiment with your session "tomorrow" (I'll get back to this "tomorrow", session and patient). And that is the attempt to allow your desires to play as small a part as possible in the analysis. *Suppress desire*. Once more, it's very easy to say but I think it's extremely difficult to do, and it may even be very difficult to know what I mean by that. So the first experiment really is this: if you catch yourself looking at your watch, and wondering when the session is going to come to an end, stop it. Try to arrange things in your consulting room in such a way that the time is obvious to you, without causing you to do this sort of thing [he most likely demonstrates looking at his wristwatch], or anything else, so that you don't have to worry about whether the session is coming to an end or not. Now the same thing applies to the weekend break and suchlike. Now if you'll do that, I would like you to consider what is meant by the word *desire*. I am saying … taking a simple example, because I say, "Don't desire the end of the session." "Don't desire the weekend break." If you do, it will interfere with your observations. There is something very peculiar about desire, as I'm using the term. It has a peculiarly devastating effect upon one's clinical observation. I won't hide that behind this I've got a deep-laid plot, which is to introduce you to the idea of giving up desire to cure your patients, and so on.

But, at the same time, I'd advise you against trying anything of that kind. Because I think unless you take this very slowly, you will find yourself in very deep water. I think it is far better to stick to what you know, and what you're used to (your methods of working), and to make any attempt of this kind very cautious, very critical, and slow. So, if you'll start off with this, and if you feel disposed to do so, to work on the system of clarifying first of all what *you* think is desire on this very narrow basis (because no great harm can be done by this—it doesn't lead very far), but what it may lead to is a definition by which you know what you mean by desire.

The desire is the future tense of it – it's what you want to happen. Memory is what you want to have happened.

(LASS, pp. 43–45)

[201]   Memory

In my experience I find nearly always that the wish to remember what the patient said, or any desire to cure the patient, invariably seems to me to crop up in the situation, and in a formulation, which is intended to keep at bay and to keep out of mind certain other feelings.

(*CWB VI*, p. 12)

From Bion's reply to the discussants of the "Memory and Desire" paper:

The discussants of my "Notes on memory and desire" help to make it clear that some of the confusion arises through the ambiguity of the terms "memory" and "desire". I realise that it would be helpful if I could distinguish between two different phenomena which are both usually and indifferently called "memory". This I have tried to do by speaking of one as "evolution", by which I mean the experience where some idea or pictorial impression floats into the mind unbidden and as a whole. From this I wish to distinguish ideas which present themselves in response to a deliberate and conscious attempt at recall; for this last I reserve the term "memory".....

(*LASS*, p. 356)

It is the wish to remember that is problematic, not "memories" that might come to one in the free-associative state of mind in the session. I was struck to hear the author Marilynne Robinson say that when she is not writing her fictional work "truly", it is not simply that she is writing "falsely", but she is writing stuff already known and now caricatured.

Michael Parsons

Memory and desire are human attributes, which analysts have in common with their patients. Divesting oneself of them might look, on the face of it, like a retreat from personal relationship to a psychological crow's-nest, allowing exact observation but little in the way of shared experience. So it is important to bear in mind that Bion (1970: 41 [*CWB VI*, p. 255]) also said that what is ordinarily called forgetting is as bad as remembering. Moreover, the clinical examples given earlier do not indicate a disengagement between analyst and patient. The woman who was contemplating a new job showed me my desire to mean more to her than her work or her mother. But that led to my realising more clearly what I did mean to her as her analyst. With the man who was warding off feelings of disorganisation, I found myself wanting memory, his memory of the course of events, and I needed to give that up. But this was in order to get closer to, not further from, what he was really bringing. In the session described at length, I was more able to be free of desire for the meaning of the patient's material. And the result? He told me about the personal meaning I held for him. It was emphasised in Chapter 1 that psychoanalysis, as a vocation which expresses the analyst's being, can only be arrived at by the analyst's immersing himself or herself in basic technique. The processes Bion describes, which might appear so transcendent as to become imper-sonal, are similarly to be found in the ordinary details of the everyday analytic interaction.

(Parsons 2000, pp. 48–49)

[202] A clock that shouts at you

... you've got to know when it's the end of the session and so on, and I wouldn't like to guarantee that even after lots of experience the sort of internal clock ticks on to the fact that it's the end of the session. I think it is one of the reasons why one should be careful to arrange one's consulting room with great attention to these details. Much more attention than we ever hear about in training or anything of that kind. To have a clock which shouts at you, as it were, something which is absolutely obvious and unmistakable so that there's a minimum of attention required on your part to it (because you've got to know it), and as I say, I think that the less one has to do with it the better.

(*LASS*, pp. 81–82)

[203] Analysts to make up own minds about what they would call "memory" and "desire"

...I suggest that every psychoanalyst should make up his mind for himself by simple experimentation as to what these terms [memory and desire] represent. For example, he should school himself to avoid thinking of the end of the session, week or term (having made previous provision for terminating the session at the correct time as a matter of administration), and when he has done this for a sufficient period without trying to hurry himself, make up his mind about what *he* would call "memory" and "desire". When he has done this he can proceed to the next stage of extending his suppressions of the experience he has discovered in this way. I must warn psychoanalysts that I do not think they should extend this procedure hurriedly or without discussion with other psychoanalysts with a view to consolidating each step before taking another.

(*LASS*, pp. 367–358)

In many statements made by Bion on "memory and desire", he describes what he is saying as a rule – and, as I have commented, he can sound like a captain issuing an order. This final quote, however, puts the onus on the individual analyst to engage in a process of discovery, rather than the application of a rule. The quote is from Bion's reply to the discussants' responses to his "Memory and Desire" paper when given in Los Angeles. The discussants were Thomas M. French, John A. Lindon, Avelino González, and Marjorie Brierley.

Chapter 14

Attention and Interpretation: A Scientific Approach to Insight in Psycho-Analysis and Groups

Introduction

Bion's way of talking in *Attention and Interpretation: A Scientific Approach to Insight in Psycho-Analysis and Groups* can result in a tendency either to dismiss or to idealise what he says. It can be difficult to find appropriate ways to think about what he is saying. I hope the quotes from Bion in this chapter will be helpful in this.

André Green commented on the book.

André Green

. . . Actually, the word "attention" is not even mentioned in the index and as to the term "interpretation". . . . In fact, the person responsible for the interpretation (my own position *vis-à-vis* this book I had to comment upon) must do away with the feeling of kinship he might be tempted to establish between himself and the object of his interpretation. To achieve this, he must free himself from his illusory possessions (assets as well as liabilities) in order to meet with a more open frame of mind what he will be faced with as intrinsically unknown. I had to shake off the feeling of how limited I was to give an account of this book in so far as it deals with matters I am not familiar with in the realms of mathematics, mysticism or Kant's philosophy to comply with the wish of the author, who expects that the reader will not so much have some knowledge transmitted to him, but rather that he will be affected by his reading.

I was then beginning to understand more clearly the reference to the word "attention", according to the meaning Freud and Bion give it as a function helping: "periodically to search the outer world in order that its data might be already familiar if an urgent need should arise" (Freud 1911, p. 220). Nevertheless, Freud adds: "Its activity meets the sense impressions half way, instead of awaiting their appearance." I then saw the object of the book as aimed not to passive reading but as meeting the reader half way. Attention was not what was in the book, it was the book itself and that is the reason why the word did not appear in the index. Yet I find it necessary to point out a difference between Freud's and Bion's uses of this function. Freud's aim is a preventive one, familiarity having to be assured in case an urgent need should arise. Bion's aim is more a provocative one, intended as it were to encourage a rushed meeting with what is unknown in both parties facing each other, to create the conditions of urgent need rather than to insure against the possible advent of the expectation of a happening.

(Green 1973, p. 115)

Notes on concepts Bion is using and developing

(I have included material from the Introduction for ease of reference.)

"O"

Bion comes to a question in later life that Freud also came to in his later life: "Why is change so difficult to achieve?" In 1920 Freud's response was to consider the inherent destructiveness of human beings. His conclusions were part of Bion's psychoanalytic inheritance. Fifty years later, Bion's response went in a different direction – to the difference between (K) (knowing) and "O" (being). The use of the letters "K" and "O" again allow us to mark a subject that can then be enquired into. The American psychoanalyst Michael Eigen puts it like this:

> What is crucial is *how one relates to* whatever one may be relating to. . . . If, for example, one's emotional reality or truth is despair, what is most important is not *that* one may be in despair, but one's attitudes *toward* one's despair. Through one's basic attentiveness one's despair can declare itself and tell its story. One enters profound dialogue with it. If one stays with this process, an evolution even in the quality of despair may begin to be perceived, since despair itself is never uniform.
>
> (Eigen 1981, p. 429)

It is not only the patient's difficulty with "being" that concerns Bion, but also the analyst's "being" properly in the session with the patient. It is worth mentioning that Bion remained strict throughout about the analytic setting.

I have included quotes from other analysts on "O" later in the chapter.

"F" (Faith)

In *Attention and Interpretation* Bion uses the term F (Faith) to describe the psychoanalyst's relation to the non-sensible world of psychic reality. How can a man so concerned with being in touch with reality take on the idea of faith as a key concept? From the point of view of science, even common sense, isn't faith delusional belief? I must confess a liking for conundrums and have grappled with this one for quite some time. Take, for example, "The Red Wheelbarrow", by American modernist poet William Carlos Williams (1883–1963). The poem describes the scene of a red wheelbarrow and white chickens after the rain. The poem was originally published without a title and was designated as "XXII" – the twenty-second work in Williams' 1923 book *Spring and All*. The scene painted for us is one that would be "seen" by the senses of sight, and perhaps smell. Yet we also grasp that the poem has considerable weight. In his use of the term F (Faith), I think Bion is talking about a faculty rather than a belief. It is not necessarily a precise faculty, there are different interpretations of the poem, but it is nonetheless a faculty.

The "Messianic idea" and the "Establishment"

In *Attention and Interpretation* Bion refers to the relationship between what he calls "the messianic idea" and the "establishment". Growth occurs if the new idea is allowed to be strong, while being rightly assessed and checked by the establishment, to ascertain real worth not just superficial daring. In order to do this, the establishment is required to allow its established ideas and practices to be put into question. Growth does not occur if the challenging idea is suppressed by the establishment through ridicule or avoidance, or if the establishment is dismissed as irrelevant or "blown up" by the idea.

Did Bion see himself as a Messiah? It does seem that Bion had grown frustrated with the external establishment (has always been frustrated with the external establishment?). The key question, however, I think, is whether he maintains a healthy robust internal establishment through which to scrutinise his emerging ideas. One view (influential in the United Kingdom) has been that he didn't – that he lost his previous rigour. My own view is that he does maintain a healthy internal establishment – but does have a sense of having a mission – perhaps always has, since surviving the First World War. I think you can hear this in the following quote from *The Italian Seminars*:

> Whatever our difficulties may be, we have to remember to be concerned not with our problems, but with the work in hand – the work which never stops whether we are there to do it or not. There was a famous warrior named Cr[i]lon to whom Henry IV said, "Go hang yourself, brave Crillon; we fought at Arc and you were not there.
>
> (*CWB IX*, p. 184)

Quotes

[204]   Suffering

> There are patients whose contact with reality presents most difficulty when
> that reality is their own mental state. For example, a baby discovers its hand;
> it might as well have discovered its stomach-ache, or its feeling of dread
> or anxiety, or mental pain. In most ordinary personalities this is true, but
> people exist who are so intolerant of pain or frustration (or in whom pain
> or frustration is so intolerable) that they feel the pain but will not suffer
> it and so cannot be said to discover it. *What* it is that they will not suffer
> or discover we have to conjecture from what we learn from patients who
> *do* allow themselves to suffer. The patient who will not suffer pain fails to
> "suffer" pleasure and this denies the patient the encouragement he might
> otherwise receive from accidental or intrinsic relief.
>
> (*CWB VI*, pp. 227–228)

Bion distinguishes between what he describes as pain "suffered" and pain "felt".
This difference is to do not with whether the experience comes from inside or
outside, but with how it is received by the person. His distinction has not been
developed in a widespread or explicit way, and this may well be because of his
use of the term "suffer". At least at first sight, the term is confusing, the notion of
"suffering" pleasure, for example, would appear contradictory. However, it does
have another meaning, one illustrated in the following Biblical quotation:

> 13   Then were there brought unto him little children, that he should put
>   his hands on them, and pray: and the disciples rebuked them.
> 14   But Jesus said, Suffer little children, and forbid them not, to come
>   unto me.
>
> (Matthew 19, 905)

Here we get more sense of a meaning of "suffer" that is also contained in its
dictionary definition, of enduring a change and bearing or allowing something
to happen. This is the meaning, I think, Bion has in mind. He suggests that an
important difference between "suffering" and "feeling" is that the former is a discovery made in contact with reality (internal and external reality). By "discover",
he conveys a sense of finding the pain or pleasure within oneself, as an experience
of what it is to be oneself. As the psychoanalyst David Bell put it: "There is not
an 'I' which discovers certain states, thoughts, feelings within itself, but more
than that, it is in the act of the discovering, in that moment, that the 'I' is itself"
(personal communication).

   In contrast to this, pain felt but not suffered may be believed to carry information only about the "torturer" and hold no meaning for the self. On the loss of
the analyst for the break, patient A may discover that he or she is someone who
misses, who can feel excluded and can be jealous. By contrast, patient B may feel

pain, but not as their own experience of loss, but as pain inflicted on them cruelly by the analyst.

Bion concludes the quote above with reference to the "suffering" of pleasure.

Clinical note

A 9-year old girl dreamt she was in the seaside resort she visited every year with her family. She was out in deep water, waiting for a wave to surf on. She could not see them, but she knew that her family were around her in the sea. She was then picked up by a wave and flung through the water. It was, she said on waking, like flying. The family around her in the sea may act as a container for her experience. This experience, like adult orgasm, falling in love, or feeling an idea come to life, has in it a moment of considerable mobility. A person may not have access to pleasure that "arises within the self", because avoidance of pain and frustration has, as a consequence, the loss of the experience of pleasure. It may also be that the "suffering" of pleasure is avoided in its own right, because it can be disruptive and unsettling.

[205]   Hallucinosis

Verbal, musical, artistic modes of communication all meet with realizations that they appear to represent only very approximately. Hallucination may be regarded, wrongly, as a representation and therefore as unsuited to some activities. As verbal, musical, and artistic transformations have compensating values arising from their being *transformations* of O, it is natural to consider the like possibility with hallucinosis. But hallucinations are *not* representations: they are things-in-themselves born of intolerance of frustration and desire. Their defects are due not to their failure to represent but to their failure to *be*.

(*CWB VI*, p. 235)

This state [hallucinosis] I do not regard as an exaggeration of a pathological or even natural condition: I consider it rather to be a state always present, but overlaid by other phenomena, which screen it. If these other elements can be moderated or suspended hallucinosis becomes demonstrable: its full depth and richness are accessible only to "acts of faith". Elements of hallucinosis of which it is possible to be sensible are the grosser manifestations and are of secondary importance; to appreciate hallucination the analyst must participate in the state of hallucinosis

(*CWB VI*, p. 250)

From *Clinical Seminars*

Hallucinosis is a word which one uses as a compact summary of an emotional experience. It has a somewhat pejorative meaning, but the thing itself has to be treated with more respect than to be deposited in a psychiatric dustbin. I would like to see the state of hallucinosis treated with the kind of respect which we expect to accord neurosis, dreams, nightmares and other mental phenomena; we can then hope to learn more about it. I would like to say to the questioner: don't bother what I think about it, but have a good look at it when you feel that you have a chance of examining a state of hallucinosis. If we can respect hallucinosis we may be regarding a future mathematician − not mere mental debris.

(*CWB VII*, p. 189)

Clinical note

After a difficult break, the patient had a "dream" that I found myself cautious about interpreting in the transference. I came to think that it was in fact not a dream, but more an "hallucination". What made it different from a dream was the assertion of possession. The man and child in the "dream" were, in fact, being asserted to be in her possession, not mine.

[206] Suffering

1. The patients, for the treatment of whom I wish to formulate theories, experience pain but not suffering. They may be suffering in the eyes of the analyst because the analyst can, and indeed must, suffer. The patient may say he suffers but this is only because he does not know what suffering is and mistakes feeling pain for suffering it. The theory will need to be such that it represents the realization in which this is possible and shows how it comes about. The *intensity* of the patient's pain contributes to his fear of suffering pain.

2. Suffering pain involves respect for the fact of pain, his own or another's. This respect he does not have and therefore he has no respect for any procedure, such as psychoanalysis, which is concerned with the existence of pain.

3. Frustration and intense pain are equated.

4. Pain is sexualized; it is therefore inflicted or accepted but is not suffered – except in the view of the analyst or other observer.

(*CWB VI*, p. 236)

[207] "O"

> Psychoanalytic events cannot be stated directly, indubitably, or incorrigibly any more than can those of other scientific research. I shall use the sign O to denote that which is the ultimate reality represented by terms such as ultimate reality, absolute truth, the godhead, the infinite, the thing-in-itself. O does not fall in the domain of knowledge or learning save incidentally; it can be "become", but it cannot be "known". It is darkness and formlessness but it enters the domain K when it has evolved to a point where it can be known, through knowledge gained by experience, and formulated in terms derived from sensuous experience; its existence is conjectured phenomenologically.
>
> The events of the psycho analytic experience are transformed and formulated. . . . Their value therapeutically is greater if they are conducive to transformations in O; less if conducive to transformations in K.
>
> (CWB VI, p. 242)

Some other analysts on "O"

Ron Britton

In a discussion of James Grotstein's *A Beam of Intense Darkness* (2007), Britton makes the following comment:

> I think talking of what is unknowable (small case) as "the Unknown", or "Ultimate reality" (upper case) invests it with grander status and supernatural qualities. As Auden said, to give something or someone a Proper Name is to acknowledge it as having a real and valuable existence. This to me gives identity to what is unknown and conjures up a world beyond the one we live in as another version of the hereafter. Grotstein tells us he agrees with Bion that man has a natural propensity to religious belief. I wholeheartedly agree with this, but it only tells us that man is capable of worshipping stones, prophets, or "the Unknowable." Such is our anthropomorphic tendency God is likely to be made in man's image, as Spinoza said, "If he were a triangle he would think God was triangular" (Loemker 1956). . . .
>
> Grotstein is likely to be criticised for some ideas and formulations where, if there is criticism, it should be of Bion. This is not uncommon; in psychoanalytic argument one can find oneself criticised for putting forward ideas that are actually those of Freud. So my criticism is of Bion when he uses proper nouns for descriptive formulations, which Grotstein adopts and perhaps develops further. In *Attention and Interpretation*, Bion (1970 [*CWB VI*]) does not take his own advice and avoid using words that are already saturated with associative meaning, such as "Mystic" for an innovator within the group, or "Ultimate reality" for

"the-thing-in-itself", Kant's noumenon. Bion says himself, "Ultimate reality is a term with a penumbra of associations, which makes it psychologically helpful, but this fact makes it unsuitable to represent something that by definition is unknowable. The same objection applies to the term 'godhead' . . ." (Bion 1970, pp. 87–88 [*CWB VI*, pp. 294–295]).

I can only say amen to that but then he does use this language even though qualifying his use of it. Language like this attracts by osmosis religious longings, by which I mean longing for a religion, that I think contaminate psychoanalytic discourse. His "O" I see as unexceptionable, like alpha and beta, though for me it always stands for ontology. Any mystical infiltration of the capital letter "O" by the reader is their own responsibility; there is inevitably a drift into treating it as a proper noun which then makes it an entity, "a Being", not simply a state of being. There is a hunger for the transcendent that attracts some people to Bion and perhaps attracted Bion – the sceptical man still contained the religious boy he once was whose mind easily filled with the hymns of his youth.

Personally, I find religious language appealing and enlightening, but I know of others who find it aversive, and this can become a barrier to reading what is often called "late Bion." This so-called "late Bion" was quite early, in fact, certainly it is well underway by 1958 when he has recourse to Braithwaite, Bradley, Poincaré, Heisenberg, and so on. It was really his centring on processes in the analyst at work that moved him on.

(Britton 2008, pp. 119–121)

Elizabeth Tabak de Bianchedi

Although I agree with Edna [O'Shaughnessy] that, from the last chapters of *Transformations* (1965 [*CWB V*]) onwards, his writings become more "pro- and e-vocative", I believe that his style, now more ambiguous and less positivistic, generates strong possibilities of evolution in those who can stand it. The sub-title of that book [*Transformations*] is "Change from learning to growth", and the notion of change and mental development is implicit in it. The important ideas of the transformations in O ("becoming", being what one is) as complementary to the transformations in K (knowing about what one is) continue to be strongly present in *Attention and Interpretation* (1970 [*CWB VI*]) and in all his later writings. And the psychoanalytic process is seen as a growing spiral of transformations in K and transformations in O.

(De Bianchedi 2005, pp. 1530–1531)

André Green

In my review of *Attention and Interpretation* in 1973, I noticed the parallel between Bion's conception of the unknowable object and Freud's ideas about the object as stated in the "Project" (1950). It is not only the object that is unknowable but also the mental space "as a thing-in-itself that is unknowable, but that can be represented by thoughts" (Bion 1970, p. 11 [*CWB VI*, p. 229]). This originary state of the unknowable thing in itself meets a final state, the one of the symbol O. Bion writes: "I shall use the sign O to denote that which is the ultimate reality represented by terms such as ultimate reality, absolute truth, the formless, the infinite, the thing in itself" (p. 26 [*CWB VI*, p. 242]). All that we know stands in between these two extremes: the unknowable beginning and end. Speaking of the aim of analysis, Bion will not claim to reach anything beyond approximation. To some extent all knowledge is a loss of absolute truth compared to the formless infinite.

(Green 1998, p. 657)

James Grotstein

The concept of "O" as a revision of the nature of the Unconscious

Bion (1965 [*CWB V*], 1970 [*CWB VI*]) would frequently cite Milton's phrase, "the deep and formless infinite" in regard to his comments about "O." He and Matte Blanco (1975, 1988) ascribe the quality of infinity (dimensionally), of infinite sets (mathematically), and of chaos or complexity cosmically to the Unconscious. Freud's and Klein's perspectives on the nature of the unconscious were fundamentally constrained by their positivistic and deterministic assumptions. The libidinal and destructive drives represented the inchoate motor of the human will and, as a consequence, of its fate or destiny. Beginning with Winnicott's (1954) concept of "chaos" and Bion's (1965) concept of "O", as well as Matte Blanco's (1975, 1988) concept of infinite sets, we begin to see a post-modern revision of the picture of the fundamental nature of the Unconscious. The "deep and formless infinite" is its nature. It is dimensionless, infinite, and chaotic, or, in Matte-Blanco's terms, symmetrical and infinitized. In other words, Bion's picture of the Unconscious, along with that of Winnicott and Matte-Blanco, conveys an ineffable, inscrutable, and utterly indefinable inchoate formlessness that is both infinite and chaotic – or complex – by nature. It is what it is and is always changing while paradoxically remaining the same. From this point of view, Freud's instinctual drives and Klein's paranoid-schizoid and depressive positions can be understood as secondary structures, strategies or filters, to assist the infant in mediating this chaos. Lacan (1966), in delineating this aspect of the Unconscious as the "Register of the Real", as distinguished from the "Registers of the Imaginary and the Symbolic", fortifies my view of Bion's conception of the Unconscious as inchoately chaotic – vis-a-vis any attempt to "understand" it or perceive it. The Unconscious, as the Subject of subjects, is "O" and is therefore, like the "Immanent God" with which it is associated, utterly uncontemplatable. The only way to access it is by resonance in "O" with it.

(Grotstein on-line communication, 1977
http://www.sicap.it/merciai/bion/papers/grots.htm)

Howard Levine

For many American analysts, the work of Wilfred Bion is an acquired taste. His papers and early books are built on a foundation of Kleinian theory that may be unfamiliar to an audience raised on ego psychology and contemporary conflict theory. *Attention and Interpretation* and the various "lectures" and "seminars" that follow, can present even more of a problem. They can require familiarity – or at least comfort and conversance – with concepts such as "alpha and beta elements", "container and contained", "waking dream thoughts", "thoughts without a thinker", and Bion's infamous Grid. The result may seem baffling and esoteric, almost cultic. Is Bion writing as analyst, existentialist, philosopher, or mystic? What is the clinical relevance of his ideas? Will the effort required to master a new technical vocabulary prove worthwhile?. . . .

It is unfortunate, even ironic, that a man who tried so hard to find a way to write and speak clearly and succinctly about the immediacy of existential experience, what he called "O", created a vocabulary that ultimately threatened to obscure his purpose. . . . The problems that confronted Bion in this effort, problems that continue to plague us all, were almost insurmountable. Chief among them is the fact that psychic reality and the unconscious, the true subjects of psychoanalytic investigation and concern, are not available for direct observation.

(Levine 2007, pp. 677–678)

Chris Mawson

[Bion's] concept of "O" still remains something of a challenge to contemporary analysts, but serves to remind us all that the phenomena we study are elusive and somehow "behind" those surface manifestations which strike our sensory and perceptual systems, and that what we normally deal with are transformations of what is really there.

(From the Melanie Klein Trust Website)

Edna O'Shaughnessy

Consider one small example of what increasingly becomes an overall style: Bion writes, "I shall use the sign O to denote that which is the ultimate reality represented by terms such as ultimate reality, absolute truth, the godhead, the infinite, the thing-in-itself" (1970, p. 26 [*CWB VI*,

p. 242]). This statement mixes the psychoanalytic idea for which the sign O was originally introduced with the vast "penumbra of associations" of an assortment of philosophical ideas. Earlier, in *Learning from Experience* (1962 [*CWB VI*]), O, as part of his exploration of K, denotes the process and experience of getting to know – in opposition to the static state of possessing knowledge. Later, as O mingles with "ultimate reality, absolute truth, the godhead, the infinite, the thing-in-itself', Bion's earlier work rather than being developed, in my opinion, is confused. Moreover, how shall a reader align O if it is to denote, among other ultimates, "the godhead", with Bion's observation about the meaning of symbols for the psychotic patient? In "The mystic and the group", Bion states, "When the psychotic symbol is met with in practice . . . it indicates that the patient is in private rapport with a deity or demon" (1970, p. 65 [*CWB VI*, p. 276]) – a statement that instantly resonates with clinical experience of psychosis in psychoanalysis. How then shall we read Bion? Is being in rapport with God and the Godhead to do with O or to do with psychosis? Or both? If both, then, if we follow through the two lines of thought, a contradiction is being embraced – with pleasures and perils for the text.

In "Dreams and Occultism", Freud observed how "when life takes us under its strict discipline, a resistance stirs within us against the relentlessness and monotony of the laws of thought and against the demands of reality testing. Reason becomes the enemy" (1933, p. 33). Contradictions have their appeal: breaking the laws of thought and reason brings a quantum of verbal fun. Yet, in scientific writings, such transgressions lead us to anything and everything we fancy – because, as is readily logically demonstrable, from a contradiction any proposition follows. Texts with contradictions risk an unending proliferation of meanings. . . .

Thus, my reading of Bion's opus is that the arresting qualities of language in his main writings free the reader's thinking, but that, as his late thinking becomes less boundaried, the defects of these very qualities make the texts too open, too pro-and e-vocative, and weakened by riddling meanings.

(O'Shaughnessy 2005, pp. 1524–1525)

Rudi Vermote

From the conclusion to a clinical paper:

In my intervention, I had made an intuitive link between clochard (tramp) – the mirror (in the dream of the patient) and Beckett's tramps in *Waiting for Godot* and the Beckett Trilogy (1979) [following which the patient began to read Beckett]. Making this link was not thought, it emerged. The intuitive link can be seen as the emergence of a constant conjunction in the patient, that found itself expressed in the image of the tramp in Beckett's work. Recognising it was not wild but based on a long and intense relationship with the patient. However, it was something new.

. . . My point is that the change in the patient happened not only by the sharing and seeing of a psychoanalytic object, but also by the change in her mental attitude by reading Beckett. It was as if the patient could enter a kind of transcendent position together with me as analyst by reading Beckett. This deep receptiveness was alien to her before. It was a new and transformative experience, not a new insight or a getting a form for what she experiences (a transformation in knowledge). It was the first time in her life and lasted for months. Therefore we may call it a transformation in O.

(Vermote 2017, p. 153)

[208] F [Faith]

> An "act of faith" is peculiar to scientific procedure and must be distinguished
> from the religious meaning with which it is invested in conversational usage.
>
> (*CWB VI*, p. 249)

> Freud said that he had to "blind myself artificially to focus all the light on
> one dark spot". This provides a useful formulation for describing the area I
> wish to cover by F. By rendering oneself "artificially blind" through the exclu-
> sion of memory and desire, one achieves F; the piercing shaft of darkness
> can be directed on the dark features of the analytic situation. Through F
> one can "see", "hear", and "feel" the mental phenomena of whose reality no
> practising psychoanalyst has any doubt, though he cannot with any accuracy
> represent them by existing formulations.
>
> (*CWB VI*, p. 269)

A colleague commented: "This development in Bion's thought sounds a guru-type
thing in its claim to see things that other people can't, to be a conduit to another
world, it arouses scepticism and is very provocative. Bion is saying that we can't
know about these things through our sense perceptions, it depends what you mean
by sense perceptions. As an analyst you feel . . . a state of mind communicates
itself, the patient communicates and shares something not totally visible externally. It is not that it is not to do with sense impressions, but with one mind communicating with another. If people have the same kind of mental apparatus those
mental apparatus's can get together. Analysts have faith that analysis will have a
positive effect – patients often lack this" (personal communication).

Michael Parsons

Bion (1970 [*CWB VI*]) starts from the observation that the happenings
which really matter in psychoanalysis cannot be perceived by the senses.
Sensory experience is important, of course. The analyst listens and
speaks, and what he or she sees of the patient is also revealing. But this
only gives imperfect access to a realm that lies beyond sense experience.
When the patient's psyche is truly touched by the analyst, and something
changes in it, the analyst "intuits" this. Bion uses this word deliberately
to emphasise that what happens in this realm is not inferred from sense-
perceptions, but is known in some different way. How, then, to conceptualise a kind of experience which carries in its nature the conviction of
truth, but which cannot be deduced from, or proved by, the empirical
experience of the senses?

"Faith" is a term denoting exactly this conviction of the reality of
something that cannot be proved by sensory experience. Bion was not

disconcerted by finding in religious thinking a concept that he needed for describing what happens in psychoanalysis. He simply brought it into his analytic thinking, tending, however, to call it "F" rather than "faith" in order to avoid the connotations he did not want. By "F" he did not mean subscribing to a belief. He was referring to a particular kind of experience. Bion could make use in this way of a religious idea because of an enlarged understanding of religion . . . Bion is able to say, for example:

Certain problems can be handled by mathematics, others by economics, others by religion. It should be possible to transfer a problem, that fails to yield to the discipline to which it appears to belong, to a discipline that can handle it. (Bion 1970, p. 91 [*CWB VI*, pp. 297–298]).

One can also import, from one discipline into another, ideas that help the second discipline handle a problem more effectively. This is what Bion is doing with religion and psychoanalysis:

All psycho-analytic progress exposes a need for further investigation. There is a "thing-in-itself" which can never be known; by contrast, the religious mystic claims direct access to the deity with whom he aspires to be at one. Since this experience is often expressed in terms that I find it useful to borrow, I shall do so, but with a difference that brings them closer to my purpose. (Bion 1970, p. 87 [*CWB VI*, pp. 294])

Bion needed the concept "faith", or "F", to describe how the truth of what happens between patient and analyst is apprehended beyond the realm of sense-perception. As Eigen (1993, p. 124) has expressed it, faith is for Bion not just a condition that makes psychoanalysis possible, but its primary methodological principle. This poses a question: If F is not directed toward the sights and sounds of sensory experience, what is the object for which F is the specific mode of apprehension? Bion's answer is: a reality, for which he uses the symbol "O", that has the quality of absoluteness. He calls it "ultimate" reality, or "absolute truth". A patient's material and way of behaving in an analytic session belong to the world of sensory experience. Bion calls them "transformations" – we might also say "expressions" – in the sensory world of the ultimate reality of that human being, which is only imperfectly revealed by what the analyst hears and sees. What is apprehended by F is the reality of the person unmodulated by the inevitable circumscriptions of it that particular instances must involve.

(Parsons 2005, pp. 28–29)

[209] Possessed

A certain class of patient feels "possessed" by or imprisoned "in" the mind of the analyst if he considers the analyst desires something relative to him – his presence, or his cure, or his welfare ... If the psychoanalyst has not deliberately divested himself of memory and desire the patient can "feel" this and is dominated by the "feeling" that he is possessed by and contained in the analyst's state of mind, namely, the state represented by the term "desire".

(*CWB VI*, p. 256)

[210] Technique for suspension of memory, desire and understanding

The nearer the analyst comes to achieving suppression of desire, memory, and understanding, the more likely he is to slip into a sleep akin to stupor. Though different, the difference is hard to define. The sharpening of contact with O cannot be separated from an increase of perception, in particular of elements of K; this sensuous sharpening is painful although partial and mitigated by the general obliteration of sensory perception. The residual sensory perception, often auditory and restricted to particular kinds of sound, is responsible for inducing a sharp and painful reaction (similar to the startle reaction seen in babies).

(*CWB VI*, p. 260)

[211]   A frightful fiend

The emotional state of transformations in O is akin to dread as it is represented by the formulation:

> Like one that on a lonesome road
> Doth walk in fear and dread;
> And having once turned round walks on,
> And turns no more his head;
> Because he knows a frightful fiend
> Doth close behind him tread.

The "frightful fiend" represents indifferently the quest for truth or the active
defences against it, depending on the vertex.

The menace to "reality" is felt to derive from: (1) the suppression of
memory, desire, and understanding, for such suppression undermines sense-
based experience which is the reality with which the individual is familiar;
(2) the increase of power of F, which reveals and makes possible experiences
that are often painful and difficult for the individual analyst and analysand
to tolerate; and (3) the peculiar type of relationship between one element
and another in the O domain. Included in this is a relationship that is indifferently expressed as spatial or temporal. Thus, in my quotation, the walker
is being "overtaken" by dread; he walks a "lonesome road". It may seem
improbable that dread should be associated with analytic progress towards
a more realistic outlook.

(*CWB VI*, pp. 259–260)

The quote is from Coleridge's "The Rime of the Ancient Mariner". To my knowledge Bion doesn't use the quote anywhere else in his writings. This is rather
unusual, as he often referred to quotes a number of times.

Frightful fiends: Frankenstein: Mary Shelley makes several allusions to "The Rime
of the Ancient Mariner" in her novel Frankenstein. The above excerpt from the
poem appears after Victor creates the Monster, abandons him, and wanders the
streets throughout the night. The quote precisely complements Victor's actions
and characterisation, because Victor was alone in his quest to create life and
fled from the horror of what he had done once reality struck him.

[212] A married/unmarried man

In the first place [eschewing memory, desire and understanding], the analyst will soon find that he appears to be ignorant of knowledge which he has hitherto regarded as the hallmark of scrupulous medical responsibility. . . . Thus an analyst may feel, to take a common example, that his married patient is unmarried; if so, it means that psychoanalytically his patient is unmarried: the emotional reality and the reality based on the supposition of the marriage contract are discrepant. . . .

In psychoanalysis such matters as the patient's marriage have to be considered deeply. Is an overt practising homosexual with several children and a wife with whom he has entered into the marriage contract married?. . . .

What matters is that to statements of a particular category [of the grid] the patient begins to add statements of a different category.

(*CWB VI*, pp. 261–263)

It may be helpful to view what Bion is saying in two stages. The first stage will not be unfamiliar to the reader. A person may be legally married, with children, without actually being emotionally married. This thought is not an unusual one – we might expect to have seen that the patient's legal state did not match his psychic reality: he may, for example, be homosexual. We are arguably prone at this stage to assume we know about people's unconscious or hidden motivations and leave it there. Bion, however, is saying something more unexpected: not just that we should put the fact of the legal marriage aside in considering the person, but that we should put it aside and observe if and when "being married" makes its presence known and in relation to what other elements in the patient's material.

Back in his 1950s paper, "On Arrogance" (*CWB VI*, pp. 131–137), Bion had observed that references to "arrogance", "curiosity" and "stupidity" occur together, and he had gone on to explore the meaning this may hold. As with the Grid, I suspect Bion is both developing new tools and also finding ways to describe what it is he has always done.

[213]   Pain

The central point appears to be the painful nature of change in the direction of maturation. It is probably idle to ask why it should be painful, why intensity of pain bears so little relationship to intensity of recognizable danger, and why pain is so feared. There is no doubt that mental pain in particular is feared in a way that would be appropriate if it corresponded directly with mental danger. The relationship of pain to danger is, however, obscure. In this it is not peculiar, for any relationship of one element of the personality with another seems difficult to determine.

(*CWB VI*, p. 265)

Clinical note

The patient said she had gone off in her mind to shopping. She was not going to let analysis interfere with what she saw as a special powerful mental capacity to cut herself off from pain. She went on to associate to a story of people who had hypnotised themselves before being executed, as well as a Chinese woman who had hypnotised herself for a caesarean section. Her belief seemed to be that there would either be no pain (through her powerful capacity to cut herself off from it) or the most terrible pain, and even extinction. She didn't know if the pain would be for good or bad – for new life or death.

[214] Controversy

Controversy is the growing point from which development springs, but it must be a genuine confrontation and not an impotent beating of the air by opponents whose differences of view never meet.

(CWB VI, p. 267)

And below, a taste of Bion's sense of humour – probably written about the same time.

Undated (1969)

Much psychoanalytic "controversy" is not controversy at all. If listened to for any prolonged period, say a year, but preferably two or three, a pattern begins to emerge, so much so that I can write a chairman's address suitable, with the alteration of a phrase or two, for practically any paper by anyone at any time. Thus:

"Ladies and Gentlemen, we have been listening to a very interesting and stimulating paper. I have had the great advantage of being able to read it in advance, and though I cannot say I agree with everything Dr X says" (chiefly because I haven't the faintest idea what he thinks he is talking about, and I am damned sure he hasn't either), "I found his presentation extremely – er – stimulating. There are many points that I would like to discuss with him if we had time" (thank God we haven't), "but I know there are many here who are anxious to speak" (in particular our resident ex-officio permanent bores whom no one has succeeded in silencing yet), "so I must not take up too much of our time. There is, however, just one point on which I would like to hear Dr X's views if he can spare the time." (At this point I prepare to give one of the favourite bees which reside in my own bonnet its periodical air-ing. It does not matter in the least how irrelevant it may be, or how unlikely Dr X is to have any views whatever on the subject, or how improbable that I would want to hear them if he had – the time has come and out it goes.) "It has often occurred to me" (and only the poor devils in my Society know how often that is) "that ... etc.... etc."

(CWB XI, p. 291)

[215]   Irreducible man

> ...the absence of memory and desire should free the analyst of those pecu-
> liarities that make him a creature of his circumstances and leave him with
> those functions that are invariant, the functions that make up the irreducible
> ultimate man. In fact this cannot be. Yet upon his ability to approximate to
> this will depend his ability to achieve the "blindness" that is a prerequisite
> for "seeing" the evolved elements of O.
>
> Reciprocally, his freedom from being "blinded" by the qualities (or his
> perception of them) that belong to the domain of the senses should enable
> the analyst to "see" those evolved aspects of O that are invariant in the
> analysand.

(*CWB VI*, p. 270)

Bion thought that through disciplining memory and desire, the analyst can become both more present and less "peculiarly" individual – observing what is essential in the patient and being what is essential in ourselves.

[216]   Sharpened to an unbearable point

. . . the analytic situation itself, and then the psychoanalytic occupation or task itself, are bound to stimulate primitive and basic feeling in analyst and analysand. Therefore, if the technique I propose for ensuring vivid appreciation of the emotional facts is as sound as I think it, these fundamental characteristics, love, hate, dread, are sharpened to a point where the participating pair may feel them to be almost unbearable: it is the price that has to be paid for the transformation of an activity that is about psychoanalysis, into an activity that is psychoanalysis.

(CWB VI, p. 276)

[217]   Remaining within himself

I cannot observe Mr X because he will not remain "inside" the analytic situation or even "within" Mr X himself.

(CWB VI, p. 282)

At a later date Bion commented:

We are generally able to understand sensual experience; so long as we can use our physical make-up we can understand certain things. We can understand, for example, that I am Bion. But here is the misleading point about visual imagery. As a result of thinking that we know who or what Bion is, we may think that we know that character because we are misled by the power of our sight, and we may, therefore, think that Bion's character ends with his skin. In fact, any psychoanalyst would be bound to feel that if there is such a thing as a mind, or character, or personality, it cannot be assumed to correspond to the physical formation. All of us need, in the analytic session, to wonder why we think there is a personality where the body lies.

(CWB VII, p. 19)

Clinical note

A very controlled patient had a sudden experience of feeling lively disgust towards me. The following day he returned in a familiar, rather haughty state of mind and declared that he knew what was going on yesterday: he had been disgusted by my sexuality. The patient was no longer "in" the experience. His discomfort in having had such an experience had been replaced by a defiant assertion that he is superior to it and "knows" already what it is about.

[218]   The group and the mystic

The group and mystic are essential to each other; it is therefore important to consider how or why the group can destroy the mystic on whom its future depends and how or why the mystic may destroy the group. I shall indicate the nature of the questions at issue since it is vital that the problem should be seen to exist. It is inherent both in the nature of man as a political animal and in the nature of psychoanalysis as the explosive force.

The relationship between group and mystic may belong to one of three categories. It may be commensal, symbiotic, or parasitic. The same categorization may be applied to the relationship of one group with another. I shall not trouble with the commensal relationship: the two sides coexist and the existence of each can be seen to be harmless to the other. In the symbiotic relationship there is a confrontation, and the result is growth-producing though that growth may not be discerned without some difficulty. In the parasitic relationship the product of the association is something that destroys both parties to the association.

(*CWB VI*, p. 287)

Interview by Anthony G. Banet Jr

If the organization does not respond to human needs, either it or the individual will be destroyed. It's like an animal that protects itself by growing a hard shell. What's going to happen when the animal grows? What's going to happen to either the shell or the animal? The ordinary bird has sense enough to crack the shell and walk out.

The curious thing is that the mind itself seems to be able to produce a shell of its own. People say things like "I don't want to hear any more of these new ideas. I've been very happy. I don't want to have my ideas upset. If you start making me think of this and that, well then, I might have to bother about the troubles of Los Angeles. Why can't I live here in peace and quiet?" I think there is always a resistance to development and change and a tendency to think what a horrible thing this maggot is that tries to animate the dung heap. . . .

(*CWB X*, p. 158)

. . . there is a most striking resemblance, say, between the *Bhagavad Gita* and Meister Eckhart – a resemblance between entirely different religions. Both of them are surrounded by this type of thinking – breaking out of one's shell – and it upsets a great many people. . . .

(*CWB X*, p. 161)

[219]   Container–contained: the stammerer

... a man speaking of an emotional experience in which he was closely involved began to stammer badly as the memory became increasingly vivid to him. The aspects of the model [container–contained] that are significant are these: the man was trying to contain his experience in a form of words; he was trying to contain himself, as one sometimes says of someone about to lose control of himself; he was trying to "contain" his emotions within a form of words, as one might speak of a general attempting to "contain" enemy forces within a given zone.

The words that should have represented the meaning the man wanted to express were fragmented by the emotional forces to which he wished to give only verbal expression; the verbal formulation could not "contain" his emotions, which broke through and dispersed it as enemy forces might break through the forces that strove to contain them.

The stammerer, in his attempt to avoid the contingency I have described, resorted to modes of expression so boring that they failed to express the meaning he wished to convey; he was thus no nearer to his goal. His verbal formulation could be described as like to the military forces that are worn by the attrition to which they are subjected by the contained forces. The meaning he was striving to express was denuded of meaning. His attempt to use his tongue for verbal expression failed to "contain" his wish to use his tongue for masturbatory movement in his mouth.

Sometimes the stammerer could be reduced to silence. This situation can be represented by a visual image of a man who talked so much that any meaning he wished to express was drowned by his flood of words.

(CWB VI, pp. 300–301)

[220]   Container–contained: sexual implications

Description 1: The signs ♂ and ♀ I call the contained and the container. The use of the male and female symbols is deliberate but must not be taken to mean that other than sexual implications are excluded.

(*CWB VI*, p. 311)

When Bion says that other factors as well as sexuality are implied in the concept of container–contained, we have tended to concentrate – with him – on these other factors – K (knowledge) and –K (anti-knowledge)] – and not on the implications of this concept for our understanding of sexuality. In fact, we potentially have a view of a sexuality driven by the instinct to "take in" and "be taken in" that is not present in Freud's model and balances Freud's model.

[221]   Container–contained: squeezed out

The container ($♀$) extracts so much from the contained ($♂$) that the contained is left without substance. A psychoanalysis is so long continued that the patient can get no further meaning from it. A converse example would be the continuation until the patient had no more patience, tolerance, fortitude, or money left. The container can squeeze everything "out of" the contained; or the "pressure" may be exerted by the contained so that the container disintegrates. An illustration would be the word used as a metaphor until the background is lost and the word loses its meaning.

(*CWB VI*, pp. 311–312)

From the 1967 *Los Angeles Seminars*

Either you squeeze the life out of the whole thing – you formulate in a way which shows that psychoanalysis is nothing new, there's nothing to it and so forth – or you can try loading the psychoanalyst with such honours that he's sunk without a trace, as I have put it. [laughter from audience].

(*LASS*, pp. 121–122)

[222]   Container–contained: greed

[A]n extremely greedy patient may want to obtain as much as he can from his analysis while giving as little as possible: we should expect this to show itself by frequent events in which the container was denuding the contained object and vice versa. The patient might show that he made enormous demands on his family but resented doing anything for it. Many patients might show behaviour of this kind on relatively rare occasions but some might show it in many activities and in striking degree as, for example, by habitual incoherence while demanding great precision of interpretation from the analyst.

(*CWB VI*, pp. 313–314)

[223] The objects are many, the relationships are not

According to his background a patient will describe various objects as containers, such as his mind, the unconscious, the nation; others as contained, such as his money, his ideas. The objects are many but the relationships are not.

(*CWB VI*, p. 324)

People tend to have a characteristic relationship between container and contained that recurs, whatever the particular objects are. Greed in the previous quote is an example of a characteristic relationship: it can be seen in the patient's relationship with his family, in his relationship with his analyst, and, one imagines, in many other areas of his life.

[224]   Negative capability

The following letter, written to Francesca Bion (who was at the time in California house-hunting), refers to Bion's paper "Negative Capability", which was published as Chapter 13, "Prelude to or Substitute for Achievement", in *Attention and Interpretation*.

To Los Angeles October 3 1967

My darling,

It already seems years since you went and this place is a bit desolate in consequence. I hope you are having a good journey. I am churning over the paper and feeling jolly glad I shan't have to give more. Wednesday. The "paper" (of course I didn't read it) went off all right. At first I thought no one was coming – only one or two there five minutes before the start. But it filled up. They all stayed (except about three) till past the end and there was no hostile demonstration.

. . . Your letter has just come in. I am so relieved and glad to have it. You must have been very tired and it is lovely of you to have written to me at once. I felt a bit as I did in the First World War – I couldn't bear to write home because I felt I couldn't *think* of home. But I was only nineteen then and there was some excuse. I too wish I was with you; it is awful to think you have to do all this load of business by yourself, and I know you must feel it a wretched responsibility to meet all the snags which are sure to crop up without a chance of talking it over. *You* have not a moment too much time – I feel it is an age to have to wait another fortnight.

Julian rang up – he said he had nearly scored twice in rugger but each time the full back had got him. He seemed to think this very unreasonable! I remember the feeling myself.

I thought the "paper" went well. Of course I spoke direct; too many "ers" I think, but I haven't spoken for a long time and I did not, as you know, relish the circumstances. I think I spoke to the point and a number of people seemed to feel that *this* time a lot more people grasped the general idea. It might have turned out anyhow – including a boycott. There is no doubt that the Klein Group has been very upset but I think they needed it. But there must have been about 130 people which is as much as anyone has a right to expect. Furthermore there was no nonsense about my going (tears of grief etc.). Just a straightforward exposition by me of my ideas about how things should go and how I at least tried to make that happen. I think the fact that it was straight forward talk, "to be continued in our next", all helped. And as I say, they stayed to the end.

I do hope you will not feel you are landed with an impossible job. I know what a terribly difficult one you have and I am sure you realize I shall do my best to fit in with such plans as you can make. Do please try to get in some rest and relaxation. It is too heavy a job for one person to tackle without some time in which to dismiss the whole job from your mind. Even in your kind of work I think you need to dismiss "memory and desire" so as to have as clear a mind as possible for the decisions. You can only do "the best you can" – not "the best". But I know you don't need to be told this.

. . . Heaven knows where anyone is safe or reasonably secure with the U.S. so shaken by Vietnam. And this country seems unlikely to get into the Common Market with the recent EEC report that we are bankrupt. Why *should* a successful Europe want a bankrupt Britain which has also a labour force completely out of hand and strike-riven?. . .

(CWB II, pp. 166–167)

[225] Negative capability

Chapter 13
Prelude to or substitute for achievement

"I had not a dispute but a disquisition with Rilke on various subjects; several things dove-tailed in my mind, and at once it struck me what quality went to form a Man of Achievement, especially in Literature, and which Shakespeare possessed so enormously – I mean Negative Capability, that is, when a man is capable of being in uncertainties, mysteries, doubts, without any irritable reaching after fact and reason." (John Keats)[1]

A number of aspects of the practice of psychoanalysis must now be discussed; I group them under the Language of Achievement. The quotation from Keats will serve as an introduction to the area to be covered. Language is loosely and widely defined to include behaviour of which it is sometimes said "actions speak louder than words". Set over against and in contrast with the Language of Achievement, I consider the language that is a substitute for, and not a prelude to, action. Language of Achievement includes language that is both prelude to action, and itself a kind of action; the meeting of psychoanalyst and analysand is itself an example of this language....

Any session should be judged by comparison with the Keats formulation so as to guard against one commonly unobserved fault leading to analysis "interminable". The fault lies in the failure to observe and is intensified by the inability to appreciate the significance of observation....

(1) "Letter to George and Thomas Keats", 21 December 1817 (in E. L. Freud 1961).
(*CWB VI*, pp. 327–328)

Dennis Duncan

The work of Wilfred Bion represents a technical as well as a theoretical revolution. Although much of his work is esoteric and difficult, it has been at a personal and simple level that he has had the widest impact on analysts. This is due to a capacity to capture images or ideas which so meaningfully relate the analyst to the inner analytic position that he feels subjectively supported, and his technical confidence is enhanced by their use. Such is his depiction of the analyst's inner situation as being "beyond memory and desire", and the poetical image, borrowed from Keats, of "Negative Capability": "that is when a man is capable of being in uncertainties, mysteries, doubts without any irritable reaching after fact and reason.

(Duncan 1981, pp. 342–343)

[226]   Negative capability

From: *Brazilian Lectures:* "São Paulo 1973"

It may be true from a macroscopic point of view to say, "Oh, he is hallucinating", or, "She is highly disturbed", but it would not be true if one could see or hear or intuit what the analysand can. Psychoanalysts must be able to tolerate the differences or the difficulties of the analysand long enough to recognize what they are. If psychoanalysts are to be able to interpret what the analysand says, they must have a great capacity for tolerating their analysands" statements without rushing to the conclusion that they know the interpretations. This is what I think Keats meant when he said that Shakespeare must have been able to tolerate "Negative Capability".

(*CWB VII*, p. 48)

[227] Hatred and sexualisation of psychoanalysis

I have rarely failed to experience hatred of psychoanalysis and its reciprocal, sexualization of psychoanalysis. These are part of a "constant conjunction". . . . the human animal has not ceased to be persecuted by his mind
and the thoughts usually associated with it – whatever their origin may be.
Therefore I do not expect any psychoanalysis properly done to escape the
odium inseparable from the mind. Refuge is sure to be sought in mindlessness, sexualization, acting-out, and degrees of stupor.

(*CWB VI*, p. 328)

[228] On the analytic position
& inhibition

What is required is not the decrease of inhibition but a decrease of the impulse to inhibit; the impulse to inhibit is fundamentally envy of the growth-stimulating objects.

(*CWB VI*, p. 330)

I was recently asked to give a paper on Bionian Technique to the Regional Bion Symposium in Los Angeles. I was to discuss what I actually use from Bion's writings in my everyday analytic work. Looking back over my analytic career, I remembered being a newly qualified analyst, and how I would look subjects up in Bion's indexes when I was unclear or troubled by something to do with a patient. The first instance of this I can remember was with a patient who was extremely inhibited. I had become aware that I was subtly – or not so subtly – attempting to reassure her that she could be less inhibited with me. I looked up inhibition, and found the quote above. I remember it had a considerable effect on me: not because I fully understood it or was sure it was envy in my patient's case, but because it put me back in the analytic position. The analyst's job is not to encourage the patient to become less inhibited, but to consider the nature of the impulse to inhibit. As I thought further about the way I have read Bion over the years, I began to realise how often it related to the question of the analytic position. If one's position is right, then one's technique flows from it. It is the analytic position that matters, not having a list of technical dos and don'ts.

On the loss of the analytic position, see, for instance, the following quotes:

268 "Interference" (*Brazilian Lectures,* Rio de Janeiro 1974, *CWB VII*, pp. 106–107);
289 Patient slides over terrifying dream (New York 1977, *CWB VIII*, p. 267);
295 Analyst's voice taken as a soporific drug ("São Paulo 1978", *CWB VIII*, pp. 373–375).

Clinical note

With a young male patient I went through a gruelling undermining of my analytic position in which I experienced losing hope that I had anything at all to offer. One helpful change in my technique was to move from largely interpreting in the transference (with his relation to his parents in mind), to the interpretation of his reaction to the analysis itself and his rivalry with me. From here I found myself conceiving of what was happening as being like an onion. With the removal of each layer, one seemed to be bringing about change, but this was immediately made the same – like the layers of an onion. The image of the onion evolved, I think, through my recovering some of my symbolic capacity. The non-symbolic experience I had been through with him told me something of his own terrible belief that he had no right to exist.

[229] The restoration of god (the Mother) and the evolution of god

What is to be sought is an activity that is both the restoration of god (the Mother) and the evolution of god (the formless, infinite, ineffable, non-existent), which can be found only in the state in which there is *no* memory, desire, understanding.

(*CWB VI*, p. 330)

This quote follows on directly from the previous quote.

The following piece is by Annie Reiner, who practised close by to Bion when he moved to California.

Annie Reiner

Ferenczi . . . delineates a response to early trauma and emotional abuse in which the child escapes the painful, emotionally deprived earthly self to seek comfort through contact with an all-knowing, omniscient part of the mind. He called it the astra (Dupont 1995, pp. 206–207), the Latin word for stars, essentially a dissociated state in which the infant's real self exists far away "in the stars". The emotional bond to the mother, already damaged by her absence or neglect, is thus further severed by the child, as is the bond to his (or her) own feelings. It is a severe fragmentation of the self in which the child is in flight from reality. Fearful of being returned to the primal states of intrauterine dissolution, the child gathers up the pieces into an omniscient false self, an illusion of wholeness or containment. In fact the self is further fragmented by this split from awareness. Ferenczi sees this flight as regressive, but also as progressive, for while there is fragmentation and "a narcotic state of relaxation", there is also the "sudden development of intelligence, even clairvoyance" (ibid., p. 203).

According to Ferenczi, the infant in contact with the astra represents an omniscient self associated with "God", a saviour and divine container. Communication with this state is later commonly viewed by the individual as spiritual enlightenment, a relationship with God. In some sense this is true, for it aims to save the child from unbearable pain. However, this "divine" container cannot really contain feelings, it contains the *fragments* of feelings, and so the child is "saved" only from *experiencing* the terror of such a disintegrated state, which continues to loom throughout his life. Understanding the difference requires us to distinguish between what is essentially a defensive act of fusion with an idealised mother, and the spiritual aspect of O as the Godhead. The former, idealised state reflects Freud's view of religion as an illusion, a primitive belief in an idealised father (or mother), while the latter reflects the Gnostic view of religion as empirical knowledge of metaphysical realities (Reiner 2009, 2012). For the Gnostics, Christ was not the literal son of a reified God, but a *symbol* of the esoteric knowledge in Christ's teachings. It is the difference between a symbol and a symbolic equation (Segal 1981), a mental representation of something as opposed to the thing itself. It is a difficult distinction, since the thing-in-itself – represented by O – cannot in fact ever be known. Both the astra and O represent states of transcending of the boundaries of the self into a deeper, more vast awareness. One cannot transcend the self, however, if one does not yet have one, and the traumatised infant who has not yet developed a conscious self has no means of understanding the reality he has become one with. He cannot transcend his reality, he can only have a phantasy of escaping it. Whatever wisdom the "wise baby" gleaned would therefore retain the stamp of infantile omnipotence of a reified God/parent. (We can also recognise this as a superego which delivers emotional relief through emotional death.)

The decisive difference lies in an understanding of mental existence as an uncertain, *ongoing* process of learning or "becoming", an open mind filled with questions, that is, space for new experience. This mind is not a fixed entity, an identification with the omniscient God/parent with ready-made answers. The capacity for what Bion calls at-one-ment with O (reality) reflects this openness of a self capable of change and growth, while the infant's foray into the infinite astral plane is an *escape* from that reality of the self. To confuse matters, however, they may be looking at the same realm of truth and ultimate reality which Bion intended by O. It is a question of what drives the leap into this other realm, for O, as Bion said, is impersonal, a non-human reality which does not change according to human whims, it just is. However, the nature of the mind which receives this knowledge changes the perception of that unchanging reality – O. A different container changes the experience of that which is contained within it. The infant views things through an undifferentiated mind which, in the case of trauma, is also a mind of fragmented sensations and perception. While the same reality (O) is observed, being experienced by a dis-organised, or pre-organised self without the capacity to attach meaning to that which has been observed, alters the perception. It reflects Freud's idea of religion, where a child identified with the phantasied omnipotent parent *is* God, a primitive oneness with the parent where the child can observe everything, but without meaning or consciousness. Describing what is necessary to the experience of O, Bion (1970 [*CWB VI*]) writes, "What is to be sought is an activity that is both the restoration of god (the Mother) and the evolution of god (the formless, infinite, ineffable, non-existent), which can be found only in the state in which there is no memory, desire, understanding" (p. 129 [*CWB VI*, p. 330]). In order to transcend that personal self into this larger realm of the infinite, one must draw upon the capacity for primal oneness with the mother as well as adult capacities for integration.

(Reiner 2017, pp. 337–342)

Sándor Ferenczi (1873–1933): Hungarian psychoanalyst and Klein's first analyst. He was a close associate of Freud.

Part III

International lectures, seminars and supervisions

Chapter 15

Visiting Los Angeles: seminars and supervision

Introduction

I was up to 360 quotes when I picked up the book on Bion's *Los Angeles Seminars and Supervision*, but it soon became clear that something was going to have to give way and make more space for what I was reading. In April 1967 Bion gave four seminars and a group supervision to members of the Los Angeles Psychoanalytic Society and Institute and to interested others. The editors of the book, Joseph Aguayo and Barnet D. Malin, transcribed the tape recordings of these presentations made by Art Malin (Barnet Malin's father). This has happened since the publication of *The Complete Works of W. R. Bion*.

One of the many interesting things about these seminars is that Bion is revisiting his work with psychotic patients. At the time of his visit, there was interest in Los Angeles in the possibility of analytic work with psychotic patients. The established view seemed to be that it was not possible, and yet there were psychotic patients requiring treatment. The Los Angeles analyst Ralph Greenson was in the audience, and I have included excerpts from two of the interchanges between him and Bion. Greenson, known internationally for his book *The Technique and Practice of Psychoanalysis* (published in 1967), was described by a colleague of mine as the "king" of Los Angeles, "like Elvis himself".

In 1967 Bion was also writing the commentary to go with his 1950s papers on psychotic patients, which were published under the title, *Second Thoughts*.

James S. Grotstein

To hear Wilfred Bion's voice again [on the tape recording] is to be overcome with so many feelings, so many thoughts, so many waking dreams. . . . These transcripts are precious for many reasons, perhaps mostly because they document a transformational moment in Bion's life and thinking. He was in the throes of creation and extension of his new ideas on the very nature of psychoanalysis itself, and he was considering uprooting his life at home to come to the foreign land of California at the height of the Western cultural insurrection of the late 1960s. . . .

(Grotstein 2013, pp. 13–14)

Quotes

[230]   The thing itself

What is perceptible is always something secondary; you see somebody flush
up, and you say that they're self-conscious, or that they're anxious, or frightened, or hostile – all of that, is really a deduction from something else. It is
not talking about the thing itself. What we are concerned with, is however,
the thing itself: the reality, the fundamental reality with which psychoanalysts
have to deal.

(LASS, p. 36)

[231]   What Bion thought was going wrong in psychoanalysis?

It may sound as if I'm stressing the obvious unnecessarily. I don't think so, because I think it is the easiest thing in the world, what with the patients trying to deny the reality of what we are trying to draw attention to, and our own dislike of what we feel we ought to draw attention to, that you can very easily get into a state in which you gradually drift into a position in which you talk not English, but jargon, and in which you talk about the non-existent. It simply becomes a complete myth. Now the serious thing for analysts about this, is that the situation gradually gets more and more intolerable. One is reduced more and more, to denying the reality of something of whose reality we have been at some point absolutely convinced, and which is the one thing that we are really in existence to deal with.

(*LASS*, pp. 37–38)

Bion advocated eschewing memory and desire in the context of believing that "something was going wrong in the work in England – not only mine" (from a letter written to his wife on 6 August 1968 [*CWB II*, p. 177]). The quote above throws some light on what he thought this to be.

[232]   Instinctive flair of very disturbed patients

... when he [the patient] wants to defend himself against psychoanalysis, what he will do as soon as he knows the analyst sufficiently well, is to stimulate the analyst's memories and desires. He will stimulate in the analyst, a wish for the end of the session, a wish to cure the patient, and heaven knows what else (there's no shortage of supply whatsoever). And when he has done that, the analyst's work deteriorates then and there. The session begins to get more and more wide of the mark, and I think that there's reason to suppose that this is deliberate. I wouldn't say conscious or unconscious (I don't really know how to use these terms with patients of that kind), but there's this sort of instinctive flair.

(*LASS*, pp. 39–40)

We hear in this quote about pressures from the patient that can cause an analyst's work to deteriorate.

[233]   The science of psychoanalysis

> I think it is our duty to be sceptical, I think it is our duty to ask questions, and to try to elicit why a particular analyst thought that a particular event took place, and why he thinks the patient was persuaded of the truth of it ... But how this is to be balanced, how you are to balance a rigorous scientific outlook with a reasonable degree of tolerance, I don't know.
>
> (*LASS*, p. 42)

The duty to be sceptical adds a balancing counterweight to any tendency to idealise practice.

[234] Freud to Lou Andreas-Salomé

Now, I'd like to read you this: it's a letter which Freud wrote to Lou Andreas-Salomé on May 25th 1916. He says, "I'm always particularly impressed when I read your remarks about one of my works." Now, this part I want to stress. "I know that I have artificially blinded myself at my work in order to concentrate all the light on one dark passage: on connection, harmony, nobility and all you call the symbolic. I refrain, frightened by the experience of such a demand; each expectation carries with it the danger to see the expected recognition as distorted, though perhaps beautified. Then you come, and add what is missing, put on the super-structure ..." – I think Freud is being a little bit complimentary – "...and link-up what was isolated with its content. I cannot always follow you. For my eyes are adapted to the dark, and cannot perhaps stand the strong light or a wide vision. But I have not quite become a mole, and so I can enjoy the prospect of a lighter and wider horizon, and indeed I would not deny its existence.

Now the point that I want to stress about that is this: that when you have a particularly dark spot, turn onto it a shaft of piercing darkness. Rid yourself of your analytic theories. Rid yourself of what you picked up about the patient; get rid of it. Bring to bear on this dark spot a shaft of piercing darkness. On the principle – if one can use such a model with accuracy – I think there's something to be said for it – that if you want to see a very faint light, the more light you shut out, the better, the bigger the chance of seeing the faint glimmer, if you're not blinded by the "light" as Freud himself describes it.

And that is why I say about this, that I have grave doubts about the tendency to feel baffled in psychoanalysis and fall back on ..., "let's have some more theory" (as if there weren't enough). The real trouble is that one is blinded by the amount of psychoanalytic experience one has got. It is very difficult to believe, because we have learned to start off with (in our own experience with analysis) such an enormous amount about what our analysts know, and we're impressed by that, whereas the real point about it is whether our analyst managed to remove from us our objection to the free-play of curiosity.

(*LASS*, pp. 50–52)

[235]   Linking up to past sessions

A patient started off a session once, by complaining very much about his
father, who he said was very insensitive, very unaware of what was taking
place. He had never really sympathised with him at all (he'd always favouri-
tised his sister)....

When I thought that this situation had evolved enough, I said to the
patient that I thought that he must have been very envious of a patient
whom he said he had seen on the day before, and that he felt that that
patient was my favourite patient, and that I was very much the father who
was not interested in him or in his development, or the kind of things he
did and so on....

When I finished, the patient said, "Yes ..." [spoken by Bion in a slow and
deliberate drawl]....

After a time, it again evolves, it obtrudes on you, and you begin to feel
that you really must know the meaning of "Yes ..." because you will have to
interpret it – it's coming up too often....

Now in this matter, I think that what the patient is saying and what the
interpretation is (which you give), is in a sense relatively unimportant. Because
by the time you are able to give a patient an interpretation which the patient
understands, all the work has been done. It's merely signalising the close of a
particular situation. So what I would say, is that any moment of the analysis,
one could say that the material could be divided into this. There's the immediate stimulus to the psychoanalyst – the immediate point (which links up
with all sorts of things which have been going on for weeks, months, years),
and which issues in the given interpretation. But the reason why it is so
important to be blind, (so that one can take in every scrap of ... every faintest
glimmer of light) is because at the time that the interpretation is given, one
should be in a position to be taking in material which will not be interpreted
probably for a long time, because the second element in what is taking place
there, is the material on which your interpretation will be based in so many
weeks, months, or possibly even years. And the more wide one's spectrum
can be, the more one can be open to all the nuances and so forth. You may
get to this stage (I think that you will) in which you are bothered by this "Yes
...". While you're bothered by it, that's *not* the time to give interpretations....

(*LASS*, pp. 53–57)

Later, when asked a question, Bion replied:

Bion: Yes ... (in a slow drawl)
[Laughter and uproar from audience].

(*LASS*, p. 70)

In his writing on eschewing memory and desire, Bion emphasises the importance of working in the present. One response I had to this was that I could not do everything all at once! My impression is that "working in the present" can cause analysts to sit on their patient's every response or, alternatively, to rather idealise (and oversimplify) the relationship, leaving out the complexities of the transference. The above quote, however, makes it clear that in the present of the session we are both to be as open as possible (and he is right that we are often more defended than we realise) while over time observing and drawing the patient's attention to patterns that emerge.

[236]   Psychotic transference

I think that there are a number of peculiar things which apply to the psychotic patient, in particular his contact with the analyst. One way of putting it in terms of transference theory, is that it is extremely tenuous. One feels it to be a sort of umbilical cord as it were – very, very tenacious, the patient sticks to you very tightly – and it's just a very thin line, a very thin connection between you and the patient.... Now, the transformation which shows itself in the consulting room is peculiar. The patient may find that he can't tolerate this very intense, very narrow limited relationship. I think there's a lot in the Kleinian theory about this, that the relationship is so intense that he projects himself into you, or takes you into him, and then he gets confused with you and cannot stand the confusion. Now, the defensive move that he makes is to change the line into a plane....The line turns into a contact with you which is – using more pictorial terms, I don't know what else to do – it turns into a sort of monomolecular film; the thinnest possible film that you can imagine. But with that, it retains its whole intensity. The patient can't understand what you say, but if you stumble over a word, he's on you like a knife. "What's that you say?" There's this absolute unfailing recognition of the slightest little defect. Everything else passes by – your interpretations if they aren't exact just don't link up....

(*LASS*, pp. 63–64)

Freud said that it was not possible to work psychoanalytically with psychotic patients. Psychoanalysis depends on being able to work in the transference, and Freud was of the view that psychotic patients did not form a transference with the analyst. Bion speaks specifically of the "psychotic transference" and describes what his experience of it is. People working with psychotic patients might find it immediately recognisable. I wondered whether I could find something by another analyst to elaborate on what he says, and I looked at various papers, but all were rather dry in comparison to Bion's description. I have found that if one stays with his description – taking it on in a way rather like a poem – that it does prompt clinical recognitions of psychotic mechanisms in neurotic patients.

[237]   Bion and Greenson

Greenson:	. . . And I think that's very admirable [suppression of memory and desire]. . . . [But is it not] a terrible stress on some patients, and shouldn't that be in some way dealt with? I think that with patients who are in analysis for a period of time and can bear this kind of stress, but now what about the patient who isn't in that state? . . .

(LASS, p. 94)

Greenson, interrupting:	No, I want to say I am talking about the danger that you seem to pose by this experiment of creating a situation in which you are dealing with a human being, a unique human being who came to you with problems and a need for help, and now, for some scientific reasons and in order to improve your own insight in time, you're going to put aside his therapeutic needs. . . .

(LASS, pp. 97–98)

Bion:	. . . what I am arguing in favour of is that one should try not to let that pressure [the patient's distress] distort one's judgment. I think that in my experience, the patient can feel something . . . about your failure to be jockeyed into a premature interpretation, which gives him something to go on with. Now, this again, is one of these experiences which I think brings it home to you, that we as psychoanalysts are dealing with forces of no mean order, that they are extremely mysterious, they cannot easily be fitted into any form of words (some of them can, but a great many can't), but I think that one can take a certain degree of comfort by that, that actually the inability to give an interpretation (the lack of knowledge about it), and the ability to tolerate the ignorance and the distress of the situation with a feeling that heaven knows what this patient is going to get up to before he turns up the next day. It self-communicates itself to the patient. . . .

(LASS, pp. 99–100)

It sounds as if each man thinks that what the other is doing with patients is somewhat dangerous. Greenson sees Bion as unsupportive and unfeeling; Bion feels that Greenson fails to see that being supportive is not sufficient in relation to psychotic mechanisms.

[238]   Why use the term mystic?

And here, I have introduced the idea of the *mystic*, which I regard as being pretty well interchangeable with the word scientist, and with the word artist. Mystic, of course, has got a much more religious connotation, but really what I mean is the same thing. It's one of these unfortunate things – I was asked by Adrian Stokes why I didn't say simply the "artist" or the "scientist". Well I don't know. I felt that I really wanted to shove it over a bit more into the realms which have been occupied so much by religion and philosophy. Because I think that what we're dealing with today is the sort of thing which is being dealt with in the past (mostly, I think, by religion), but it has been talked about anyway by philosophers. I think that the philosophical version is so sophisticated, of course, it's only available to relatively few people; with religion it is quite different.

Now, the point that I want to make about this is this: that the mystic is a person who invariably claims direct contact, usually with God. . . .Now the point about that is, that we are doing something similar when we work on what we might just call hunches. . . .

(*LASS*, pp. 115–116)

Adrian Stokes (1902–1972): Painter, influential art critic and author. He was also analysed by Klein and seems to have been at Oxford at around the same time as Bion. Bion studied history, Stokes philosophy. Stokes was a member of the "Imago Group", which met regularly for nearly 18 years to discuss applications of psychoanalysis to philosophy, politics, ethics, and aesthetics; it included Hanna Segal among its members.

[239]   Invariants: a clinical example

[T]he patient's apparently talking quite obviously and clearly about a particular society, a particular group known to him, in these external terms. As the analyst, you begin to feel that this situation is evolving. This isn't *really* simply the external society that he's talking about – it is that, it has got that meaning, but one is not going to bother him with that because he knows it already, that's why he's talking about it. I give a patient such an answer. He has been talking about people, he has been talking about London and Edinburgh, and I draw his attention to the fact that these are not simply London and Edinburgh. They are names of places where it was once a father and mother. It is simply a way of describing not the father and mother, but the place where the father and mother were until something or other happened to them, which has turned them simply into a place. And then, that these other objects which he's been mentioning are really felt to be the children of this pair (these two objects which have now turned into places) and from that, to give the interpretation that it is in fact himself, "only he himself is now split up. The parents have been attacked, they are destroyed, so that they are only places where parents used to be, and he himself has been destroyed in the process, in the sense of being split up into a whole lot of particles which can only be described in terms of these various people, with names, and so forth. People and objects. It can be, in the case that I'm thinking of, a great mixture of things which are just persons and things, and all of them are representing parts of his own personality.

I give the patient the interpretation, and the next thing that he does, is to start on a series of hypochondriacal complaints. And in short, to sum the thing up, one would say the rest of the session is spent in his describing a hypochondriacal state. Now, what has happened there is, that the external objects, these external objects have been taken into him, and they have now been transformed and turned into objects like his spleen, his hernia, and so on. But they are the same objects.

(*LASS*, pp. 117–118)

[240]   Electricity

Now it's no good, Faraday being able to understand electricity. He has got (or the community has got) to make Faraday's ability available in such a way that you and I can go and turn on the switch there and the room is flooded with light without having to be abstruse physicists or mathematicians, and so forth. The direct contact which Faraday has got with the reality, the ultimate reality of electricity, is therefore made available to lesser mortals like ourselves. We learn a set of rules, and deal with it.

(*LASS*, p. 118)

I would like to continue this further, and suggest about it that psycho-analysis is tapping emotional forces which we ourselves have not yet fully experienced.

(*LASS*, p. 141)

Faraday (1791–1867): One of the most influential scientists in history, it was due to Faraday's efforts that electricity became practical for use in technology. Albert Einstein kept a picture of Faraday on his study wall.

[241]   An object with no regard for one's personality

Bion: I would have said that, "You feel that you have something very bad inside you. And although you describe this as something which is outside of you and slashes your wrists and arms and so forth, actually I think it is felt to be an object which is inside you, which has no regard for your personality or even your anatomy, but breaks out by cutting you from inside outwards. . . .

You are again afraid here, of being surrounded by an extremely cutting, painful, dangerous excretion, urine, in which it cuts into you, and destroys you, because it is such very, very, bad stuff; it's nothing good, it's something very bad. . . .

(*LASS*, pp. 139–140)

The patient is cutting herself. The question being asked is how one can work analytically with such a patient. Bion gives an example of how he might speak to her.

[242]   To say that she seemed to be hostile was putting it very mildly indeed

To say that she seemed to be hostile was putting it very mildly indeed. The abuse became much more violent and in the course of this, she slithered off the end of the couch onto the floor, appeared to be frightened by the fall, which led to still further abuse and violence. . . .

(LASS, p. 175)

Now, I'd like just to mention the term "free-floating attention". The idea being that this is the term for the appropriate state of mind of the psychoanalyst. No countertransference, no nonsense of that sort, free-floating attention. Or, as I have put it, get rid of your memory and your desire, so that you expose yourself to the full treatment. . . .

(LASS, p. 182)

. . . it's not enough to be analysed – that is a kind of minimum requirement. It is not even enough to know your job. You really have to be the kind of personality who will do the job, while this kind of business is going on. . . .

(LASS, p. 184)

Greenson: Aren't you describing a situation with a patient whom you are trying to analyse, in which an acute emotional crisis or storm erupts, which can't be handled by analytical methods. . . . I wonder what you did, besides what you told us so far, that she was able to go out on her own steam and you were able to sleep that night.

Bion: The kind of thing that would happen would be, I would say: "Let me draw your attention to the fact that you extremely angry. Reply, if you could make a statement about it." "Oh, so you do think I'm just a nasty little bitch, a horrid little girl." "No, I don't. You are thirty; you are much more dangerous than being just a horrid little girl. This is not just a horrid little girl." It sounds fine. As I say, I could hardly hear myself say that.

Greenson: Yes, but I would submit that's not an interpretation; what you are saying is trying to bring her back to some piece of reality.

(LASS, pp. 186–187)

Bion: If it is legitimate to say that this is an interpretation, do you get certain patients in whom you do not interpret to expose

the unconscious, but interpret in order to expose what ought
to be the conscious? I certainly think, in my experience with a
psychotic patient, that this is really the difficulty. . . .

(*LASS*, p. 188)

We hear Bion's wry sense of humour in his description of the pandemonium that
unfurled in the consulting room. This is the second quote that includes discussion
between Bion and Greenson. From Bion's point of view, everything that happens
in the room is part of the analysis. He attends to the non-verbal and pre-verbal
material as a part of this, interpreting actions and symptoms. Much of what Bion
interprets is to do with reality and the patient's anxiety about it, rather than with
unconscious conflict. Greenson comments that he would not include some of the
patient's behaviour and some of Bion's interventions as being analytic.

In the LA seminars Bion uses the model of a spectrum. The analyst is to become
more adept to working at the extreme ends of the spectrum, outside what can
be verbalised and symbolised. One sees above the significance of his category
of "beta-elements" (raw unsymbolised stuff) and his emphasis on the analyst's
sensitivity to "wave lengths" we are unused to dealing with – one has to consent
to being disturbed.

[243]   Omnipotent use of sight

I think that one aspect of this situation is really closely related to hallucination, to omnipotence, to greed, and so on in this way. Let's put it in pictorial terms, in terms of the infant. The infant cannot tolerate the frustration of not having the breast. He cannot have the breast because it has been removed, but he discovers at some point that he can have an experience which is like being omnipotent. He can take the breast into himself, even when it is not in contact with his body, and he can do this through his visual senses. In other words, you can get the sensation of being able to suck at the breast, or to take the breast into yourself through your eyes, when you can't take it in through your mouth, or even through your nose – it's too far away. Now all this, I think, tends to invest in a certain class of patients who can't tolerate frustration – a heavy investment in the sense of sight. Because you can do things with sight, which you can't do through any other sense, or through any other organs of your body....

(*LASS*, p. 202)

[244]   Omnipotence and helplessness

... you know, one never gets omnipotence unless the patient is feeling helpless. It is always legitimate to suppose that the two go hand in hand, and you
can't get one without getting the other. The more helpless the patient is, the
more they become omnipotent.

(LASS, p. 210)

Clinical note

A patient who has been in analysis with me for a long time – in fact, for the longest
time of all my patients – was more moved by our recognition that his omnipotence
was inextricably linked to his helplessness than perhaps by anything else.

[245] Manufacturing something that explains why you feel as you do

Now, it seems to me, here is another thing with this patient, he's got a great store of activities which will help to explain why he's feeling as he does. He takes drugs, you see, for that accounts for that. You all know if you take drugs, you have certain symptoms and so forth. But his trouble is, if he didn't take drugs, he'd have the same symptoms. So he has got to be delinquent. He's got to be selectable, he's got to be these various things as a sort of method of explaining why he feels as he does.

I would almost put it as a kind of homemade analysis. It is terrible to have feelings which you can't understand at all. Therefore, manufacture something which explains why you feel like that. Get drunk. That explains why you see things, and why you have such odd ideas. You're just drunk and everybody knows that's what happens to you when you're drunk. But if you hadn't got drunk, and you saw those same things, that would be terrible.

(*LASS*, pp. 247–248)

[246]   How eschewing memory and desire affect the session

The pattern of analysis will change. Roughly speaking, the patient will not appear to develop over a period of time but each session will be complete in itself. "Progress" will be measured by the increased number and variety of moods, ideas and attitudes seen in any given session. There will be less clogging of the sessions by the repetition of material which should have disappeared and, consequently, a quickened tempo within each session every session.

(LASS, p. 275)

[247]   The move to Los Angeles (1968)

The previous quotes from the Los Angeles seminars are from Bion's visit there in 1967. The Bions set out on 25 January 1968 to live in Los Angeles, where Bion continued to write, practise, teach, and to develop his ideas, until he returned to England in 1979, shortly before his sudden illness and death.

Letters from England

Francesca Bion went ahead of Bion to find a house for them in Los Angeles. Bion, still in England, wrote to her there.

> July 29 1967
>
> I am beginning to feel restive and that it is time I had some "thoughts", but I realize it is only the third day of the holiday. It's a bore your not being here...
>
> In the course of my gloomy feelings I could not help thinking what the original Pilgrim Fathers must have felt like when they set out for America. At first it seems a bit far-fetched, to say the least, but I am not so sure that it is. I *do* regret leaving England; I do feel anything but confident about the kind of reception one will get there. Yet I am not sure that the stories told us are quite as easily explained as people think. There *is* much pessimism in the U.S. about psychoanalysis: there ought to be more pessimism about it here. But I feel doubtful about what can be done, not least by myself, either here or in the U.S. What else *can* one feel? And how is it to be put to the test except by going?
>
> (CWB II, pp. 165–166)

> October 11
>
> ... I think our decision to leave has stirred up quite a bit here in our colleagues. I answered queries in the (extended) Klein group tonight. It was clear that they were jolly glad to get it and I think they were again very much impressed. Indeed I do feel that what I have been saying is requiring a new orientation in all practising analysts....
>
> (CWB II, p. 169)

> October 14
>
> ... I am just back from Ishbel's – I saw the portrait. I think I am in rather a tense position. She said she had made me rougher – had not put in my benign look but more the tension of when I am talking about work. Personally I think she is too polite to say, as I think, that it shows my bad temper. I

don't think you would like it but she says she will show it to you when you return and you can judge for yourself.

... I am surprised to find how indifferent, except for occasional pangs, I feel about leaving England. It is sad to feel one is *not* sad. Once I would have thought it impossible to leave one's country and one's friends, but somehow things change so much that it is not so. Still I think it must be because one's whole attitude has altered. ...

(*CWB II*, pp. 169–170)

Francesca Bion

Our peripatetic years began in 1967 when Bion was invited to work for two weeks in Los Angeles where a few analysts were interested in the theories of Melanie Klein and hoped to persuade a Kleinian-trained analyst to move to California to work with them.

Our decision to uproot ourselves in January 1968 was not an easy one; we had doubts and fears about the wisdom of such a major upheaval and worried about leaving the family. But on the plus side it offered Bion the possibility of freedom to work in his own unorthodox way a freedom he felt he did not have within the Klein group. He had for a long time experienced a sense of being, as he expressed it, "hedged in."

Many of the British psychoanalytic community were shocked and baffled; as well as genuine regret at losing him, the reactions ranged from surprise to the assumption that it was his way of going into retirement, to incomprehension, to disapproval and to dire warnings of culture shock and imminent racial bloodbaths in a land of drug addiction and weird cults. The dangers to be faced turned out to be of a somewhat different kind from those visualised by the prophets in London: the likelihood of being sued by paranoid patients; of being prevented from practising by the authorities on the grounds of lack of American medical qualifications; of not having a leg to stand on in a court of law as a "resident alien"; of actively hostile neighbours; even the possibility of making an adequate income was in doubt for a time. These were the serpents in that Garden of Eden where the sun shone, the flowers bloomed all year and the swimming pool beckoned.

Change the vertex again – as Bion might say – and I see many valuable, long-lasting friendships, generous hospitality, wonderful art exhibitions, thrilling orchestral concerts and recitals at the Music Centre and UCLA. Our experiences were as diverse as the country itself and its inhabitants. I must pay tribute here to our many Californian friends for their help, support and invariably stimulating company. I miss them still.

The anxieties associated with the fundamental change in professional status and the loss of a sense of security (probably illusory even in one's own country but usually assumed to exist) added stresses to the already difficult job of psychoanalysis. But from what Bion told me and what I sensed, his work did not suffer; his courage and characteristic reaction to a challenge were beneficial stimulants.

A society fed on distortions of the truth, facts spiced with phantasy, lying by omission, the encouragement of false expectations, presents a rocky foundation for a structure based on truth, but psychoanalysis has to be practised in the real world, however adverse the circumstances.

In late 1971, when we had been in California for almost four years, Bion wrote in his *Cogitations*, "The relationship between myself and my colleagues in Los Angeles could be accurately described as almost entirely unsuccessful. They are puzzled by, and cannot understand me – but have some respect even for what they cannot understand. There is, if I am not mistaken, more fear than understanding or sympathy for my thoughts, personality or ideas. There is no question of the situation the emotional situation – being any better anywhere else." Nevertheless I am sure that California provided the environment, both emotional and physical, in which he could break free, develop further his individuality, think what he called "wild thoughts", give free rein to "imaginative conjectures" – there is always the chance that they may turn into realisations.

In the mid-70s, the growing interest in so-called "Kleinian" analysis caused consternation in the "traditional" American Psychoanalytic Society. Bion said, in a 1976 interview, ". . . American psychoanalysts think that psychoanalysis will be undermined by sanctioning psychoanalysts who support the theories of Melanie Klein." He was reluctant to be drawn into this kind of controversy, regarding it as an irrelevant waste of time. He succeeded in preserving his independence by remaining an "outsider"; he was not a member of any American psychoanalytic society, institute or group.

(Francesca Bion 1994, pp. 99–101)

The view from Los Angeles

Joseph Aguayo

Visitors included Hanna Segal, Herbert Rosenfeld, Donald Meltzer, and Wilfred Bion, among others [starting in the mid-1960s]. These small meetings initially started as clinical lectures and seminars held in private homes, but as interest blossomed and attendance grew, these meetings were moved to larger venues such as the Beverly Wilshire Hotel. Looking back several years later, Grotstein gave his study group the moniker "The Four Horsemen of the Apocalypse" for having brought Kleinian ideas to Los Angeles. . . . Bion was the first Kleinian analyst invited to live and work in Los Angeles by this group. . . . Shortly after relocating, Bion realised he needed other colleagues to join him, both for support and to meet the growing demand for Kleinian analytic and supervisory services. Other Kleinian analysts, such Albert Mason and later, Susanna Isaacs Elmhirst, also accepted invitations to join him in Los Angeles.

The Los Angeles analysts could not have known the significance of their invitation to Bion. A number of important issues in his psychoanalytic career crystallised as he now turned seventy. Bion had been both president of the British Psychoanalytical Society and chair of the Melanie Klein Trust in the period from 1962 to 1967. His oft-cited comment rendered in his 1966 paper, "Catastrophic Change", namely ". . . loading up the psychoanalyst with such honours that he's sunk without a trace" may have reflected his weariness of having such an administratively burdened schedule in London, among other things. It is hard to imagine that all this work had not compromised the time that he could devote to his passion of theorising and writing about psychoanalysis. Bion evidently decided that the interest in his work shown in Los Angeles was serious and significant enough to warrant his move there. In addition, he arranged to take on no administrative and leadership responsibilities there. His hope was for a receptive enough environment that would give him ample time to continue his research and writing.

Bion had some sense that his work, particularly on the treatment of borderline and psychotic patients, would be well received in Los Angeles. As mentioned, there was tremendous interest in the claims made by Kleinians that they had had some limited success in the treatment of psychotically disturbed patients. Many physician-analysts in attendance at Bion's 1967 Los Angeles seminars had extensive experience working with hospitalised psychotic and near psychotic patients (Greenson 1965; Wexler 1965), and they were quite interested to hear new ideas on how to go about doing such difficult work. All the clinical examples given by Bion in the Los Angeles seminars were of psychotic and borderline patients, and the transcripts make clear that these examples struck a responsive chord. . . .

I have maintained elsewhere that Bion himself may have felt quite intrigued by why his paper ["Notes on Memory and Desire"] created such a controversial stir in Los Angeles. As attested to by the various commentaries written on this paper – and published in The Psychoanalytic Forum – some American analysts were quite enthused while others were shocked and appalled by Bion's ideas, such as the active abandonment of memory for previous sessions.

More importantly, this "here and now" technique of active and receptive listening also implicitly challenged ego psychological assumptions regarding the importance of the patient's early history, its careful reconstruction and interpretative understanding in the past-to-present transference. Bion's "Notes on Memory and Desire" was exceedingly compressed, direct, and forthright, almost to the point of being strident. The responses to the paper demonstrated some interest but much incredulity and utter bewilderment regarding just what Bion was attempting to convey. Interestingly, Los Angeles analyst John Lindon, the editor of The Psychoanalytic Forum, expressed his own appreciation of Bion's work in his own separate discussion, finding it ". . . provocatively nihilistic of all that we have learned as psychoanalysts. . ."

In light of the fact that few American analysts were familiar with his publications, Bion spoke plainly and directly to his American colleagues, inviting them to ask him questions, repeatedly if need be, so that he could clarify his intended meanings. In these 1967 seminars, Bion shunted aside his dense, epistemological style of communication, particularly with regard to his emerging ideas on analytic technique. Rather than take exclusive aim at the patient's pathology, Bion also took up the problematic nature of the analyst's subjective processing capacities. These Los Angeles seminars demonstrated an alternative to a dense, theoretical exposition – he worked with the technical implications of the analyst's potentially problematic reactions to working with his disturbed patients.

(Aguayo 2017, pp. 42–46)

[248]   Letter: something was going wrong in the work in England

The Other Side of Genius: "Letters to Francesca"

1968 August 6

My darling,

...Very "enthusiastic" reception [in Buenos Aires] and although I think I now know better than to allow myself to be taken in by it, it is a comfort and a nice change after Los Angeles analytic "enthusiasm". However, I am quite sure that the astringent atmosphere of Los Angeles is better for *me* – if we can stand it. I hate to think of the time you are having and the anxiety you have to put up with. I am glad to hear of the family and that you think they are having the holiday they need. In a peculiar way I feel I am having the work I need. Something was going wrong in the work in England – not only mine. I can't, as you know, pretend I like it, but there it is....

(*CWB II*, pp. 176–177)

What was going wrong with the work in England? An indication of what Bion thought has already been seen in the Los Angeles Seminar quote (*LASS*, pp. 37–38) in which he talks about the powerful effect on the analyst of the patient's denial of what the analyst is drawing attention to, but also the analyst's own dislike of remaining close to painful psychic realities. Both exert a subtle pressure that can cause the analyst to drift into a jargon version of theory. I found myself reminded of his arrival at Northfield Hospital back in the 1940s to find his desk covered with request slips to either get away or to stay away from the hospital. To reiterate a point made in the Introduction: Bion was struck by there being a lack of discipline, and he turned his attention to the identification of a common enemy. In the First World War the enemy was the "Boche" who could come over the hill behind the huts of the rebellious Welsh miners on whom Bion has had the guns turned. At Northfield hospital the enemy is identified as "neurosis". In relation to what was going wrong with the work in England in the 1960s, the enemy is identified as "memory and desire". Did Bion think there was a lack of discipline in psycho-analysis? A prevalent view in England is that Bion is becoming increasingly less disciplined himself from the mid 1960s. Bion's view, I think, is the opposite.

[249]   Reverence and awe

Synopsis and notes of a paper given at a joint meeting of the Los Angeles Psycho-Analytic Society and Institute, and the Southern California Psycho-Analytic Society on 20 April 1967 in the Mount Sinai Hospital Auditorium. There is no record of the actual presentation.

From *Further Cogitations*

March 1967

... If psychoanalysts can abandon themselves to analysis in the psychoanalytic sessions, they are in a position when recollecting the experience in tranquillity to discern their experience as part of a greater whole.... My example, which I have called "Reverence and Awe", is taken from the analysis of a patient who came to me after an experience of many years of analysis. He had no doubt at all that he had benefited greatly from his experience, and yet he was dissatisfied. I expected to find that greed played a large part in his make-up, but from what I knew of his analyst I thought it very unlikely that this point had not been adequately dealt with....

The patient was a man of medium height, fifty-three years old, with greying hair and an alert and lively manner. He at once embarked on a torrent of free associations plentifully sprinkled with information about various psychoanalysts whom he had known. The information was mostly trivial, but I was given to understand by his manner that he had plenty more....

After he had gone on pouring out material of this kind for some five or ten minutes, I stopped him and said he was showing me that there was very little about being an analysand that he did not know.... He complimented me on the brilliance of my interpretation and indicated what a relief it was to find that I was not wedded to any rigid psychoanalytic theories [recounted by Bion with humour!]....

[The patient] constantly reverted to feelings of admiration, which were not only clear in the transference but cropped up again and again in situations outside analysis altogether. Many times I had to give interpretations showing him that he was virtually worshipping "God", although he had repeatedly said that he was not religious and had no belief in God. I pointed out that his reactions to the "God" in whom he appeared emotionally to believe were hostile because He could not stand up to intellectual scrutiny. His reactions reminded me very much of the savage who is supposed to beat his gods if they do not grant his wishes. He seemed finally to accept that he felt an intense need for someone or something for which he could entertain feelings of reverence and awe. His resentment was related to his inability to feel this in any particular instance....

There is a great difference between idealization of a parent because the child is in despair, and idealization because the child is in search of an outlet for feelings of reverence and awe.

The answer to the question – which is it? – will not be found in any text-book but only in the process of psychoanalysis itself....

(*CWB XI*, pp. 272–280)

[250]   A bad psychoanalyst?

From *Further Cogitations* (1968–1969)

10 May 1968

Technique

Why am I such a bad psychoanalyst? Cannot just be age because have always been aware of this, though sometimes it is the suspicion that it is the inadequacy of psychoanalysis itself and not just me. But this is based on a mistaken idea of psychoanalysis as a body of knowledge or a therapeutic procedure rather than as a research into the domain of the mind itself, an expedition.

(*CWB XV*, p. 62)

This entry was followed shortly by:

[*Fourteen pages of notes dealing with his anxieties connected with the (analytic) practice and fears of finding himself in an intolerable situation – the outstanding impression is one of anger, hostility and self-dissatisfaction. F.B.*]

Francesca Bion (*CWB XV*, p. 62)

Francesca Bion decided not to include these notes.

[251]   I and Thou

From *Cogitations* (1958–1979)

[Transcription of a tape recording.]

8 August 1978

Many mystics have been able to describe a situation in which it is believed that there really is a power, a force that cannot be measured or weighted or assessed by the mere human being with the mere human mind. This seems to me to be a profound assumption which has hitherto been almost completely ignored, and yet people talk about "omnipotence" as if they knew what it meant and as if it had a simple connotation. Martin Buber came much closer to recognizing the realities of the situation when human speech is resorted to. [I and Thou: "The attitude of man is twofold in accordance with the two basic words he can speak. The basic words are not single words but word pairs. One basic word is the word pair I–You.... This is different from the basic word I–It."] When one talks about "I–You", the significant thing is not the two objects related, but the *relationship* – that is, an open-ended reality in which there is no termination (in the sense that this is understood by ordinary human beings). The language of ordinary human beings is only appropriate to the rational, can only describe the rational, can only make statements in terms of rationality.

(*CWB XI*, p. 343)

Chapter 16

Brazilian Lectures

Introduction

In his seventies, Bion travelled to destinations in South America, North America and Europe to give lectures, seminars and supervisions. People were impressed by his physical strength and athleticism as well as by the content of what he said. The following quotes are from these visits. The intense exploratory nature of his earlier work of the 1960s gives way to a format in which we get a more relaxed access to the wisdom of his years and the detail of his clinical thinking with many different kinds of patients. The various pieces were recorded and later transcribed, and the fact that he spoke, rather than wrote, them may also contribute to the less dense content. In a rather dour British way, he is also very funny.

These pieces are, in many ways, the most accessible and easily quotable of his work, and I have added fewer commentaries (there are more commentaries again when we get to his novel). I do, however, want to make a general point: I think there is a detectable change as one goes through the lectures, seminars and supervisions, the later ones having more sense of a mission.

Quotes

[252]   Ur

From "1973 São Paulo"

I shall start with a fable, in the guise of an historical account of the Royal Cemetery at Ur. On the death of the king the entire court processed into an excavation, since called "The Death Pit", and there, dressed in their finery and jewels, took a drug from a small cup later found by each body.

Five hundred years later, without any publicity, the tombs were robbed. It was a courageous thing to do because the Cemetery had been sanctified by the death and burial of the Royal Family. The robbers were the patrons of the scientific method: the first who dared to break through the ghostly sentinels of the dead and their priestly attendants.

This primitive reconstruction, which is not history, archaeology or art, might be categorized from a religious, aesthetic or scientific vertex. In Grid terms we might say that it is a C category construction [dream/myth]. . . .

We have no way of guessing what the tomb robbers subsequently felt. I still consider that they must have been brave men to dare to rob the treasures hidden in a spot which was guarded by evil and dangerous spirits. Similarly in psychoanalysis: when approaching the unconscious – that is, what we do not know, not what we do know – we, patient and analyst alike, are certain to be disturbed. Anyone who is going to see a patient tomorrow should, at some point, experience fear. In every consulting room there ought to be two rather frightened people: the patient and the psychoanalyst. If they are not, one wonders why they are bothering to find out what everyone knows.

(CWB VII, pp. 9–10)

[253] Inappropriate causes of financial fluctuations

From "1973 São Paulo"

Continuing this use of fable into the domain of finance: money was early used as a mode of communication in religious observance, the communication then being between corporeal beings like humans, and others such as the ghostly sentinels at Ur. Later, it was used by the Anglo-Saxons as "wergild" to compensate for the loss of life or blood, and "bride-purchase" to compensate for the loss of a bride from the membership of a group. The convenience of this method of communication, analogous to the convenience of speech, made it suitable for take-over for purposes of exchange and communication in commerce.

Psychoanalysis may be regarded as a response to the inappropriate; from that awareness arose the search for the cause of the inappropriate. In finance the inappropriate has not yet been discovered. Consequently, fluctuations in exchange are sought in the realms of the appropriate. The causes of the fluctuations will have to be sought, not only in the rational world of finance, but also in the continued survival of these primitive, and now no longer recognized, basic roots – religious and tribal (as described in my fable). Money does not work in accordance with rational, economic laws alone.

(*CWB VII*, pp. 9–10)

[254]   Giving an interpretation

From "1973 São Paulo"

I think most psychoanalysts know what it feels like to be giving an interpretation in front of the patient. It sounds simple. It is difficult to say why it is not. One would have to say, "If it is as easy as you think, you go and try it." If you *can* try it, and if neither you nor your patient have what we loosely call a breakdown, and survive, then both people will be mentally stronger after the experience. The writer, Bagehot (1872), said, "Strong men are attracted by strong ideas, and strong ideas attract strong men and make them stronger". In psychoanalysis two people dare to ask questions about what they have forgotten and about what they do not know, and at the same time must be capable of living in the present. As a result they do get stronger.

(*CWB VII*, p. 11)

From *Clinical Seminars:* New York 1977

The analyst is trying to help the patient to dare to be himself, to dare to have enough respect for his personality to be that person. The analytic experience, in spite of all the appearance of comfort – comfortable couch, comfortable chairs, warmth, good lighting – is in fact a stormy, emotional experience for the two people. If you are an officer in a battle you are supposed to be sane enough to be scared; but you are supposed also to be capable of thinking. It sounds ridiculous to say that people sitting in a comfortable room in full peace time have to be capable of anything – but they do. The analyst is supposed to remain articulate and capable of translating what he is aware of into a comprehensible communication. That means that he has to have a vocabulary which the patient may be able to understand if given a chance to hear what the analyst has to say. It sounds absurdly simple – so simple that it is hard to believe how difficult it is.

(*CWB VIII*, pp. 242–243)

Bagehot (1826–1877): Editor-in-chief of *The Economist* for 17 years.

[255]   Past, future and present

From "1973 São Paulo"

Over and over again, these names, like "past", "future", "good old days", are in fact names of a feeling in the present, and that is why they are so important.

(*CWB VII*, p. 14)

[256]   Problem for which the patient seeks help

From "1973 São Paulo"

In the practice of psychoanalysis the patient will make a statement. One part of it consists of what he already knows; another part is the attempt to formulate the problem for which he seeks help.

(CWB VII, p. 20)

Thomas Ogden comments that the question Bion asks the presenting analyst far more often than he asks any other question is, "Why is the patient coming to analysis?".

Thomas Ogden

. . . . It seems to me that, in each instance Bion poses this question, he is implicitly asking the presenter to think of the patient as unconsciously bringing to each session an emotional problem for which he has been unable to find a "solution" . . . , i.e. a problem with which he has been unable to do psychological work.

(Ogden 2007, p. 1190)

. . . The analyst's task, for Bion, is to help the patient to live with his pain long enough to do analytic work with it. There is some aspect of the patient that comes to the analyst for analysis. Bion is continually listening for the (often very muted) voice of that part of the patient, and for hints from the patient, concerning what emotional problem this aspect of the patient is trying to think/solve. If the patient is not using the analyst as an analyst (for example, by behaving as if he expects the analyst to be a magician who will turn the patient into the person who he wishes to be), Bion asks himself (and often asks the "dreamt-up" patient) what the patient thinks analysts do. Perhaps second only in frequency to Bion's question "Why has the patient come for analysis?" is his question "What does the patient think analysis is?" And he often comments in response to the patient's idea, "That is a very strange conception of analysis." Helping the patient and giving the patient the "correct" analysis (a genuine analytic experience) are, for Bion, one and the same thing.

(Ogden 2007, p. 1195)

[257] Palinurus

From "1973 São Paulo"

The god Somnus appears disguised as another god and in this guise seduces Palinurus, saying: "You are tired; it is a fine night, the fleet is going by the guidance of your ship; there is no danger; you can go to sleep and I will guide the ship." Palinurus replies, "I am not such a fool as to be taken in by a smooth face. I would never trust the smooth face of the sea and the air", and he ties himself to the helm. The god then takes a branch, dips it in the waters of Lethe, and scatters it over Palinurus who is thereby rendered helpless. The god immediately hurls Palinurus into the sea with such violence that part of the ship is torn away at the same time. That is a moral story, a *serious* moral story. If we ask ourselves what words we should have to use to tell that story today, we should have to talk about things like memory, desire, drugs (the waters of Lethe), violence and great hostility.

To continue the story – Aeneas sees his helmsman has gone, his ship is veering wildly and the fleet has nothing to navigate by. He says: "Poor Palinurus! How sad that you should be taken in by something so commonplace as the smooth appearance of the sea." Nobody gains anything. Aeneas cannot believe he has a faithful, experienced helmsman; Palinurus cannot feel that his leader knows anything about his fidelity or his ability.

(*CWB VII*, p. 22)

Aeneas is taken in by appearances and loses the anchor he could have had in his knowledge of the character of Palinurus.

On returning from the war and having completed his degree Bion worked as a teacher at his old school Bishop Stortford. He was falsely accused by one of the boy's mothers for improper behaviour with her son. The Headmaster told him to leave. Bion said he would leave at the end of the term:

It was a hideous term at a hateful place and I did not know to whom to turn. I realized years later that I should have demanded legal advice in considering the possibility of an action for damages. But the stormy seas of sex I could not navigate any better than Palinurus. I visited the bottom of this monstrous world beyond the stormy Hebrides. How deceptively calm that term, how friendly were my friends!

(*CWB II*, pp. 16–17)

[258]   I don't understand: I'll kill it

From "1973 São Paulo"

"Here is something I don't understand – I'll kill it". But a few might say, "Here is something I don't understand – I must find out".

(*CWB VIII*, p. 21)

Keeping to this primitive area of alpha-elements, the human animal might say, "Here is something that frightens me, let me hide and watch it", or if it became braver, "Let me go nearer and sniff it", using its olfactory senses.

(*CWB VIII*, p. 31)

As analysts and patients ourselves in analysis we can come to realise just how quickly we turn from what frightens us, so quickly that we may not even have known the feared situation to be there. Bion, who had much more frightening times in his life than many determinedly continued to explore more primitive and frightening areas of life.

[259] Feeble ideas but powerful emotions

From "1973 São Paulo"

We bring into the open certain elements of an analysand's past, not because we think they are particularly valuable, but because they are not valuable for him to have in his luggage. If we bring them to the surface then he can forget them. Those memories, past or future, which he does not know seem to have a great deal of power; they are what I would call feeble ideas but powerful emotions.

(CWB VII, p. 33)

[260]   Patient can't make use of what he already knows

From "1973 São Paulo"

Any words which I employ in an attempt to convey something to you are extremely inadequate; it depends on your being friendly enough and tolerant enough to be able to bring my statement into contact with your hearing. Some patients cannot do that, nor can they listen to what they themselves say. They have no respect for what they already know, so that their experience and knowledge are of no use to them. The question is not simply one of the relationship of the patient to the analyst, but the relationship of the patient with himself which may be so bad that he cannot even make use of what he already knows.

(*CWB VII*, p. 53)

[261]   Anxiety in children

From "1973 São Paulo"

Making use again of the story about the infant and mother, the mother can be glad to be able to say, "This child is ill". Before long the infant turns into a child and finds it much easier to say, "I've got a stomach ache", because it has no word for anxiety, and in any case I doubt whether a child ever considers that there is anything peculiar about being anxious. I have no doubt at all that children, from a very early age, feel anxious, but they have no language in which to express it and do not consider that feeling anxious is anything out of the ordinary. If they dislike it they have to say something like, "I've got a stomach ache".

(*CWB VII*, p. 57)

[262]   Tension

From "1973 São Paulo"

One fundamental matter with which we are all concerned is tension. Sometimes there can be so little tension between two people that they fail to stimulate each other at all. At the other extreme, the differences in outlook or temperament are so great that no discussion is possible. The question is, can the society or group or pair find the happy mean which is tense enough to stimulate but belongs to neither extreme, either lack of tension or too much? Can a nation achieve both sufficient homogeneity and sufficient tension?

This problem applies also to the categories of science and religion. How is a proper balance to be achieved between a scientific vertex which could be said to be devoted to truth or the facts, and a religious vertex which could equally be said to be devoted to truth? Similarly, the sincere artist is also concerned to depict truth. If Vermeer can paint the little street in Delft, and if people can look at it, then they will never see a street in the same way again. The painter has brought about a change in the individual which makes it possible for him to see a truth that he has never seen before. It would seem absurd if the tension between these three groups – science, religion and art – which are all fundamentally devoted to the truth, was either so slack or so tense that they were unable to further the aim of truth.

(CWB VII, p. 62)

[263]   Flash of the obvious

From "1973 São Paulo"

Q: How did you come to realize the advantages of suppressing memory and desire during the analytic session?

Bion: I found that I could experience a flash of the obvious. One is usually so busy looking for something out of the ordinary that one ignores the obvious as if it were of no importance. Indeed, one of the reasons for thinking it is time to give an interpretation is that nobody has seen something that is obvious.

(CWB VII, p. 67)

José Américo Junqueira de Mattos

What struck me from the very beginning of my analysis was the extent to which Dr. Bion was attentive to all I said and how seriously he took it all. (This observation may seem obvious, but I did learn from him that the obvious is not always easily seen. I even think that sometimes the obvious may be the most difficult. I might say without exaggeration that, to a great extent, my analysis with Dr. Bion was the "discovery" and recognition of the obvious).

One day, after stating several associations, I feel silent. Then, Dr. Bion told me that he saw no sense in what I had said and asked me what I thought about it. After reflecting on this, I told him that I thought nothing at all. No doubt, what I had said was unimportant. After this, Dr. Bion told me something I was never to forget: "If you think that what you said is unimportant, why did you say it at all? Do you think that you are so rich that you can afford to waste time and money to come here and say futile, unimportant things?"

I realized that my association contained some things I knew and others I ignored. His function was to show me the underlying meaning that I ignored. Thus I clearly perceived – once again, the obvious – that I only took from analysis what I put into it. I started to feel responsible for everything I put into words and to follow the simple rule, telling everything that would come in my associations. . . .

I soon learnt – obvious once more – that he wanted to say exactly what he did say. "I mean what I say and I say what I mean", he told me once, probably paraphrasing Shakespeare.

(Junqueira de Mattos 2015, pp. 8–9)

[264]   Is Bion a mystic?

From "1973 São Paulo"

Q: Can this method of observing what occurs in the session, when suppressing memory and desire, be differentiated from the non-scientific method, that is from mystical practices suppressing the lower ego to reach knowledge, truths, which are unknowable in other ways?

Bion: My knowledge of mysticism is through hearsay and I am, therefore, not qualified to express an opinion which might have greater weight attached to it than it deserves. There is an ever-present danger of our not very great knowledge of psychoanalysis conferring undeserved authority on what we say.

(*CWB VII*, p. 68)

From *Cogitations*

8 August 1978

Many mystics have been able to describe a situation in which it is believed that there really is a power, a force that cannot be measured or weighted or assessed by the mere human being with the mere human mind. This seems to me to be a profound assumption which has hitherto been almost completely ignored, and yet people talk about "omnipotence" as if they knew what it meant and as if it had a simple connotation.

(*CWB XI*, p. 343)

[265] What has frightened the patient

From "1974 Rio de Janeiro"

You are in your consulting room; you say that you are a psychoanalyst; you have your name on the door; for some reason a person has come to see you. You are at his disposal, you are free for fifty minutes, and during that time, if he will tell you what he wants, you will answer it if you can. I do not know why that patient thinks it worth his time and his money to come and see me, and I would not like to say that I know that he is spending all that time and trouble without some reason until I have heard more of what he has to say for himself. Suppose he says he is terrified that he might kill his children, or his mother or father. One would like to know how the patient comes to know that. I would say, "You have known yourself for a long time so you must have some kind of evidence which has led you to suppose that that is what you would do. You have evidence which I have not – that doesn't mean that you are wrong, but you haven't made it clear to me." One is not saying the patient cannot or will not do it, because he can do what he likes. I might continue, "Although you haven't made me frightened by what you have told me, there must be some reason why you have frightened your-self; you have frightened you – so much so that you have even come here today. You must have some evidence which has frightened you, although you haven't made it clear to me what that evidence is – so far."

(*CWB VII*, p. 79)

[266]   Grown man cannot bear to be reminded of what he was like

From "1974 Rio de Janeiro"

The grown man cannot bear to be reminded of what he was like by the behaviour of his children, because he cannot bear to be reminded of a part of his still existing mind. He does not like the experience of living with his family and he does not like psychoanalysis. We are trying to introduce him to a character which we think it would be worth his while to respect, namely, himself: either himself as he was once, or to introduce what he was once to himself as he is today. These two people dislike each other and do not want to be introduced. Not only do they hate each other, but they hate this psychoanalyst who is trying to introduce them.

(*CWB VII*, p. 88)

...There is a complication; you will not be surprised that we shall now look at it. The baby in us hates the grown-up; the hate is mutual. Tomorrow one of our patients may show every sign that he does not want to grow up – he thinks it is a bad idea. He would rather remain a baby all his life.... Equally, the analysand does not want to be reduced, as he fears he will be, to the state of mind of child or infant. But it is not something which is over and done with once and for all. We remain human animals: sometimes young human animals; sometimes one can say we are grown-up human animals. Can they be made to work together? Can they co-operate enough to pro-duce, to use metaphor, binocular vision, bi-mental perception?

(*CWB VII*, p. 104)

Howard B. Levine

It may be very useful for the analyst to ask him or herself in relation to every patient:

What areas of himself does he want to know nothing about? ... As we listen to this story, we can get a chance of learning something about what he has chosen to know and from that, some idea of what he has chosen not to know: the self that he doesn't want to know!

"The self that we do not wish to know"! Doesn't that lie at heart of every encounter with the unconscious?

(Levine 2015, p. 100)

[267]   Silence

From "1974 Rio de Janeiro"

A group of people are not always talking; they are sometimes silent and that silence is a part of what they are doing. In English we even have an expression, "a pregnant silence". It expresses it very well. There are some silences which are nothing; they are mathematically zero. But there are times when a zero is put between the figures 1 and 1 and it turns it into one hundred and one. Similarly, there are some silences which turn the preceding sounds and the succeeding sounds into a valuable communication. A good poet uses ordinary words and ordinary silences, but the use to which he puts them turns both the words and the silences into something which is extraordinary. In analysis you may be able to distinguish the silences which you have a chance of observing.

(*CWB VII*, p. 105)

[268]   "Interference"

From "1974 Rio de Janeiro"

When you are talking to your patient you can sometimes see and feel that he is not attending to you. At the same time you can feel that he is attending to *something*; the conversation between the patient and analyst is being interfered with. That is what I mean by interference. Are you going to pay attention to what he tells you, or what your books have told you, or are you going to pay attention to the interference? This is the difficulty about practical psychoanalysis; this is the difficulty about tomorrow's sessions. It is no good saying, "You are not free-associating", or, "This patient doesn't talk to me, I can't do anything about him". You can be silent; and you can listen. You can stop talking so that you can have a chance to hear what is going on. What you have to listen to then is psychoanalytic "interference", just as somebody had to listen to radio interference.

(*CWB VII*, pp. 106–107)

[269]   Psychoanalytic non-sense?

From "1974 Rio de Janeiro"

But the extraordinary thing is that when you are looking at a genuine Picasso you get a feeling, "You know, I think I see what this chap means – it's not quite what I could interpret as 'that's my wife', but I can say 'that is about something; that isn't about nothing'". That painting by Picasso is not adequately mathematized by the zero 0. You may feel that you do not really know enough to be able to understand what Picasso shows you.

You may give your analysand a correct interpretation, an interpretation which you are sure expresses the truth, and yet the patient may say, "I don't understand this psychoanalytic nonsense!" You can only say, "Well, you feel that it is nonsense; but perhaps you may feel it is 'non-sense' later" – and leave it at that. Many of our interpretations which are obvious to us as psychoanalysts may seem extremely obscure to the patient. He may sincerely say, "I think it's nonsense". But sometimes analysis is accompanied by the growth of mutual respect. The parents may have had something to teach the child. Today the grown-up child knows more than he used to know, but he is also the child who could teach him something. After all, the child must have known enough to have grown up and still to be surviving. Sometimes analysis is accompanied by growth of the analysand's respect for himself.

One can identify oneself with the analyst, or one can identify oneself with the analysand. One can feel, "I can understand that he doesn't understand my interpretations, but as a matter of fact I have no reason to alter my interpretation; I think it is true. I can quite see that he thinks it's nonsense. Time will tell." Time is telling.

(*CWB VII*, pp. 108–109)

[270]   Smashing up is not the whole truth

From "1974 Rio de Janeiro"

...a patient can be dominated by the feelings of fear of his being extremely destructive, of his feeling that even if he loves something he loves it in the way that he loves his food – he chews it up and turns it into faeces and urine. That is fairly easily and quickly understood by the child, but it is a long time before a child is able to learn that as a result of what he eats he does in fact grow. By the time he is able to stand against the wall and see that last time he was four feet three, but that now he is four feet three and a half inches tall, the conviction that he destroys what he eats has become firmly established. Analysis would be like being able to introduce him to the idea that he has grown, and introducing that idea to his feelings of depression, hopelessness, boredom and anger. He has often heard "You *are* a naughty boy; why do you break everything up?" He cannot say, "I have only been breaking up my breakfast – or my lunch or my tea – because I hope to be bigger" – as a child he cannot argue like that. These two people – the destructive, hopeless, despairing person, and the creative, constructive one who grows – do not meet unless we can manage to introduce them to each other in analysis. We are not attempting to show the patient how bad he is or to make him feel he will never be any good. We are trying to show him why he is so depressed, and that although he may know nothing about it he actually makes something out of his food which is not only faeces and urine. The girl has a chance of feeling that she may be able to make babies and that can bring a certain degree of relief. The boy, on the other hand, hears that his little sister can make babies, but that he cannot. It is easy for him to understand that; it is much more difficult for him to understand what good he is. Even in genital intercourse the man can feel that his contribution is slight indeed; even if he can have intercourse, what he does is very little compared with what the breast does – or his mother, or his sister. The analytic experience is not simply to find out about the boy or girl, the man or woman, in the sense of finding out what their faults and mistakes are. It also means giving them a chance to see that it may be perfectly true that they smash things up, but it is not the whole of the truth.

(CWB VII, p. 113)

[271]   On failing a candidate

From "1974 Rio de Janeiro"

Q: *Bearing in mind your references to the respect due to the human mind and personality, what do you think are the factors or motives that should lead one to fail a candidate?*

Bion: . . . I would not feel disposed to qualify somebody who disliked people unless the people were likeable. Most of the time we have to deal with people who have failed, or who are not very good at their job. Those are the people that we have to make able to be good at their job. Someone may have made a mess of everything he has ever had – education, fortune, married life, all of it – and yet will expect an analyst to make a success of him; and the analyst is expected to make a success of making a success of such a person. He will not do that if he dislikes people.

(*CWB VII*, pp. 115–116)

[272]   Countertransference is unconscious

From "1974 Rio de Janeiro"

Counter-transference is a technical term, but as often happens the technical term gets worn away and turns into a kind of worn-out coin which has lost its value. We should keep these things in good working condition. The theory about a counter-transference is that it is the transference relationship which the analyst has to the patient without knowing he has it. You will hear analysts say, "I don't like that patient, but I can make use of my counter-transference". He cannot use his counter-transference. He may be able to make use of the fact that he dislikes the patient, but that is not counter-transference. There is only one thing to do with counter-transference and that is to have it analysed. One cannot make use of one's counter-transference in the consulting room; it is a contradiction in terms. To use the term in that way means that one would have to invent a new term to do the work which used to be done by the word "counter-transference". It is one's *unconscious* feelings about the patient, and since it is unconscious there is nothing we can do about it. If the counter-transference *is* operating in the analytic session the analysand is unlucky – and so is the analyst. The time to have dealt with it was in the past, in the analyst's own analysis. We can only hope that it does not use us too much and that we have had enough analysis to keep the number of unconscious operations to a minimum.

(CWB VII, p. 116)

Bion in New York

One of the essential points about countertransference is that it is *unconscious*. People talk about "making use of" their counter-transference; they cannot make any use of it because they don't know what it is. There is such a thing as my emotional reaction to the patient; I can hope that through my awareness of the fact that I have human characteristics like prejudice and bigotry I may be more tolerant and allow the patient to feel if my interpretation is or is not correct. That is a transient experience. It is one reason for calling it "transference"; it is a feeling or thought or idea you have on your way to somewhere else. When you are in the presence of something which you have learnt to call a transference can you feel more precisely what it is at the time? It depends on what the patient says to you being allowed to enter into you, allowed to bounce off, as it were, your inner being and get reflected out.

(CWB VIII, p. 245)

Paula Heimann, one of Bion's two supervisors during his analytic training, wrote a ground-breaking paper on countertransference (at around the time when Bion would have been in supervision with her). Heimann (1950) first notes the "basic assumption" that the analyst's unconscious mind is in contact with the unconscious of the patient. She argues that feelings coming up in the analyst can be a leading sign of what is occurring unconsciously. It is clear in her paper that the analyst needs to be skilled in detecting what belongs to themselves and what feelings are, in fact, a newly emerging light being thrown on the patient. Heimann expresses the concern, which Klein also had, that talk of the countertransference may be used to obscure the analyst's shortcomings. It is possible that one reason for Bion's emphasis in his later writings on the unconscious nature of countertransference is that he thinks sight has been lost of the depth of the forces under observation.

[273]   The shadow and the source of illumination

From "1974 Rio de Janeiro"

> Further questions to be resolved are: is it a past, future, or contemporary state which is casting its shadow on the present screen on which we hope to delineate it? Stating this in psychoanalytic terms: the screen is the transference; the interpretation is to determine what it is that is being "transferred". In pictorial terms: there is the shadow; where is the source of illumination?
>
> (*CWB VII*, p. 118)

Bion's reference to a shadow falling on the screen brings to mind Freud's well known comment of the "shadow of the object".

Sigmund Freud

> So we find the key to the clinical picture: we perceive that the self-reproaches are reproaches against a loved object which have been shifted away from it on to the patient's own ego.
>   . . . the shadow of the object fell upon the ego.
>
> (Freud 1917 SE 14, pp. 248–249)

[274]   Friendliness of patient

From "1974 Rio de Janeiro"

Very frequently analysts seem to allow themselves to be preoccupied with why patients fail to come and thus do not recognize the reciprocal mystery – why they do come. The investigation should not ignore either polarity. Sometimes patients keep on coming when one feels that it is hard to see that it is worth their while in time or money, but they must be getting something out of it, and they must think it is worth while. It is a fact which the analyst should never allow to disappear below his conscious horizon. It is absurd for analysts to talk about the hostility of patients and so on – we know there is plenty of hostility; but the surprising thing is that there is apparently such a great supply of friendliness. People actually do their best to co-operate. They get to the consulting room, even when they feel sure that they cannot do anything when they get there.

(*CWB VII*, pp. 140–141)

[275]   Letting a child do whatever it likes

From "1974 Rio de Janeiro"

One of the dangers of letting a child do just whatever it likes is that it does not simply do just whatever it likes. The moment it is aware that not even its mother or father can watch what it is up to all the time, and it is therefore free to do what it likes, the child at once and automatically reconstitutes the missing parent. You have probably seen one of your own children solemnly go and stand in a corner as a kind of punishment for some crime that we have heard nothing about. But that reconstituted parent has insufficient knowledge or experience to be a parent – it is simply part of the child. So that the failure of the parent to impose some discipline means that the place of a potentially sensible or wise person is taken by an inexperienced conscience and a disciplinary system which is so severe that the child may break down under its own discipline.

(CWB VII, p. 151)

[276] Construction: much to be said for a short story

From "1974 São Paulo"

The view, expressed by Freud, which I found has a great deal of meaning for me is that many of these interpretations are almost meaningless, but these constructions are not. I remain unexcited by being told that I am omnipotent, or that I am helpless. I do, however, feel slightly more interested if somebody says that I think I am God; if it means nothing else, at least it means that somebody is being rude. To that extent it is an improvement on being told that one is omnipotent. But I would go further; I would like the individual concerned to tell me what sort of god I was behaving like. There is a large variety of gods which one's behaviour could resemble. If the individual, instead of being rude or hostile, would tell me which kind of god I resembled, I would find that construction much more meaningful and comprehensible. There is much to be said for a short story which I can understand and which, therefore, is a vehicle which communicates meaning. For example, if somebody said that I am like the god of Babel, that I am so jealous and envious that I would not like anyone to climb up a higher tower than the pedestal on which I was happening to sit myself, that I would like to make them so confused and on such bad terms with one another that they would not be able to construct a better and higher and more glorious tower – if I were given that sort of interpretation I would feel that I had a clearer idea (although I might not like it) of how I appeared to somebody else. That is why I am more in favour of the construction. ...

(*CWB VII*, p. 195)

I think the construction/short story is, at least partly, what Bion meant in *Elements of Psycho-Analysis* (1963) by "myth" (one of the three "dimensions" of psycho-analytic objects – sense, passion and myth).

[277]   Hospitalised patient

From "1974 São Paulo"

Q: What is the analyst to do if the patient suffers a psychotic episode and has to be hospitalized?

Bion: If the minimum conditions for analysis still exist I continue to analyse the patient. Putting the patient into hospital has little to do with the patient's personality; it has more to do with the public, or the family, or the people who are feeling inconvenienced – perhaps seriously so – by the patient. If the patient is going about wanting to murder his fellows that is very inconvenient indeed. Extremes of this kind are easy to comprehend; it is more difficult when the person in question is a nuisance – like Solzhenitsyn. Should he be hospitalized in a psychiatric "cancer ward", or just exiled? This matter of diagnosis is often a question of what degree of irritation or annoyance or inconvenience the person is creating. However, as analysts with a prejudice in favour of the individual, we would like to know what *kind* of nuisance the person was. Even if we narrow it down sufficiently to use some term like "psychosis" we would like to know which particular variety of psychosis.

(*CWB VII*, pp. 195–196)

Chapter 17

Clinical Seminars and Four Papers: "Brasilia 1975"

In 1975 Bion spent the month of April in Brasilia, giving lectures and clinical seminars. He preferred to have no more than 6 people in his seminars.

Quotes

278 One's behaviour has to be a compromise
279 Question asked by the patient
280 Flooding with information
281 Transference interpretations
282 Investigate the thing that obtrudes

[278]   One's behaviour has to be a compromise

We tend to forget that we may be much more used to analysis than the patient is. It would be quite natural to me to sit there silently and hear what the patient has to say, but the patient might not be able to stand that. A patient coming to me for the first time might be so frightened at such peculiar behaviour that he would get up and walk straight out. So as usual we come back to this point: in *theory* we can read what we like in all these great books on analysis; in *practice* we have to have a feeling about what the patient can stand. One's behaviour has to be a compromise; one has to have some concern and make allowances for the patient to whom this is such a frightening experience. I think this is an argument in favour of our behaving in a fairly conventional manner to make it easier for patients, who are under a strain anyway, to say whatever they want to say.

(*CWB VIII*, p. 10)

[279]   Question asked by the patient

Presenter: [The patient] asked "Why do I come here?". . . .

Bion: I think I should simply . . . say to her, "You have posed the question; perhaps later on you will be able to say what the answer is!", or simply say, "You have posed the question". I would rather leave her the chance of saying what the answer is when she has found it. . . .

It sounds to me as if she has come into this room where there are two people and has started asking questions about what they are doing. It would be much easier if one could say that there is a little girl watching what these two people are up to.

(CWB III, pp. 14–15)

[280]   Flooding with information

Bion: Yes, you often get a patient who, in contrast to saying nothing at all, floods you with information. I gather that this is happening here [in the case being presented]. Ordinarily one expects there to be some kind of structure to which the total communication conforms. But if the patient is always changing the subject he isn't really conversing; he is flooding you with free associations, not assisting you, not keeping you informed so much as keeping you unable to give an interpretation. But I don't think I would be inclined to stop him until I got a clearer idea of what he was up to. . . .

Presenter: I have the feeling that the patient didn't change the subject – he only apparently changed it.

Bion: This feeling of yours is where the interpretation comes from. Otherwise, if you interpret all these various changes of subject, you miss the point, you miss the subject which hasn't changed. When you begin to feel that all these different free associations are not really different ones, because they have the same pattern, then it becomes important to wait until you know what that pattern is. . . .

With this patient you can feel that he wants, or ought, to get back to work, and that it is a serious business that he is absent. But the analyst has to be ruthless; he has to resist the pressure because his business is not whether somebody gets back to work or not, but that somebody be given the correct analysis. . . .

The patient will push you, give you so much material that you feel, "If I go on listening to this I shall never know what interpretation to give because there are so many associations". You have to try to resist that, to insist to yourself that you are going to go on listening to what he has to say until you are convinced that you want to say something. Otherwise you can find yourself in the horrible situation of spending your life giving what you think is an interpretation that somebody else would give, instead of giving the interpretation *you* want to give. I don't think you can ever do good analysis if you are not satisfied with what you say.

(*CWB VIII*, pp. 19–22)

[281]   Transference interpretations

One gives interpretations like, "You are feeling that I am . . .", not because
the analyst is a person of any importance, but because it gives the analysand
a chance of recognizing what sort of person he himself is. If he is capable of
love and affection and gratitude, it is important that he should know that –
and so on through the list of his capacities and incapacities. In analysis it is
possible to see the kind of relationship that the patient is able to have with
somebody who is not himself.

(*CWB VIII*, pp. 35–36)

[282]   Investigate the thing that obtrudes

It is often helpful to go to the very thing which obtrudes: if you feel that the patient is able to make you feel guilty or frightened or anxious, that is what you need to investigate.

(*CWB VIII*, p. 113)

Chapter 18

Bion in New York and São Paulo: "New York, 1977"

The 1977 visit to New York was Bion's first seminar there. He wrote an author's note to accompany the publication of *Bion in New York and São Paulo*.

AUTHOR'S NOTE

I thank all who participated in these discussions with their objections and agreements. Many who read this book will feel that my replies are inadequate and incomplete. That they are inadequate I must admit; that they are incomplete I regard as a virtue especially if it stimulates the reader to complete the answers. I wish the reader as much enjoyment as I had in speaking; if it sends him to sleep may I wish him "Sweet Dreams and a profitable awakening".

W.R.B.

(*CWB VIII*, p. 231)

Quotes

[283] Resting with the patient

To return to this simple poem of Kipling's ["The Elephant Child"] – "I give them all a rest". When we are in the office with a patient we have to dare to rest. It is difficult to see what is at all frightening about that, but it is. It is difficult to remain quiet and let the patient have a chance to say whatever he or she has to say. It is frightening for the patient – and the patient hates it.

(CWB VIII, p. 239)

Clinical note

I began to notice that I was going off in my mind while with the patient, not in an associative way but more as an escape. I became interested in the fact that I could not "rest" between thoughts while at the same time remaining with him. When it came up in the material, I talked to him about his experience of my pausing after something has been understood. He hated any idea of my resting. He said he never rested and believed he only ever would be able to when absolutely everything was done. He would either have "to be severely injured and unable to move, or dead" before he could rest. Shortly after this, a dream he had, in which he took my chair, helpfully enabled us to robustly address his putting himself in my place. Following this, and for the first time, he remained in the waiting room for me to collect him instead of hastily appearing in the corridor down which I was walking. He said he had been off in his thoughts and hadn't heard me coming. There was an element of dismissiveness in this, but more importantly, something had happened between us that was not being controlled by his anxiously attentive mind. He had let me collect him. Some days later I heard that he had been able to rest at home (rather than only collapse in exhaustion). He had sat back in his chair and "for once" let his thoughts wonder freely.

Rudyard Kipling

"The Elephant's Child"

I keep six honest serving-men
They taught me all I knew;
Their names are What and Why and When And How and Where and Who.
I send them over land and sea,
I send them east and west;
But after they have worked for me,
I give them all a rest.

Just So Verses

[284]   Free association

What the patient says can be used by the analyst as a free association. {This may be mistaken by the analysand as a way of ignoring the facts which he has communicated. It is necessary for the analyst to be clear in his mind that this is not so.} In due course a pattern will emerge which can then in its turn be interpreted. As a by-product the patient can discover who he is. So few people think that it is important to be introduced to themselves, but the one partner the patient can never get rid of while that patient is alive is himself.

(*CWB VIII*, p. 241)

[285]   Characters in search of an author/"thoughts in search of a thinker"

Freud said it is important to analyse the Oedipal situation. What is the Oedipal situation? Who are the characters? Father, mother, child? Can you be sufficiently exposed to the change that occurs when a patient walks into your office to be able to communicate first of all with yourself? To do this you have to forget, denude, your mind of what you know, so as to have yourself free to what is going on. Then as you watch the "screen", can you see any pattern flicker into position? Who are the characters who are in search of an author? You will have to be the author; and when you have this play clear you could mention it to the patient – that would then be your interpretation. I have also described it as "thoughts in search of a thinker"; I have to be exposed to it on the off-chance that some stray thought might lodge itself in my mind – or if not mine, the patient's. It might then be verbalized.

(CWB III, pp. 246–247)

Readers may be reminded of *Six Characters in Search of an Author* (1921) by Luigi Pirandello, in which a rehearsal is interrupted by the arrival of six strange people. The Director of the play, furious at the interruption, demands an explanation. The Father explains that they are unfinished characters in search of an author to finish their story. The Director initially believes them to be mad, but as they begin to argue among themselves and reveal details of their story, he begins to listen. . . .

Bion saw the play in 1964 and wrote to his children about it:

The Pirandello which we saw on Friday is *Six Characters in Search of an Author*. It is a very good play, but what was so interesting to me was the clarity with which Pirandello brought out the author's dilemma, namely the struggle of the ideas to find expression and then the problem of making them true without their being so unaesthetically expressed that they are incomprehensible or too unacceptable on the one hand, or, on the other "artistic" or acceptable but so distorted as to lack all honesty or integrity. The ending is too melodramatic I have always thought, but even that was well done. It could be argued that a good play will always get through but I think it indisputable that the better the play the more there is to get lost on the way.

(CWB II, p. 200)

[286]   Patient best colleague

The patient knows much more about what it feels like to be him or her than any analyst. So it is important to work on the basis that the best colleague you are ever likely to have – besides yourself – is not an analyst or supervisor or parent, but the patient; that is the one person on whom you can rely with confidence to be in possession of the vital knowledge. Why he doesn't simply make use of it I don't know. The human being is an animal which is dependent on a mate. In analysis it is a temporary mate; when it comes to life itself one would prefer to find somebody not oneself with whom to go through the rest of one's living days. The biological unit is a couple.

(*CWB VIII*, p. 255)

From *The Italian Seminars*

We could say that there is one collaborator we have in analysis on whom we can rely, because he behaves as if he really had a mind and because he thought that somebody not himself could help. In short, the most important assistance that a psychoanalyst is ever likely to get is not from his analyst, or supervisor, or teacher, or the books that he can read, but from his patient. The patient – and only the patient – knows what it feels like to be him or her. The patient is also the only person who knows what it feels like to have ideas such as that particular man or woman has. That is why it is so important that we should be able to hear, see, smell, even feel what information the patient is trying to convey. He is the only one who knows the facts; therefore, those facts are going to be the main source of any interpretation, any observation, which we are likely to be able to make.

(*CWB IX*, p. 103)

James Gooch

When he made interpretations he always made it clear what the evidence was – he was meticulous about that. It was not a pronouncement, but a theory or an educated guess, and only I could know whether there was any truth in it or not. I increasingly could feel in the music, and the dance, the cadence . . . the timbre of his voice that he was speaking to me from his heart; that he had to be having an emotional experience himself to be speaking to me that way. So even though he wouldn't tell me what his associations were, it was clear that he was in touch with something within himself that had been evoked by me. As a matter of fact, it was not an uncommon thing for him to say, "Even though I tell you almost nothing about myself, you're likely to know a great deal about me based on what I'm able to understand about you and what I'm not able to understand in you.

(Culbert-Koehn 2011, pp. 79–82)

[287]   The intuition which is blind and the concept which is empty

After a time it becomes unmistakable that the way in which you talk to your patients seems to have an effect on them. Nobody can tell you that – you have to find it out for yourself. You have to be a practising analyst before you discover that it is worth your while talking to patients in the way that *you* talk to them – never mind whether it is sanctified by appearing in one of the Collected Works. That experience convinces you that it is worthwhile having some respect for your Self – for what you think and imagine and speculate. There is a curious kind of conviction about these occasions where what you say has an effect which is recognizably similar to your theories. A "marriage" is taking place between you and you; a marriage between your thoughts and your feelings. The intuition which is blind and the concept which is empty can get together in a way which makes a complete mature thought.

(*CWB VIII*, p. 257)

[288] The interpretation of dreams ⇌ the interpretation of facts

No, but I suggest that somebody here should, instead of writing a book called "The Interpretation of Dreams", write a book called "The Interpretation of Facts", translating them into dream language – not just as a perverse exercise, but in order to get a two-way traffic.

(CWB VIII, pp. 262–263)

We tend to assume that waking reality is reality, and dreams are not real. In the dream world the opposite is true: it is the dream that is real. Bion wants to look from both directions, not just from that of waking reality.

[289]   Patient slides over terrifying dream

A patient may say, "I had a terrifying dream last night". This is said so quickly that it almost passes notice. "Terrifying" dreams, "terrifying" experiences – we hear it over and over again. But if you are sensitive you may begin to feel that there is something about it which is beyond just an ordinary statement. There are feelings which patients themselves slide over; they don't want to tell you how terrified they are and how unpleasant it is. If they do get to the point of admitting that, the chances are that they will say, "I was all right until I came to see you, but since then I have been terrified; I get frightened of almost anything I have to do". Of course you are not trying to frighten the patient; but you are trying to make him aware of the fact that he has that feeling of terror. A certain type of patient slides over many remarks inviting you not to pay attention to them and agreeing that they have made progress, are so much better. The next thing you hear is that the patient has committed suicide. The feelings have been of such intensity that while passing off the phrase, "I had a terrifying dream", he does not allow you or himself to know how appalling these feelings are.

(*CWB VIII*, p. 267)

Bion in New York and São Paulo: "São Paulo, 1978: Ten Talks"

The 1978 South American visit was Bion's third to São Paulo and his fourth to Brazil, which meant that his method of presenting his subject was somewhat familiar to those taking part.

Quotes

[290]   Storm

The analytic experience is potentially a nasty one both for the analyst and the analysand, although the analyst is more used to it. It is like being at sea: it is just as stormy for both people, but one of them may not be able to stand the storm. Here it is an invisible storm; these are storms of emotion. Psychoanalysing a patient causes an emotional disturbance; sometimes it creates so much emotional disturbance that it is not even confined to the consulting room – the waves spread out to the patient's husband, wife, children or other relatives. So it is not surprising if they also spread to the analyst. It is not possible to be an analyst, any more than a sailor or a soldier, without knowing this turmoil, this storm which is raging.

(CWB VIII, p. 146)

[291]   The analyst sensed to be thinking

People often fail to realize that besides talking, analysts also listen....

There are cultures which expect people always to be talking, always making a noise, so that anybody who is thinking is assumed to be doing nothing. The analyst has to be able to respect and pay attention to his own intuition while pressure is put on him to say something, or to do something, or to touch the patient, and to give up remaining in silence where he can at least hear himself think.

(*CWB VIII*, pp. 199–200)

[292]   You can walk out if you like

Bion: If the patient says, in effect, that he is going to pick and choose what to listen to, one could say, "Well, I hope you will be able to choose the right things. I can see that I may be telling you somethings that you don't want to learn or to hear or to see. I can't do anything about that – go ahead by all means." I have sometimes said to patients, "If what you say is right, then I am the wrong person to come to. You hate being with me here; you hate what I say to you; you don't want to hear it. That is no problem because, as you know, there are plenty of other analysts. The door isn't locked, so you can walk out if you like." We are trying to show patients something we think would be good for them to know. So whatever they say, we should not lose sight of that fact; we are there to help. We don't agree with patients that we are there to cause trouble or to make things difficult for them. They are free to think what they like, but we are also free to be what we want to be. This patient seems to want to force you to be the sort of person that would suit *him*. You may want to be helpful, but there is a great difference between being helpful because you want to be, and being helpful because you are forced to be.

(*CWB VIII*, pp. 222–223)

[293]   Analyst as mirror

The oracle at Delphi was supposed to have carved into the stone, "Know thyself". So the idea that it is useful and helpful to 'know thyself' is not new. In that sense we are trying to say, "I will help you to know yourself. If you tell me something, I will tell it back again to you in a way in which you may be able to see yourself. I am trying to be a mirror which doesn't tell you who I am – that is of no importance whatsoever – but who *you* are. The only thing I can do to help you is to reflect back to you who you are, so that you can see in what I say to you an image of yourself. If you don't want to know what you look like, I don't mind – you need not look to me to reflect you; you can find a different mirror." We would like, if we could, not to be too turbulent a mirror, because if we can remain steady, then the patient can get a clearer image of who he is. If we change too much, then it becomes a distorting image.

(CWB VIII, p. 223)

[294]   Long detained in that obscure sojourn

I recall a patient who talked freely and easily; he said that he didn't have dreams and that he had no imagination. For month after month he came to every session, never failed, never had an illness, never caught cold. When he got onto the couch he seemed to have some difficulty about which I did not bother much because it appeared to be simply a question of adjusting his clothes and his comfort. But after about three months I began to think this was very peculiar.

He always lay in a slightly awkward position on the couch; he would lie flat and then raise his head as if he were struggling against some sort of opposition and trying to see his feet. He did that three or four times. I had no idea what he was doing or even how to tell myself what this peculiar movement was. He was so co-operative, so rational, and I was kept very well informed. He said that he only slept an hour or two each night and worked for about sixteen hours a day, seven days a week. There were no complaints when I took a break or at week-ends; no disturbance, no depression, whereas with other patients I am used to some kind of reaction to the fact that I am stopping.

I thought I would change my vertex because I could not see anything very much from where I was observing the patient. When I did that, it occurred to me that his precise and exact position on the couch could be comprehensible if he were lying on the edge of a precipice. And then his posture began to look like a cataleptic attitude. Indeed, the whole analysis began to look like a compulsive ritual – the same hour, the same behaviour, no diversion from that position at all. The more I saw of him the more I thought that these were not ordinary communications and that my interpretations themselves fitted into the pattern. I wondered what kind of psychiatric diagnosis I could make. The nearest I could get to one was that the total situation in the consulting room was a *folie à deux*, and that I was just playing a part in this relationship. Then I began to look at and listen to the behaviour of both these people, one of whom was myself. I continued to observe and listen to that peculiar conversation. The "free associations" and the interpretations fitted in beautifully. You could call it the marriage of two minds – but there was something wrong with it. You could not call it homosexual; you could not call it heterosexual. In fact you could not call it sexual at all – not if the word "sex" means the kind of thing that it means in botany, or physiology, or what I call psychoanalysis. . . .

I tried giving it a location; I talked about his "feelings", and the sort of thing he did "up here", in his head. It was clear that he did not understand what I meant – or thought it was just nonsense anyway. He didn't say that; he was polite – he simply ignored any reference to "up here" or "down there". So I fell back on still talking about his "Self". I said, "Now you are talking as if your Self was located in your spleen". Sometimes I could have said that it was located in his adrenals, but I didn't have to because he talked about people who "ran away", or people who were "very aggressive". I was able to say, "This person who you say runs away, and this person you say is very aggressive, are the same person. I think they are your Self". This peculiar mobility became more and more pronounced; I had to go on chasing this Self around what seemed to be various anatomical areas.

It became evident that the Self was not within the limits of what I call the body. I had to extend my interpretations over an area which had different boundaries – indeed it had *no* boundaries. In order to express it at all I would have to borrow a term like "infinity". It reminded me of Milton's words which express it so well: "Won from the void and formless infinite". He speaks about being "long detained in that obscure sojourn"; about outer and inner darkness, middle darkness and "up to re-ascend though hard and rare". That is a good description of this patient, as if he had descended into what psychoanalysts call "the unconscious" and remained there a long time – "though long detained in that obscure sojourn", "and up to re-ascend". But when he does re-ascend, instead of emerging into the realms of light, he finds himself blinded.

(*CWB VIII*, pp. 323–325)

A long quote, but I hope the reader will find it to be a very interesting one.

[295]   Analyst's voice taken as a soporific drug

Similarly, there are patients who get a "nice" sensation from the sound of your voice and possibly from the sound of their own. So analyst and analysand settle into a meaningless debate because it feels so "nice". The patient feels something which is analogous in physical terms to being stroked; the one mind has a caressing, soothing effect on the other and the mutually gratifying seduction goes on unobserved by either party – so much so that it is forgotten that the patient has come for help. The patient has forgotten it; the analyst has forgotten it; they are locked in a mutually gratifying experience. It may be a long time before the patient becomes aware of discomfort. It is as if he had access to some soporific drug so that he cannot tell you where the pain is. Here again it is useful to change the vertex so that if you cannot see the pain from one position you may be able to see it from another.

(*CWB VIII*, pp. 373–374)

I have read a psychoanalytic paper in which the writer said that in cases where death was certain the analyst should give up making interpretations and resort to reassuring and comforting statements. I would not want to be told nice stories, whether they were psychoanalytical or religious or any other variety of pleasurable and gratifying seductions. I think that if I had never known the truth or wanted to hear the truth before, I would want to hear it in a serious situation.

It is questionable whether any patient ever comes to a psychoanalyst unless they feel the situation is desperate; it is usually a last resort when everything else has failed. So in spite of appearances to the contrary the whole weight of the experience when a patient comes to see an analyst suggests that the patient himself feels that he needs a powerful injection of truth even though he may not like it.

(*CWB VIII*, p. 375)

Chapter 20

The Tavistock Seminars

Introduction

Had Bion lost the incisiveness of his thought in these last years? In large gatherings at the Institute of Psychoanalysis and the Tavistock Clinic there was a certain disquiet in the audience about his demeanour and his silence. Was he behaving like a "guru"? Here is a view from a patient of his in Los Angeles:

James Gooch

Have any of you been to hear Bion give a talk? Well, let me tell you it was an experience. And he referred to them as experiences. He would have an assigned subject, he never read anything . . . he only spoke extemporaneously. He spoke for a few minutes and then he expected the audience to respond with comments or questions or whatever they wanted to . . . and then he would sit down and shut up and he would not budge . . . until somebody said something. You would feel like you were going to explode until somebody began to have dialogue with him.

(Culbert-Koehn 2011, p. 82)

Quotes

[296]   Being analysed traumatic

Seminar 1, 28 June 1976

It took me a very long time to realize that the actual experience of being psychoanalysed was a traumatic one, and it takes a long while before one recovers from it.

(*CWB IX*, p. 7)

This quote is the first sentence of the first of the Tavistock seminars. It was the year of the record-breaking heatwave and drought, and the videotape of the seminars shows Bion wearing a short-sleeved, open-necked shirt rather than his usual long-sleeved shirt, bow-tie and jacket.

[297]   Morality is basic

Seminar 1, 28 June 1976

28 June 1976

Bion: The impression I get about morality is that it is basic. I have been
struck by the fact that making a faintly disapproving noise will cause
an infant to shrink back as if something very terrible has happened.
I don't get the feeling that there is any conscious idea of what the
crime is; in fact, the nearest that I have got to Melanie Klein's statement of it is, "free-floating anxiety". It is an anxiety without any
concept attached to it – so much so that I think the growing creature does its best to find a crime to fit the feeling. So there is no
difficulty about rationalization, no difficulty about having rational
feelings for regarding someone as a criminal or thinking of oneself
as one. And if the worst comes to the worst, the person can always
commit a crime to match the feeling, so that the morality will actually precipitate the crime as a kind of therapeutic attempt; the person concerned can feel, "Yes, I may feel guilty, but who wouldn't?
Look what I have done." In reality, I think that someone can really
commit a murder in order to be able to feel that at least his murderous feelings of guilt are rational. But all this usually means is that the
so-called rational event is one that we are capable of understanding according to our logical rules. That is a matter of our human
limitations – it has nothing to do with the universe in which we live.
Another trouble is the sense of guilt that can be so enormous that
the person concerned tries to get rid of it, tries to embrace a sort
of theory or idea that is absolutely amoral.

(CWB IX, p. 14)

Sigmund Freud

"Criminals from a Sense of Guilt"

The invariable outcome of analytic work was to show that this obscure
sense of guilt derived from the Oedipus complex and was a reaction to
the two great criminal intentions of killing the father and having sexual
relations with the mother. In comparison with these two, the crimes committed in order to fix the sense of guilt to something came as a relief to
the sufferers. . . .

In order to answer the second question we must go beyond the scope of psycho-analytic work. With children it is easy to observe that they are often "naughty" on purpose to provoke punishment, and are quiet and contented after they have been punished. Later analytic investigation can often put us on the track of the guilty feeling which induced them to seek punishment. . . .

A friend has since called my attention to the fact that the "criminal from a sense of guilt" was known to Nietzsche too. The pre-existence of the feeling of guilt, and the utilization of a deed in order to rationalize this feeling, glimmer before us in Zarathustra's sayings "On the Pale Criminal". Let us leave it to future research to decide how many criminals are to be reckoned among these "pale" ones.

(Freud 1916, pp. 332–333)

[298] Pretending to care, beginning to care

Seminar 1, 28 June 1976

Nearly everybody has been taught to bother about other people, to be concerned for them. That can also be one of these tricks learnt in the course of one's life – how to be *just like* a loving or affectionate person takes the place of *becoming* one. That is one of the solutions that put a stop to growth and development.

In analysis you have to be sensitive to the situation where the patient is talking very clearly, very comprehensibly, about his concerns for this or that cause or institution. In crude situations it is fairly easy to detect – yes, he is terribly concerned for the unfortunate people in – somewhere quite a long way away (there is no danger of having to do anything). So you begin to be suspicious that he is being just like a concerned person, just like a doctor, just like an analyst – and so forth through the list. But at some point it can become clear to you that a change has taken place: the patient is, in fact, bothered by something he can do something about. Then it becomes important to be able to draw his attention to this: that while he is talking in the same way as yesterday, or last week or last year, it doesn't sound as if that is the case. Of course, you do not want to be flattering, but the patient is much more likely to believe that you are saying this to suggest some improvement.

(*CWB IX*, pp. 14–15)

[299]   Observation

Seminar 2, 4 July 1977

I am thinking of Freud's constant reference to Charcot's insistence on observation – that seems to me to be the absolute essence of it: observation. But what are we observing? Even the language we use is not adequate for the sort of difficult job that we do. We have to use the word, "observation", as a kind of metaphor, an approximation. In *Paradise Lost*, Milton talks of the situation in which he cannot fall back on his eyes because he is blind; he says he hopes he will be able to "see and tell of things invisible to mortal sight". We cannot hope for that, but somehow we do observe things that are very often not observed in the ordinary course of social intercourse. It would be useful if we could formulate in our own minds what it is that we are observing; it is a question which crops up all the time if we are doing this kind of work. Therefore, it needs to be kept in constant repair. How would you formulate it if you were trying to convey it to somebody else? What form of words would you use? It is curious that we do, in fact, resort to words; it is probably partly because the ability to talk articulate language is our most recent acquisition. But, of course, we are having to borrow words that have been used and formulated for quite other purposes, when the kind of thing that we are wanting to use them for now wasn't even over the horizon.

(*CWB IX*, pp. 17–18)

[300]   Questions and answers

Seminar 3, 5 July 1977

I am reminded of the quotation from Blanchot, told me by André Green: *"La réponse est le malheur de la question"* (which I translated, and he agreed with it, as "The answer is the disease, or misfortune, of the question"). In other words, *that* is what kills curiosity. When you have the question answered, that's the end of your curiosity if it is allowed to happen too often. Unfortunately the whole of childhood is taken up by having questions answered – you learn quite early definitions like, "children should be seen and not heard", and are intelligent enough to learn early on to keep your mouth shut because of what you might get put into it if you open it.

Although it is easy to give a kind of mental answer like so many psycho-analytic interpretations, in fact it is much more difficult to say that there really does seem to be a sort of two-way traffic even with regard to thought. So the sort of mental nourishment to which one is subjected from an early age, and which one is very eager to lap up, then builds up a barricade against any sort of illumination whatever – unless, of course, you happen to be one of these pernicious creatures like me. I got a reputation even by the time I was eight as a joke because I was always asking so many questions; I had the answer pushed at me by what happened to the Elephant's Child who asked the crocodile questions.

(*CWB IX*, p. 33)

Rudyard Kipling

"The Elephant's Story"

Originally the elephant had a short nose the size of a boot, flexible but useless for grasping things. One little elephant was insatiably inquisitive. He asked so many questions that all his relations spanked him. One day he asked:

"What does the Crocodile have for dinner?"
They all spanked him and told him to hush. Then he asked Kolokolo Bird, who told him to go the Limpopo River and find out. On the way there he met and asked the Bi-Coloured-Python-Rock-Snake, who also spanked him. Then he came to the river and found the Crocodile, who told him to come and hear the whispered answer. When he came close, the Crocodile caught him by his nose and tried to pull him into the water.
The Elephant's Child resisted, helped by the Bi-Coloured-Python-Rock-Snake, but his nose was pulled out into a long trunk before the

Crocodile let go. He found he could use it to swat flies, pick grass, and gather mud to cool his head. It was also useful for picking up litter and for spanking his relatives when he got home. Eventually they all went to the river to get trunks from the Crocodile, and nobody spanked anybody any more.

(With thanks to the Kipling Society website www.kiplingsociety. org.uk for the summary of the story of "The Elephant's Child")

[301] Vogue

Seminar 6, 5 July 1978

I would like to say a bit more about that from a rather different approach – namely "vogue", meaning by that a very powerful force. It is not recognized as that because usually these fashions – subsidiaries of the same thing – are extremely ephemeral. But vogue is not; it is a very powerful characteristic, one that carries with it a pressure to conform to the prevalent fashion. It may sometimes be delayed: the fashions of today won't become general for, say, another year, and then they become commonplace. Psychoanalysis was all the fashion at one time; psychoanalytic terms were bandied about with the greatest of freedom by people who usually didn't know what they meant and wouldn't undergo the long discipline required to find out.

In the same way, you find that you can become a fashion yourself – you are under extreme pressure to act or behave as if you were a person of importance when you know perfectly well that you are not, and you know perfectly well that that fashion will change in a matter of hours, days or weeks. It is the vogue, and for the time being you are under its pressure. It then becomes clear that the honours are showered upon you in the hope that you will not emerge from deep under to the abuse levelled against you.

(*CWB IX*, p. 64)

[302]   Being callous

Seminar 8, 28 March 1979

It is a curious fact that even in physical medicine doctors or surgeons can become callous; having to deal constantly with physical pain, they become almost insensitive to it. There are occasions when it erupts: I had the experience of a surgeon and an anaesthetist having such a nice time that they failed to observe that the child on the operating table had very nearly died. They suddenly ceased enjoying the joke and started putting emergency measures into action – unfortunately too late. [See *All My Sins Remembered*; *CWB II*, p. 40]

We can become callous to the actual nature of the pain, whether it is physical or mental. I know from my own experience that one loses sight of the fact that the patient is suffering – and you are helped by the patient to lose sight of that. A patient may be so amusing that the session is quite enjoyable; it seems almost unkind to remember that that patient has come because he is suffering.

(CWB IX, p. 88)

From *All My Sins Remembered*

The operation was a simple one, not likely to present any difficulty to a really capable surgical technician. Clearly there would be no point in alarming the parents of the child in advising the operation for cleft palate. The anaesthetist was capable; she was also beautiful – no point in alarming anyone by causing them to question her cosmetic qualifications. They looked beautiful in the curriculum vitae. It was a beautiful curriculum vitae; it was also a beautiful day and the surgeon was in a good humour. He and his anaesthetist engaged in amusing banter as the operation proceeded with exemplary smoothness.

"I think her heart has stopped beating sir", said the House Surgeon.

"Good Lord!" said the surgeon. "Quick! When? ... Massage her heart!"

No good; no good. The child is dead.

No more. Quite spoilt our day. House Surgeon's job to tell the parents – there's been a slight mishap. As you would know – anyone would know – there was nothing technically wrong with the operation.

(CWB II, p. 40)

[303]   On collateral circulation: where the real trouble lies

Seminar 8, 28 March 1979

The numbers of things that make the cooperation between analyst and analysand very vulnerable are legion – there is no limit to them. We can only hope to be able to detect, in time, whatever is menacing that particular attempt at a creative cooperation between the two people. One comfort we have is that, in a way, analysis is not very important; it is a temporary affair and a temporary association. So we can talk about "transference" and "countertransference"; it is transferred, it is on the way, but the real point about it is that people are constantly having an uncomfortable relationship with each other – it may be with a group of people or with an individual person – and frequently the obstruction to the comfortable or pleasant relationship causes a collateral circulation to set up. If two people cannot succeed in the aspiration to become husband and wife, then they can fall back on the physical solution of it by turning it into a kind of successful sexual experience. I pick on that deliberately because we are so used to hearing that it is sexual inhibitions that cause trouble – and so they do. But sexual freedom also causes trouble; it is a method of finding a collateral circulation to avoid the difficulties of what one might call a spiritual relationship between two people – if that doesn't have too much of a moral connotation. But people can crave for a relationship that is additional to a purely sexual one; or they can crave for a physical relationship in addition to a purely intellectual discussion. I don't think these things are settled by simply feeling, "Oh, yes, sexual inhibitions." That is one possibility, but what we really need is to be able to detect where the blockage occurred and what form the collateral circulation has taken. I am sure that analysts who work with children must be familiar with the situation in which they feel that the real blockage is something between the husband and wife, and the collateral circulation is to send their child to an analyst. So the analyst + child is a kind of collateral circulation of something that lies outside that relationship. This is one of the complexities of our approach to these difficulties; that is why I say it is the old system of co-ordinates by which one can localize the pain. It is quite easy to flog away at the relationship between analyst and analysand, to go on analysing ad infinitum – as I said before, transference, countertransference and so forth – without really being able to locate where the real trouble lies.

(CWB IX, pp. 88–89)

[304]   The mind has a kind of skin

Interview by Anthony G. Banet, Jr. 1976

It seems to me that one could say that the mind has a kind of skin that is in contact with somebody else. For example, we are talking together. Why? How? I may quite mistakenly think I know what you're asking me and what you're telling me, but why? What are these senses? If it is a question of my sense of touch, I can say that it's the skin. But what is this mental skin that enables two people to be (although it is a metaphorical use of the term) in "contact"? We borrow the term from the physical world, but it isn't touching. One can feel it; he can bring his mind (as Dr Johnson says) up against the other person....

(*CWB X*, pp. 161–162)

Chapter 21

Four Discussions with W. R. Bion: "Los Angeles 1976"

Quotes

[305]   Why not whore?

Q: . . . I had a patient last week who was very keen that I call her by her first name, very upset that I would not . . ..

Bion: It is difficult to say because I wasn't there. I might have said to the patient, "I think you must be very afraid of what I would call you if I were honest. . . .

Q: . . . she would get irritated with your reply and insist that you call her by her first name. . . .

Q: She wants sex with other men besides her husband, therefore in her view she must be a whore. . . .

Bion: In view of what you are saying I think I would try to draw her attention to the way in which she wishes to limit my freedom about what I call her. It is just as much a limitation if the patient wants you to give the correct interpretation. Why shouldn't I be free to form my own opinion that she's a whore, or that she is something quite different? Why be angry with me because in fact I am free to come to my own conclusions?

Q: Her fear is that your own conclusion will be that she is a whore.

Bion: But why shouldn't I be allowed to come to that conclusion?

Q: So you conclude that she is a whore – now where are you?

Bion: But I haven't said that I do. The point I want to show is that there is a wish to limit my freedom of thought. To exaggerate it for the sake of clarity. It is ridiculous for a patient to come to see a doctor and say, "Doctor, I've got a lump in my breast. Now, I don't want to hear anything about cancer or anything of that kind". Is the patient coming for a diagnosis? If not, what is she coming for? It is not fundamentally different if the patient wants to lay down the law beforehand about what you are to think or feel about her.

(CWB X, pp. 73–74)

The quote is from one of the four two-hour discussions at the Veterans Administration Hospital, Brentwood, Los Angeles, in April 1976. The group of about 25 was composed of psychiatric residents, psychotherapists and psychologists.

[306]   "Penetrating Silence"

... it would be a good thing for all of us to remain silent, and if you could simply note what you then hear. Some of it would seem to be immediately obtrusive, other parts of it not so clear, but gradually perhaps you would be able to hear even things like your heartbeat.

(CWB XV, p. 33)

[307]   Kellogg's Cornflakes

From "New and Improved" (1977)

. . . there is always something better – new and improved. I borrow that title from Kellogg's Cornflakes. I don't know what happens to the "new and improved" things; they are often successful – or at any rate successful as far as the technicians are concerned. It is a very seductive idea – one could almost sum it up in one word – cure. It carries with it a connotation of good times coming, an improvement, *better*. We have to be aware of that because there may not be much more we can hope for than that we shall continue to float when the thing that is really flourishing is the turbulence, the turmoil, the upheaval.

(*CWB XV*, p. 49)

[308]   On the need for discipline

From "New and Improved" (1977)

. . . All this sounds like saying, "All you have to do is let your imagination rip – just think anything you please". But that isn't good enough; there has to be some sort of disciplinary framework; a skeleton, some sort of bony structure. There is no escape from the discipline of psychoanalysis. It is very difficult to understand why we should have to go through such a frightful discipline, and equally difficult to guess in what way it will pay off at some future date. But it is somehow necessary so that even your imagination cannot be allowed to develop into an imaginative orgy.

(CWB XV, p. 53)

Chapter 22

The Italian Seminars

Introduction

Claudio Neri

I came to know Bion as a consequence of meetings I had with two other people – namely, Francesco Corrao and Parthenope Bion Talamo.

Francesco Corrao was the most brilliant and creative of the Italian psychoanalysts. It was he who introduced Bion's ideas to Italy and arranged for his books to be translated. I remember a remark of his: "It is possible to love someone's mind; well, I loved Bion's." At the time of my meeting with Bion, Corrao was president of the Italian Psychoanalytic Society (SPI) . . .

Parthenope – Bion's daughter – had studied philosophy in Florence; she had then moved to Rome, where she was living with her cellist husband. She was in personal analysis with Adda Corti and was waiting to be accepted by the SPI as a candidate. . . .

Corrao, Parthenope, and I decided to issue a joint invitation to Bion from the SPI and *Il Pollaiolo* to hold a series of seminars in Rome. I wrote to Bion, who politely accepted. . . .

There was a huge sense of expectation, and additional space was created in a room at *Il Pollaiolo* to accommodate more people . . .

My first impression of him was as a grandfather. Parthenope had a little girl, one or two years old, towards whom Bion's attitude was absolutely that of an equal. He told me he was trying to learn Italian from his granddaughter. I was also impressed by his great physical vigor: Bion was a real athlete despite his eighty years. . . .

The Roman seminars

Bion always stood while conducting his seminars; his presentation was rich in biblical metaphors and quotations from the poets.

During the seminars certain ideas that have remained the corner-stone of my activity ever since crystallized in my mind. The first is that

Bion should be read in literal terms. He says and writes exactly what he thinks. He says and writes what he thinks as directly and clearly as he can express it. Bion also does his best to see that the emotions connected with the content of a communication are incorporated in that communication. The second idea concerns the way he induced oscillations between D and PS in his audience.

One understood little of what he said. The impression was gained that Bion had an outline in his mind from which he presented various extracts. It was more a matter of seizing hold of fragments of images and thoughts.

Everyone – including myself – joined in the debate, seeking Bion's approval. His bearing was so powerful, the level of fascination he inspired so high, and his delivery so ad hominem that he, at least in part, generated the kind of dependence that he later interpreted as a mass phenomenon. Although there was much anxiety, enthusiasm was predominant. There was no doubt about it. Fornari was bewildered, Corrao fascinated. . . .

I realized that my own and my colleagues' idea of a "Bion of the generation of "68", an anarchic Bion, needed to be reconciled with the reality we had experienced of a "Colonel Bion", a "soldier Bion", and a "Bion who demands discipline".

Bion's roots lay in Imperial Britain and India. He had a powerful sense of the establishment and of belonging. However, this also enabled him to be very original.

(Neri 2015, pp. 23–27)

Quotes

[309]   Raft

Seminar 2, 9 July 1977

To make that point clearer, using a pictorial image: a party of some five people were survivors from a shipwreck. The rest had died of starvation or had been swept overboard from the remnants of the raft. They experienced no fear whatsoever – but became terrified when they thought a ship was coming near. The possibility of rescue, and the even greater possibility that their presence would not be noticed on the surface of the ocean, led them to be terrified. Previously the terror had been sunk, so to speak, in the over-whelming depths of depression and despair.

So the analyst, in the midst of the noises of distress, the failure of analysis, the uselessness of that kind of conversation, still needs to be able to hear the sound of this terror which indicates the position of a person beginning to hope that he might be rescued.

Consider this patient who smells the possibility that the analyst could nourish him, but also that the analyst might devour him. Let us put that into more rational terms: will the analyst understand him? Or will the analyst shut him up in a mental hospital so he will never escape?....

(CWB IX, pp. 119–120)

Following the battle of Amiens, Bion was granted leave much sooner than he expected: his seniors perhaps concerned both about his being war-exhausted (he had been in action for 18 months), and his burning anger. In the following quote he describes being near to safety but still under fire. (A longer version of this quote is in Chapter 2, "Leave".)

From *War Memoirs*

...The leave warrant was the most demoralizing part of it. It makes you so careful when you feel you are so near safety as that.

(CWB III, p. 157)

[310] The psychoanalytic raft and the addiction to cures

Seminar 2, 9 July 1977

The analytic situation stimulates very primitive feelings, including the feelings of dependence and isolation; they are both unpleasant feelings. It is not, therefore, really surprising if one of the pair, and probably both, is aware that the psychoanalytic raft to which they cling in the consulting-room – beautifully disguised, of course, with comfortable chairs and every modern convenience – is nevertheless a very precarious raft in a tumultuous sea. Besides the various theories and interpretations to which the analyst gives expression, there needs to be an awareness that the two people are actually engaged in a dangerous adventure. There is always a tendency to snatch at some piece of material – some psychoanalytic theory or idea – as a kind of lifebelt which would help to keep the two feeling that they are still alive and floating. A common piece of wreckage is the idea of a "cure"; we snatch feverishly at the latest bit of cure that is available in order to keep afloat. That is something the analyst should be able to resist because, while it may have a temporarily curative effect, if it is constantly repeated then it becomes an addiction – the pair get addicted to cures. And in this peculiar sphere with which we are concerned, there are any amount of cures floating around. So it is a good thing if the analyst – in so far as he identifies himself with the responsible person – resists too many of these cheap cures which can be built into an elaborate structure so that, before you know where you are, the raft which is made of bits of wreckage turns into a delusional system which is a veritable *Titanic*. As we all know, the *Titanic* was unsinkable, it was the latest thing – but it hit up against a fact, and that sank it.

(*CWB IX*, pp. 122–123)

[311]   Wild thoughts

Seminar 4, 13 July 1977

I have spoken of it before as a situation in which all sorts of thoughts are flying around – the patient gets rid of all his thoughts which then, in my pictorial imagination, are flying around. If you can be wide open, then I think there is a chance that you might catch some of those wild thoughts. And if you allow them to lodge in your mind, however ridiculous, however stupid, however fantastic, then there may be a chance of having a look at them. That is a matter of daring to have such thoughts – never mind whether you are supposed to have them or not – and keeping them long enough to be able to formulate what they are.

(*CWB IX*, pp. 140–141)

From *Clinical Seminars:* "São Paulo 1978 Ten Talks"

Parents say, "Why can't you children play properly? what are you quarrelling and fighting about all the time?" But the children don't know what they are fighting about; they would have to be prophets to know. Similarly with the thought without a thinker, the thought which is looking for somebody in whom "it could be thought about"; or, from the point of view of us as individuals, the wild thought which is in the air but which nobody has dared to think so far because we are afraid of being asked, "Why are you playing with that dirty idea? Why do you play with these nasty thoughts? You ought to be good – a nice girl, a nice boy, a nice psychoanalyst". It is difficult to stick to one's right to be a nasty psychoanalyst who has nasty thoughts and who is willing to give a home to still more nasty thoughts. I suggest that you do that with one of these wild thoughts whether it be called dirty, nasty, psychotic, banal or ordinary.

(*CWB VIII*, p. 327)

How can we tell the difference between what Bion describes as "catching a wild thought" and wild analysis? The question of whether one can corroborate the "wild thought" is important, as is trying to sense whether one is oneself (as the analyst) engaged in modification or evacuation. An illustration of evacuation would be coming up with something – apparently imaginative – in order to evade the uncomfortable guilt-inducing experience of feeling one has nothing to offer the patient. An illustration of modification is when the "wild thought" evolves out of a "not knowing" that leans beyond memory and desire.

[312]   Passion of love

Seminar 7, 16 July 1977

Horace was another inhabitant who is supposed to have lived geographically in this area. His "Ode to Pyrrha" has worried a great many people: in it he describes the painful consequences of having fallen in love with Pyrrha's golden hair. In navigating that particular sea, he appears to have come to shipwreck and has hung his dripping clothes as a memorial to the experience. I find it very moving to see portrayed on the walls of an Etruscan tomb the costume presumably worn by the inhabitant. That is a pictorial representation of what looks remarkably like a similar state of mind: it seems to be expressing a similar difficulty with regard to the passion of love. Clearly there seems to be something which brings two different human beings together; whatever the outcome of their coming together, whether it is shipwreck or continued journey, it appears to be a very stimulating experience. So those who are disposed to launch themselves on the stormy seas of love are risking a painful and frightening experience of shipwreck. Our problem here involves not only being able to think intellectually, but also being able to feel emotionally. Let me put the question again: what wild thoughts and what wild feelings are you prepared to risk giving a home to?

(*CWB IX*, p. 168)

Horace

Odes

translated by John Milton
To Pyrrha

What slender youth, bedew'd with liquid odors,
Courts thee on roses in some pleasant cave,
Pyrrha? For whom bind'st thou
In wreaths thy golden hair,
Plain in thy neatness? O how oft shall he
Of faith and changed gods complain, and seas
Rough with black winds, and storms
Unwonted shall admire!
Who now enjoys thee credulous, all gold,
Who, always vacant, always amiable
Hopes thee, of flattering gales
Unmindful. Hapless they

To whom thou untried seem'st fair. Me, in my vow'd
Picture, the sacred wall declares to have hung
My dank and dropping weeds
To the stern god of sea.

(I, 5)

[313] Discovery of dependence and discovery of being alone

Seminar 9, 17 July 1977

...even an infant seems to be able to tell when it is all alone and also when the object on which it depends is present. In that respect the discovery and awareness of dependence, and the discovery and awareness of being all alone, are fundamental. Those fundamental feelings, thoughts and ideas can still be stirred many years later.

(*CWB IX*, p. 184)

Parthenope Bion Talamo

Bion's first daughter, Parthenope, translated at all *The Italian Seminars* in the summer of 1977 – both Bion's English into Italian and the questions and comments of the Italian participants into English for Bion. "It was an exceptional *tour de force* on her part" (Francesca Bion 2005, p. 97).

Tragically, Parthenope died on 16 July 1998, in a car accident, together with her younger child, Patrizia.

Anna Baruzzi

Parthenope has gone; her bright star was extinguished too soon. . . .

Parthenope had a very broad mind that she carried modestly and with great reserve: a genuine desire for knowledge, a rare intellectual honesty that instilled respect and was reflected in her clear, clear eyes that opened wide as she listened, like the eyes of a little child.

Talking to Parthenope brought the serenity transmitted by people who know how to be really in contact with the saddest events, with great suffering. Sometimes she would fall into a gloom, and her eyes darkened, as if she were carrying a very heavy burden: the burden of all human beings, her own particular burden, and the enormous one already borne by her father.

But she was also an authentically cheerful person, with a great sense of humour, with a silvery laugh which often, I noticed at the time, faded into a gloomy smile which I later came to think belonged to little Parthenope whose mother had died too soon.

Parthenope had a great capacity for contact with people, and understood them, so she had lots of friends all over the world and in Italy, where she had put down roots to an extraordinary degree. She very much liked having ideas that she stood up for like a warrior, but she was really interested in, and knew how to value, other people's ideas.

She would listen attentively, and then express a point of view of her own which was plainly full of respect; this meant that it was possible to remain in "loyal disagreement" with her. I remember the respect with which she approached her psychoanalytic training with the Società Psicoanalitica Italiana from the first discussions onwards; she had a completely non-cynical trepidation that always struck me.

So she had gradually succeeded, with great commitment, in being Parthenope, and also Bion's daughter.

(Baruzzi 2011, pp. 31, 33–35)

Messages from the bion97 list

The news of Parthenope's death was communicated to the bion97 mailing list by Mario Perini. Here are two of the messages posted:

Two days ago the dearest among the dears, a sweet and courageous person faxed me counting five hundred letters she should had sent me and also shared with me our common love, music, for I had discovered an unknown Brazilian author who studied with Brahms, and she and Luigi heard the rare CD I sent her. As usual, I was also trying to help her with a paper that contained more than it should, . . . How could I imagine that this was the last message from her? . . . No more talks about dogs, about Jacqueline du Pré (her schooldays friend), about zaferano in the rizzo . . . about life and our respective families. The dignity and seriousness that she carried on an impossibly heavy load, a load that more fragile beings would never be able to carry (we all know that other distinguished psycho-analysts' sibships were not able to), namely, the paradoxical luck/unluck of being the daughter of a sincere, lovable and lovely person such as Dr Bion was, will remain as a lesson to all of us. . . .

Paulo Sandler (bion97 mailing list, Friday, 17 July 1998, 13:35)

Dear Listmembers,

I came back to Italy (not yet at home, though) a few days ago, but it's only today I feel I can try to write down some words to the list about the death of Parthenope. I felt (and still feel) overwhelmed and empty: unable to find any suitable words to talk about it and thoughts to think about it. . . .

I was this morning at Parthenope's home in Collegno, Torino, and met Luigi – her husband – and Alessandra – her eldest daughter. All that remains of her family. – They asked me to thank you for all that was written in the last month on this list about Parthenope. They felt their mourning was shared. . . .

Silvio A. Merciai (Thursday, 27 August 1998, 23:18)

I am indebted to the website written and compiled by Silvio A. Merciai. See www.sicap.it/merciai/parthenope/parthenope.htmf

Chapter 23

"A Paris Seminar"

Quotes

[314]   If the acorn said, "Oh, they're just roots"

In an analytic situation the analyst is concerned with trying to make conscious, trying to bring to awareness something which the patient has often spent his life trying to make unconscious. There are two people in the room who come together at the same time, in the same place, but the directions in which they are thinking are different. They could agree if the analyst consented to become very disturbed and afflicted with the same kind of neurosis or psychosis as the patient, but it is usually supposed that the analyst should not lose his capacity for being aware of the world of reality, although he may be drawing attention to a world of a different form of reality. The simplest example I can give is this: we are in the state of mind which is usually known as being awake or conscious and aware of what is taking place – so we think. But when we are asleep we are in a different state of mind. This division into day and night is not very illuminating, but I think it is useful if one can retain the valuable quality of being able to go to sleep, as well as the valuable quality of being able to wake up. That "marriage" often seems not to be harmonious. For example, patients may admit that they had a dream but they don't take it seriously; they don't feel disposed to tell you where they dreamt and what they saw. They say, "Oh, I just dreamt it".

I don't know why they "just dreamt it". If the acorn said, "Oh, they're just roots", what would one think? After all, even an acorn on an oak owes something to the roots. So what is one to make of a patient who thinks he "just dreamt it"? Freud considered that dreams ought to be treated with respect – I think that is the most important part of his work, but I don't believe we have got anywhere near to reaping the consequences of treating dreams with respect.

(CWB IX, p. 206)

[315]   Roots

Even using the language I know best, I cannot tell you what an "artist" is; I prefer you to go beyond that word and see what I am trying to convey to you by this very inadequate word. It is certainly not somebody who is able to deceive your eyes, to make you think that there is a tree there when there isn't one, but somebody who has made you able to see there really is a tree there and its roots even if they are underground. I suggest that behind this forty-two-year-old man is hidden a person, and that person has roots, an unconscious which, like the roots of a tree, is hidden from sight. There are not only branches which are ramified and have veins, but under the surface it has roots. So when this person comes into your room, what do you see? I am not asking simply what do you see with your eyes, but also what does your intuition enable you to see?

(CWB IX, p. 205)

[316] Beautiful

It is very important to be aware that you may never be satisfied with your analytic career if you feel that you are restricted to what is narrowly called a "scientific" approach. You will have to be able to have a chance of feeling that the interpretation you give is a beautiful one, or that you get a beautiful response from the patient. This aesthetic element of beauty makes a very difficult situation tolerable.

(*CWB IX*, p. 211)

Francesca Bion

All beautiful things moved him to tears – whether it was poetry, prose, music, painting, sculpture, or the Norfolk landscape, its sea birds and its skylarks. In a letter written to me a few days after we first met he said, "It is a marvellous moonlit night with the wind sighing gently in the pine trees. There is a line of Flecker's which goes, "For pines are gossip pines the wide world through". It has always stuck in my mind since I first came across it when I was at Oxford. Arthur Bryant and I used to learn quite a lot of verse when I was up. But I think I learnt most during the first war. My biggest feat was in 1918 when our battalion had no tanks left, and I and a dozen of my men had to fill a gap in the line with our machine guns. Our last night before relief I was with a colonel of the Royal Scots and it became clear as we were talking that a German night attack was starting. As everything that could be done had been done he said, "Let's talk about something decent". So we talked about the Roger de Coverly essays while the Germans shelled to bits our water-logged line of shell holes and earthworks. The colonel got killed a little later and I, still having nothing to do, learned *L'Allegro* and *Il Penseroso* from a Golden Treasury I had with me.

("Envoi", Francesca Bion 1981, pp. 262–263)

Roger de Coverley: The Roger de Coverley essays were published by Joseph Addison and Richard Steele between 1711 and 1712 as part of a daily periodical called *The Spectator*, which aimed to "enliven morality with wit and to temper wit with morality". Offering comment on a wide range of subjects, from the latest fashions to serious disquisitions on literary criticism and morality, *The Spectator* included epistles from Sir Roger de Coverley, who was Addison's invented character, epitomizing the life and times of a member of the English landed gentry.

L'Allegro and *Il Penseroso: L'Allegro,* meaning "the happy one" in Italian is a pastoral poem by John Milton published in 1645 alongside a contrasting pastoral poem entitled *Il Penseroso* ("the melancholy one"). The poems are long. Below are the first and the last two lines from each of them.

L'Allegro

Hence loathed Melancholy,
Of Cerberus, and blackest Midnight born,
. . .
These delights if thou canst give,
Mirth, with thee I mean to live.

Il Penseroso

Hence vain deluding Joys,
The brood of Folly without father bred,
. . .
These pleasures, Melancholy, give,
And I with thee will choose to live.

Part IV

A Memoir of the Future

Chapter 24

Introduction

1973

    The thing I am supposed to be writing ... is I think about done. It seems pretty unreadable to me but I hope it's not as bad as it seems. I cannot say I feel any real hope about getting it published, let alone sold after that. ... But writing books is no way of making a living – that's clear.

(CWB II, p. 235)

A Memoir of the Future was written in the later years of Bion's life, mostly while he was in California. At around the same time Bion reread his *War Memoirs 1917–1919*, written in 1920, and wrote two volumes of autobiography: *The Long Week-End* and *All My Sins Remembered: Another Part of a Life*.

The *Memoir* is nearly a third of Bion's output: it takes up three volumes of the *Complete Works*. All that it is possible to do here is to give the reader some taste of it. Reading the *Memoir* one becomes slowly increasingly involved. I hope the same will be the case with the quotes. Bion hoped readers would involve themselves in the books and be affected not by his "stuff", but by what it might bring up of their own "stuff".

A Memoir of the Future is made up of three books:

The Dream
The Past Presented
The Dawn of Oblivion

With the help of Francesca, Bion also wrote A Key to *A Memoir of the Future* to accompany the novel.

The characters

To help with the reader's sense of the characters in the novel, I include an abridged version of Paulo C. Sandler's vivid description of them.

Some characters were borrowed from "mental health enhancing" sources, such as Conan Doyle's work, Milton and Wordsworth poetry. Some of them come from interests shareable with any human being. For example, dinosaurs of bygone eras, who sunk under their own weight.

"Alice" is the first character to be introduced, with more than a passing resemblance with Carroll's creation. She "lives" in a kind of idealized wonderland as a typical woman from the upper gentry: "intelligent and blonde", she functions as Roland's pseudo-wife and mistress of the second character to appear:

"Rosemary" is a daughter of a whore who belatedly discovers herself as a strong willed and physically strong person. She derives those features from a hard lower classes life and suffering. Rosemary proves to "be" hellishly smart. She is the ablest character in [perceiving] what real life is all about, in displaying much less mindlessness than the other characters. . . . Rosemary has, as any person, her weaknesses – including a thirst for domination that will lead her to marry someone she does not love. "Roland" and his friend "Robin". . . . They are at the same time infantile and grown-ups, a type often found. They display paradoxical features, like real persons. Both "are" simultaneously educated and rude, cowards and reckless, mildly able to think in what concerns to concrete matters and much more prone to act-out with no thinking at all between the impulse and action.

"Tom" is a lustful lout who works in menial jobs at Roland's farm.

"Man" Significantly, Bion gives him the name of "Man". He impersonates a kind of cloudy, contemptful, callous, objective, aloof post-Nazi military commander. At first he seems to be the devil incarnate. He is not – because two other characters, named Du (in volume I) and thereafter simply Devil (in volume III) will take care of this duty, as "Man" fades out. He develops as the true boss of the "stage", imposing his will under many guises, including gunpoint.

A great deal of sophisticated psycho-analytical postures, and keen epistemological and social comments are put into Man's "mouth", specially in vol. I. "Man" features the darkness of authoritarianism, omnipotence and lust. He is helped by police forces, and pseudo-physicians. They are skilled in inflicting unnecessary pain. In volume II "Man" enlists in his hosts the services of another seminal character:

"Priest", who mixes deep theologic knowledge, wisdom, with callousness, lack of scruples, and opportunism. "Priest" is at first named "Paul" but soon the more general denomination emerges and lasts until the end.

Other characters are an astronomer called "Edmund", a Boy, an Old Woman, a Small Mo, a Big Bro, a Big Sister, a Small Bro, a certain Half Awake, a Schoolboy, an Apparition.

"Arf-arfer", an infantile alliteration of "Our Father" mixes God and Devil. In the Jewish-Christian-Muslim tradition, it is less awe-inspiring that fear-impinging. It is one of the main characters of volume I but fades out in volume II and III.

Doctor, who "is" a physician, Voice, Somites, Forty-seven, and Twenty-two as well as other ages appear in volume III, as matured hindsight of a whole life made of doubts, limitations, mistakes, and changes. Even PS and D are characters, as a kind of homage to the realness and usefulness of Klein's discoveries. Ghosts of old comrades-in-arms of W.W. I also obtrude, filling the author with guilt for having survived: Ghosts of Tonks, Arthur, O'Connor, Stokes. Even the author "died" in some extent, so a Ghost of P.A. also appears.

One may say that "Bion" "Myself" "PA" is a triple character that represents the author in three guises:

"Bion" is the less important and more despised of them. "Myself" is the growing, matured product of something or someone that is socially known by the name of "Bion".

"P.A." (from Psycho-Analyst) is a professional psycho-analyst. One may safely state it is a synthesis of Bion and Myself. . . . It is the more serene character of the whole book, displaying Bion's "reverence and awe" to psycho-analysis P.A. It is a most uninvolved being. It is undoubtedly a technical hint to an analyst at work, who should exercise a discipline on memory, desire, and understanding. He is less prey of projective identifications.

One may hypothesize that the author is also composed by Priest, Man, Robin, Alice, Rosemary, Roland, that is, all characters of the book. Internal reflections, scientific and psycho-analytic thinking appear in the guise of talks between those characters. They can be seen as the author's part objects, too. As an artistic or scientific work, the author's experience is just a conveyor of universal invariances of psychic reality. Specially in volume III, the characters mirror not just a maturing Bion, trying to learn from experience, but any maturing human being.

"Sherlock Holmes" is a borrowed character, highly respectful to the original. "He" displays the "Falstaff argument" as advanced before, being a real-fictitious character famous worldwide despite never enjoying (or suffering) concrete existence. Sherlock "is" accompanied by his faithful, sometimes foolhardy Dr. Watson. Bion borrows them paying homage to something that enhanced his mental health in difficult times. They illustrate reality, hallucinosis, thought processes and give a hint to the analyst in a plot where Bion himself is criticized and shown in what concerns to some paranoid features.

In a certain part of the book, the character "Bion" is infatuated with his secular titles, pretensions to immortality and self-importance. He accuses Watson of being unreal. Watson strikes back, fulminating the doctor's arguments and displaying the "himself" is more known worldwide whereas Bion and psycho-analysis are not. Sherlock is not entirely in agreement with this way of dealing with him [Bion], he hope's Watson was not too rough. To which Watson answers: "Real people have to be treated roughly if the universe of discourse is to made safe form imaginary people".

A relatively unknown and minor Conan Doyle's creation, Mycroft Holmes, Sherlock's older brother also appears. And the indefectible Moriarty, as a kind of Devil incarnate.

(Paulo Cesar Sandler, "Bion's work presented: *A Memoir of the Future*, Some Thoughts on its Oblivion and Dawn", see http://www.funzionegamma.it/wp-content/uploads/ bion-work20e.pdf)

Chapter 25

"Book I: The Dream"

Book I: The Dream

The story takes place in an England that has been taken over. We are in the rural Britain of Bion's holidays from boarding school, and some of the locations and incidents are taken directly from that time. At the centre of the drama are two couples, Alice and Roland (the master and mistress of the house) and Rosemary and Tom (the servants). As the household awaits the arrival of the invaders, the air is thick with seduction: between the servant Rosemary and her master Roland; Mistress Alice and servant Tom, and Rosemary and Alice. Two invaders appear and take all the possessions in the house. Roland abandons Alice to her fate and walks to Munden. Alice and Rosemary are taken prisoners. At Munden, Roland comes across a friend, Robin. The two encounter an enemy soldier whom Roland beats to death. The men become fugitives, are captured and escape again. A character called "Man" arrives, one of the invading force. The action then gives way to discussions between the characters, and new characters enter. The narrator is divided into Bion, P.A. (psychoanalyst) and Myself. We see the arrival of fictional characters, including Sherlock Holmes. Some characters remain anonymous – for example, "a nurse". The dinosaurs arrive! Reference is made to Shakespeare, Milton, Plato and Kant, and also to the author of the *Bhagavad-Gita*. The book ends in a dialogue between "Myself" and "Bion".

Quotes

317   "Softly breathing bronzes"
318   Alice and Rosemary
319   Roland and Robin
320   Captain Bion's Soliloquy
321   Dinosaurs, Oedipus, "Why war?"
322   "Thoughts without a thinker"
Other analysts on "thoughts without a thinker"
323   Potency
324   Words to "trap" meaning like a sculpture "traps" the light

[317]   Softly breathing bronzes

From the "Pro-logue"

The "softly breathing bronzes" of whom Virgil speaks in his tribute to Marcellus can be described as a poetic formulation of a visual image. The same is true of the heroes rescued from the black night that engulfed the many brave men before Homer immortalized Agamemnon; or the sculptures conjured from the marble by Michelangelo or Praxiteles. They can be re-buried. Confronted by a work of art, there are "clever men" who can see that it is genuine and worth a lot of money, but they may *not* see what the artist has revealed.

To turn to psychoanalysis: the erudite can see that a description is by Freud, or Melanie Klein, but remain blind to the thing described. Freud said infants were sexual; this was denied or reburied. This fate could have befallen the whole of psychoanalysis had there been no one to confer, as Horace said of Homer, immortality.

If psychoanalytic intuition does not provide a stamping ground for wild asses, where is a zoo to be found to preserve the species? Conversely, if the environment is tolerant, what is to happen to the "great hunters" who lie unrevealed or reburied?

(CWB XII, pp. 14–15)

Bion has long been interested in the difference between "animate" and "inanimate". The "softly breathing bronzes" are animate, the artist has breathed life into the sculptures. The artist can rescue a hero "from the black night" by recording and immortalising them in their aliveness. Bion has something he wants to record in his *Memoir* that he does not want to be "denied or reburied" – but how to do it?

[318] Alice and Rosemary

It was typical of these times: an eternity of boredom displaced without warning by flaming dread. Alice and Roland waited with ashen faces and staring, questioning eyes. The pounding footsteps fused with their pounding hearts – battered from without and within. The door crashed open and a woman half fell into the room.

She was gorgeously dressed in a quilted, crimson gown. With open mouth she looked from Alice to Roland, stammering with fear. "Oh, Miss! I'm sorry, Miss. I couldn't help it, Miss! You sent me away before! I couldn't . . . the last train couldn't go. They stopped it and turned us off."

A car in the yard started up and drove away, the sound of its engine fading into the distance. Then silence flowed back into the room where the three had stopped to listen. Alice recovered her voice first. "Rosemary! What are you doing here?" Roland relaxed as if resigning further part in the talk. He noticed that Rosemary was naked but for the gown and ill-fitting shoes. Roland excused himself. "Must see to the cows; bye-bye", and he bowed himself out of the scene.

The two women faced each other, Alice's restrained, good taste contrasting drably with the tattered splendour of her maid's finery. Alice was tense; Rosemary stared as if unable to comprehend her mistress's incomprehension. "You can't send me away! They will catch me, like they did before, before I got to the train." "You must go! – at once!"

"I can't. I won't! How can you be so cruel?" Alice stretched out her hand as if to compel her towards the door. The movement released something in Rosemary who at once held Alice's hand and bathed it in kisses. Alice was angry, frightened, tense. "Go! Go! you fool! Can't you see? You put us all in danger!"

"I won't! I'm frightened!"

"Fool! There's nothing to be frightened of." As she said it she was aware of the fear in her own voice. "Let me go!" Alice struggled to free herself. Rosemary was startled by her own success. "Oh, Miss! Forgive me. I'm sorry, really I am", but she did not let her advantage go. Alice, weakened by the months of anxiety since the day the invasion had become inevitable, was no match for her maid. Rosemary knew something of that bright world outside. Alice and Roland existed in a cocoon of fear that gripped them like steel; Alice did not know the world of which Rosemary had had a glimpse.

Alice struggled furiously to free her hands, both now gripped by her maid. "Please forgive me!" Frightened and humiliated, "Let go! How dare you!" Her maid stared uneasily into Alice's frightened face. It was fear now . . .

not anger. Rosemary's flood of apology and prayers for forgiveness did not cease. Nor did she loosen her grip. "Let go!" Alice could hardly hide that she was near to tears. Her background of wealthy home, conventional schooling and religion did not provide her with the dam to hold back her fear.

She was standing very near to the bed behind her. In her anxiety Rosemary had pressed her mistress ever nearer to it and a last struggle to release her wrists led Alice to pull Rosemary to her. Both girls fell over onto the bed, Rosemary uppermost. Rosemary's anxiety and guilt were overcome by lusty strength; Alice's weakness inflamed her passion.

The physical contact, her body against the young girl beneath her, caused Rosemary to stare intently into the tear-soiled face. All guilt and subordination gone, she pressed Alice's head back, exposing her throat. She forced the eyelids apart and peered into her eyes. Then she laughed — no trace of shyness now but frank curiosity. "Why — they are blue! Such a pretty blue too! Not dark and brown like mine." Alice was indeed a pretty and intelligent blonde, contrasting with her maid's dark colouring. The convention of the superiority of wealth combined with Alice's striking looks served to dim the power of real beauty. Alice's advantages were in eclipse. It was Rosemary who was flushed, the physically dominant, privileged girl.

Both girls were ignorant of sensuous pleasure. For Rosemary, the vital force coursing through arteries, battering her heart and temples, brought thoughts from a reservoir unknown to her. As she gazed she knew triumph. When Alice at last brought herself to meet her maid's stare, the past had gone as if it had never been. Not only had her situation changed, she had herself become the home of feelings that might have belonged to someone else, they were so strange.

Rosemary adjusted her position. The slum child, robust and dominant, luxuriated in the physical mastery. "They are the same as we are; just as bad if we teach them what we know." The response from her mistress was unmistakable. Alice had for so many years been starved of passionate life that she was vulnerable to her maid's manipulations. As soon as she had elicited the proof she wanted, Rosemary tossed the hair back from her eyes, sat up and rested on the edge of the bed. Alice also rose, but it was a new Alice, rosy, submissive. "What does madam wish now?" Rosemary half turned, but without looking directly at her "servant" held out her hand. "The nail file, please, Alice." "Will that be all, Ma'am?" "All for the present; get on with tidying the room till I want you." Alice flushed with pleasure, but this time she was angry and resentful too. When Rosemary looked at Alice she too was aware that Alice's new-found beauty reflected a complex emotion. She might have said something if she had not at that moment seen a face in the mirror beyond Alice's shoulder. She spun round startled. Rosemary's sudden movement made Alice follow her gaze; it was only Roland.

(*CWB XII*, pp. 20–23)

The invading forces are moving through conquered rural England. Roland and Alice (master and mistress of the house) have decided not to flee and remain in their house, awaiting the arrival of the invaders. Rosemary, the maidservant, had left, but now returns. A colleague described the scene as "strange – it varies a lot, you just have to go with it and see what it suggests to you" (personal communication).

[319]   Roland and Robin

When the Munden farm came in sight he realized he had no idea why he had come. Who was in occupation? What was he to do? England was a prison; it had been "pacified" – like hell it had! How the larks sang! He had not heard them like that before. He crouched behind the pigeon cote where he commanded a good view of the homestead and stared at its door as if willing someone to come out. Suddenly he thought he heard his name whispered from behind. He listened; it was a beautiful day, so still that all he could hear were the larks and a convoy on the main road. He began to relax. He was hearing, as if for the first time, country sounds in his own land. The voice came again, this time more urgent. Keeping his head down, he replied, "Robin". . . .

(CWB XII, pp. 32–33)

After dark Roland joined Robin, who questioned him closely, in whispers, over and again – was he sure, quite sure, that no one had seen him at any time on his way to Munden? Why had he come? His old friend was not pleased to see him. On the other hand he did not want him to go. "After all, they might see you going." Roland was affronted. "I don't know how I'm to get food for you; you haven't brought your own I suppose?" "I say, old man, don't bother! I can scrounge for myself – you know I can. You remember, with the Boche. . . ." The idea filled Robin with terror. "The Boche! My dear man, where have you been? These people aren't the Boche!" "Oh, I'm sorry" – Roland was angry and sarcastic – "I thought they had declared war again." "Forget it. The Nazis were kind and good. A bit sentimental and damnably incompetent, but this lot – you've got something to learn. Do you know what happened in that last battle? Well, it was the last. There's no army; there's no nation. Do you know". . . . They were interrupted. Stealthy steps were coming upstairs. They stopped outside the door which was ajar. It was pushed open by a dark, stocky man. Roland found himself looking down the long barrel of an automatic. Robin held his hands as high above his head as he could get them. The movement was instantaneous and distracted the man's attention from Roland. Roland, surprised into action, leaped at the man who fired – too late. Whether he was stunned by the fall, Roland did not know, for he was bashing his skull in with the man's rifle in a paroxysm of fear and rage. "You damned fool! Look what you've done now! No time. Out of here! They must have heard the gun. Out! you fool, there's not a moment to lose." They rushed, almost threw themselves, down the stairs and into the darkness of the yard. They were sobered into silence by the

stillness of the night. "As fast as you can. Puckeridge [Roland]! You damned
fool! You damned, damned fool."

(*CWB XII*, pp. 37–38)

In a scene that comes shortly after the previous quote, Roland (master of the
house) goes to a nearby farm, Munden, and finds his neighbour, Robin, hiding in a
pigeon cote. A man with a gun enters, and Roland "bashes" his skull in with a gun.
In Bion's autobiographical description of school holidays in *The Long Weekend*
he describes being at Munden as a boy when a man killed himself in the pigeon
cote. This, I think, is the one description Bion gives throughout his writings of the
experience of killing.

[320]   Captain Bion's soliloquy

CAPTAIN BION: I stared at the speck of mud trembling on the straw. I stared through the front flap at the clods of earth spouting up all round us. I stared at the dirty, strained face of my driver Allen – my strained face as I sat by me; at the boomerang that Allen sent me from Australia. I got out and hovered about six feet above us. I knew "they" would . . . and saw trees as woods walking. How they walked – walk! walk! they went like arfs arfing. Arf arf together, arfing's the stuff for me, if it's not a Rolls Royce, which I'd pick out for choice. Then a nice little Ford bright and gay, and when they came to that ford, styx I say, Valiant for S'truth passed over and all the strumpets sounded for him on the uvver side. Cooh! What "appened then? "E talked a lot more about Jesus and dog and man and then "e sez, all sudden like, Throw away the uvver crutch! Coo! Wot "appened then? "E fell on "is arse. And "is Arse wuz angry and said, Get off my arse! You've done nothing but throw shit at me all yore life and now you expects England to be my booty! Boo-ootiful soup; in a shell-hole in Flanders Fields. Legs and guts . . . must "ave bin twenty men in there – Germ'um and frogslegs and all starts! We didn't "alf arf I can tell you. Let bruvverly luv continue. No one asked "im to fall-in! No one arsed "im to come out either – come fourth, we said and E came 5th and "e didn't 1/2 stink. Full stop! "e said. The parson "e did kum, "e did qwat. "E talked of Kingdom Come. King dumb come.

(*CWB XII*, p. 57)

The whole of the short Chapter 12 is the soliloquy of Captain Bion – reproduced here in full. In the soliloquy he refers to seeing "trees as woods walking". In his autobiography, *The Long Weekend,* we hear his actual wartime experience of "men as trees, walking".

From *The Long Weekend*

And then I realized, in one of my repeated glances in the direction of the trees, that they were not trees but our infantry advancing in line with their rifles slung on their shoulders. I had imagined that infantry used their rifles for shooting; not so – not in Ypres Salient. Imaginary security; imaginary aggression? Yet men died.

(CWB I, p. 149)

From <i>A Key to A Memoir of the Future</i>

..."I see men as trees, walking", New Testament, St Mark viii.

(CWB XIV, p. 226)

The blind man at Bethsaida

23 So He took the blind man by the hand and led him out of the village. Then He spit on the man's eyes and placed His hands on him. "Can you see anything?" He asked.

24 The man looked up and said, "I can see the people, but they look like trees walking around."

25 Once again Jesus placed His hands on the man's eyes, and when he opened them his sight was restored, and he could see everything clearly. . . .

(Mark 8 23–24)

[321]   Dinosaurs, Oedipus, "Why war?"

> The tyrannosaurus provokes intrinsically an equal + opposite reaction – the
> stegosaurus. The stegosaurus sinks under its own "maginot line", its defen-
> sive armour which is its own weakness and makes its own armament, its
> own weight, under which it sinks. The self-destructive elaboration is blind to
> the quality which is to lead to its own destruction. . . . If the Oedipus story
> is the weapon that reveals homo, it is also the story that conceals, but does
> not reveal, that by which it will destroy itself.
>
> (*CWB XII*, p. 62)

"Why war?"

The following passages are reproduced from the Introduction. Parthenope Bion
Talamo has commented that Bion talks surprisingly little about man's aggression.
His interest in the above quote is in an auto-destructive mechanism in people in
which it is our armour that also destroys us.

What defensive armour does Oedipus have? Isn't he bravely pursuing the truth?
Bion holds him up as a symbol of inquiry – he does, however, also refer to the
arrogance of Oedipus.

From here my own thoughts were along the following path:

Oedipus, of course, doesn't just want to kill his father and marry his mother –
he actually (if unknowingly) does it, and in so doing he breaches the generational
divide between parents and children. Does Oedipus also go where he ought not to
in his relation to knowledge? On the surface, he seems very justified in his pursuit
of answers: he is trying to save Thebes from a plague, after all. His relation to
knowledge, however, results in gaining information while lacking the wisdom –
the developmental achievement of wisdom – to bear what he discovers. On realising his patricide and incest, he takes out his own eyes, and we see the deterioration
of his character in the following book.

I think what the Oedipus story may reveal about "that by which we could
destroy ourselves" is that the accumulation of "knowledge" as a reaction to Oedipal smallness and exclusion is like the weighty armour of the stegosaurus or the
building of the Maginot line – it makes us more vulnerable to destruction, not less.

This fits with what Bion says about humankind being "clever monkeys". At the
time of his writing in the 1970s, he had particularly in mind the construction of nuclear
weapons – the accumulation of knowledge without the wisdom to use it safely.

Tyrannosaurus: One of the last non-flying dinosaurs to exist before their extinction 65 million years ago, up to 50 different species of Tyrannosaurus once
ranged across much of the North American landmass. The Tyrannosaurus Rex

had the biggest bite force of any animal that has ever lived, before or since. Its skull was significantly larger and different in other ways – it was extremely wide at the rear but had a narrow snout, allowing unusually good binocular vision. Its name, derived from Ancient Greek, means "tyrant lizard" and it was at the apex of its food chain.

Stegosaurus: Far older in the timeline than Tyrannosaurus, this genus of armoured dinosaur lived 150–100 million years ago across land that would later become North America and Portugal. It is thought their spiky tails were most likely used to deter predators while their array of plates along their spine may have been used to attract mates. They were herbivores, and their name means "roof lizard" – perhaps because their plates look like tiles on a roof. Stegosaurus had a relatively low brain-to-body mass ratio.

The Maginot Line: Line of forts along the French border with Switzerland, Germany and Luxembourg, the Maginot Line was named after the French Minister of War, André Maginot, who was responsible for advocating its creation from 1926 until his death in 1932. Designed to deter the Germans from invading France, it did not work, because between May and June of 1940 the Panzer tank divisions simply powered their way through the hills and marshlands of the Ardennes, which Maginot had considered impenetrable and had therefore not bothered to fortify.

[322]   "Thoughts without a thinker"

Roland's voice (*the enunciation is clear and precise. He is himself not visible and as he talks he becomes progressively more a disembodied thinker and finally pure thought without a thinker*). . . .

A similar seepage from the domain of religion may likewise be traced to the inability to respect the "thought without a thinker" and, by extension, the "relationship without related objects". How this has affected even so-called practical thinking is seen in the difficulty of the "public" to grasp that an analogy is an attempt to vulgarize a relationship and *not* the objects related. The psychoanalytic approach, though valuable in having extended the conscious by the unconscious, has been vitiated by the failure to . . . understand the function of "breast", "mouth", "penis", "vagina", "container", "contained", as analogies. Even if I write it, the sensuous dominance of penis, vagina, mouth, anus, obscures the element signified by analogy. . . .

(*CWB XII*, pp. 69–70)

We tend to be dominated by what we can see, and as a consequence we are dominated by objects – penis, vagina, mouth, anus. Bion focused on the relationship between objects, something we cannot "see" or do not know how to look for. However, what are we to make of his talking about the intervening process without there being any objects on either side? The "thought without a thinker", the "relationship without related objects"? Is it partly a form of training one's mind to attend to the relationship and not the objects? It is also a way of turning things around. Instead of a relationship emanating from the objects, we might say that there are key relationships that objects take up if they get themselves in the right position to "receive" the relationship.

Other analysts on "thoughts without a thinker"

Some embrace Bion's concept, others are critical of it.

Giuseppe Civitarese

Sense, sensible, sense-able: the bodily but immaterial dimension of psychoanalytic elements
    . . . the concept of thought without a thinker. Might it not be, precisely, the "unthought known" (Bollas 1987) – what the body (not another part of the mind) knows but the mind does not? Things that may be, but

of which one cannot speak? The pre-reflective horizon of *Dasein* considered by Heidegger to determine at all times the way we experience reality? Conversely, thought without a thinker could be understood as abstract thought, not anchored in the body and in a single individuality.

(Civitarese 2015, p. 303)

Dasein: Existence or determinate being.

Paulo C. Sandler

Michelangelo said that the sculpture was already in the stone; oxygen is already there waiting for someone to breathe it in. Free associations are considered as freely floating immaterial "entities", arising from the person's mind, waiting to be thought, whose links can be grasped by intuition. In the session, the truths of the patient "float" in the "atmosphere" and may – or may not – be picked up. The same was true of $E = mc^2$, of Oedipus: they were truths of the universe that existed well before there was an Einstein, a Sophocles or a Freud to think them.

(Sandler 2006, p. 191)

Hanna Segal

I was often struck by the conciseness and power of some of his formulations. For instance, his saying, "No breast, therefore a thought". . . . Bion puts it into a nutshell – an unforgettable formulation – and in doing that also adds an important element. His formulation emphasises what is implicit in psychoanalytical thinking, but never clearly stated, namely that thought and thinking are necessarily self-conscious, a Cartesian "I think, therefore I am" (One could almost reverse this: "I *am*, therefore I think). The person must be aware, consciously or unconsciously, that thoughts are *his* thoughts, not to be confused with independent things. When a thought is not self-conscious, at its worst it becomes a hallucinated voice, a foreign body in one's mind. Curiously, much, much later in his development, Bion stated that there are thoughts without a thinker. To my mind this is irreconcilable with "No breast, therefore a thought". And I think that here we part company. Bion's first statement is to my mind a most fruitful abstraction and conceptualisation from actual clinical experience, which makes it impossible to think of a thought without the thinker. Thinking and thoughts are a function and product of one's own personality. "Thoughts without thinker" seems to be more like a rather mystical kind of philosophy. Of course, there are ideas in the air, often formulated by many people in different ways, sometimes formulated only by a great thinker like Freud conceptualising the unconscious. But those ideas in the air still arise out of people thinking.

(Segal 1998: paper given to a British Psychoanalytical Society conference in commemoration of Bion's birth in 1897)

[323]   Potency

ROSEMARY: Men seem to attach great importance to conflict, rivalry, victory. Even in private affairs I couldn't make a man think that there was any importance in what I thought or felt about him. He talked and acted as if the only matter of consequence was whether he was successful. I suppose he thought I would then be bound to fall in love with a man of such capacity and brilliance. To the end he never entertained the possibility that I loved *him* and couldn't care less about his successes.

BION: Is that true? I would be surprised if you did not find, if you were honest with yourself, that you cared a lot about his success.

ROSEMARY: He had some distinction; it was the most boring part about him. Why, even in sexual love he was convinced he had to be potent. He couldn't believe that I might love him and therefore be capable of helping him to be potent.

BION: I am sure there are many men who have no doubt of the woman's ability to make fools of them. In technical terms, there are plenty of men who are sure the woman can "castrate" them. All states exist, from primitive fears of the female genital – as expressed in visual prototypes of a vagina dentata – to fears that the woman would rejoice in triumphing by humiliating the man.

MAN: There is certainly a profound belief in the pleasure of triumphing over and humiliating the rival. That state of mind is common enough and it is feared by man or woman. It, and the fear of it, can be generated by the experiences of the child.

BION: Its efficacy depends on belief. But there can be innumerable reasons for fear, including fear of the pleasures of cruelty.

(CWB XII, p. 162)

[324]   Words to "trap" meaning like a sculpture "traps" the light

MYSELF: Perhaps I can illustrate by an example from something you do know. Imagine a piece of sculpture which is easier to comprehend if the structure is intended to act as a trap for light. The meaning is revealed by the pattern formed by the light thus trapped – not by the structure, the carved work itself. I suggest that if I could learn how to talk to you in such a way that my words "trapped" the meaning which they neither do nor could express, I *could* communicate to you in a way that is not at present possible.

BION: Like the "rests" in a musical composition?

(*CWB XII*, p. 176)

Chapter 26

"Book 2: The Past Presented"

The story itself retreats somewhat and to the fore comes a series of dialogues and discussions. In the dialogues one can hear Bion addressing criticisms that have been made over the years. For example his drawing on the work of the mystics. He is clear that he is not a mystic – he is a psychoanalyst. There is no longer a narrative voice, the reader is to enter the debates through different voices. The action is now taking place in the 1970s. England is not at war. Alice and Roland entertain many guests, some of whom we have already met in Book One. The debates then move to the kitchen, Rosemary is the new lady of the house and is to marry Man. When Robin and Roland rail against Rosemary, Man shoots Roland. Rosemary and Man ruthlessly dominate the others. The book ends with "Time Past's" party, including a resuscitated Roland and an exchange between P.A., Ghost of P.A. and the Ghost of Auser (this quote is in the chapter on Last Quotes).

Quotes

325 Alice wakes from a dream
326 Zoo
327 Augmenting the boundaries of perception
328 Centre of one's own personality
329 I died on the Amiens-Roye road
330 God not interested in religion
331 DU
332 Facts, beliefs and treacle wells
333 Do you take God and the Devil seriously?
334 P.A. (Psychoanalyst) and the Priest
335 A solemn and incomprehensible conversation between Bion's parents
336 Freud at 82
337 In love with being seduced
338 P.A. soliloquy
339 Regret

[325]   Alice wakes from a dream

ROLAND: What's the date?

ALICE: No idea; does it matter?

ROLAND: Of course it matters! Wake up!

ALICE: Oh, sorry sir. Tuesday, nineteen seventy. . . .

ROLAND: You aren't awake. It is Tuesday though. I have to be up
             because I must go to Munden.

ALICE: Yes. Yes – I must have been dreaming. What's the –

ROSEMARY: Yes, Ma'am? You told me to call you.

ALICE: Yes, of course. Breakfast at half past seven. My God! I've got
             a headache.

ROLAND: You're dreaming.

ALICE: My headache is no dream I can tell you. You're off are you?
             See you at lunch. Rosemary, I've had an awful dream.

                                                    (*CWB XIII*, p. 5)

[326]   Zoo

DOCTOR: . . . I don't think, with my limited knowledge, I could venture on describing what the physiology or embryology of the growth process is.

P.A.:   Nor would I like to suggest a psychoanalytic formulation. But here is the trouble. While I am "considering", someone rushes in with the "answer" and there's no catching up with an "answer". You might as well try to catch a bandersnatch. "Any stigma will serve to beat a dogma". But the hunt which we could only match in our nightmares would be one in the vast deserts in which roam the fearsome and dangerous creatures known to us only in the pale illumination of daylight and waking thoughts as "answers", "dogmas", "scientific facts", "triangles" – and their close relatives, "eternal triangles". I would include in my psychoanalytic zoo a whole series of fascinating animals – if I were sure they would not escape and roam the world as the latest and most beautiful new-born facts.

ALICE: Such as? You fascinate me, I confess. Do show me your zoo!

ROLAND: Trust a woman to go off on a side-track!

P.A.:   Allow me to conduct you round the cages of my psychoanalytic zoo. Of course the names are somewhat forbidding, but the creatures themselves are beautiful and ugly. Ah! Here is Absolute Truth – a most ferocious animal which has killed more innocent white lies and black wholes than you would think possible.

ROLAND: You muddle it with your puns.

ROBIN: Call it paronomasia – more scientific.

ALICE: It sounds like a very attractive flower.

P.A.:   Only a flower of speech. Throw hither all your quaint enamelled lies that on the green turf suck the honied showers. "Blind mouths", as Ruskin showed you, would have to learn to read.

ALICE: I learnt to read years ago.

P.A.:   That is what we all think, but in fact the greatest thinkers are very difficult to read unless you find great readers to read them.

ALICE: But I was a *great* reader as a child.

P.A.:   You may have been – but now you are a grown-up and have an enormous amount of knowledge – or is it bilge? – to fall back on. . . .

We were just coming to the twins, Absolute Space and Absolute Time. . . .

ROBIN: And decent people like me cannot even think of the roars of cosines and the bellowing of tangents and the whistling of borogroves –

                                                                    (*CWB XIII*, pp. 22–23)

Bion is aware of the risk that his own "animals" could themselves be picked up as banners or slogans – a sentimental heroism, rather than a clinically based discipline.

Bandersnatch: Fictional creature from the nonsense poem, "The Jabberwocky", found in Lewis Carroll's sequel to *Alice in Wonderland*, the novel *Through the Looking-Glass, and What Alice Found There* (1871). Described only as "frumious" (another nonsense word) in "The Jabberwocky", there is a more detailed description of the bandersnatch's speed and snapping jaws in his later 1874 poem, "The Hunting of the Snark".

Borogroves: Nonsense word from Lewis Carroll's poem, "The Jabberwocky"; all we learn about them from this work is that they are "mimsy".

Lewis Carroll

Jabberwocky

'Twas brillig, and the slithy toves
Did gyre and gimble in the wabe;
All mimsy were the borogoves,
And the mome raths outgrabe.

"Beware the Jabberwock, my son!
The jaws that bite, the claws that catch!
Beware the Jubjub bird, and shun
The frumious Bandersnatch!"

He took his vorpal sword in hand:
Long time the manxome foe he sought –
So rested he by the Tumtum tree,
And stood awhile in thought.

And as in uffish thought he stood,
The Jabberwock, with eyes of flame,
Came whiffling through the tulgey wood,
And burbled as it came!

One, two! One, two! And through and through
The vorpal blade went snicker-snack!
He left it dead, and with its head
He went galumphing back.

"And hast thou slain the Jabberwock?
Come to my arms, my beamish boy!
O frabjous day! Callooh! Callay!"
He chortled in his joy.

'Twas brillig, and the slithy toves
Did gyre and gimble in the wabe;
All mimsy were the borogoves,
And the mome raths outgrabe.

John Milton

Lycidas

Ye valleys low, where the mild whispers use,
Of shades, and wanton winds, and gushing brooks,
On whose fresh lap the swart star sparely looks,
Throw hither all your quaint enamelled eyes,
That on the green turf suck the honied showers,
And purple all the ground with vernal flowers.

Lines 136–141

Blind Mouths: The metaphor of "blind mouths" refers to the ministry of the church in its two different offices – that of bishop who should "see" their flock, exhort secular powers to rule wisely and be their conscience, while the pastor should "feel", ensuring he remains closely bound up with the trials and tribulations of his flock. A "blind mouth" is therefore a castrated religious institution that can neither guide the powerful nor care for the weak.

[327]   Augmenting the boundaries of perception

P.A.:   It may be a peculiarity of the human mind that events are thought to be sequential and even consequential.

ROBIN: You don't suggest they all happen at once?

P.A.:   No, I don't. I am saying that "cause and effect" are words which are appropriate to the human mind and only appear to inhere in things and characters *not* the observers.

EDMUND: Isn't this coming near to denying the existence of the environment?

P.A.:   No; I am suggesting that we are unable to free ourselves from our prison of sense even though something can be done to augment the boundaries of perception. Had Aristarchus lived a few hundred years, he might have been able to use the two hundred inch reflector at Palomar, or the radio telescope at Jodrell Bank. As far as we know, he couldn't.

PAUL: As far as we know –

P.A.:   That is what I have been saying – as far as we know, but I do not think that we should deliberately go on to say, "Thus far and no further".

(*CWB XIII*, pp. 26–27)

Cause and effect

Bion's point that our conception of cause and effect has more to do with our own minds than what might "actually" be occurring in the external world is not an unusual view. What, however, does Bion mean by "something can be done to augment the boundaries of perception". What equivalent might there be today of the hypothetical putting together the imaginative capacity of Aristarchus to conceptualise the relation between the sun and earth differently, and the advanced telescopic equipment of today? Bion has been working on this question in one form or another throughout his psychoanalytic work and perhaps throughout his life.

Anyone who has had an analysis knows first-hand how, through the analytic work, they become able to see more of their emotional and external reality. Personal analysis, Bion says, is fundamental. He is also interested in how the conscious mind can be trained to be less limited by existing assumptions and advocates an intentional diminution of information from the senses to augment the boundaries of intuitive perception.

Aristarchus of Samos (c. 310 – c. 230 BC): Ancient Greek mathematician and astronomer, was the first person to declare himself for the heliocentric world view – that is, to argue that the Earth goes round the Sun (and not the other way round). He was also theorised that the other stars he could see were suns just like ours but much further away. He couldn't be proved right until the invention of the telescope.

Palomar: The Palomar Observatory in San Diego County, California operates three active research telescopes (the 200-inch Hale Telescope, the 48-inch Samuel Oschin Telescope and the 60-inch Telescope) and has been at the forefront of astronomical research since it opened in the mid-1930s. Founded by George Ellery Hale, a founder of Caltech and graduate of MIT, with a grant from the Rockefeller Foundation, the Palomar Observatory opened in 1928 and has been training astronomers ever since.

Jodrell Bank: Jodrell Bank in Cheshire, UK, is the site of a 90-m-high radio telescope first established in 1957 by Sir Bernard Lovell, a radio astronomer at the University of Manchester. His work on radar during WWII led him to research cosmic rays, and discoveries with the Lovell Telescope have informed astrophysics in multiple ways including research into meteors, quasars, pulsars, and space probes.

[328]   Centre of one's own personality

P.A.:   It is as difficult to see the centre of one's own personality. Distracted and fascinated by what is not one's self, the periphery is substituted for the centre.

(*CWB XIII*, p. 35)

[329] I died on the Amiens–Roye road

P.A.: A runner who was crouching beside me in a shell hole had his thoracic wall blown out, exposing his heart. He tried to look at the ghastly wound across which an entirely ineffectual field dressing dangled. "Mother, Mother – you'll write to my Mother, sir, won't you?" "Yes, blast you", I said. If I could believe in God I would ask him to forgive me. "Dieu me pardonnera. C'est son métier."

ALICE: I thought you were supposed to be cured of such irrational guilts.

P.A.: Who said they were irrational? Or that one would not sometimes see sufficiently clearly to know one was damned – rationally?

PAUL: You are angry with her; why, what has she done?

P.A.: I am sorry if I was rude; I didn't mean it. I use the saddest words in the language – "I didn't mean it to happen." They hang across the gaping wound of my mind like a ridiculous field dressing. August 8, 1918, that was.

. . . .

As far as I am concerned the ideas *hold me* whether I like it or not. I would not go near the Amiens–Roye road for fear I should meet my ghost – I died there. For though the Soul should die, the Body lives for ever.

(*CWB XIII*, pp. 37–38)

The runner is Sweeting.

Dieu me pardonnera. C'est son metier: God will forgive me. It is his job.

Heinrich Heine (1797–1856): German critic & poet.

[330]   God not interested in religion

P.A.: So many of your famed religious talk as if the God in which they believe is keenly interested in religion. I can understand religious professors being interested in God, but I cannot see why God should be.

(*CWB XIII*, p. 38)

[331]   DU

DU: . . . Remember that fellow who sniped you down the path at Berles-aux-Bois? He was only bored, poor chap.

ROLAND: I'm no snipe.

DU: You would never have "seen" the joke if he hadn't been feeling hot, bored, drinking warm Bocks and wishing he was in Germany and not on that lousy West Front where it was all quiet and nothing to do.

ROLAND: What were *you* doing anyway?

DU: I was keeping quiet, lying as close to your CNS [central nervous system] as I could get and trying to make you have the sense to lie flat on the ground – drowned in adrenal stimulation.

ROLAND: At least I got back to lunch.

DU: Just – thanks to me, not your bloody heroism and conceptual rubbish.

(CWB XIII, p. 58)

Who or what is DU? I have spent a not inconsiderable amount of time trying to work out more about this. In the quote above, DU puts Roland in contact with his military past fighting in France. It may be relevant that DU's name is French (translated as "some or any"). In the quote above he saves Roland's life – in what is an incident that actually happened to Bion. DU saves him by keeping him quiet when he is full of "adrenal stimulation".

Du is also the familiar "you" in German.

[332] Facts, beliefs and treacle wells

P.A.: . . . I mean I am careful to choose what I know and what I believe and, to the best of my capacity, not to mix them up. Because I do not take to be true what humans tell me are the facts, it does not mean that I fall back on "believing" a lot of twaddle as if I had to keep my mind full at all costs. Or the reverse – empty – like a kind of mental anorexia nervosa. . . .

ROSEMARY: Were those facts when you said all that about "masochistic cravings"?

P.A.: No, they were attempts at formulating a particular instance of belief. If I were an artist I would try to formulate it in terms of painting or music.

ROSEMARY: I would like to hear you sing it –

P.A.: I doubt it – any more than you like my verbalization. And you remember what the dormouse said about drawing a treacle well.

ROSEMARY: No, I don't. What's all this about a dormouse?

ALL (*except Man*): Not know the Dormouse? Well! Not know *Alice*?

ROSEMARY: I'm very ignorant. The only Alice I know is my maid.

P.A.: Anyhow, I cannot sing it or draw it even in the way I might draw treacle.

ROSEMARY: I think you must be crazy. I don't understand a word you say. Or perhaps I am crazy not to understand.

ROLAND & ROBIN: Not crazy.

P.A.: Nor was Alice, nor Lewis Carroll. But I think he gave a fine representation of it – even a remarkable expression of psychosis.

ALICE: I hope you are not going to make out that the Alice books are psychotic. I loved them. They are still favourites of mine.

(*CWB XIII*, pp. 72–73)

Here – paraphrased – is what the dormouse in Lewis Carroll's *Alice in Wonderland* says about drawing a treacle well:

Three girls lived at the bottom of a well on treacle. Where did the treacle come from? You can draw water from a well, so you can draw treacle from a treacle well. The girls were learning to draw.

The pun hinges, of course, on the two different meanings of "draw". Bion is poking fun at the notion that one can have anything one likes just by believing it to be true (having one's treacle just by drawing it). Bion says he is careful about what he believes. He may be responding to his critics, who view him as believing religious "twaddle".

[333]   Do you take God and the Devil seriously?

P.A.: . . . just as serious psychoanalytic interpretations are thought often to be jokes. God and Devil are frequently not taken seriously.

ROLAND: Do you mean to say you take them seriously?

P.A.: Of course I do – I am a psychoanalyst.

ROLAND: Quite. I thought psychoanalysts didn't take religion seriously.

P.A.: How could I possibly be concerned with people without taking seriously one of their outstanding features?

ROBIN: I thought psychoanalysis was all sex.

P.A.: Since psychoanalysis is a human interest you would naturally assume, without having to be told by a psychoanalyst, that it was sure to be sexual – "all sex", as you call it. As psychoanalytic theories are about, or purport to be about, human beings, you would feel they should resemble real life, real people. If so, sex ought to appear somewhere in the theories.

ROLAND: But not everywhere. . . .

ROBIN: Well, you are the first psychoanalyst I have heard of who believes in God or God incarnate.

P.A.: I did not say I believed in it, but certainly I cannot imagine doing anything else or using such capacity for belief as I have for any purpose other than for facts.

ROLAND: You mean you believe nonsense, and what is nonsense that is what you believe?

P.A.: Already you are mis-representing and mis-understanding me to say I believe in a particular form of religious non-sense. I do not. I would subscribe to this belief in the doctrine dogma of God incarnate if it were also understood to include belief in the Devil incarnate. . . .

P.A.: Anyone who aspires to the initiative in matters which are ordinarily thought of as spiritual or religious or artistic is in for trouble with his contemporaries. The fate of the reputation of outstanding artists, scientists and religious leaders would be more comprehensible to us ordinary human beings if we could conceive of the domain more widely, in the way that the domain of mathematics has had to be widened – almost to the point of notoriety – to accommodate new kinds of figures and their manipulation.

(*CWB XIII*, pp. 79–81)

[334] P.A. (Psychoanalyst) and the Priest

PRIEST: The most profound expression of despair known to us was, "Why has thou forsaken me?"

P.A.: This discovery is one which all are afraid to make. A theory that the human animal is not going to call on God to do for him what he must do for himself in loneliness and despair cannot be formulated; any formulation is a substitute for that which cannot be substituted. . . .

(*CWB XIII*, pp. 106–107)

ROSEMARY: Sit down all of you. You two (addressing Priest and P.A.) have arrived at an agreement. I am glad –

PRIEST: It is more apparent than real.

P.A.: We have arrived at the same fence at the same time and that gives an illusion of agreement liable to obscure the fact that we are on different sides of the fence.

(*CWB XIII*, p. 153)

The crucifixion of Jesus

Around the ninth hour, Jesus shouted in a loud voice, saying "Eli Eli lama sabachthani?" which is, "My God, my God, why have you forsaken me?"

(Gospel according to Matthew 27: 46)

[335]　A solemn and incomprehensible conversation between Bion's parents

P.A.:　. . . I remember my mother asking my father if he had ever experienced what a poet said – "Sometimes a light surprises the Christian while he sings" – and his reply, after a moment of thought, that he had not. I remember the sudden onset of tropical night, the lamp-lit room and the frighteningly solemn and incomprehensible conversation. Why were they sad? Experience has not answered.

(*CWB XIII*, p. 114)

"Bion came from a Protestant missionary family, Swiss Calvinist of Huguenot origin on his father's side, and Anglo-Indian on his mother's" (Bion Talamo 2005, p. 183).

William Cowper

"Sometimes a light surprises the Christian when he sings"

Sometimes a light surprises
The Christian while he sings;
It is the Lord who rises
With healing in his wings:
When comforts are declining
He grants the soul again
A season of clear shining
To cheer it after rain.
In holy contemplation
We sweetly then pursue
The theme of God's salvation,
And find it ever new.
Set free from present sorrow
We cheerfully can say,
Now let the unknown morrow
Bring with it what it may.
It can bring with it nothing
But He will bear us through;
Who gives the lilies clothing
Will clothe His people too:
Beneath the spreading heavens
No creature but is fed;
And He who feeds the ravens

Will give His children bread.
Though vine nor fig-tree neither
Their wonted fruit should bear,
Though all the field should wither,
Nor flocks nor herds be there,
Yet, God the same abiding,
His praise shall tune my voice;
For, while in Him confiding,
I cannot but rejoice.

William Cowper (1731–1800): Son of a clergyman who was connected to the Royal Court. At the age of 6, on the death of his mother, he was sent to boarding school, where he had terrible experiences. He then moved to Westminster school, where he learned about life in fashionable society. He courted a lady for seven years but was refused permission to marry her. He attempted unsuccessfully to be a lawyer. He was supported financially by friends. When, at the age of 33, he was about to be publicly questioned to discover whether he was suitable for a particular public post, he had a nervous breakdown. He was severely depressed and suicidal and was placed in a private asylum. In the process of his recovery, he had a conversion experience and became a Christian.

[336]   Freud at 82

P.A.:   Freud wrote an outline of psychoanalysis when he was eighty-two; this "Outline" seemed simple and therefore easy. So it is – for anyone who has spent the previous eighty-two years doing the work.

(*CWB XIII*, p. 124)

[337]   In love with being seduced

ROSEMARY: . . . if I go on like this I shall "fall in love" – with Man.

P.A.: No, you are only falling in love with being seduced.

ROSEMARY: You again? So you think I am being seduced?

P.A.: No, I think you are in love with seduction. You made Alice fall in love with being seduced. She was starved and you were starved, so it was hardly surprising that you were both vulnerable – susceptible to the allurement of physical sex, she perhaps more than you, because in her "bin", as you call it, she was starved of physical sex in a way which you couldn't experience in your slum. Neither of you knows the first thing about love. . . .

(*CWB XIII*, p. 137)

P.A.: Your feelings are one kind of evidence. But don't make the mistake of acting as if you had a different sort of evidence. Alice *feels* you love her, but the feeling leads her to suppose facts. She thinks she can depend on you; she can't. If she cannot depend on herself she would be unwise to depend on anyone else.

(*CWB XIII*, p. 168)

[338]   P.A. soliloquy

P.A.:   Do I choose to be or not to be? That fellow Shakespeare put words to the emotional problem that is still not solved. . . .

Is it the sleeper only who poisons his dreams with his mental excrement? Or he who cannot dream of destroying the world but has to transform his dream into a bomb that poisons us with his atomic debris?. . . .

"Oh my, I don't want to die, I want to go home", we used to sing. That was true; we hoped that the ugly reality would not penetrate the joke armour-plate. The armour-plate of a tank was penetrable; we were bewitched, bemused, "probability"-dazzled cowards. "Probably" we would not be killed; "probably" we would survive to inhabit a new heaven and a new earth – "après la guerre". I did not know I loved life so much. I survived to foot the bill; fight a war and spend the rest of life paying the bill for all those shells and tanks and bullets and the state of mind used to provide an armour more impenetrable than "gloire" or "flannelle". "*Ante Agamemnona multi*". . . . I remember, am still penetrated by the memory of brave men whose name did not "live for evermore". "With whatsoever emphasis of passionate love repeated" the echo of their name is faint at last, "soft as old sorrow, bright as old renown"; it fades and dies. Why do I mind this grizzly, victorious lout? It is not death I fear, but the shame of knowing a few, only a few, of the multitudinous shabby failures. There goes the bell again! Telephone? Alarm? Come in. From that warfare there is no release – *après la guerre fini*. Come Phorbas! Come, come. As torrents in summer suddenly rise, though the sky is still cloudless . . . Mene huic confidere monstro? Not bloody likely! Ecce deus . . . ecce homo . . . take your choice. Sleep or wake – : you pays your money and you takes your choice".

(*CWB XIII*, pp. 162–164)

William Shakespeare

Hamlet

"To be, or not to be: that is the question:
Whether 'tis nobler in the mind to suffer
The slings and arrows of outrageous fortune,
Or to take arms against a sea of troubles,
And by opposing end them? To die: to sleep;
No more; and by a sleep to say we end

The heart-ache and the thousand natural shocks
That flesh is heir to, 'tis a consummation
Devoutly to be wish'd. To die, to sleep;
To sleep: perchance to dream: ay, there's the rub;
For in that sleep of death what dreams may come . . .
. . . Soft you now,
The fair Ophelia! – Nymph, in thy orisons
Be all my sins remembered."

(Hamlet, Act 3, Scene 1)

"*Ante Agamemnona multi*" Line from Horace's *Odes.*

Vixere fortes ante Agamemnona
multi; sed omnes illacrimabiles
urgentur ignotique longa
nocte, carent quia vate sacro.

There lived many brave men before Agamemnon,
but they are all buried unwept
and unknown in long night,
because they lack a holy poet.

(Book 4, verse 9)

The phrase, "Soft as old sorrow, bright as old renown" comes from Henry New-bolt's poem "Homeward Bound":

Henry Newbolt

"Homeward Bound"

After long labouring in the windy ways,
On smooth and shining tides
Swiftly the great ship glides,
Her storms forgot, her weary watches past;
Northward she glides, and through the enchanted haze
Faint on the verge her far hope dawns at last.
The phantom sky-line of a shadowy down,
Whose pale white cliffs below
Through sunny mist aglow,
Like noon-day ghosts of summer moonshine gleam – –
Soft as old sorrow, bright as old renown,
There lies the home, of all our mortal dream.

Sir Henry Newbolt (1862–1938): English poet most famous for a poem entitled *Vitaï Lampada,* in which the call to duty as a colonial Englishman was enshrined in a popular public-school-boy cricketing phrase, "Play up! Play up! and play the game!" It was widely lampooned by those opposed to the First World War as the scale of the slaughter became evident, and this association may well have been in Bion's mind when quoting this line from another Newbolt poem. During the First World War Sir Henry Newbolt worked for the War Propaganda Bureau, whose task was to promote public opinion in favour of the war.

"Après la guerre": "When the war is over". "Gloire" means "glory" and "Phorbas" was an Ancient Greek king said to attack pilgrims on their way to the Oracle at Delphi. *"Mene huic confidere monstro"* is from *The Aeneid* by Virgil and means, "Shall I trust such a depraved wretch". *"Ecce deus"* means "Behold, God" in Latin, while *"Ecce homo"* means "Behold the man" and are the words attributed to Pontius Pilate when presenting a scourged Jesus Christ, bound and crowned with thorns, to the hostile crowd shortly before his Crucifixion.

[339]   Regret

ROSEMARY: No, it is Time Past's party.
PRIEST: That is P.A.'s party.
P.A.: No, my party is not times past. Always the mistake of thinking the past is owned by psychoanalysis; the past is owned by Regret.

　　Regret is a guest at a psychoanalytic party but is not the host; nor is psychoanalysis the domain of Regret. Regret is so vain that it is regarded as important and treated with deference in religion.

(CWB XIII, pp. 173–174)

The meaning of "regret" in religious thought and practice includes remorse, repentance, having a conscience about, contrition, and guilt.

Chapter 27

"Book 3: The Dawn of Oblivion"

Bion's growing interest in the foetal "dawn" of life is introduced through the character Em-mature – who makes the following comment: "This book is a psycho-embryonic attempt to write an embryo-scientific account of a journey from birth to death overwhelmed by pre-mature knowledge, experience, glory and self-intoxicating self-satisfaction". The reference to "oblivion" in the title includes human-kinds potential for blindness and senselessness.

In the quotes the reader will see Bion portraying himself at different ages.

Quotes

340 Q&A
341 Em-mature
342 Tibs
343 Devil
344 No answering god replied
345 Ordered up the line
346 Difficult to give an interpretation which is distinguished from a moral accusation
347 Vagina and penis both important channels
348 Do you never want to give help?
349 We do not know much about the world we live on, or the minds we are.
350 The liquid environment
351 Cruelty and love
352 Bion's belief that he would survive and the cost of war
353 Aroused by something I can't smell, touch, hear or see
354 Compassion
355 Eyes that have seen colossal storms
356 Pleasure and pain
357 Klein Freud Charcot
358 Pre-natal experiences
359 Body and Mind, Psyche and Soma

[340]   Q&A

Q: Can you give me . . . oh it's you is it?

A: Alas! yes.

Q: I don't see why you say Alas!" I don't mind meeting you! Why. . . .

A: I thought you were going to ask what it's about.

Q: Oh no. I read the last one.

A: Splendid! Did you like it?

Q: No. Is this as bad?

A: Worse.

Q: How interesting: I must get it.

A: I said "worse".

Q: That's what made me want it – I don't see how it could be.

(CWB XIV, p. 4)

[341]   Em-mature

EM-MATURE: This book is a psycho-embryonic attempt to write an embryo-scientific account of a journey from birth to death overwhelmed by pre-mature knowledge, experience, glory and self-intoxicating self-satisfaction. I was spared any knowledge of the courtship of my sperm with my ovum, but many years later was given to understand that my ancestors had a long and disreputable history extending to the day when an ancestral sperm, swimming characteristically against the current, lodged in a fallopian tube to lie in wait for an unknown ovum. The history of my ovum appears to be virtually non-existent. My sperm impetuously penetrated a Graafian follicle before my ovum had time itself to escape penetration. I cannot vouch for the truth of these tales which became known to me through scientific hearsay many years later. I admit responsibility for what I have experienced, but not for the distortions of scientific sense. I acknowledge dependence on sensible and experienced transcriptions; I cannot promise communication of pure non-sense without the contamination by sense. I shall not repeat my apology for having to borrow the language of experience and reason despite its inadequacy.

My earliest experiences were of something touching what I later heard was "me". The changes in pressure in the fluid surrounding me varied from what Me called pleasure to what Me called pain. My optic and auditory pits at the age of three or four somites received sound and light, dark and silent, not usually increasing beyond nice and nasty, but sometimes making Me feel more inanimate than animate.

(*CWB XIV*, p. 5)

Bion would have been fascinated by Piontelli's (1992) findings, which demonstrate connections between psychoanalytic evidence and observational data on behavioural and psychological continuities between pre-natal and post-natal life.

(Mawson, *CWB XIV*, p. 205)

[342]   Tibs

BOY: Smash it down on the pot and that sets Tibs [the cat] off to a good start and we have to catch her before she gets up a tree. You have to be jolly quick though. . . .

GIRL: . . . Tibs doesn't like you. Mummy, he chased Tibs till Tibs had to run up the tree. . . .

TIBS: *(soliloquizing and licking her whiskers)* The tree and I understand each other – though he is rather rooted in the past.

TREE: *(soliloquizing)* I live on earth and water, and even my leaves and branches when they break out feed and feed on air.

(CWB XIV, pp. 14–15)

In *The Long Weekend* Bion speaks of himself and two other adolescent boys chasing Tibs the cat. I have included this quote because we see here in the *Memoir* the voices also given to Tibs and to the Tree!

[343]   Devil

DEVIL: You are not by any chance addressing me, are you? Are you one
of the people whose God is the Devil? I do not cultivate theories;
theories are a symptom of gregarious animals when they function as members of a group. I am special, individual, a victim of
disapproval.

(*CWB XIV*, p. 23)

In a scientific meeting of the British Society, attention was drawn to how ani-
mated the discussion became when it was about the Devil. Bion's description of
the Devil as "special, individual, a victim of disapproval" may contribute to an
understanding of why that might be.

[344]   No answering god replied

SIXTEEN YEARS: I read a great deal; I also played hard.

PRIEST: And prayed hard.

SIXTEEN YEARS: I may even have done that, but no answering god replied
and I gave it up. The devil wasn't much use either.

(CWB XIV, p. 33)

[345]   Ordered up the line

P.A.:   Right – let's start. I remember how I felt when I was Twenty-
             one. We had just been ordered up the Line; I was terrified. I
             did not like the prospect at all. The orders were that we must
             not allow the enemy any rest, but carry on the pursuit now
             he had been beaten and a great gap torn in his lines by our
             victory on August 8th. Unfortunately I had been decorated
             for gallantry. Twenty-one knew I was terrified and hadn't the
             courage to get the doc to invalid me out. I knew I had not the
             courage for "heroic" deeds. Besides, I had "flu; my runner was
             given a bottle of phyz to dose me with. No one knew what I
             was suffering from so it was called p.u.o. – pyrexia of unknown
             origin. I hoped my death would be painless and sudden. The
             infantryman by my side had a hole in his belly. We looked at
             him coldly. "He's a gonner – why waste time looking at him?
             Come on – zero hour." I scrambled out of the trench and
             started walking forward. I inhibited – as I learned to call it
             later – any whisper of fact to burst through my p.u.o. . . . .
                                                    (*CWB XIV*, pp. 44–45)

ROLAND: Well, what happened?
P.A.:   I caught up with my leading tank. I knew the long-range naval
             guns must get us. "Get out!" I told them, "and walk behind till
             it gets hit". I set the controls at full speed and got out myself. It
             raced – for those days – ahead so we could hardly stumble up
             with it. And then – *then!* – the full horror came on me. Fool!
             What had I done? As I scrambled and tripped in my drunken
             influenza to catch up with the tank, in the shadow of which I
             had ordered my crew to remain sheltered, my ice-cold reality
             revealed a *fact*: The tank, in perfect order, with guns, ammuni-
             tion and its 175-horse-power engines, was delivered into the
             hands of the enemy. Alone, I alone, had done this thing! My
             pyrexia left to rejoin its unknown origin.
PRIEST: How did you get in – by beating your hands on the cold steel
             doors?
P.A.:   I was in; I did get in. A high-velocity shell struck; without
             thought I shot out of the hatch as the flames of petrol swathed
             the steel carcass. Are you hurt, sir? No – fell on my arse. Are
             you all right, sir? Of course! Why? Home – quick!
                                                       (*CWB XIV*, p. 46)

[346] Difficult to give an interpretation which is distinguished from a moral accusation

P.A.:   That is one component of the practice of psychoanalysis which is constant even if not constantly perceived. Guilty feelings are unwelcome and even in infants easily evoked. It is difficult to give an interpretation which is distinguished from a moral accusation.

ROLAND: Surely this is a defect of psychoanalysis?

P.A.:   Certainly; but when I agree, you and others are therefore liable to assume that it is psychoanalysis only that suffers from that weakness, whereas I believe that this is a fundamental experience. It is this fundamental experience that underlies Plato's dialogue between Socrates and Phaedrus which is being revived here – a few hundred years later – in this discussion.

(*CWB XIV*, p. 50)

Socrates and Phaedrus: The Phaedrus dialogue, by Plato, was written around 370 B.C. and features a conversation between Socrates and Phaedrus, which takes place out in the woods. It covers diverse topics, including the reincarnation of souls, the wisdom or otherwise of consummating love affairs invoking the famous image of the charioteer who must command two horses, the good horse who is controlled by its sense of shame and the bad horse who is overcome by desire; and how to practice an art properly – that is, to practice an art one must know what the art is *for* and what it can help one to achieve.

[347]   Vagina and penis both important channels

ROLAND: . . . a vagina is a real and important canal. So is a penis.

(*CWB XIV*, p. 55)

[348]   Do you never want to give help?

ROLAND: But do you never give any help?

ROBIN: Suppose they come to you for help.

P.A.: Naturally I should hope that I was the sort of character who would want to help them; but I would like to have the discipline to confine my efforts within the limits of my capacity.

(*CWB XIV*, p. 64)

In his discussions of eschewing memory and desire, Bion has included the desire for cure as an impediment to the analyst's availability for the work to be done. There is perhaps an echo of people's questioning response to this in the above quote: "But do you never give any help?"

[349]   We do not know much about theworld we live on, or the minds we are

P.A.:   No. "God is, or is not" is only a human formulation in conformity with human principles of thinking. It has nothing to do with the reality. The only "reality" we *know about* is the various hopes, dreams, phantasies, memories and desires which are a part of us. The other reality exists, *is*, whether we like it or not. A child may want to punish a table for hurting him when he suffers a contusion. But he may desire to punish himself for "suffering" a contusion. He may ultimately be compelled to believe that, in addition to these facts, there is a table that is neither good nor bad, like it or not, forgive it or punish it. We may decide to punish our god, punish ourselves for believing in "it" or "him" or "her". It will not affect the reality which will continue to be real no matter how unsearchable, un-knowable, beyond the grasp of human capacity it is/not is. After all, we do not know much about the world we live on, or the minds we are.

(*CWB XIV*, p. 67)

[350]   The liquid environment

P.A.:   Lack of choice means that each of us still retains his fishy qualities.

ROBIN: Fish out of water.

P.A.:   Not quite. When we abandon our liquid environment for a gas-
            eous one we take our liquid with us. Like fish, we can still smell by
            cause of the mucus preserved in our respiratory passages by the
            glands that maintain our watery medium although we have moved
            into a gaseous one.

ROBIN: I don't see what we are to do about it, or what it has to do with
            us.

P.A.:   You would if you caught what is called "a cold"; or if your tears
            began to flow. The liquid environment which we take with us or
            manufacture inside is useful for making it possible to see or smell,
            or even to provide for the germ plasm which we produce when
            we transfer to a gaseous medium like air. But if it is over produc-
            tive, then the mucus makes us feel we are about to drown; we
            can't smell, we can't see for tears, we can't find a repository for
            the superfluity of seminal or ovarian fluids.

ROBIN: If all these generations of our human development are repeated in
            each individual, I can see it might also apply to the mind or psyche.

P.A.:   It is sometimes illuminating to think so.

                                                              (CWB XIV, pp. 69–70)

In this third book particularly Bion is interested pre-birth and evolutionary vestiges. He draws attention to the liquids in us, enabling life, but if excessive drowning us. We have a psychic equivalent in our carrying something atavistic in us
(ancient and primitive).

[351]   Cruelty and love

P.A.:   Cruelty is a very early form of love. The baby bites the nipple and proceeds to bite all the food it loves. It would soon find that the food would "bite it back" again if it did not chew it; but it may be too afraid to chew it. Wrong either way.

(CWB XIV, p. 73)

[352]   Bion's belief that he would survive and the cost of war

P.A.:   In situations of great danger I always had a belief that I would probably survive. Had I realized – been compelled by some dreadful
wound to realize – that such a belief was nonsense, I would have
dodged the danger. Nobody told me – nor would I have understood
them if they had – that war service would change utterly my capacity
to enjoy life. Are we, even today, prepared to tell our children, or
our children's children, what price they would have to pay if they
served their fellows? Are we to tell them not to do it, that it might
cost them too much? What would it cost them if they did not serve
their fellow men? Socrates chose not to run away after his sentence
by the court of fellow Athenians. When remonstrated with, he said
it was his free choice. For *that* freedom he paid the price knowingly.

(*CWB XIV*, p. 74)

[353]   Aroused by something I can't smell, touch, hear or see

P.A.:   . . . Increasingly I am aware that there is something more than that which presents itself to my senses – sound, sight, hearing, touch. I have feelings that are aroused by something that I do not smell or touch or hear or see. My perceptions are not fine enough – blunted by the constant battering of sensuous reality. I shall not live long enough to reach *those* facts except in rudimentary degree. . . .

(*CWB XIV*, pp. 80–81)

[354]   Compassion

P.A.: I do not think we could tolerate our work – painful as it often is for both us and our patients – without compassion. I see no reason for postulating an external source, independent of man, from which compassion flows.

(*CWB XIV*, p. 87)

[355]   Eyes that have seen colossal storms

ALICE: You say you have never had direct experience of a mysterious event; do you mean by that that you have not been in a room at the time when someone, not you, was under the influence of a mystical force?

P.A.:   I have had no evidence that either I or the other was passing through such an experience. I only remember two or three occasions when an analysand of mine actually claimed a mystical origin for the event. I have been more impressed when the individual was not consciously making such a claim.

ROBIN: Why? Surely 'unconscious' claims are far more open to mis-interpretation.

P.A.:   Agreed – I do not wish to decry the events of which I know nothing. But I have been compelled to notice that 'fashions' in beliefs, in theories, in varieties of psychoanalysis and in psychoanalysts, are as plentiful as fashions in cosmetics. I suspect that the fundamental source of fashion, whether in people, religions, 'scientific' theories or holiday resorts is, or ought to be, one goal of our curiosity. As individuals we cannot hope to do more than reach some outlying, peripheral goal and please ourselves by claiming that it is ultimate truth; or alternatively fall into despair at discovering our insignificance.

ROLAND: Most people with any common sense know that.

P.A.:   "Most people with any common sense" are, in my experience, very few people indeed. Common sense is only rarely in fashion. "Real" common sense, in contrast to cosmetic common sense, tells too many uncomfortable things. "Eyes that have seen colossal storms and terraqueous convulsions" are not likely to be sought after if they reveal danger and the emotional state appropriate to it.

(*CWB XIV*, p. 90)

From *A Key to A Memoir of the Future*

"Eyes that have seen colossal storms and terraqueous convulsions" a reference to Thomas Hardy's *Tess of the d'Urbervilles*, ch. 43: ". . . gaunt spectral creatures with tragical eyes – eyes which had witnessed scenes of cataclysmal horror in inaccessible polar regions of a magnitude such as no human being had ever conceived, in curdling temperatures that no man could endure; which had beheld the crash of icebergs and the slide of snow-hills by the shooting light of the Aurora; been half blinded by the whirl of colossal storms and terraqueous distortions."

(*CWB XIV*, p. 171)

[356]　Pleasure and pain

P.A.:　　Pleasure, particularly sexual pleasure, is one of the earliest pleasing events to be appreciated. Thanks to Freud it is not difficult to detect the existence of that pleasure.

ROLAND:　Surely that is general. I have always regarded Freud's discovery as somewhat naïve and over-rated.

P.A.:　　Freud himself was astonished that something so commonplace should create such a furore – but it did. Today, the theories of psychoanalysis have to be formulated in tired language and it is thought that the *meaning* of Freud's formulations is correspondingly tired. Illnesses don't become tired, and mental pain is as fresh and lively as ever it was. People who complain of mental pain are regarded as being as unreasonable as an ancient Egyptian would have been had he complained about what *we* diagnose as syphilis. Mental pain is regarded, even today, as a fuss about nothing. *Theories* are discussed – rarely the pain the sufferer inflicts or embodies. I remember being called to see a German prisoner of war who complained of pains in his wrists which had been caused, he said, by the British who chained his hands together when he surrendered at Narvik. A German naval officer captured at the same time was called to interpret. I could do nothing because the officer, instead of translating, made use of the opportunity to express his contempt for the man and for the British for resorting to such barbarous tricks. I did not respond to his own self-hate for surrendering either to us or, as I began later to suspect, to the Nazis.

(*CWB XIV*, p. 97)

[357]   Klein, Freud, Charcot

P.A.:   ... Many analysts repudiate Klein's extension of psychoanalysis as elaborated by Freud. I found it difficult to understand Klein's theory and practice though — perhaps because — I was being analysed by Melanie Klein herself. But after great difficulty I began to feel there was truth in the interpretations she gave and that they brought illumination to many experiences, mine and others, which had previously been incomprehensible, discrete and unrelated. Metaphorically, light began to dawn and then, with increasing momentum, all was clear.

ALICE: Did you remain convinced by further experience?

P.A.:   Yes — and no. One of the painful, alarming features of continued experience was the fact that I had certain patients with whom I employed interpretations based on my previous experience with Melanie Klein, and though I felt that I employed them correctly and could not fault myself, none of the good results that I anticipated occurred.

ROBIN: In other words the objections raised by contemporary psychoanalytic colleagues to Kleinian theories were being supported by your own experience of futility?

P.A.:   That was indeed one of my anxieties and one I did not feel disposed to ignore.

ROLAND: But you must have ignored it. Did you not feel you had a vested interest in continuing to support psychoanalysis, Kleinian or otherwise?

P.A.:   I was aware that I would be likely to cherish my preconceptions. Every now and then something would occur that convinced me I would be foolish to abandon my ideas as if they were clearly wrong. In fact it was clear that they were not always wrong. So — it became a problem of discrimination.

ROLAND: What led you to persist?

P.A.:   Partly a chance recapitulation of Freud's description of the impression created on him by Charcot's insistence on continued observation of facts — unexplained facts — until a pattern began to emerge; partly his admission that the "trauma of birth" might afford a plausible but misleading reason for believing that there was this caesura between natal and prenatal. There were other impressive "caesuras" — for example, between conscious and unconscious — which might be similarly misleading. Melanie Klein's interpretations began to have a vaguely but truly illuminating quality. It was as if, literally as well as metaphorically, light began to grow, night was replaced by dawn. I was aware, with a new comprehension, of the passage of Milton's invocation to light at the commencement of the Third Book of *Paradise Lost*. I re-read the whole of *Paradise Lost* in a way which I had not previously done, although I had always been devoted to Milton. This was true likewise of Virgil's *Aeneid* – though it involved much painful regret for the way in which I had wasted and hated the privilege of being taught by certain schoolmasters whose devotion had but a sorry response from me. Let me now praise men who ought to have been famous. For my own pleasure I write their names: E. A. Knight, F. S. Sutton, Charles Mellows. Later came the debt to my friends whom I will not name lest it cause embarrassment.

ROBIN: I appreciate the point, but I would like to know more about the "illumination".

P.A.:   Had you not better ask yourself to whom you owe such illumination as has saved your journey from being plunged in everlasting night or, worse still, in the blaze of everlasting certainty and good fortune?

(*CWB XIV*, pp. 121–122)

Bion's analytic position?

A noticeable number of analysts in England have thought that Bion lost his analytic position in the mid 1960s and do not give weight to his later work. On his part, Bion thought something was going wrong in psychoanalysis in England. From comments he makes, he thought we underestimate the subtle attack on our capacity to think and that we cover over the problem by turning to theory.

A related question sometimes asked is whether one can understand his later work without knowledge of Klein's work. On hearing that I was going to Los Angeles to give a paper, more than one colleague commented, "they won't want to hear about Klein"! I thought I would have a look for references to Klein in his later writings and see what he himself might say about Klein after his move to Los Angeles. I came across the above quote, in which he says Melanie Klein's interpretations began to have a vaguely but truly illuminating quality.

In the quote Bion also refers to "the continued observation of unexplained facts until a pattern began to emerge". I think it is on the practice of this that the scientific basis of our work rests. It is of central importance that our observations should be as differentiated as possible from the psychoanalytic theory we draw on in understanding their meaning. What Bion means by observation is not a detached intellectual position. We would not be able to observe the internal world in this way. It involves allowing the patient to have as great an impact on us as possible.

John Milton

Invocation to light

Paradise Lost

HAIL, holy Light, offspring of Heaven first-born!
Or of the Eternal coeternal beam
May I express thee unblamed? since God is light,
And never but in unapproached light
Dwelt from eternity-dwelt then in thee,
Bright effluence of bright essence increate!
Or hear'st thou rather pure Ethereal Stream,
Whose fountain who shall tell? Before the Sun,
Before the Heavens, thou wert, and at the voice
Of God, as with a mantle, didst invest
The rising World of waters dark and deep,
Won from the void and formless Infinite!

[358]   Pre-natal experiences

P.A.:   . . . the fetus must have inherent characteristics which sooner or later become apparent. If the fetus subsequently becomes an intelligent or wise or gifted man or woman, why should it not, as it approaches full term, show prototypes of the sort of behaviour expected of children and adults? It occurred to me that a fetus might hear noises, see sights, smell odours, in a watery fluid such as the amniotic fluid and meconium. The significance of this did not become apparent at once, but I felt that past experiences with patients would have been less obscure if I had dared to imagine that the emotions displayed might be pre-natal. They were often expressed in a manner which differed from commonly accepted modes of expression.

ALICE: How did that differ from any other person?

P.A.:   That is what I asked myself. I wondered whether the highly endowed fetus might employ the mechanisms which psychoanalysis had made familiar in the treatment of children and adults, even before birth, precociously. Such a precociously developed fetus could try to rid itself both of the senses when they became sensitive to changes of pressure in the watery medium, and of the feelings, "emotions" of sub-thalamic intensity; it might be prey to experiences unmodified in the way we expect them to be by the "higher" centres. Then comes the "trauma of birth". . . .

BION: In the meantime – if I may join in the discussion – his premature personality continues its life in uneasy proximity with his post-mature lodger in the same physical soma. Sometimes the psycho-somatic partner demonstrates his soulful qualities; sometimes his soma-psychotic demands acknowledgment and recognition of his physical and psychotic gifts. I describe the situation in naïvely pictorial terms. There are other descriptions, but most of them have been impregnated with pejorative connotations.

ALICE: Such as "hypochondria"?

BION: Yes; or "crazy", or "insane", or "difficult", or "tiresome".

(*CWB XIV*, pp. 124–126)

[359]   Body and Mind, Psyche and Soma

TERM: I am *mind* and my mental membranes make me able to reach far beyond my feet.

EM: Now you have muddled me. I shall be *body*; forever I shall gird at your mind.

MIND: Hullo! Where have you sprung from?

BODY: What – you again? I am Body; you can call me Soma if you like. Who are you?

MIND: Call me Psyche – Psyche-Soma.

BODY: Soma-Psyche.

MIND: We must be related. . . .

BODY: . . . It is the meaning of pain that I am sending to you; the words get through – which I have not sent – but the meaning is lost.

MIND: What is that amusing little affair sticking out? I like it. It has a mind of its own – just like me.

BODY: It's just like me – has a body of its own. That's why it is so erect. Your mind – no evidence for it at all.

MIND: Don't be ridiculous. I suffer anxiety as much as you have pain. In fact I have pain about which you know nothing. I suffered intensely when you were rejected. I asked you to call me Psyche and promised to call you Soma.

SOMA: All right Psyche; I don't admit that there is any such person other than a figment of my digestion.

PSYCHE: Who are you talking to then?

SOMA: I'm talking to myself and the sound is reflected back by one of my fetal membranes.

PSYCHE: Your fetal membranes! Ha, ha! Very good! Is that your pun or mine?

SOMA: It's the only language you understand.

PSYCHE: It's the only language you hear. All you talk is pain.

SOMA: All you respect is pain or lack of it. The only time I can get any-thing over to you is pain-talk from the hills.

                                        (*CWB XIV*, pp. 8–9)

BION: . . . the individual often behaves as if his wisdom and intelligence would be contaminated if he allowed himself to recognize that his body thought. . . .

                                        (*CWB XIV*, p. 128)

In this conversation we hear reference to the language of the body and the language of the mind: two different languages. We are more used to conceiving of the mind/body relation in terms of the representations of the body in the mind. Bion has the body speak its own language.

While the primary link between body and mind in Freud's model of the body/mind relation is sexuality, by contrast, the primary link we see in Bion's model of the body/mind relation is one of K, the "knowing" of the mind by the body and the body by the mind.

From here my own thoughts were along the following path:

Might the mind–body relation be specifically affected by the Oedipus complex? Freud's account of the Oedipus complex foregrounds sexual desire rooted in the body. In the resolution of the complex, the child both gives up the parent as the sexually desired object and also introjects parental authority into his or her own self (superego). The child is thus both withdrawing bodily sexual desire back from being focused on the parents and, at the same time, gaining a strengthened, more independent mind. Might we consider that the body of the young Oedipus (male or female), into which the sexual desire for the object has been withdrawn, could now depend more on the containment of the mind, and the mind (now more independent of the object) depend more on the containment of the body? Does a healthy experience of the Oedipal couple facilitate the "coupling" of the mind and body in the child? This can be at least tentatively investigated clinically. Do changes in the patient's relation to the Oedipal couple augur in detectable changes in their mind/body relation?

Part V

Epilogue

Chapter 28

Last quotes

Introduction

The Bions returned to England in 1979, moving into a house in Oxford at the beginning of October. Bion died on 8 November 1979.

Francesca Bion

> It has been suspected and believed that Bion wanted to return to England because he knew that he faced imminent death, but although it would have been natural for him to accept that at the age of eighty-two his days were numbered, taking steps to keep a foothold in California and agreeing to work with a group in Bombay in January 1980, were not the actions of a dying man – unless he is given to gross denial. Bion was, above all else, scrupulously honest with himself and others.
>
> He became ill in the third week of October: myeloid leukaemia, diagnosed on November 1st, developed with extraordinary rapidity and, mercifully, quickly led to his death on November 8th.
>
> (Francesca Bion 1994, *CWB XV*, pp. 105–106)

Isabel Menzies-Lyth

> . . . He said to us that day, "Life is full of surprises, mostly unpleasant", because he had just heard he'd got leukaemia. . . . He was reading a book which he had been given by his son, called *Far Pavillions*, about India. You know he was brought up in India . . . That was the last time we saw him.

> BP: How long before he died?
>
> IML: The beginning of the following week. That was a Friday afternoon and I think he died on the Monday or Tuesday.
>
> BP: So it was very rapid?
>
> IML: Ah, well yes, it's difficult, you know, with these old people with leukaemia . . . I don't know whether his was a sudden onset or

quite what it was. Anyway he didn't survive a week after that . . .
(Pause) It was a great loss, great loss to all of us . . . His wife is
still here, she lives down the road.

(Pecotic 2002, p. 33)

Quotes

From Francesca Bion's "Envoi"
Francesca Bion after Bion's death

360   A present to you
361   Ghost of P.A. and the Ghost of Auser
362   And did you find it interesting?
363   From that warfare there is no release
364   One never knows which side up the leaf will land
365   Last quote

From Francesca Bion's "Envoi"

On the blank pages [of Bridges' *Spirit of Man*] he wrote some poems and quotations of his own choice, among them a poem by Flecker, "To a Poet a Thousand Years Hence . . ."

> I who am dead a thousand years
> And wrote this sweet archaic song
> Send you my words for messengers
> The way I shall not pass along.
> I care not if you bridge the seas
> Or ride secure the cruel sky
> Or build consummate palaces
> Of metal or of masonry.
> But have you wine and music still,
> And statues and a bright-eyed love,
> And foolish thoughts of good or ill,
> And prayers to them who sit above?
> How shall we conquer? Like a wind
> That falls at eve our fancies blow,
> And old Maeonides the blind
> Said it three thousand years ago.
> O friend unseen, unborn, unknown,
> Student of our sweet English tongue,
> Read out my words at night alone,
> I was a poet, I was young.
> Since I can never see your face
> And never shake you by the hand,
> I send my soul through time and space
> To greet you. You will understand.

He died as he had lived – with courage. He accepted the end of his life philosophically, adhering to his belief in the advice, "Do not strive officiously to keep alive." On 14 November we stood in Happisburgh churchyard on the cliffs high above the North Sea. Here, in his "beloved Norfolk" of bracing winds, wide skies, bright light, dear to him since boyhood, the ashes were buried; here he was always happy.

He would often quote this poem of George Herbert's on waking to a morning of sunlight – hastening to add that many thought it poor verse, but he found it beautiful.

> *"Virtue"*
>
> Sweet day, so cool, so calm, so bright!
> The bridal of the earth and sky –
> The dew shall weep thy fall tonight;

> For thou must die.
> Sweet rose, whose hue angry and brave
> Bids the rash gazer wipe his eye,
> Thy root is ever in its grave,
> And thou must die.
> Sweet spring, full of sweet days and roses,
> A box where sweets compacted lie,
> My music shows ye have your closes,
> And all must die.
> Only a sweet and virtuous soul,
> Like season'd timber, never gives;
> But though the whole world turn to coal,
> Then chiefly lives.

Our grand-daughter, aged seven, put into words what so many of us felt after Wilfred's death – "I didn't realize I knew Grandpa so well." His love, wisdom, affectionate humour, sympathetic concern permeated our lives. I believe we shall continue to feel, sometimes with surprise, that we didn't realize we knew him so well.

(CWB II, pp. 263–265)

Francesca Bion after Bion's death

I have included this piece to let readers know something about Francesca Bion's life after Bion's death. She died in 2015, 36 years after Bion. During these years she did considerable work in the editing and publication of Bion's writings and recordings. Analysts from countries around the world speak warmly of her support of their study of Bion. With Chris Mawson, she edited *The Complete Work of Bion* and was present at its launch. The following quote is from Paulo C. Sandler's obituary for her.

Paulo C. Sandler

. . . You all know what happened after this [Sandler's account of her adult life up to meeting Bion – see the earlier entry on Francesca Bion]: the widowed Francesca married with the widowed Dr Bion and she had not only the opportunity of mothering Dr Bion's daughter Parthenope, but to enjoy maternity twice, with Nicola and Julian. Both Dr Bion and Francesca were fortunate enough: Peter, Luigi and Nitaya graced their life with music – literally and metaphorically, with four granddaughters and two grandsons, including a pair of twins! Most of you know that Parthenope was an analyst, Nicola is an editor, first at Oxford University and now at Tate Modern and Julian, an internationally acknowledged physician, an authority in intensive care.

I may just tell that she dignified faced the last two serious "catastrophic changes" in her life, the death of Dr Bion and the death of Parthenope and her lovely daughter Patricia, in 1998. . . .

From 1983 to 1993 my contact with Mrs Bion followed on in epistolary forms as well as by frequent phone calls. . . .

With the exception of two, Francesca answered all from the 300 and plus queries [for the translation of *A Memoir of the Future*]: full of witty, wise, good humored as well sad comments about human life and the criminal idiocy of politicians. I never heard any comment that could be prejudiced and no gossips at all. She prized intelligence but not erudition . . . She had to review Bion's manuscripts and found the correct phrases – which are reproduced not only in the Brazilian edition (from 2002 to 2007) but now in the *Complete Works*. . . .

Francesca was awarded with a Honorary Membership by the British Psychoanalytic Society: she phoned me to tell this: "Now, like you, I am a Honorary Member!" . . .

In 2013, we talked by phone for the last time. She asked me: "When you will come here to visit me again? I am 90 and I will not be around for too much time." . . . She well knew that I was severely ill in that time. I was not able to go; since then, my correspondence with her was made though Nicola, who was able to deal with e-mails and inherited her mother's forbearance and graciousness.

Nicola and Julian invited me to Francesca's burial: Julian wrote me in the next day of her death. . . . I wished to write this obituary, but my mourning took an excessive time to be dispelled: only now I found the internal means to do it, to live without Francesca.

(Paulo Cesar Sandler, personal communication, September 2015)

[360]   A present to you

1971 Los Angeles: a letter to his children

From *The Other Side of Genius*

As Mummy and I were sleeping the profound sleep of innocence there was suddenly a devilish and horrible noise. "There's that bloody picture down again", I thought angrily, determined not to be fooled again as I was last time when it nearly brained us and I thought it was an earthquake. Well, this time it wasn't the picture. Mummy dived to get under the bed – she couldn't, it is too low and there is no room. I took my usual precautions – got under the bed clothes. This scheme – of which I make a present to you – has always worked and is a sovereign cure and protection against mosquitoes, 5.9 howitzer shells, tigers, phosgene, mustard gas, bad dreams and earthquakes. You cannot always tell which is which when you are asleep and it's very useful to have something which is a cure for the lot.

(*CWB II*, pp. 226–227)

[361]   Ghost of P.A. and the Ghost of Auser

From *A Memoir of the Future, Book 2: The Past Presented*

The quote is a conversation between the Ghost of Auser (Asser, Bion's the second in command at the Battle of Amiens), P.A. (Psychoanalyst) and Ghost of P.A. (Ghost of Psychoanalyst).

GHOST OF AUSER: Aren't you . . .?

P.A.:   No, I'm P.A.

GHOST OF AUSER: You reminded me of – ah, there you are! I thought I might find you here.

GHOST OF P.A.:   When you knew me I was a ghost of myself – at Berles-aux-Bois. I loved you, but I couldn't save you.

GHOST OF AUSER: Never mind, old boy. You were wonderful! Sorry I lost my tank, but there were a lot of them and they shot me through the heart. What's this dismal hole? Seems to be some sort of Transit Camp. . . .

GHOST OF AUSER: (to P.A. and Ghost of P.A.) Well, how's things? How have you been getting on? It's jolly nice seeing you again – I hope you are glad to see me too.

P.A.:   I am indeed – but truth to tell I've always been afraid of meeting you.

GHOST OF AUSER: Afraid of meeting me – whatever for? You were one of the bravest men I ever met! I wanted to get a V.C. – one better than you.

GHOST OF P.A.:   You only saw me wearing my Hero dress. . . .

P.A.:   Ask my ghost what spectacle was presented by those of us who lived to grow old.

GHOST OF P.A.:   Do you think I was any better *before* English Farm?

P.A.:   On consideration – no; nor after. The actions of the just – the generous man – stay just; the mean man stays mean. Whatever the dress in which we clothe our "selves" the structure lives longer than the character we hang upon it – the "glories" of our blood and state.

GHOST OF AUSER: I wanted to ask you – did we win?

(*A long, long silence.*)

(*CWB XIII*, pp. 189–191)

From *A Key to A Memoir of the Future*

English Farm   the name of a minute area in the mud of the battlefield of Ypres.

(*CWB XIV*, p. 169)

[362]   And did you find it interesting?

The last lines of Bion's novel *A Memoir of the Future*

ROBIN: Why catastrophe?

P.A.:   Because unless the human animal learns to become expert in discrimination, he will be in imminent danger of the *wrong* choice.

ALICE: Nuclear war, for example.

P.A.:   There are no labels attached to most options; there is no substitute for the growth of wisdom. Wisdom or oblivion – take your
choice. From that warfare there is no release.

On a separate page:

A: *I see you turn to the last page as you always used to do.*

Q: *Of course. Last time you told me how much it had cost you to publish. Did
you find it interesting? How was America – North and South?*

A: *Marvellous; a nice change from the Third Battle of Wipers.*

Q: *Lots more since then. And more to come – which reminds me; I must rush; I
have a date to meet Fate.*

A: *Bye-bye – happy holocaust!*

And on a separate further page:

... & EPILOGUE

... FUGUE

... DONA ES REQUIEM ... MANY

*All my life I have been imprisoned, frustrated, dogged by common-sense, rea-
son, memories, desires and – greatest bug-bear of all – understanding and being
understood. This is an attempt to express my rebellion, to say "Good-bye" to all
that. It is my wish, I now realize doomed to failure, to write a book unspoiled by
any tincture of common-sense, reason, etc. (see above). So although I would write,
"Abandon Hope all ye who expect to find any facts – scientific, aesthetic or religious – in this book", I cannot claim to have succeeded. All these will, I fear, be seen
to have left their traces, vestiges, ghosts hidden within these words; even sanity, like
"cheerfulness", will creep in. However successful my attempt, there would always
be the risk that the book "became" acceptable, respectable, honoured and unread.
"Why write then?" you may ask. To prevent someone who KNOWS from filling the
empty space – but I fear I am being "reasonable", that great Ape. Wishing you all
a Happy Lunacy and a Relativistic Fission...*

(*CWB XIV*, pp. 136–138)

[363] From that warfare there is no release

From *The Italian Seminars*

To fall back again on the simple model of actual physical warfare: if, by any chance, we survive, we can learn something about ourselves. A book written in the First World War described a situation of perpetual and never-ceasing war – the war of the mind. The writer quoted the statement which was made long before psychoanalysis had even been thought of: "From that warfare there is no release". Here we can make breaks in this discussion, take rests, but that does not mean that the warfare takes a rest – it does not. Disease – mental disease, physical disease – does not take a holiday. That is why we have to be so robust, so healthy. Whatever our difficulties may be, we have to remember to be concerned not with our problems, but with the work in hand – the work which never stops whether we are there to do it or not. There was a famous warrior named Cr[i]lon to whom Henry IV said, "Go hang yourself, brave Crillon; we fought at Arc and you were not there.

(*CWB IX*, pp. 183–184)

[364]   One never knows which side up the leaf will land

From *The Italian Seminars*

> Bion: I thank you very much for that expression of gratitude. I hope it doesn't appear to be ungracious if I say that I can compare your description of my contributions with the fact of which I am aware and which I don't very much like. The nearest image I can give to it is this: like a leaf falling off a tree – one never knows which side up it will land.
>
> (*CWB IX*, p. 194)

The quote is from the last moments of *The Italian Seminars* on 17 July 1977. Earlier in the seminar Bion has referred to the time when he had been Director of the London Clinic. As some readers will recall, a number of the clinic rooms were up in the attic of Mansfield House, reached by steep steps. Concerned that patients or candidates may hurt themselves by falling and the potential risk of patients throwing themselves out of a window, Bion went to investigate. He had all the possible changes done (these are pretty limited), but couldn't make it a foolproof setting. As he continued to talk I think one can hear his deep awareness that he has encouraged people to think more of the thoughts that might usually be held off. He cannot guarantee which side up the leaf will fall – whether or not the result will be fruitful, welcomed – and is aware of having to leave people to it.

Bion's comment "like a leaf falling off a tree – one never knows which side up it will land" reminded me of a poem by Walt Whitman.

Walt Whitman (1819–1892)

Leaves of Grass

As I lay with my head in your lap, Camerado,
The confession I made I resume – what I said to you in the open air I resume:
I know I am restless, and make others so;
I know my words are weapons, full of danger, full of death;
Indeed I am myself the real soldier;
It is not he, there, with his bayonet, and not the red-striped artilleryman;
For I confront peace, security, and all the settled laws, to unsettle them;
I am more resolute because all have denied me, than I could ever have been had all accepted me;
I heed not, and have never heeded, either experience, cautions, majorities, nor ridicule;

And the threat of what is call'd hell is little or nothing to me;
And the lure of what is call'd heaven is little or nothing to me;

. . . Dear camerado! I confess I have urged you onward with me, and still
  urge you, without the least idea what is our destination,
Or whether we shall be victorious, or utterly quell'd and defeated.

[365]   Last quote

From Bion's Introduction to his anthology of poems (unfinished)

From Francesca Bion's "Envoi"

It is easy in this age of the plague – not of poverty and hunger, but of plenty, surfeit and gluttony – to lose our capacity for awe. It is as well to be reminded by the poet Herman Melville that there are many ways of reading books, but very few of reading them properly – that is, with awe. How much the more is it true of reading people.

Someone asked, "Why climb mountains?" "Because they are there" was the reply. I would add that there are some who would prefer to postpone the exercise till their rugosities, heights, depths and declivities have been worn to a uniform flatness. The Grand Canyon will be tamed; Everest, Kanchen-junga neon-lit; the pass of Glencoe deserted by its ghosts; Nanda Devi no longer the home of the Seven Rishis; the Master of Stair a phantom without bones. William Blake, in Gnomic Verses said, "Great things are done when men and mountains meet". . . .

(*CWB II*, p. 263)

Timeline

1897	Born 8 September, Muttra, India.
1905	Sent at age of 8 years to Bishops Stortford boarding school in England, never to return to India.
1915	Leaves school (just before his 18th birthday) and joins the 5th Royal Tank Regiment as an officer.
1917	20 November: The Battle of Cambrai; Bion is awarded the DSO (Distinguished Service Order) and the French Legion of Honour.
1919–21	Queen's College Oxford. Bion reads History, captains the swimming team and obtains a rugger blue. He meets H. J. Paton, Professor of Philosophy, through whom he becomes interested in Kant.
1921–22	Attends Poitiers University to "improve his knowledge of French literature and language" (to my knowledge, he only mentions this once in his writings – in his novel).
1922	Returns to Bishops Stortford school to teach.
1923	Studies medicine at University College London; works with Wilfred Trotter, a surgeon and author of *Instincts of the Herd in Peace and War* (1916).
1932	Joins the staff at the Tavistock Clinic, and also works part-time at the Maida Vale Hospital for Epilepsy and Paralysis, and then at the Institute for the Scientific Treatment of Delinquency (now called the Portman Clinic).
1934	Samuel Beckett begins psychotherapy with Bion.
1935	14 October: Bion takes Beckett to a lecture given by Carl Jung at the Tavistock Clinic.
1937	Meets the psychoanalyst John Rickman and goes into analysis with him. This is brought to an end in 1939 by the advent of the Second World War. The two men go on to become colleagues.
1938	Begins his training at the Institute of Psychoanalysis.
1940	At the outbreak of the Second World War, joins the RAMC [Royal Army Medical Corps]. He instigates leaderless groups for the

	selection of officers and, together with Rickman, sets up the Northfield experiment.
1940s	Writes a number of papers for medical journals about Northfield and related subjects.
1945	His first wife, the well-known actress Betty Jardine, tragically dies in childbirth, leaving a baby daughter, Parthenope, whom he brings up.
1945	With the war over, returns to the Tavistock and develops a method of group therapy and a new theory of group dynamics.
1945	In November, resumes his analytic training and begins analysis with Melanie Klein. Paula Heimann is one of his supervisors.
1946	Klein publishes "Notes on Some Schizoid Mechanisms".
1948	Bion qualifies as a psychoanalyst.
1950	1 November: gives his Membership paper "The Imaginary Twin" to the British Psychoanalytical Society [*CWB VI*].
1951	Rickman dies, aged 60.
1951	Bion marries Francesca McCallum (née Purnell). They have two children: Julian, born in July 1952, and Nicola, born in June 1955.
1952	"Group Dynamics: A Re-View", published in the *International Journal of Psycho-analysis (IJPA)*.
1953	Finishes his analysis with Klein.
1953	Gives his paper "Notes on the Theory of Schizophrenia" at the International Psychoanalytical Association (IPA) Congress in London.
1954	"Notes on the Theory of Schizophrenia" published in the *IJPA*.
1955	Gives his paper "Development of Schizophrenic Thought" at the IPA Congress in Geneva.
1956	"Development of Schizophrenic Thought" published in the *IJPA*.
1956–62	Director of the London Clinic of Psychoanalysis.
1957	"Differentiation of the Psychotic from the Non-Psychotic Personality" published in the *IJPA*.
1958	"On Hallucination" published in the *IJPA*.
1958	"On Arrogance" published in the *IJPA*.
1959	"Attacks on Linking" published in the *IJPA*.
1960	Melanie Klein dies, aged 78, on 22 September.
1960–67	Chairman of the Melanie Klein Trust – he took over directly from Klein.
1960	*Learning from Experience* published.
1961	Gives his paper "A Theory of Thinking" at the 22nd IPA Congress in Edinburgh.
1962	"A Theory of Thinking" published in *IJPA*.
1962–65	President of the British Psychoanalytical Society.
1963	*Elements of Psycho-Analysis* published.
1965	*Transformations: Change from Learning to Growth* published.
1965	"Notes on Memory and Desire" given to the British Psychoanalytical Society on 16 June.

1967	Invited to work for two weeks in Los Angeles.
1967	"Notes on Memory and Desire" (a brief paper, only three pages long) appears in a Californian publication, *The Psychoanalytic Forum*.
1967	*Second Thoughts: Selected Papers on Psycho-Analysis* published (the papers of the 1950s and early 1960s collected together and published together with a "Commentary", which contains his "second thoughts" on the papers).
1966–68	Member of the Training Committee.
1968	Decides to move to Los Angeles.
1968	August: invited to work in Buenos Aires for two weeks.
1969	August: Invited to Amherst College in Massachusetts for a Group Relations conference.
1970	*Attention and Interpretation: A Scientific Approach to Insight in Psycho-Analysis and Groups* published.
1969–71	"A time of adjustment, of building up a practice, and of setting to work on 'The Dream' which became the first book of the trilogy *A Memoir of the Future*" (Francesca Bion 1994, p. 101).
1972	Gave three talks to the Psychoanalytical Society in Rome.
1973–74	Brazilian lectures.
1973	Comments in a letter to his children that his novel *A Memoir of the Future* is "about done". The first volume, *The Dream*, is published in 1975, followed by *The Past Presented* in 1977, and *The Dawn of Oblivion* in 1979. The three were to be finally published in one volume in 1991.
1974	Invited to Rio de Janeiro for two weeks, followed by one week in São Paulo.
1975	Visits Brasilia for a month.
1976–79	Visits include Topeka, Kansas; London, including *The Tavistock Seminars* (four times); Rome, *The Italian Seminars* (twice); Lyon; Paris; New York; and Washington, DC.
1977	Works on his autobiography; his novel, *The Memoir of the Future*, is "already done" (Parthenope Bion Talamo).
1978	Two weeks in São Paulo.
1979	Early in 1979 the Bions decide to return to England.
1979	Dies of leukaemia on 8 November.

Bibliography

Abel-Hirsch, N. (2010). The life instinct. *International Journal of Psychoanalysis*, *91*: 1055–1071.

Aguayo, J. (2017). The early psychoanalytic work of James Grotstein (1966–1981): Turning a Kleinian/Bionian tide away from American ego psychology. In: A. Reiner (Ed.), *Of Things Invisible to Mortal Sight: Celebrating the Work of James Grotstein* (pp. 1–18). London, Karnac.

Aguayo, J., & Malin, B. D. (2013). *Wilfred Bion: Los Angeles Seminars and Supervision*. London: Karnac.

Bagehot, W. (1872). *Physics and Politics*. London: Kegan Paul, Trench, Trubner and Co, 1903. Reprinted Kitchner, ON: Batoche Books, 2001.

Barker, P. (1991). *Regeneration*. New York: Viking.

Baruzzi, A. (2011). Introduction. In: P. Bion Talamo, *Maps for Psychoanalytic Exploration* (pp. xxi–xxiv). London: Karnac, 2015.

Beckett, S. (1952). *Waiting for Godot*. In: Samuel Beckett, *The Complete Dramatic Works*. London: Faber & Faber, 1986.

Beckett, S. (1957). *Happy Days*. In: Samuel Beckett, *The Complete Dramatic Works*. London: Faber & Faber, 1986.

Beckett, S. (1961). *Endgame*. In: Samuel Beckett, *The Complete Dramatic Works*. London: Faber & Faber, 1986.

Beckett, S. (1959). *The Beckett Trilogy: Molloy, Malone Dies, The Unnameable*. London: Calder.

Bion, F. (1981). Envoi [to *All My Sins Remembered*]. In: *The Complete Works of Bion, Vol. II* (pp. 261–265). London: Karnac, 2014.

Bion, F. (1985). Foreword [to *All My Sins Remembered*]. In: *The Complete Works of Bion, Vol. II* (p. 7). London: Karnac, 2014.

Bion, F. (1990). Foreword [to *Cogitations*]. In: *The Complete Works of Bion, Vol. XI* (p. 7). London: Karnac, 2014.

Bion, F. (1994). The days of our years. In: *The Complete Works of Bion, Vol. XV* (Appendix A, pp. 91–111). London: Karnac, 2014.

Bion, F. (2005). Editorial note [to *The Italian Seminars*]. In: *The Complete Works of Bion, Vol. IX* (p. 97). London: Karnac, 2014.

Bion, W. R. (1957). Differentiation of the psychotic from the non-psychotic personalities. In: *Second Thoughts* (pp. 43–64). New York: Aronson, 1967.

Bion, W. R. (1962). *Learning from Experience*. London: Heinemann.

Bion, W. R. (1963). *Elements of Psycho-Analysis.* . London: Heinemann.

Bion, W. R. (1965). *Transformations.* . London: Heinemann.

Bion, W. R. (1970). *Attention and Interpretation.* London: Tavistock Publications, 1970.

Bion Talamo, P. (1997). Aftermath. In: C. Mawson (Ed.), *The Complete Works of Bion, Vol. III* (pp. 307–310). London: Karnac, 2014.

Bion Talamo, P. (2005). Bion, Wilfred Ruprecht (1897–1979). In: A. de Mijolla (Ed.), *International Dictionary of Psychoanalysis* (p. 183). New York: Thomson Gale.

Bion Talamo, P. (2011). *Maps for Psychoanalytic Exploration.* London: Karnac, 2015.

Bollas, C. (1987). *The Shadow of the Object: Psychoanalysis of the Unthought Known.* London: Free Association Books.

Birksted-Breen, D. (2003). Time and the après-coup. *International Journal of Psychoanalysis, 84* (6): 1501–1515.

Britton, R. (1994). Publication anxiety: Conflict between communication and affiliation. *International Journal of Psychoanalysis, 75*: 1213–1224.

Britton, R. (1998). Taming Wild Thoughts. By W. R. Bion [Book review]. *International Journal of Psychoanalysis, 79*: 817–819.

Britton, R. (2003). Common and uncommon ground: Panelist's response. *Journal of the American Psychoanalytic Association, 51* (4): 1335–1337.

Britton, R. (2008). *A Beam of Intense Darkness*: Wilfred Bion's Legacy to Psychoanalysis by James S. Grotstein. London: Karnac; 2007. *Fort Da, 14* (2): 117–123.

Britton, R., Chused, J., Ellman, S., & Likierman, M. (2006). Panel II: The Oedipus complex, the primal scene, and the superego. *Journal of Infant, Child and Adolescent Psychotherapy,* 5(3): 282–307.

Britton, R., Feldman, N., Stein, R., & Tucker, S. (2010). Roundtable Discussion 2, 31 March 2007. *The Psychoanalytic Review, 97* (2): 303–335.

Bronstein, C. (2015). Bridging the gap: From soma-psychosis to psychosomatics. In: H. B. Levine & G. Civitarese (Eds.), *The Bion Tradition* (pp. 239–251). London: Karnac.

Brown, L. J. (2005). The cognitive effects of trauma: Reversal of alpha function and the formation of a beta screen. *Psychoanalytic Quarterly, 74*: 397–420.

Brown, L. J. (2012). Bion's discovery of alpha function: Thinking under fire on the battlefield and in the consulting room. *International Journal of Psychoanalysis, 93*: 1191–1214.

Civitarese, G. (2015). Sense, sensible, sense-able: The bodily but immaterial dimension of psychoanalytic elements. In: H. B. Levine & G. Civitarese (Eds.), *The Bion Tradition* (pp. 297–306). London: Karnac.

Conci, M. (2011). Bion and his first analyst, John Rickman (1891–1951): A revisitation of their relationship in the light of Rickman's personality and scientific production and of Bion's letters to him (1939–1951). *International Forum of Psychoanalysis, 20*: 68–86.

Culbert-Koehn, J. (2011). An analysis with Bion: An interview with James Gooch. *Journal of Analytical Psychology, 56* (1): 76–91.

De Bianchedi, E. T. (2005). Whose Bion? Who is Bion? *International Journal of Psychoanalysis, 86* (6): 1529–1534.

Duncan, D. (1981). A thought on the nature of psychoanalytic theory. *International Journal of Psychoanalysis, 62*: 339–349.

Dupont, J. (Ed.) (1995). *The Clinical Diary of Sándor Ferenczi.* Cambridge, MA: Harvard University Press.

Eigen, M. (1981). The area of faith in Winnicott, Lacan and Bion. *International Journal of Psychoanalysis, 62*: 413–433.

Eigen, M. (1993). *The Electrified Tightrope*. Northvale, NJ: Aronson.

Feldman, M. (1993). Aspects of reality, and the focus of interpretation. *Psychoanalytic Inquiry*, *13* (4): 274–295.

Ferro, A. (2011). Clinical implications of Bion's thought. In: C. Mawson (Ed.), *Bion Today*. Hove: Routledge.

Ferro, A. (2015). Changes in technique and in the theory of technique in a post-Bion field model. In: H. B. Levine & G. Civitarese (Eds.), *The Bion Tradition* (pp. 189–200). London: Karnac.

Flynn, D. (2014). On the "correlation" and disruption of knowing (Bion, "K"). Paper read at the Institute of Psychoanalysis/University of Essex joint event, "Bion and Observation", and at St John's College Oxford, Philosophy/Psychoanalysis research seminar.

Freud, E. L. (Ed.) (1961). *Letters of Sigmund Freud, 1873–1939*. London: Hogarth Press.

Freud, S. (1911). Formulations on the two principles of mental functioning. *Standard Edition, 12.*

Freud, S. (1916). Some character-types met with in psycho-analytic work. *Standard Edition, 14.*

Freud, S. (1917). Mourning and melancholia. *Standard Edition, 14.*

Freud, S. (1919). The "uncanny". *Standard Edition, 17.*

Freud, S. (1920). *Beyond the Pleasure Principle. Standard Edition, 18.*

Freud, S. (1923). *The Ego and the Id. Standard Edition, 19.*

Freud, S. (1930). *Civilization and Its Discontents. Standard Edition, 21.*

Freud, S. (1933). *New Introductory Lectures on Psycho-Analysis. Standard Edition, 22.*

Freud, S. (1950 [1895]). Project for a scientific psychology. *Standard Edition, 1.*

Frost, R. (1923). *Collected Poems by Henry Frost*. Vintage Classics. Philadelphia, PA: Henry Holt.

Green, A. (1973). On negative capability: A critical review of W. R. Bion's *Attention and Interpretation. International Journal of Psychoanalysis*, *54*: 115–119.

Green, A. (1992). Cogitations: By Wilfred R. Bion, edited with a Foreword by Francesca Bion [Book review]. *International Journal of Psychoanalysis*, *73*: 585–589.

Green, A. (1998). The primordial mind and the work of the negative. *International Journal of Psychoanalysis*, *79*: 649–665.

Greenson, R. (1965). The working alliance and the transference neurosis. *PsychoanalyticQuarterly*, *34*: 155–181.

Greenson, R. (1967). *The Technique and Practice of Psychoanalysis*, Vol. 1. New York: International Universities Press.

Grotstein, J. (1981). Who is the dreamer who dreams the dream, and who is the dreamer who understands it? In: J.S. Grotstein (Ed.), *Do I Dare Disturb the Universe? A Memorial to Wilfred R. Bion* (pp. 357–416). Beverly Hills: Caesura Press.

Grotstein, J. (2007). *A Beam of Intense Darkness: Wilfred Bion's Legacy to Psychoanalysis*. London: Karnac.

Grotstein, J. (1997). Bion's Transformation in "O" and the concept of the "Transcendent Position". Available at: http://www.sicap.it/merciai/bion/papers/grots.htm

Grotstein, J. (2013). Foreword. In: J. Aguayo & B. D. Malin (Eds.), *Wilfred Bion: Los Angeles Seminars and Supervision*. London: Karnac.

Guntrip, H. (1967). The concept of psychodynamic science. *International Journal of Psychoanalysis*, *48*: 32–43.

Heimann, P. (1943 [(1991)]). Some aspects of the role of introjection and projection in early development. In: P. King & R. Steiner (Eds), *The Freud–Klein Controversies*

(1941–1945) (pp. 502–530). London: Routledge, 1991. Republished in: M. Klein, P. Heimann, S. Isaacs, & J. Riviere (Eds), *Developments in Psychoanalysis* (pp. 122–169). London: Hogarth, 1952.

Heimann, P. (1950). On counter-transference. *International Journal of Psychoanalysis, 31*: 81–84.

Hinshelwood, R. D. (1997). The elusive concept of "internal objects" and the origins of the Klein group 1934–1943. *International Journal of Psychoanalysis, 78*: 877–897.

Hinshelwood, R. D. (2013). *Research on the Couch: Single Case Studies, Subjectivity and Psychoanalytic Knowledge*. London: Routledge.

Horovitz, M. (2015). A scream lurking in his silence [trans. A. Weller]. Paper presented at the Bion International Conference 2016, Milan.

Joseph, B. (1959). An aspect of the repetition compulsion. *International Journal of Psychoanalysis, 40*: 213–222.

Junqueira de Mattos, A. J. (2015). Impressions of my analysis with Dr. Bion. In: H. B. Levine & G. Civitarese (Eds.), *The Bion Tradition* (pp. 5–22). London: Karnac.

Kant, I. (1929). *Critique of Pure Reason*, trans. N. Kemp Smith. New York: Macmillan [*Kritik der reinem Vernunft*: First edition 1781; second edition 1787].

King, P., & Steiner, R. (1991). *The Freud–Klein Controversies 1941–45*. London: Tavistock/Routledge.

Kipling, R. (1906). *Puck of Pook's Hill*. London: Macmillan & Co.

Klein, M. (1935). A contribution to the genesis of manic-depressive states. *International Journal of Psychoanalysis, 16*: 145–174; reprinted in: *The Writings of Melanie Klein Vol. 1: Love Guilt and Reparation* (pp. 262–289). London: Hogarth Press, 1975.

Klein, M. (1946). Notes on some schizoid mechanisms. *International Journal of Psychoanalysis, 27*: 99–110.

Klein, M. (1957). Envy and gratitude. In: *The Writings of Melanie Klein, Vol. III: Envy and Gratitude and Other Works* (pp. 176–235). London: Hogarth Press.

Klein, M. (1958). On the development of mental functioning. *International Journal of Psychoanalysis, 39*: 84–90.

Khan, M. M. R. (1975). Introduction. In: D. W. Winnicott, *Through Paediatrics to Psycho-Analysis*. The International Psycho-Analytical Library, 100. London: Hogarth Press and the Institute of Psycho-Analysis.

Lacan, J. (1966). *Ecrits*, trans. Bruce Fink. New York: W.W. Norton, 2002.

Laplanche, J., & Pontalis, J. B. (1973). *The Language of Psycho-Analysis*, trans. D. Nicholson-Smith. London: Hogarth Press and the Institute of Psycho-Analysis.

Levi, P. (1963). *La Tregua*. Turin: Einaudi. *The Truce*, transl, S. Woolf. London: Bodley Head, 1965.

Levine, H. B. (2007). Truth, growth, and deception: The late seminars of Wilfred Bion: *The Italian Seminars/The Tavistock Seminars*. By Wilfred R Bion, 2005 [Book reviews]. *Journal of the American Psychoanalytic Association, 55* (2): 677–685.

Levine, H. B. (2015). Commentary on supervision, A42. In: H. B. Levine & G. Civitarese (Eds.), *The Bion Tradition* (pp. 99–104). London: Karnac.

Loemker, L. (1956). Letter LX. (Lvi): Spinoza to Hugo Boxel. In: *The Chief Works of Benedict de Spinoza* (Vol. 2). Chicago, IL: University of Chicago Press. [Original letter written in 1662.]

Lyth, O. (1980). Wilfred Ruprecht Bion (1897–1979). *International Journal of Psychoanalysis, 61*: 269–273.

MacNeice, L. (1936). *The Faber Book of Modern Verse*. London: Faber & Faber.

Masson, J. M. (1985). *The Complete Letters of Sigmund Freud to Wilhelm Fliess 1887–1904*. Cambridge, MA: Belknap Press, of Harvard University Press.

Matte-Blanco, I. (1975). Creatività ed ortodossia. *Rivista Psicoanalisi, 21* (1): 223–289.

Matte Blanco, I. (1980). *The Unconscious as Infinite Sets: An Essay in Bi-Logic*. London: Karnac.

Mawson, C. (2011). *Bion Today*. Hove: Routledge.

Mawson, C. (2014). Editorial comment [in: *Key to a Memoir of the Future*]. In: *The Complete Works of W. R. Bion, Vol. XIV* (p. 205), ed. C. Mawson. London: Karnac.

Mawson, C. (2015). Psychoanalytic intuition and imagination. Unpublished paper presented at the Institute of Psychoanalysis, London, Saturday 11 July: Observation II: Clinical Concerns and Research on the Couch.

Menzies Lyth, I. (1981). Bion's contribution to thinking about groups. In: J. Grotstein (Ed.), *Do I Dare Disturb the Universe* (pp. 661–666). Beverly Hills, CA: Caesura Press.

Money-Kyrle, R. (1978). *The Collected Papers of Roger Money-Kyrle*. Strath Tay: Clunie Press.

Neri, C. (2015). A long meeting with Bion. In: H. B. Levine & G. Civitarese (Eds.), *The Bion Tradition* (pp. 23–28). London: Karnac.

Ogden, T. H. (2003). On not being able to dream. *International Journal of Psychoanalysis, 84* (1): 17–30.

Ogden, T. H. (2007). Elements of analytic style: Bion's *Clinical Seminars*. *International Journal of Psychoanalysis, 88* (5): 1185–1200.

Ogden, T. H. (2008). Bion's four principles of mental functioning. *Fort Da, 14* (2): 11–35.

O'Shaughnessy, E. (1981). A commemorative essay on W. R. Bion's *Theory of Thinking*. *Journal of Child Psychotherapy, 7* (2): 181–192.

O'Shaughnessy, E. (1999). Relating to the superego. *International Journal of Psychoanalysis, 80*: 861–870. Reprinted in: C. Mawson (Ed.), *Bion Today*. Hove: Routledge.

O'Shaughnessy, E. (2005). Whose Bion? *International Journal of Psychoanalysis, 86* (6): 1523–1528.

Parsons, M. (1986). Suddenly finding it really matters: The paradox of the analyst's non-attachment. *International Journal of Psychoanalysis, 67*: 475–488.

Parsons, M. (2000). *The Dove that Returns, The Dove that Vanishes*. London: Routledge.

Parsons, M. (2005). Mankind's attempt to understand itself: Psychoanalysis and its relation to science and religion. *Fort Da, 11* (2): 18–33.

Pecotic, B. (2002). The life of Isabel Menzies-Lyth. *Organizational and Social Dynamics, 2* (1): 2–44.

Piontelli, A. (1992). *From Fetus to Child: An Observational and Psychoanalytic Study*. London: Routledge.

Pirandello, L. (1921). *Six Characters in Search of an Author: A Comedy in the Making*. New York: Dutton, 1922.

Pistiner de Cortiñas, L. (2016). Les Fleurs du Mal: anti-emotions and the destruction of meaning. "Attacks on Linking" revisited: Variations on hypocrisy, cynicism and fanaticism. Paper presented at the Bion International Conference, Milan.

Poe, E. A. (1848). To Marie Louise. In: *The Complete Tales and Poems of Edgar Allan Poe* (p. 80). New York: Barnes & Noble, 1992.

Poincaré, H. (1914). *Science and Method*. New York: Dover Publications.

Pritchard, F. H. (1925). *Fifty Stories from Uncle Remus*. London: Harrap, 1958.

Reiner, A. (2009). *The Quest for Conscience and the Birth of the Mind.* London: Karnac.

Reiner, A. (2012). *Bion and Being: Passion and the Creative Mind.* London: Karnac.

Reiner, A. (2013). Recollections of Wilfred Bion. *DIVISION/Rev.,* 7: 17–19.

Reiner, A. (2017a). Ferenczi's "astra" and Bion's "O": A clinical perspective. In: *Of Things Invisible to Mortal Sight: Celebrating the Work of James S. Grotstein.* London: Karnac.

Rickman, J. (2003). *No Ordinary Psychoanalyst. The Exceptional Contributions of John Rickman,* ed. P. King. London: Karnac.

Sandler, P. C. (2006). The origins of Bion's work. *International Journal of Psychoanalysis,* 87 (1): 179–201.

Sassoon, S. (1984). *Collected Poems.* London: Faber & Faber.

Segal, H. (1952). A psycho-analytical approach to aesthetics. *International Journal of Psychoanalysis,* 33: 196–207.

Segal, H. (1964). Symposium on fantasy: Fantasy and other mental processes. *International Journal of Psychoanalysis,* 45: 191–194.

Segal, H. (1981). Notes on symbol formation. In: *The Work of Hannah Segal. A Kleinian Approach to Clinical Practice* (pp. 49–68). New York: Jason Aronson.

Segal, H. (1998). Introduction. *The Bulletin of the British Psychoanalytical Society,* 4.

Segal, H. (2007). *Yesterday, Today and Tomorrow.* Abingdon: Routledge.

Sodré, I. (1994). Obsessional certainty versus obsessional doubt: From two to three. *Psychoanalytic Inquiry,* 14 (3): 379–392.

Spillius, E. B. (1983). Some developments from the work of Melanie Klein. *International Journal of Psychoanalysis,* 64: 321–332.

Spillius, E. B. (1993). Varieties of envious experience. *International Journal of Psychoanalysis,* 74: 1199–1212.

Steiner, J. (1987). The interplay between pathological organizations and the paranoid-schizoid and depressive positions. *International Journal of Psychoanalysis,* 68: 69–80.

Steiner, J. (2000). *A Mind of One's Own: A Kleinian View of Self and Object,* by Robert Caper [Book review]. *Journal of the American Psychoanalytic Association,* 48 (2): 637–643.

Symington, N. (1990). The possibility of human freedom and its transmission (with particular reference to the thought of Bion). *International Journal of Psychoanalysis,* 71: 95–106.

Taylor, D. (2011). Commentary on Vermote's "On the Value of 'Late Bion' to Analytic Theory and Practice". *International Journal of Psychoanalysis,* 92 (5): 1099–1112.

Teising, M. (2005). Permeability and demarcation in the psychoanalytic process: Functions of the contact-barrier. *International Journal of Psychoanalysis,* 86 (6): 1627–1644.

Tracey, N. (2000). Thinking about and working with depressed mothers in the early months of their infant's life. *Journal of Child Psychotherapy,* 26 (2): 183–207.

Trotter, W. (1916). *Instincts of the Herd in Peace and War.* London: Unwin; Fourth impression, with postscript, New York: MacMillan, 1919.

Tustin, F. (1981). A modern pilgrim's progress: Reminiscences of personal analysis with Dr. Bion. *Journal of Child Psychotherapy,* 7 (2): 175–179.

Vermote, R. (2017). Reaching the transcendent position by a borderline patient in reading Beckett. In: A. Reiner (Ed.), *Of Things Invisible to Mortal Sight: Celebrating the Work of James S. Grotstein.* London: Karnac.

Watson, S. (2002). Complexity and the transhuman. *Organizational and Social Dynamics,* 2 (2): 245–263.

Wexler, M. (1965). Working through in the therapy of schizophrenia. *International Journal of Psychoanalysis,* 46: 279–286.

Williams, W. C. (1923). *Spring and All*. Paris: Contact Publishing.

Winnicott, D.W. (1954). Mind and its relation to the psyche-soma. In: *The Maturational Processes and the Facilitating Environment: Studies in the Theory of Emotional Development*. London: Hogarth Press and the Institute of Psycho-Analysis, 1965.

Winnicott, D. W. (1987). *The Spontaneous Gesture. Selected Letters of D. W. Winnicott*, ed. F. R. Rodman. Cambridge, MA: Harvard University Press.

Wittgenstein, L. (1922). *Tractatus Logico-Philosophicus*. London: Routledge & Kegan Paul.

Index